WARMING UP TO THE COLD WAR:
CANADA AND THE UNITED STATES' COALITION
OF THE WILLING, FROM HIROSHIMA TO KOREA

When U.S. President Harry Truman asked his allies for military support in the Korean War, Canada's government, led by Prime Minister Louis St-Laurent, was reluctant. St-Laurent's government was forced to change its position, however, when the Canadian populace, conditioned to significant degrees by the powerful influence of American media and culture, demanded a more vigorous response. *Warming Up to the Cold War* shows how American cultural influence overtook waning Canadian nationalism.

Comparing Canadian and American responses to events such as the atomic bomb, the Gouzenko Affair, the creation of NATO, and the Korean War, Robert Teigrob traces the role that culture and public opinion played in shaping responses to international affairs. With penetrating political and cultural insight, he examines the Cold War consensus between the two countries to reveal the ways in which Canada cited 'homegrown' rationales to justify its increasing subservience to American strategy and posturing.

Full of fascinating insights, *Warming Up to the Cold War* is essential reading for anyone interested in the Cold War, the role of culture in politics, and the history of United States–Canada relations.

ROBERT TEIGROB is an assistant professor in the Department of History at Ryerson University.

ROBERT TEIGROB

Warming Up to the Cold War

Canada and the United States'
Coalition of the Willing,
from Hiroshima to Korea

UNIVERSITY OF TORONTO PRESS
Toronto Buffalo London

© University of Toronto Press Incorporated 2009
Toronto Buffalo London
www.utppublishing.com
Printed in Canada

ISBN 978-0-8020-9923-5 (cloth)
ISBN 978-0-8020-9615-9 (paper)

Printed on acid-free paper

Library and Archives Canada Cataloguing in Publication

Teigrob, Robert, 1966–
   Warming up to the Cold War : Canada and the United States' coalition of
the willing, from Hiroshima to Korea / Robert Teigrob.

   Includes bibliographical references and index.
   ISBN 978-0-8020-9923-5 (bound).   ISBN 978-0-8020-9615-9 (pbk.)

   1. Canada – Foreign relations – 1945 – Public opinion.   2. Canada –
Relations – United States.   3. United States – Relations – Canada.
4. Cold War – Public opinion.   5. Cold War – Press coverage – Canada.
6. Cold War – Press coverage – United States.   7. Public opinion – Canada –
History – 20th century.   8. Nationalism – Canada – History – 20th century.
9. Nationalism – United States – History – 20th century.   I. Title.

   FC249.T43 2009   327.71009′044   C2009-900601-4

University of Toronto Press acknowledges the financial assistance to its
publishing program of the Canada Council for the Arts and the Ontario Arts
Council.

University of Toronto Press acknowledges the financial support for its publishing activities of the Government of Canada through the Book Publishing
Industry Development Program (BPIDP).

This book has been published with the help of a grant from the Canadian
Federation for the Humanities and Social Sciences, through the Aid to
Scholarly Publications Program, using funds provided by the Social Sciences
and Humanities Research Council of Canada.

Contents

Acknowledgments   vii

Introduction   3

1 The Bomb: 'Pax Anglo-Saxonia' or 'Too Much Power'?   19

2 Espionage: 'Soviet Method Revealed!'   54

3 The Cold War and the Third World: 'Time to Lay Bogey of British Imperialism'   92

4 NATO: 'Our Only Present Means of Salvation'   127

5 Korea: 'From an Imperial Frying Pan into an American Fire'   168

Conclusion   225

Notes   233

Bibliography   263

Index   273

Illustrations follow page 120

Acknowledgments

Many thanks to my mentor and friend Beth Bailey, whose imprint upon this book, and upon my broader development as a historian, is without parallel. Beth helped me conceive of the project, and provided invaluable commentary, encouragement, and assistance throughout, including prudent advice on marketing the manuscript to the presses.

Fredrik Logevall, Alex Lubin, Eric Porter, and Rebecca Schreiber read earlier drafts of the manuscript, and each provided timely and judicious comments. Advice from Gordon Morrell and Katrina Srigley helped to prepare a version of chapter 3 for publication in the *Canadian Review of American Studies* (37.3 [2007]), and I am in their debt for their insightful suggestions and wider counsel and support. It is truly an honour to enjoy the benefit of assiduous readings from individuals of such diverse and renowned expertise.

It has been a pleasure to work with University of Toronto Press. Editor Len Husband championed the project enthusiastically and tirelessly from the beginning, and provided sound advice and support throughout. Managing editor Frances Mundy and copy editor Ken Lewis were always responsive and insightful in their recommendations. The anonymous readers at UTP offered constructive and expeditious advice on strengthening the manuscript, and I thank them for taking the time to provide such sensitive readings.

I gratefully acknowledge the financial support provided by research and travel grants from Ryerson University and Nipissing University.

Finally, my thanks to all those who have supported me over the many (many) years required to obtain a doctoral degree. Colleagues and students, first at Nipissing and now at Ryerson, have made professional life a pleasure. My friends and family have displayed unwavering support, and I would like to thank, in particular, my father, a historian in his own right, for promoting my interest in the field (I know of no other family, for example, that commemorates Guy Fawkes Day on an annual basis!). Jon Gil Bentley, the most brilliant individual I have ever known, encouraged me to pursue a career in academia, and I am grateful for his exhortations. Greatest debt is owed to my partner, Suzanne Zerger. As she begins the task of writing her own book, I can only hope to provide a level of encouragement and sound advice that approaches her contribution to this one.

WARMING UP TO THE COLD WAR:
CANADA AND THE UNITED STATES' COALITION
OF THE WILLING, FROM HIROSHIMA TO KOREA

Introduction

In the summer of 1950, a folksy, plain-spoken American president made a case for war which would not be unfamiliar to twenty-first century audiences. The emerging conflict in Korea, President Truman insisted, was merely one component of a wider struggle against a unitary global enemy who seamlessly coordinated all challenges to the United States and its interests. The North Korean attack, he continued, was the work of 'bandits and thugs' whose primary motivation lay in their revulsion for Western freedom. Truman's rhetoric eschewed diplomacy, context, and nuance in favour of simplistic analogies, toughness, and decisive action, and conflated American values and aspirations with those of humanity as a whole – an orientation shared by other influential observers. To *Newsweek*, the president 'spoke from the heart of his country, and indeed, of the free world. He spoke not only as Commander-in-Chief of American armed forces but as World Chief of Police.' And while Truman hoped to build a broad international coalition to further his aims, he made it clear that the United States would go to Korea alone if necessary. Here, then, was a powerful manifestation of long-standing American notions of exceptionalism, unilateralism, chosen-ness, and national destiny.[1]

Such narrowly nationalistic calls to arms would appear at cross-purposes with the United States' goal of coalition building, particularly when one desired international partner, Canada, shared a common border, language, and – as a consequence – unparalleled access to American views. Indeed, a similar approach to rallying U.S. public and Congressional support taken in the run-up to the 2003 invasion of Iraq did much to encourage Canadian citizens to insist that their government opt out of that operation. In 1950, however, the scenario was reversed: the ruling Liberal government denounced – privately – Truman's rashness and oversimplification, offered only tokenist naval support, and called for a diplomatic rather than military solution to the crisis. The Canadian public and press corps, meanwhile, insisted upon a large-scale injection of ground forces. This endorsement for an American-led war was unprecedented in Canadian history and, even in the context of the Cold War, serves as a singular moment. What led Canadians to sign on with such apparent enthusiasm to a battle, and wider global confrontation, which was built so firmly upon the discourses of American nationalism?

In seeking to answer this question, I provide a comparative analysis of the emergence of the Cold War consensus in the United States and Canada, pointing to the ways in which 'nation' interacted with other markers of identity as citizens from both countries negotiated their responses to the emerging world order. Of particular interest is the role of American popular and public culture in creating the conditions for Canadians' widespread endorsement of a U.S.-led, global anti-communist campaign. My analysis suggests that while support for the Cold War consensus was built upon distinctly national idioms, Canadian nationalism tended to wane while its American counterpart expanded as anxieties over the global standoff with the Soviets intensified. And while this trend in Canada was certainly enhanced by the unprecedented volume and intensity of American anti-communist discourse available to Canadians following the Second World War, the latter utilized a host of 'home-grown' rationales to justify their increasing subservience to the American 'grand strategy' of containment. On the whole, Canadians believed themselves to have agency in this process, to have made this choice based on their own assessment of the costs (national sovereignty) and benefits (deliverance from 'world slavery').

At the same time, many Canadians responded to the unprecedented intimacy of the post-war bilateral alignment with a good deal of hesitancy. At the heart of these apprehensions lay persistent anxieties over the nature and fate of Canadian national identity itself. Indeed, following the Second World War, a confluence of domestic and international pressures led many to believe there was a great deal more at stake in the debate over Canadian identity than at any time previous. The global influence of Britain, and along with it the military and economic guarantees on which Canada had traditionally relied, was on the wane. The United States, like Canada a British settler society but one whose population, military and economic might, and territorial ambitions had continually eclipsed – and sometimes endangered – those of its northern neighbour, had emerged as the globe's leading power. At the same time, many feared that the Americans' main rival, the Soviet Union, sought nothing less than complete domination of the globe, and that Canada might serve as its initial target for gaining a foothold in the Western Hemisphere. Meanwhile, powerful voices the world over maintained that the war had laid bare the futility of national allegiances, and that humanity's continued survival in the atomic age required a vigorous internationalism overseen by an effective, egalitarian United Nations. Within Canada, francophones angered over repeated military conscriptions in defence of the British Empire increasingly conceived of themselves as a distinct, potentially independent, entity. And chronic population shortages would rekindle traditional concerns over the effects of non-'Nordic' immigrants on the nation's values and unity.

These forces pulled in multiple directions and raised fundamental questions about post-war national alliances that would bear directly upon issues of national identity. Should Canada draw closer to Britain in an attempt to reinvigorate the weakening Commonwealth? Should it attempt to deflect Soviet attentions by refusing to align with the United States, or would such neutrality in fact tempt a communist takeover? Should it forge new multilateral alliances with other lesser powers in order to uphold both national security and national autonomy? Should it downplay or repudiate the nation-state model altogether and work toward the establishment of an authoritative world government? Or should it deepen its connections to a newly preponderant United States, a state that traditionally served as the foil for Canadian identity – and the nation's most discernible threat? In the end, the latter course was adopted (though after the establishment of NATO, this quiescence was often soft-pedalled by emphasizing the multilateralism and international partnership ostensibly enshrined by that treaty). Advocates of continentalism had succeeded in obliging Canadians to coexist with the United States, and yield to its dictates, to degrees that appeared unthinkable just a few years earlier.

My primary interest lies not in whether this alternative was the wisest, nor in whether the Canadian state possessed sufficient agency to adopt any other bearing under the circumstances; scholars have wrestled with these matters, and arrived at a variety of conclusions, since the moment these fateful steps toward continental integration were taken.[2] Rather, I seek to measure how public consent – in Cold War parlance, 'consensus' – for this reorientation of national allegiances was achieved. Did the development of consensus in Canada imply or require American coercions? As a corollary, did there exist a truly 'Canadian' position on the Cold War?

In order to measure this phenomenon, I focus on the period from

1945 to 1950, and analyse representations of Cold War 'high politics' found in public and popular culture. I survey the mass print media (e.g., *Life, Time, Saturday Evening Post* in the United States, *Maclean's, Saturday Night, Canadian Forum* in Canada, as well as major daily newspapers from both countries), publications from racial minorities, academic organizations, and advocacy groups, texts of political speeches, polling data, and, to a lesser extent, radio broadcasting, film, and popular literature.

Notwithstanding the breadth of these sources, the bulk of my analysis is drawn from readings of the mass print media's response to issues of global significance in the early Cold War. As communications theorists and media analysts have shown, the news media plays a foundational role in simultaneously manufacturing and reflecting public opinion and policy-making, and is therefore a vital resource for gauging local, regional, and national attitudes. Some theorists go so far as to suggest that the media constitutes the single most influential institution in a liberal democracy – in large measure because it mediates the conversation between citizens and officials. As the authors of *Negotiating Control: A Study of News Sources* argue, 'Journalists are the living public for politicians and officials, and therefore their "public" debates are primarily with them.' In other words, for officials at least, the media and public are often viewed as synonymous. Politicians seeking public assent, therefore, are particularly beholden to the views expressed by dominant news organizations, and my study points to several instances where the press exerted considerable sway over the crafting of both domestic and foreign policy. Citizens, for their part, rely heavily on the media in order to comprehend conceptions of, and to formulate their own relationship toward, public and 'national' attitudes.[3]

In the era covered by this study (significantly, just prior to the advent of television), the print media's influence in both Canada and the United States was particularly formidable. In the years immediately following the Second World War, per capita sales of magazines and daily newspapers in both nations reached their apex; in fact, Canadian dailies boasted a combined circulation that exceeded the number of households in that country. For its part, Canada has a unique relationship with the communications industry: along with the nation's transportation infrastructure, communication has long been viewed as a core ingredient in binding together a sparsely populated and regionally disparate nation. Accordingly, Canadian media institutions hold a vaunted position in the national imagination, a notion that has contributed to a history of intensive communications analysis among Canadian scholars of international renown such as Harold Innis, Marshall McLuhan, and Northrop Frye. In all, as historian Paul Rutherford has written, particularly in Canada, and particularly in this era, 'the press acted as an agent of consensus: the habitual consumption of its messages united people otherwise divided by distance, religion, language, or class.'[4]

This is not to say that the views of the media and the average citizen were one and the same during this period, despite the aforementioned proclivity of officials toward this conflation. For one, corporate news media organizations constitute elite and interested parties that replicate dominant power structures and ideologies, an understanding foundational to media analysts such as Noam Chomsky and Todd Gitlin. Further, theories of cultural reception developed by British cultural theorist Stuart Hall, among others, illustrate the central role played by audiences in the interpretation and modification of all cultural products, suggesting that meaning (or, more narrowly, 'public opinion') is made collectively by all participants in the process; I have endeavoured wherever possible to be attentive to this interplay in the determination of public views. It is also important to acknowledge the growing power of radio broadcasting over the formulation of citizen attitudes; unfortunately, the paucity of existing tapes or transcripts, particularly from the Canadian side, hampers a fuller accounting of this aspect of mass media.[5]

In an effort to trace the shifting currents of popular attitudes toward the early Cold War, I examine national responses to a series of episodes and issues vital to both Canada and the United States: the development and use of the atomic bomb; the so-called Gouzenko Affair, which revealed the presence of Soviet spying operations in North America; the process of decolonization, a phenomenon which accelerated after the war, but one that was complicated by the emergence of a bipolar world order; the creation of NATO, which formalized the Cold War bifurcation; and the Korean War, which required Western nations to demonstrate their stated allegiance to American containment strategy.

I refer to these issues as 'vital' in the sense that they impacted citizens on both sides of the border in rather direct ways and/or involved some form of state-level, concrete action. As such, and unlike, say, the 'fall' of China or the Soviet takeover of Czechoslovakia (traumatic though they may be), debates over the issues I have chosen were required to move beyond the level of abstraction: the bomb was developed by citizens of both countries, and the bombings were carried out in their names; Russian espionage demonstrated that Soviet machinations were directed at North American, not merely European targets; the economies and identities of Americans and Canadians were thoroughly connected – though in divergent ways – to the colonial order; Canada was one of the early advocates for the creation of NATO, while the United States soon became the primary architect and, for all intents and purposes, administrator of the treaty; both nations would commit fighting forces, and endure combat losses, in Korea.

I was drawn to this topic for several reasons. For one, since the mid-1980s, cultural historians have brought attention to the fact that the Cold War was a cultural phenomenon, as much as it was a political, diplomatic, and military confrontation. Under this analysis, U.S. governmental and private cultural initiatives aimed at establishing and safeguarding domestic and international consensus are viewed as foundational to the extension of post-war American hegemony. The best of these works do not eschew the particular historical, materialist context (including the diplomatic, political, and economic milieus) in which cultural forms and practices developed; rather, they point to the ways in which culture shapes and is shaped by domestic and foreign policy-making. These studies also bear out the notion that the material 'realities' that defined bipolarity – embodied by slogans such as 'the iron curtain,' 'the free world,' 'the vital centre,' and 'Judeo-Christian Civilization,' as well as images of falling dominoes and maps of nations swallowed whole by the red seep of communism – represent mutable and contingent historical constructions: accordingly, the political 'centre' could shift radically and abruptly during the era, sharp divisions over core components of Judeo-Christian Civilization could appear between and within its constituent religious groups, and some residents of the free world could be decidedly un-free.[6]

Taken together, these studies of Cold War culture suggest that the strident anti-communism that characterized the domestic and foreign policies of Western nations was an outcome of both an undeniably hostile Soviet Union and an oftentimes calculated embellishment of that hostility. At the outset of the Cold War, those most responsible for that embellishment included political and cultural elites who utilized fears of communism in order to safeguard and extend their influence. American historian Eric Foner summarizes the myriad functions of anti-communism in his country:

> Business used it to tar government intervention in the economy with
> the brush of socialism, physicians to denounce proposals for national
> health insurance as 'socialized medicine.' Anticommunism became a tool

wielded by Republicans against the legacy of New Deal liberalism, employers against labor unions, white supremacists against black civil rights, and upholders of sexual morality and traditional gender roles against homosexuality and feminism.[7]

At the same time, elites throughout the West often mismanaged and oversold Cold War linguistic and visual symbols, resulting in a collective hysteria that went beyond these 'opinion makers'' own requirements, and over which they ultimately had little control. Studies of Cold War culture also suggest that the enforced unanimity of 'consensus' was continually challenged, resisted, and refashioned by individuals and groups whose interests it did not serve.

Yet despite this scholarly outpouring, cultural historians have largely ignored the impact of American popular discourses on Cold War policies and attitudes in Canada. There are many explanations for this, foremost among them a kind of unexamined assumption that citizens of Canada and the United States shared a common view of the emerging international rift. Canadians, it is believed, were firmly 'on side,' an impression that explains the absence of official U.S. cultural initiatives in Canada, a comparative dearth of attention from U.S. intelligence agencies, and past and current scholarly inattention to Cold War distinctions between the nations. Yet, from the start, Canadian voices raised doubts about the desirability of a U.S.-led anti-Soviet campaign. And when they did, official and private Canadian *and* American proponents of anti-communism were quick to impugn the dissenters. In this sense, a program of didactic 'cultural exchange' was in fact directed at Canada, though it is best characterized as a private, ad hoc initiative. One of the questions raised by this study, then, involves the effectiveness of – or need for – state promotion of culture; in this context, at least, the United States appears to have achieved a great deal of influence over popular and public discourse through largely private initiatives, and despite a fair measure of hostility to that perceived encroachment.

My primary motivation, however, is to emphasize the importance of national and other identities to the analysis of U.S.-Canadian Cold War relations and consensus formation. Past, and often exaggerated, characterizations of the essential congruity between and within Canadian and American society on 'core' issues cannot accommodate the sometimes fundamental differences exhibited by residents of both nations on a host of important matters. Failure to fully historicize Canadian-American relationships and perceptions of national character and interest has on occasion led to surprise and resentment among U.S. leaders when, for instance, Canadians pressed their government to adopt policies that did not conform to those of the United States. In Canada, an often reflexive anti-Americanism has relied on a similar – and equally spurious – flattening of difference *within* American society: U.S. leadership, the argument goes, represents and reflects U.S. society more or less precisely; U.S. society is uniform (and, often, uniformly evil), and so on. Redressing these misconceptions requires an appreciation for the role of culture and public opinion in the development and understanding of international relations; for the forces which built and resisted the Cold War consensus in both societies; and for the role of the U.S.-Canada border in accentuating or eliding perceptions of difference.[8]

Like their counterparts in cultural studies, those working in the fields of diplomatic history and international relations have also tended to overlook the impact of American culture on Canadian Cold War attitudes, a disregard that has been defended by a series of interrelated though sometimes contradictory assumptions. The first of these is the notion that the elemental contours of Canadian foreign policy were determined behind closed doors and only at the highest levels of government; public attitudes, under this schema, simply did not matter. This supposition is not without at least some merit: particularly during this era, Canadian politics was perceived as a 'mandarin' affair, with mid-century sociologist S.D. Clark arguing that Canadians were far less likely to question their leaders than citizens of the United States, even at the height of the McCarthyite purges. Canada's War Measures Act (1939–46), one that was a good deal harsher than that of either Britain or the United States, would only further this national timidity: the act allowed Mackenzie King's Liberal government unprecedented powers throughout much of the 1940s to suppress opposition by banning organizations and publications and interning 'enemies of the state.' Diplomatic historian Denis Smith sums up the resulting ambiance: 'Public discussion of foreign policy was limited not only by an indifferent and ill-informed parliament, but by an undeveloped academic community and the existence of only a tiny core of journalists with serious interest in international affairs.'[9] Thus, the argument goes, the opinions of ordinary Canadians on matters of international relations counted little, if they indeed existed at all; where they did exist, they more or less mirrored those of their government.

The aforementioned qualifications notwithstanding, evidence (often provided by these same diplomatic historians) suggests that at many key junctures Canadian ruling elites were forced to pay particular attention to public attitudes; as such, public opinion not only mattered but departed in important ways from that laid down in Ottawa. For instance, Dean Acheson, briefing President Truman in preparation for a 1947 visit with Canadian leaders, suggested that Truman prod the Canadians toward acceptance of mutual defence. At the same time, Acheson acknowledged that moving away from Britain and closer to the United States is 'a considerable political risk for the present Government' in Canada. In 1948 the Canadian ambassador to Washington, Hume Wrong, noted that Article 2 of NATO, which broadened the organization's mandate to include the peacetime promotion of stability and development, was insisted upon by Canadian officials who feared that a purely military alliance would spark a public backlash. And it is now clear that the Canadian governmental opposition to U.S. policy in Korea was driven to a significant degree by public relations concerns among leading Liberal Party officials. In each case, Canadian policy-making was mediated in some measure by the existence of an engaged constituency. The refusal to fully account for the public influence over foreign policy renders John Lewis Gaddis's critique of U.S. diplomatic historiography apt in the Canadian context as well: 'Somehow,' he observes, 'in our preoccupation with archives, theory, quantification, methodology, and historiography, we've lost sight of something Presidents Roosevelt and Truman never forgot: that they operated within a highly contentious domestic political environment from which they could rarely insulate the conduct of foreign policy.'[10]

Some Canadian historians justify their slighting of Cold War public opinion for reasons similar to the ones utilized by scholars of American culture who dismiss Canada as a productive region of inquiry: namely, the supposition that, owing to their common cultural and ethnic past, their sound wartime alliance, and their unshakable commitment to liberal internationalism, Canadian and U.S. attitudes were more or less synonymous. Moreover, and by extension, neither nation experienced much internal challenge to the so-called Cold War consensus. This unanimity was reinforced, so the argument goes, by the nature and extent of the messages inundating Canada from the south. 'The Canadian-American border was an information highway,' explains Robert Bothwell, 'with American issues and commentary speeding north for packaging (sometimes) into Canadian editions, or (more often) consumed raw. Canadians watched American movies, read American periodicals and sat entranced in front of American television.' Under this state of affairs, writes Denis

Smith, 'Canadians depended heavily for their judgment of world affairs on the American news services and American political columnists syndicated in the Canadian press.' Yet the same author identifies, only a few pages on, 'the Canadian tendency *from the beginning* to discount the extremes of American Cold War rhetoric' (emphasis mine).[11] If this disparity between Canadians and Americans did indeed exist, how can we account for it?

What makes the task of identifying Canadian Cold War positions particularly challenging is the exceedingly complex network of national and international dynamics that forms the backdrop for the array of culture available in that country. As the majority of Canadians spoke the same language as their larger neighbour, the protection offered by language in many other cross-border contexts was negated. By the 1920s, for instance, the number of American magazines available to Canadians outnumbered locally produced publications eight to one, and the most successful of these – *Ladies' Home Journal, Saturday Evening Post, McCalls,* and later *Time* and *Reader's Digest* – regularly outsold the most popular Canadian periodicals by wide margins. As Bothwell's quote indicates, Canadian domestic media operations carried U.S. articles and broadcasts (often without clear provenancial information) alongside locally produced material. Moreover, given that the majority of Canadians lived within a hundred miles of the border, many residents could tune into American broadcasting directly. Viewed only from this angle, it would not appear difficult to theorize a homegrown Canadian culture industry struggling, mostly in vain, to stake out an independent national position in the face of a hegemonic, imperialist ideological invasion from the south. Canadian media historian Mary Vipond demonstrates that both English- and French-Canadian elites from the era played upon this 'invasion' hypothesis in order to press for protectionist legislation against the encroachment of American culture.[12]

Such simplistic models of hegemony, however, ignore the elitist bent of Canadian cultural institutions, which tended to cast themselves as defenders of 'civilized' society against the 'tyranny' of the middle- and low-brow leanings of their American neighbours. There is more than a remnant in this anti-American posture of the British idea of Canada in the first place: as a bulwark against the expansion of American ideals and interests on the continent. Ryan Edwardson's recent work on the shifting conceptions of Canadian identity reveals that despite its early pedigree, this anglophilic approach to national arts and media content – what he terms 'Masseysim,' after Vincent Massey, the idea's most powerful exponent – dominated the Canadian intellectual sphere until the 1960s. Elitism on this scale can hardly be expected to generate views that truly represent the full range of the Canadian constituency, and, indeed, it is possible to find instances of various individuals and groups in Canada using elements of the sometimes more egalitarian U.S. culture to counteract the condescension of their own – as a form, then, of resistance. Further, as was the case in the United States, influential Canadians utilized opportunities furnished by the Cold War to suppress alternatives to the status quo; to a great degree the story of the conflict in both countries is the story of those who, as cultural theorist Ann McKinnon has written in another context, 'have the power to produce discourse, who symbolically limit the world.'[13] These vigorous attempts to construct, rather than consult, public opinion regarding Cold War policy frequently relied on the strategy, expressed notoriously by Michigan senator Arthur Vandenberg, of 'scaring the hell' out of average citizens in order to achieve state objectives.

Accordingly, it is vital to pay heed to the myriad viewpoints expressed by residents of various identities in both nations, and to Canadians' especial identification with region and chronic inability or unwillingness to subscribe to a cohesive national identity. In so doing, the simple dichotomies too often endorsed by Canadian nationalists between two fixed, discrete, nation-based attitudes, or between cultural imperialists and victims, begin to lose their value. What is needed in their stead is a mindfulness that hegemonic confrontations operate both within and across national borders; further, actors on both sides of the power/resistance nexus often look beyond the category of nation to build alliances aimed at reifying or confronting authority. Moreover, like the media theorists discussed above, scholars of Cold War culture have increasingly acknowledged the role of audience agency in the interpretation and relative influence of foreign cultural products, leading the field away from rigid concepts of 'cultural imperialism' and toward nuanced portrayals of mutual cultural transfer, 'transculturation,' and hybridity.[14]

It is likewise important to bear in mind that U.S. culture, even during the high point (or nadir) of consensus, was never a unitary entity. By applying models of discursive fluidity to the analysis of Cold War culture operating *within* U.S. boundaries, researchers have concluded that claims of a stable mid-century national unity have often been overstated, further challenging the notion of a simple reproduction of a monolithic U.S. Cold War ideology in Canada. If Canadians did rely to a great extent on U.S. attitudes, and those attitudes have now been revealed to comprise an enormous variety of often contradictory impulses, a rather linear schema necessarily fractures into a series of context-specific inquiries: Which attitudes? Among whom? During what time period? Austrian historian Reinhold Wagnleitner, who came of age in the midst of a massive U.S. State Department effort to sell the virtues of American liberalism in his country, notes that his generation learned many of their critical attitudes of the United States from the multifarious voices of Americans themselves (though generally not the ones officially sanctioned by the State Department). The success of U.S. culture internationally, then, has produced in various international contexts what René-Jean Ravault terms a 'boomerang' effect.[15] In sum, if new scholarship about Cold War culture in the United States suggests a much less vigorous Cold War unanimity than originally posited, and these contests over the American narrative were exported northward via an 'information highway,' massive reliance on U.S. cultural exports may not translate in all cases into a buttressing of consensus in Canada.

In keeping with the discussion of the influence of the U.S. media in Canada above, it should be noted that examples of U.S. attitudes originating from the 'opinion-making,' mainstream organizations would have been available to a great many Canadians, and especially anglophones, through a variety of channels: in their original format (in the dozens of U.S. publications sold in both countries such as *Time*, *Life*, or the *New York Times*, in broadcasts from northern U.S. stations, in films imported to Canadian theatres); in reprints or rebroadcasts provided by Canadian media outlets (which I have identified as such where possible); and from Canadian editors, columnists, and other intellectuals who scanned cultural production from the United States, Britain, and elsewhere in order to reproduce and interpret information and opinion they considered relevant to their readers.

Given this context, I make little effort to discuss whether a given story, idea, or debate that received widespread coverage in the U.S. mass media was also generally known in Canada; because of the communications environment outlined above, it simply was (though the degree to which American issues and opinions influenced Canadians differs, matters, and is, to the extent possible, measured in the following chapters). As Canadian cultural theorist W.H. New observes, 'the *presence* of the USA in Canadian daily life' is redoubled by 'the *preoccupation* with American behaviour and recognition,' a combination of circumstances not unique to Canada, but one that is arguably as potent in that country as anywhere else on the globe (italics in original).[16]

By contrast, the much broader range of U.S. opinion that existed outside the mainstream (but nonetheless might represent a great many Americans on any given issue) often originated from constituencies that lacked the means to reach an extensive audience, even within the United States: that is, from racial advocacy groups, religious bodies, left-ist organizations, and other voluntary and/or progressive groups and individuals. Unless specific evidence suggests the contrary, I assume that these more wide-ranging and often more critical perspectives would be largely invisible north of the border. Canadians arguing for or against American attitudes, then, possessed a highly circumscribed knowledge of those attitudes, a state of affairs that constitutes one of the principal leitmotifs of this study. To sum up, in assessing Canadian views of the United States and the potential impact of American culture in Canada, I focus chiefly on what Canadians saw, and only secondarily on whether those understandings of the United States were comprehensive and/or 'correct.'

This study is organized into five chapters, each of which deals with one of the issues I termed 'vital' above. In chapter 1, I find that while Canadians expressed high levels of approval for the atomic bombing of Japan, their analysis of the event exposed certain orientations that appear out of sync with the emerging Cold War bipolarity. Bomb-related discourses suggest that Canadians felt a wariness regarding *both* American and Russian expansionism following the war, and feared that the Bomb would be utilized to remake the post-war world on decidedly American terms (a prospect that was frequently celebrated in the United States). Even so, Canadians appeared far more sanguine about prospects for 'the atomic future' than their counterparts in Europe, a circumstance which I suggest reflects a heavy reliance on U.S. reportage regarding the potential peacetime applications of atomic energy.

In chapter 2, assessment of reactions to Soviet espionage in North America finds a substantial retraction of a good deal of post-war idealism on both sides of the border. The Gouzenko Affair revealed the limits of purported commitments to liberal values and tolerance at home, as well as multilateralism abroad – commitments that many in both nations had previously claimed as 'core values.' In short order, these ideals gave considerable ground to ideas that had recently been declared anachronistic, even suicidal: nationalism, power balancing, counter-subversion, and regional defence arrangements. And while many in Canada adopted or mirrored U.S. perspectives on the implications of Russian spying, others posited direct and deliberate counterchecks to often reactionary U.S. views, though these counterchecks frequently represented simplistic reversals of perceived American attitudes. In other words, this backlash against perceived American meddling in an 'internal' affair led some in Canada to utter facile Soviet apologetics that could be turned against them by Red-baiters from both nations – thus abetting the acceleration of the anti-communist crusade.

In the third chapter of this study, I demonstrate that ideas and policies relating to colonialism and race provide a measure – not the sole yardstick but one of the more revealing – of professed commitments to the postwar ideals of 'One World' multilateralism, national self-determination, and individual freedom and equality operant in the United States and Canada. Here I find that while residents of both geographies frequently expressed paradoxical and often delusional views of their own nation's relationship to imperialism, many anglophiles in Canada expressed highly intransigent defences of the practice based on the perceived need to place national security over the concerns of Third World peoples. Moreover, many of these imperial defenders addressed American anti-imperialists directly, avowing that the latter's 'myopic' idealism would tip the global balance of power in favour of the Soviets. In short, this chapter demonstrates that the degree of antipathy to communism in either country tended to ebb and flow according to issues that had as much to do with an array of national identities and interests as they did straightforward assessments of the Soviet threat. I also find that by tapping into a tradition of anti-colonialism that had deeper roots south of the border, some Canadians were able to find, in advance of even traditional anti-imperial constituencies in the United States, elements of neo-imperialism in the emerging 'grand strategy' of containment.

Chapter 4 concerns the debate over the establishment of NATO, an organization that formally committed the Canadian state to the global containment strategy. Remarkably, this ultimate subservience of national interests to those of a U.S.-led military alliance was not debated with much intensity in Canada, nor did the U.S. media play a perceptible role in convincing Canadians to sign on to an American-dominated anti-communist bloc. Rather, Canadians found their own reasons for endorsing this move – many of which involved a seemingly wilful denial of probable outcomes – and at the same time rather mercilessly silenced dissenters. These phenomena complicate both the characterization of

Canadian consensus formation as an end product of 'imperialistic' processes, as well as the mythic self-conceptions of moderation and tolerance that supposedly inoculated Canadians against the fanatical Red-baiting they ascribed to American political culture.

The analysis in chapter 5 of the early debates surrounding the Korean War finds that Canadians and Americans alike expressed hesitation over the prospect of making sacrifices on behalf of a people represented in popular narratives as fundamentally backward and alien. Given these depictions of Asian 'others,' I demonstrate that participation in Korea was promoted in public discourse, not as an act of altruism toward a sovereign and imperilled people, but as a means of Western self-preservation. Canadians faced special anxieties over participation, as the conflict involved the unprecedented step of following the United States, rather than Britain, into war. Those in Canada supporting the mission sought to assuage these concerns by overstating the multilateral character of the operation, de-emphasizing the importance of Canadian nationalism in the face of a wider threat to Western civilization, or by linking U.S. tactics and goals in Korea to those practised abroad by the British Empire for centuries. It is also clear that Canadian officials, who sought to maintain a sense of proportion regarding the true threat to their nation represented by the conflict, were pressed into sending ground troops to Korea by a public that had, with notable exceptions, become true believers in the anti-communist cause.

A brief conclusion summarizes the book's principal findings: while Canadians had traditionally derided the perceived excesses of their southern neighbours, by the end of the period under study, much of the disapproval had vanished from Canadian depictions of the United States – or, rather, had been transferred to communists and Russians. A portion of this shift can be attributed to the markedly unambiguous and disparaging portrayal of communism found in post-war American culture, yet particular conditions within Canada made many of its citizens unusually receptive to these views.

However, the experience of being identified internationally with U.S. decision-making in Korea, at the same time that American discourse grew increasingly reactionary, spurred a desire among Canadians to distance their policy from that of their neighbour and to reinvigorate a relatively dormant nationalism. By the time the Cold War entered its second decade, then, many Canadians moved from expressing muted hesitations about the bilateral Cold War alliance to outright opposition, facilitating the development of a distinctly Canadian response to

the bipolar order. And, in no small irony, that distinct stance appropri-
ated a great deal from various constituencies in Canada – among them,
francophones, progressives, anti-imperialists, and religious and peace
groups – branded previously as 'un-Canadian' for daring to resist Cold
War orthodoxies.

1 The Bomb: 'Pax Anglo-Saxonia' or 'Too Much Power'?

It has become axiomatic to declare that the atomic bomb produced a 'revolution in human consciousness.' Still, the collective sense of arrest that followed the news of 6 August 1945, the immediate awareness that existence had forever changed and that all aspects of the known world must now be reassessed through the prism of atomic fission, may yet astound the modern observer. While many of these first appraisals retain – in their prophetic bleakness – the power to chill, others proved inadvertently, if still darkly, comic. Take the case of Ross Harkness, war correspondent for the *Toronto Star* on assignment in the United Kingdom. Writing just one day after the world learned of the shocking new weapon, Harkness culls information from British scientists – who, because of the sensitivity of the knowledge they hold, 'must remain nameless' – and learns that the splitting of the atom portended a marvellous future for Canada. Appearing less like a prudent journalist than a modern St John channelling an updated Revelation, Harkness avers that he 'was shown a vision of a remade Canada, with the climate of California, its topography of mountains, valleys and rivers altered better to suit men's needs, and barren lands made fruitful by the magic of atomic energy.' Simply decanting 'atomic heat' into the Great Lakes – thereby transforming them into 'great radiators' – would eradicate the dreaded Canadian winter itself; likewise, the removal of polar ice caps would moderate the insufferable climate of the Maritime Provinces and do away with meddlesome icebergs. Well into the article, Harkness acknowledges the potential dangers of such interventions, though the projected 'unfortunate results' merely involve aggravated residents of the southern United States, whose climate might become uncomfortably warm, rather than the slapdash ruination of global ecosystems.[1]

Harkness's buoyant tone – buoyant, at least, to a generation unac-
quainted with the perils of global warming – clearly represents a desire
to provide a soothing counterpoint to the terrifying news from Japan. It
is also a dispatch whose unbridled optimism is uncharacteristic of most
Canadian reports; indeed, it is far more redolent of the earliest American divinings of the atomic future than the more restrained stories printed in Canada. Curiously, despite these national discrepancies in media
representations of the bombings, Canadians would come to articulate
more sanguine views about the 'atomic future' than citizens of all other
nations polled, save the United States, in the first years of the atomic
age.

This set of circumstances provides a précis of the principal themes of
this study: first, perceptible and sometimes significant national distinctions are evident in a survey of Canadian and American attitudes toward
international affairs (in this case, between mainstream media representations of the promise and peril of nuclear fission); second, their unrivalled access to U.S. attitudes meant that Canadians came to view the
geopolitical landscape, at least in part, through American eyes (here, in
their upbeat forecasts for the atomic future). Though by no means a new
phenomenon, Canadians' receptivity to U.S. representations of global
affairs would reach a high-water mark in the 1940s, spurred first by the
Second World War alliance and then by Cold War fears of an impending
all-out battle between the democratic and communist worlds. Because
the Bomb marks a suitable division between these hot and cold wars, and
because it served as a medium through which all significant issues of the
day could be interpreted, analysis of American and Canadian attitudes to
the bombings serves as an apt starting point for this comparative study of
the formulation of a global, U.S.-led anti-communist consensus in both
nations.

Much has been written about the impact of the atomic bomb on Americans' popular consciousness, and this scholarly outpouring is fully warranted: the weapon was developed and utilized under U.S. leadership,
and when its nuclear monopoly ended, the United States participated
in a frightening arms race whose effects were manifest in nearly every
aspect of national life.[2] Moreover, as the nation constituted one of the
two principal combatants in a potential nuclear conflict, many citizens
considered it their responsibility to avert a nuclear Armageddon, and
thus moved to the forefront of the global anti-nuclear movement. Nor
is this a purely 'historical' preoccupation. Nuclear anxieties continue to
shape American politics and society to a degree that is, arguably, unparalleled among twenty-first-century nation-states.

That public attitudes to the development and use of the Bomb receive less notice in accounts of post-war Canadian culture should not be unexpected; that they appear only peripherally, if at all, is more remarkable. The nation was a U.S. ally when the weapon was utilized against the Japanese, and Canada's scientists and especially its uranium played important roles in the Manhattan Project. As wartime alliances gave way to the bipolarity of the Cold War, Canada's geographical proximity to both the United States and the Soviets made nonchalance toward atomic weaponry challenging, to say the least. Nevertheless, existing analysis of early public responses to the issue is marked by a largely unexamined assumption that Canadian attitudes more or less mirrored those of their American counterparts, that distinctly Canadian perspectives on the Bomb did not exist. In the analysis that follows, I argue that they did.

Some of the questions that form the basis of a cross-cultural assessment of Bomb-related attitudes are closely tied to the weapon's immediate military/strategic objectives: Was the bombing necessary? Should it be a source of pride? How did it intersect with existing attitudes toward the enemy, in particular, and non-European peoples, in general? Did the detonation of the Bomb also explode commonly held assumptions about the social, political, and economic realms?

Most importantly for the purposes of this study, discussions about the Bomb provide a synopsis of the ways in which Canadians and Americans were thinking about vital post-war international issues before a rigidly enforced Cold War orthodoxy constricted the range of acceptable discourse. As such, they provide at least a starting point to questions of whether Canadians expressed a distinctive, autonomous attitude toward the post-war order and the emergent bipolarity. Furthermore, this survey speaks to the manner in which Canadians responded to an uneven communications landscape, one in which much of their news and popular culture was imported from the United States. Under which circumstances did Canadians adopt, resist, or refashion messages from the south? What factors led residents on either side of the border to accentuate or minimize 'nation' as a locus of identity on the eve of the Cold War?

I do not attempt, in the chapter which follows, to outline the long-range attitudes toward the new weapon in either country, nor to provide a comprehensive comparison of all Bomb-related thinking between Americans and Canadians. Rather, I focus on the period from 6 August 1945, when the first bomb fell on Hiroshima, to the beginning of February 1946, when the case of Igor Gouzenko, a Soviet cipher clerk who defected to Canada with information about a Soviet spy ring in Canada, was made public. As chapter 2 will demonstrate, this latter event would push post-war thinking among both Canadians and Americans in a fundamentally different direction.

Though many quite correctly regard the bombing of Japanese cities as the first operation of the Cold War, it is also true that discussions over the use and future of atomic weapons took place in an atmosphere of much greater tolerance than the period following the ultimate breakdown – generally associated with the March 1947 implementation of the Truman Doctrine – in East-West dialogue. In Canada, these debates took place against the backdrop of an emerging post-colonial, nationalist identity, one fostered to a great degree by pride over the nation's contributions to both global wars, as well as by direct state sponsorship: namely, the overtly unifying agendas, in a country disposed toward regional and/or British loyalties and concerned about American dominance, of federally sponsored cultural institutions like the Canadian Broadcasting Corporation (established in 1930) and the National Film Board (1939). Indeed, according to some Canadian nationalist readings, the period immediately preceding the entrenchment of the Cold War represents a brief flickering of the possibility for true Canadian autonomy before bipolarity subsumed the nation's interests to those of the United States.[3]

At first glance, a survey of nation-based differences in early U.S. and Canadian debates over the Bomb does not reveal especially substantial discrepancies. This is hardly surprising given the degree of U.S. material that constituted Canadians' daily news and cultural diet since the advent of mass culture. In this sense, parsing a truly 'Canadian' perspective can be exceedingly difficult, as that perspective is 'always already' Americanized in some measure. The instances of Canadian 'exceptionalism' outlined below, where they exist, are differences of degree and even then find parallels, antecedents, and links to U.S. cultural production being crafted beyond the mainstream. In fact, as I argue in the Conclusion, the 'America' that many Canadians utilized in order to construct a frequently contrapuntal national identity was something of a straw figure, one assembled from the patently constricted range of representations of American identity and cultural opinion available beyond U.S. borders. Conversely, access to more reliable delineations of the full diversity of American expression may have led even the most ardent Canadian nationalists to conclude that the border separating the nations was more porous than they imagined (and, perhaps, hoped). Still, 'nation' emerges as a useful category of analysis in the discussion of post-war public opinion, though one that must be weighed in concert with the variables of region, religion, class, gender, and, in particular, race.

The first reports of the Bomb's detonation that reached the Canadian public included many of the tropes that appeared in the U.S. press. Journalists expressed, in turn, a mixture of awe and horror, coupled with a relief that it had been utilized by, not against, the Allies; hope that the conflict in the Pacific would soon be over; pride in their nation's role in a revolutionary scientific development; frequently wild conjectures about the technology's applicability to all manner of military and peacetime functions; and concern over what the splitting of the atom meant for the global balance of power, the recently created United Nations, and the fate of humanity. Though each of these themes found expression through distinctly national idioms, it was in their assessment of these latter geopolitical implications that U.S. and Canadian opinion exhibited the greatest variance.

While major Canadian dailies led off their August 7 editions with headlines that emphasized the horrors of the Bomb's destructive force (reflecting at once the fear that would become synonymous with the entire nuclear era), these newspapers almost invariably paired these apocalyptic warnings with celebrations of Canada's role in the affair. Toronto's *Globe and Mail*, like most other publications, seemed to have trouble framing the event in appropriately stirring language. Its headline, 'Atomic Bomb Rocks Japan,' was subtitled 'Cosmic Energy Harnessed to Unleash Greatest Force Ever Discovered by Man'; the accompanying Canadian Press article suggested that, in addition to fearing for humanity, Canadians should feel a swell of pride at the dawning of the atomic age. It began: 'Japan rocked today under the most devastating destructive force ever known to man – the atomic bomb – and Canadian science and Canadian uranium played a large part in this epochal achievement.'[4] Those who expressed insecurities about the nation's international standing, a more or less permanent guild in Canadian society, might well find succour in the mighty atom.

Assorted headlines likewise warned Canadians, on the one hand, that a 'terrifying power menaces [the] globe,' one that 'seared to death' and 'burned alive' its victims and could well 'destroy civilization,' and boasted, on the other, of 'Canada's intimate part' in its creation. An extensively reprinted Canadian Press story pointed out that nuclear physics itself had been born in Canada at the turn of the century under the guidance of McGill University's 'Lord [Ernest] Rutherford.' That the (largely unrealized) international prestige many journalists expected to follow had been won at the cost of uncounted civilian lives and at the possible expense of the future of humanity – surely the most Pyrrhic of triumphs – was not addressed directly, but the chilling connection seemed to haunt many of these reports. Manhattan Project scientist Leo Szilard's comment on the sudden celebrity of his colleagues – 'mass murders have always commanded the attention of the public' – could also be affixed to the circumstances surrounding Canada's heightened status, but none of the nation's leading dailies dared make this move directly. The communist *Canadian Tribune*, meanwhile, exhibited no dis-ease whatsoever, reporting 'universal rejoicing in Canada' over both the bombing and the Soviet entry into the war against Japan.[5]

Some of the scientists involved, for their part, were able to navigate the apparent chasm between horror and fulfilment by taking responsibility only for the 'pure science' of atomic fission and not its practical application on the battlefield. Dr Charles Camsell, deputy minister of mines, participated in the project to utilize Canadian uranium in the Bomb's development on the condition that he not be told 'any more about it than necessary'; it may be this wilful compartmentalizing that allowed him to depict the affair, just days after a second bomb devastated Nagasaki, as 'a romantic story.'[6]

That Canadian journalists were far more likely than their American counterparts to point out that an international coalition, not merely U.S. scientists, produced the Bomb should come as no surprise. C.D. Howe, Canada's minister of munitions and supply, made triumphal claims to the press and the House of Commons regarding the nation's vital contributions, and given the secrecy surrounding the research, reporters had little else to go on.[7] (To be fair, Howe acknowledged that Canada did not have, nor did it want, the ultimate secret to the Bomb, a fact that owed much to the expense involved in nuclear weapons production as well as the belief that the nation's atomic allies would protect it should a threat materialize.) While it is true that Canadian scientists and laboratories did play an important role in the research on nuclear fission, given the small scale of the wartime operation north of the border and the fact that these scientists were not privy to the ultimate secrets of the Bomb's detonation, American commentators can be forgiven for downplaying the international perspective.

In fact, U.S. politicians and reporters were prone to depict the Second World War itself as an American, rather than Allied, victory, and the Bomb as the crowning achievement of this rather unilateral triumph. President Truman, notes cultural historian John Fousek, 'emphasized that this remarkable achievement was made possible by the unique know-how, material abundance, and physical security of the United States,' and that

the United States alone would decide about future control and application of atomic power, views that carried the day in many American publications. 'Prometheus, the subtle artificer and friend of man, is still an
American citizen,' proclaimed *Life*. Some in the United States, like NBC
radio commentator H.V. Kaltenborn, acknowledged that 'Anglo-Saxon
science' had unlocked the atom's secret; none would go as far as Toronto's *Globe and Mail*, which called the successful detonation a seemingly
equivalent 'Anglo-American-Canadian victory' (a clunking appellation
to be sure, but one that, unlike the more inclusive term 'Allied,' elevated
Canada to 'Big Three' status at the expense of the excluded Soviets).
The *Halifax Chronicle-Herald* expressed a similar theme with still greater
inelegance, citing the Bomb as proof of the supremacy of 'English-speaking brains.' And when the Canadian press ran syndicated American stories about the Bomb's development that failed to account for Canada's
role, readers were quick to point out the oversight.[8]

Many of these same reports made clear that Canada's heightened significance in the atomic age went well beyond its contribution to nuclear
research: as in the case of the other known uranium-rich region, the
Belgian Congo, Canada's vast stores of fissionable material ensured that
the nation would be valued by its friends and targeted by its enemies
(though precise delineations of 'friend' and 'enemy' remained murky
in the days following the war's end). 'Nature in its bounty,' proclaimed
a *Vancouver Sun* editorial, 'looked after our stock-pile of uranium'; now
it would be up to Canadians to ensure that the nation will 'never be left
behind in the race to apply atomic secrets.'[9] In fact, warned many commentators, given that wars would no longer be fought over now outmoded resources such as oil (!) but over access to uranium, Canada might
rightly expect to be at the centre of the next global conflict. At the very
least, Canada's international standing – and again it bears repeating, like
that of the Belgian Congo – would experience remarkable gains. Heady
days, indeed, for a nation seeking to establish its standing as a partner,
rather than drudge, to the major international powers.

Less ubiquitous in Canadian publications, though still marked in its
distinctiveness from that of the mainstream U.S. press, was an almost
immediate willingness to take on (though often tepidly) moral issues
surrounding the use of atomic weaponry. In the United States, Lawrence
Wittner observes, 'the communications media generally told the story in
a way that failed to contest the necessity or desirability of the bombing.
They rarely, if ever, discussed the Bomb's victims or showed pictures of
them; instead, they carried upbeat accounts of postwar reconstruction in

the two Japanese cities.' While these latter themes found their way into many Canadian newspapers and magazines – often in accounts mined from the Associated Press – these publications also provided stories and editorials that reflected, or at least acknowledged, worldwide controversy over the bombing. Opinion polls confirmed that while majorities in both countries approved the action, a greater percentage of Canadians disapproved or were undecided.[10]

It is noteworthy that this debate among Canadians did not entail finger pointing at the United States; Canadians of differing perspectives on the issue spoke in collective terms about the Allied, rather than solely American, utilization of the Bomb. As the editors of the democratic-socialist *Canadian Forum* wrote, 'The atomic bomb represented the culmination of a process in which the American-British-Canadian forces have earned for themselves an unchallenged and unchallengeable reputation. We are the great destroyers.'[11] Though the bombing of Hiroshima and Nagasaki was undertaken without Canadian assistance, the perception of shared responsibility is perhaps not surprising. Since the beginning of the conflict, Canada's press had spoken in the language of a unitary effort against the Axis powers; what is more, having imbricated Canadian politicians and scientists so thoroughly in the triumph of nuclear fission, as illustrated above, simultaneous attempts on the part of the press to wash the nation's hands of the ultimate ends of that project would appear blatantly disingenuous.   In later decades, many Canadian nationalists, falsely romanticizing Canada's non-nuclear status as ethical rather than economic and strategic in origin, would point to the bombing as confirmation of the moral bankruptcy of U.S. leaders, but the early analysis carried none of those intimations.

That said, the tenor of most articles willing to wrestle with the morality of the Bomb amounted to a kind of hedging approval based on the special circumstances generated by the war, with the caveat that future use would be judged more starkly. According to *Saturday Night*, a liberal, highbrow news weekly, atomic strikes against Japan were 'part of a necessary campaign for the maintenance of peace and something resembling justice upon the surface of the earth; but we cannot assume that the atomic bomb will always be at the disposal of the better side and the side to which we belong.' Though the bombings were needed in order to save Allied lives, 'there is,' they conceded, 'no guarantee that what has happened this week to Hiroshima may not happen at some remote date to Montreal or Edmonton.'[12]

This kind of relativism lay at the heart of a kind of stock 'by-any-means-necessary' defence of Allied tactics in the 'Good War': since freedom had been imperilled by tyranny, we should not become paralyzed by protracted hand-wringing over the means to an ultimately noble end. Many reiterated uncritically the justifications provided by Truman and adopted by mainstream journalists in the United States: the Bomb saved Allied lives, Hiroshima was primarily a military target, the Japanese had been warned, and in 'total war,' civilian targets were fair game. A *Saturday Night* editorial of September 8, provocatively titled 'Should We Have Used It?' concedes that loss of civilian lives on this scale might be difficult to stomach, but maintains that the methods of total war had, after all, been learned from the enemy. 'We said we would teach the Hun [and by extension, it seems, the Japanese] what war meant, as he had taught others.' Still, this bombing was undertaken 'reluctantly, in the cause of human freedom,' and full justification for the Bomb's use on the Japanese would only be realized if that specific, exceptional usage serves to end all future war.[13]

More forceful condemnations were rare. In their August 10 column 'Atomic Bombing – the Moral Issue,' *Vancouver Sun* editors criticized as 'superficial' claims by American commentators that because it kills swiftly and 'painlessly,' the atomic bomb is more humane than conventional weaponry. The 'horror' of the Bomb 'weighs on the consciences of the less calloused among the western peoples,' they chided, before falling back on the already standard mantras, as if sheer repetition would serve to unburden those same troubled consciences: the bombing saved both Allied and Japanese lives, and may be the instrument that finally 'banish[es] war.' The editors of *Canadian Home Journal*, a monthly directed at middle-class women, appended a sobering epilogue to their editorial about September's cover girl: 'But as we go to press, Japan has reeled under the impact of atomic bombs. This terrifying destruction has broken, with scarcely less shattering impact … upon our concepts of strategy, of statesmanship, and of Christian morality.' 'Destruction on such a scale is revolting,' conceded the leftist *Toronto Star*, but added: 'To tolerate it, one has to recall the years of Japanese atrocities …'[14]

More than one analyst contextualized Hiroshima and Nagasaki as merely the final, most brutal step in the progression of total war, one whose antecedents included Japanese bombing of Chinese cities in 1937, German terror bombing, and the Allies' incendiary bombing of Dresden and Tokyo. Opinion remained divided, however, as to whether the deployment of atomic bombs represented an organic – and therefore, morally consonant – development in the *technique* of mass killing, or an ethically indefensible departure from conventional weaponry. *Life* editors held that Hiroshima was an inevitable continuation of a process initiated in 1937 by the enemy, writing: 'From the very concept of strategic bombing, all the developments – night, pattern, saturation, area, indiscriminate – have led straight to Hiroshima.' In the Anglican serial *Canadian Churchman,* Vancouver clergyman Cecil Swanson countered that the Bomb marked a new low in the conduct of warfare, writing, 'If we never thought war evil before, surely we must do so now, and bend all our energies towards developing world peace.' The *Calgary Herald* responded to Hiroshima with unreserved pessimism, asking, 'What hath man wrought?' and calling the Bomb's development not a triumph but 'a matter for regret' that may become 'a noose to hang the entire human race.' The *Canadian Forum* held that the nation's role in developing the reprehensible weapon meant Canada bore new and heavy responsibilities to ensure a just peace – that is, 'if we want to erase the memory of American-British-Canadian bombing.'[15]

Although many of these ruminations do not represent an especially thorough cross-examination of the decision, they constitute an admission, largely absent in the United States, that the ethics surrounding the bombing of Japan were legitimate points of discussion. By contrast, a study of fourteen major U.S. columnists' references to the bombing found that only one columnist made more than passing mention that the action may have been immoral, or even that others may regard it as such.[16]

In rare instances, a Canadian journalist wrote against the notion that, when it comes to deployment of nuclear weapons, there exist both good and evil pretexts. Willson Woodside, a regular *Saturday Night* contributor on the subject of international affairs, advised that 'the moral question involved should be long debated by the conscience of Christian people, unless we are to surrender to the Machiavellian principle, adopted by the Nazis, that what serves our purposes is right.' Such views found particular favour in publications from Quebec, a province whose largely Catholic makeup and resentment toward past British rule yielded Canada's highest rates of anti-imperialism, isolationism, and pacifism. Montreal's *Le Devoir*, an elite French-nationalist daily, levelled particularly vigorous denunciations. Its first report on the Bomb included subtitles that pointed to the 'moral problem' posed by the new weapon, to Tokyo's protests against 'the massacre of innocent civilians,' and to the fact that the *Osservatore Romano,* the *de facto* voice of the Holy See, condemned the action. In the following issue, *Le Devoir* found itself agreeing with the official Japanese claim that the bombing's indiscriminate killing of civilians was reminiscent of Genghis Khan, though the paper added an unsettling qualifier: 'But the Mongols were not fighting in the name of democratic civilization.' To find equally forceful condemnations from anglophone publications, one must look beyond the mainstream press: the Canadian branch of the Christian-pacifist organization Fellowship of Reconciliation, for one, called the bombing an 'atrocity' whose architects 'stand condemned before the bar of justice and mercy.'[17]

In large-circulation English-language publications, however, it was left to readers themselves to articulate such positions in letters to the editor, often in response to the standard editorial justifications of the bombings summarized above; in this instance, it appears that the cool *realpolitik* advanced by some in the mainstream press could not fully account for the sense of horror and shame experienced by many average citizens after August 6. Responding to the justifications offered by the author of 'Should We Have Used It?' a reader counters that 'the means determine the end. If the means are inhuman and immoral, the result will be inhumanity and immorality.'[18] An especially heated debate played out in the 'Letters' column of the *Globe and Mail* – perhaps English Canada's most influential daily – with some citizens expressing outrage over the actions of the Allies, and others providing (often reactionary) defences of the Bomb's use. Whether the elevated principle for which Allied lives were sacrificed had now been tarnished was open for debate; less disputable was the fact that the Bomb itself had fractured a portion of the unanimity that marked Canadian public attitudes to the war.

It should not be surprising that in these debates race provided a significant, if not the most significant, subtext to these arguments over the Bomb's use. For the Allies, the Second World War was fought in profound contradiction, waged as it was (particularly in the public realm) against the abhorrent racial initiatives of the Axis and at the same time in full accordance with notions of Anglo-Saxon supremacy. In his survey of the racial underpinnings of the war in the Pacific, John Dower identifies the Second World War as a watershed in racial thinking: 'fueled by racial pride, arrogance, and rage on many sides,' it also 'brought about a revolution in racial consciousness throughout the world that continues to the present day.' What one writer terms the 'claims of blood and history,' advocated most chillingly by the Nazis but utilized in varying degrees by all of the war's major participants, grew less palatable in light of the discovery of the death camps.[19] The contest over the shifting meaning of race and nation after Auschwitz was fought on many fronts, including the debates over the morality of the bombing.

A frequent justification in both the U.S. and Canadian media centred on the idea that the Japanese deserved such a payback after the 'treachery' of Pearl Harbor. It is important to note that the theme of treachery was not associated solely with the events of 7 December 1941, nor was such an attitude limited to the character and actions of Japan's wartime leaders. Dower's study reveals, using textual analysis familiar to practitioners of post-colonial theory, that this trait was believed to inhabit the Japanese 'national character' itself, a category that conflated race, culture, and nation. That profound contradictions plagued many of these supposed immutable national/racial characteristics – the Japanese were at once childlike in their simplicity and cunningly deceptive, frail and superhuman, primitive and frighteningly advanced – did little to impede the overarching trajectory of this racial project: that is, to render the Japanese 'a uniquely contemptible and formidable foe who deserved no mercy and virtually demanded extermination.'[20]

Variations on this stance found greatest expression in the United States (the recipient of the 'treachery,' after all), but numerous correlates appeared north of the border and particularly in newspapers from the West Coast, a hotbed of anti-Japanese sentiment long before the war. Here, significant Japanese populations had resided – and to the chagrin of many in the WASP majority, flourished – before twenty-two thousand were forced to relocate to internment camps in the interior (an action patterned after Roosevelt's Executive Order 9906). 'No tears of sympathy will be shed in America for the Japanese people,' the *Omaha Morning World Herald* assured; not to be outdone, the *Vancouver Sun* led off a report that the victims of Hiroshima perished in temperatures of two trillion degrees with the headline 'Hot Enough for Satan Himself.'[21]

Readers would have been fully conditioned, then, to interpret properly a *Globe and Mail* editorial cartoon from 9 August 1945, entitled 'Avenging Genii': the cartoonist contends that it was the 'Jap sneak attack on Pearl Harbor' that opened the bottle of Allied science, producing an angry, anthropomorphic cloud branded 'Atomic Bomb' that reaches back over the Pacific with merciless – but fully warranted – fury.[22] The deceitful enemy had reaped his just desserts. And like Truman himself, many readers and journalists on both sides of the border were quick to point out that it was not only 'Allied science,' but Providence itself which had endowed Anglo-Saxon nations with the ultimate weapon, governed as those nations were by singular measures of sound judgment and temperance (the annihilation of two Japanese cities notwithstanding).

Many Canadian readers defending the use of the Bomb likewise employed the language of racial hierarchy and caricature, arguing, for instance, that 'you can't call the Japs "humans,"' or that their 'fiendish treatment of the white races' warranted apocalyptic payback. This latter reader recommended further bombing as 'a swift and merciful way of clearing a heap of filth from the path of human progress,' rather than requiring that the 'white races ... pour out the flower of their manhood' in order to achieve global stability. These oafish rants were not the sole province of 'the masses'; as Canada's own prime minister wrote in his diary shortly after Hiroshima, 'It is fortunate that the use of the bomb should have been upon the Japanese rather than upon the white races of Europe.'[23]

Such attitudes cannot be excused, but their foundations must be contextualized as products of both a horrific and protracted conflict, and of concerted efforts undertaken by the governments and mainstream press of all countries involved in the war to motivate citizens toward specific national objectives. Anti-Japanese racism had a long and troubling history in both Canada and the United States, but accounts of the indisputable grisliness of the Pacific war presented in press releases and official speeches, and by often hyper-nationalistic journalists, served to amplify pre-existing prejudices to unprecedented levels. An appreciation for the 'true' degeneracy of the Japanese, a trait ostensibly laid bare by Pearl Harbor, was cemented in the popular imagination by such actions as the torture and execution of the Doolittle flyers (an event further immortalized – and simplified – by the 1944 release of Hollywood's *The Purple Heart*), the Bataan Death March, and the deployment of kamikaze pilots. Each of these events was real and appalling; it is also true that in each case, Allied governments rendered them in a manner aimed at reinforcing anti-Japanese hysteria *and* disclosed them to their citizens months after they occurred, timing the release of information to meet specific public relations objectives. While the above incidents involved American fighting forces, the Canadian military had its own troubling encounter with the Japanese in a brief and catastrophic attempt to garrison Hong Kong on behalf of the British in 1941. Of the 1,975 Canadian troops involved, 290 died and 483 were wounded when the Japanese attacked, and 287 more died in dreadful conditions as POWs.[24]

Nor did reports of similar acts by Allied soldiers – wholesale torture and execution of prisoners, the sinking of hospital ships, and the shooting of unarmed civilians, sailors who had abandoned ship, or pilots who had bailed out – reach the West until the conflict was over. And one category of Allied atrocities that did receive occasional disclosure – the wide-

spread mutilation of Japanese war dead for souvenirs – did not generate
a groundswell of public revulsion (as it undoubtedly would have were
the victims German or Italian soldiers).[25] While wartime propaganda is
not solely responsible for the manufacture of these attitudes, the era's
dominant discourse served to harden and intensify existing racial thinking to degrees that led some to accommodate, and even applaud, atomic
annihilation of civilians.

Race, too, was a central component of many objections to the Bomb,
though many opponents employed the concept in ways that pointed to
the embryonic 'revolution in racial consciousness' given momentum by
the war. A letter to the *Globe and Mail* condemned the extermination
of civilians for the sins of their leaders as a crime against 'Heaven and
humanity,' one which strips the Allies of the moral authority to try Nazi
leaders at Nuremberg. 'Such wholesale, indiscriminate destruction is
not according to our traditions,' the reader continued, suggesting that
claims of the innate racial and cultural superiority of Anglo-Saxons had
been called into question as a result. Another reader, exemplifying the
centrality of Christianity to mid-century national and racial identity, was
more explicit about the Bomb's challenge to existing racial hierarchies;
she expressed sorrow that Anglo-Saxons had produced, used, and, most
repugnant of all, 'gloated' over the Bomb, since 'we are supposed to be
a Christian nation, and our big ally is supposed to be a Christian nation.'
Still another contended that frequent journalistic references to the Japanese as sub-humans had been stripped of their efficacy. 'Does it matter
what color or race a dog is as long as he acts like a dog? Is a weapon less
diabolical according to which side uses it for mass destruction?'[26] Here
as elsewhere in Canadian denunciations of the bombing, the skin colour
of the Japanese is not referenced directly. As such, race was introduced,
not as a variable in the decision to deploy nuclear weaponry against the
racially 'Other' Japanese, but because the atomic act reflected badly on
the supposed moral superiority of 'we' Anglo-Saxons.

South of the Canadian border, letters condemning the bombing in
major publications (a very small percentage, indeed, notes historian
Maureen Fitzgerald) were invariably met with a barrage of angry rejoin-
ders.[27] More profound debates about the ethics of the Bomb were carried in the publications of religious, progressive, and racial advocacy
organizations, while especially cogent critiques of the bombing emerged
from African-American publications.

Some black publications in the United States sought to leverage African-
American participation in the Manhattan Project toward heightened

group recognition, a tack also adopted, as I discuss above, by Canadians insecure about their nation's international standing ('Negro Scientists Help Produce 1st Atom Bomb,' headlined the *Chicago Defender*). The prevailing attitude, however, was summed up in publications like *Crisis*, *Ebony*, and the *Pittsburgh Courier*. In these pages, the war did not represent a simple morality play between oppressors and liberators. Rather, post-war resistance among Western democracies to the dismantling of colonial empires, as well as segregation, racism, and economic disparities within the United States, led some to argue that the Russians exhibited a greater commitment to freedom and equality than the West, and that U.S. claims to moral leadership rang hollow. The use of the Bomb was simply further proof of the moral bankruptcy of the Anglo-Saxon world, which had, since the dawn of colonialism, extended and maintained domination over people of colour through superior weaponry; thus, Hiroshima and Nagasaki represented, not a souring of the principled values of the West, but the continuation of its violent, totalizing trajectory.[28]

Here, race was front and centre to analysis of the Bomb's use, an analysis that in many respects displayed a greater sophistication and depth (Stalin's purported commitment to freedom aside) than that of either the U.S. or Canadian mainstream. The skin colour of the Bomb's victims, held the black press, facilitated the decision to use the weapon, a conclusion skirted entirely by Bomb opponents north of the border but supported by the private declarations of leaders like Mackenzie King and by studies like Dower's. A U.S. poll conducted in the fall of 1945 found African Americans and the 'well-to-do and the well educated' displayed strongest support for the position that no bombs should have been used, or that they should have been dropped first on an unpopulated region.[29] The condemnation of the bombing among African Americans, it appears, was not limited to the elites who wrote for black publications. (And while the opposition among the affluent and well educated may be read as reflecting greater measures of humanitarian sentiment, it is also true that working-class Americans bore a disproportionate degree of combat losses; desire for both reprisal and for an immediate end to the conflict among this demographic may go far in explaining class discrepancies over this issue.)

Though it would be instructive to identify what mainstream and minority Canadians would have made of such views, this remains a matter of conjecture for a number of reasons. First, given the white makeup and client base of major media organizations on both sides of the border, Canadian readers would have no more access to African-American opinion than white residents of the United States. Second, as market conditions – including but not limited to intensive competition from the south – rendered all but the most successful Canadian publications unprofitable, newspapers and magazines produced by and for Canadians identified as 'non-white' simply did not exist during this period; as historian Robin Winks observes, intermittent attempts to establish a sustainable African-Canadian periodical for the country's approximately twenty thousand blacks failed for a variety of reasons, including competition from African-American publications like *Ebony* and *Crisis* (which included frequent references to black life in Canada in order to attract subscriptions from that country). Finally, the fact that the principal target of Canada's stifling War Measures Act turned out to be not fascism but an older foe of the Canadian establishment – individuals, organizations, and publications on the left – served to silence many advocates of aggrieved populations in Canada.[30]

This paucity of print offerings was made up for in marginal degrees by the greater breadth of views presented in the nation's mainstream media (a phenomenon discussed in greater depth below); still, the absence of the truly oppositional viewpoints, like those offered by alternative media organizations in the United States, served to constrain discursive possibilities in Canada. In other words, while Canadians could count on a greater range of perspectives from their mass print media, these perspectives more nearly represented the sum total of views at their disposal than was the case in the United States. This state of affairs may go far in explaining, for instance, the failure among Canadians to make connections between race and the Bomb's victims, not merely its developers.

Some found an antidote to the guilt and horror surrounding the bombings by underscoring the anticipated benefits of nuclear technology. As demonstrated at the outset of this chapter, experts and laypersons from all over the globe weighed in at once, and often with unfettered imagination, about the Bomb's implications for the social, environmental, and extraterrestrial realms. Scientists of diverse and often unspecified credentials forecasted an existence remade for the better – one marked by inexpensive interplanetary mass transit systems, free and limitless energy for all, the eradication of poverty and disease, even cows whose atomic milk would fortify iron-deficient children – if the human species could slough off its seeming obsession with self-annihilation (an obsession that itself might be stamped out by the universal prosperity provided in this atomic Eden). This 'either/or' dichotomy (either humanity will perish, if it utilizes the atom for war; or the future will be idyllic, if the technology is employed in the name of peace) plagued post-Hiroshima analysis, foreclosing the possibility that 'atomic energy might be *both* mankind's scourge and benefactor.'[31] Only a few analysts provided bleaker predictions about such phenomena as uncontrollable chain reactions, enduring radiation, or long-term environmental damage. It was in the area of scientific conjecture that Canadian publications were especially reliant on foreign opinion in the days and weeks following Hiroshima, as editors culled stories from United States and British wires or sent reporters abroad for firsthand interviews. The Canadian scientific community, it appears, did not possess the real or perceived authority, or perhaps the will, to contribute to these debates to the degree exhibited by their international counterparts.

A review of this atomic-age forecasting points to discernible, nation-based distinctions in the scientific messages Canadians received (and reprinted) from abroad. American analysts and experts displayed a greater inclination to soothe the fears of jittery citizens about nuclear technology, while British sources tended toward darker scenarios; Canadians, when provided the opportunity, steered something of a middle course. In a representative U.S. article reprinted by the *Ottawa Citizen*, Associated Press science editor Howard Blakeslee assured readers that dire warnings about catastrophic damage to the earth's environment had been overstated, and that while atomic detonations create 'a little bit' of radioactivity, these elements are emitted naturally by the air, soil, and 'particularly from the walls of great buildings.'[32] Forward-thinking, optimistic, and technologically capable, the United States would, these commentaries assured, manage the new technology for the good of humanity.

Such views, which would soon be buttressed by a massive public-relations campaign conducted by U.S. government agencies like the Atomic Energy Commission, drew heavily on America's utopian tradition; they also, by implicitly or explicitly framing the bombing of Hiroshima and Nagasaki as somehow essential to the understanding and development of the atom's peacetime applications, 'facilitated the process by which Americans absorbed Hiroshima and Nagasaki into their moral history.' According to sociologists Leonard S. Cottrell, Jr, and Sylvia Eberhart, these optimistic commentaries appeared to reflect and reinforce surprisingly optimistic attitudes circulating among the American public as a whole. In a 1946 study that attempted to reconcile Americans' prevailing expectation of future atomic war with their relative indifference over that possibility, Cottrell and Eberhart pointed to their subjects' widespread belief that, based on 'the inexhaustibility of scientific invention,' researchers would soon provide a defence against nuclear weapons.[33]

The reports from Britain – a nation that suffered greatly in the war, might be the battleground in the next, and now inhabited a world where the United States, not Britain, had the last word – were more dire. The sense of gloom and condemnation reflected in these articles exhibited at least some correlation to public opinion: polls found that while only 21 per cent of British residents opposed the bombing, the figure was more than double that of U.S. respondents. Writing from the *Ottawa Citizen*'s London bureau, A.C. Cummings reported that Britons were, in the main, 'astonish[ed] and appal[led]'; still, some scientists in that country looked forward to the use of 'precision blasts' to improve the English climate or to break up polar ice fields in order to access mineral resources beneath them. While no nation exhibited a monopoly on either calamitous or Panglossian forecasting, Canadians closely attuned to the emerging nuclear debates could insert without difficulty the category 'nation' into their appraisals of whether the atomic age portended good or ill. Beyond the presence of both U.S. and British reports reprinted in Canadian publications, though, it was hardly a fair fight: according to one report, by 1929 Canadians spent one dollar on British magazines for every $100 they spent on those American, a gap that had likely widened in the interim.[34]

It is notable, given the above discrepancies, that a multi-nation poll of June 1946 revealed that with the exception of the United States, Canadian respondents expressed 'the most favorable assessment of the prospects for atomic energy in any country surveyed': 38 per cent believed atomic energy would do more good than harm, with only 26 per cent responding that it would do more harm than good. A January 1946 poll asking whether the splitting of the atom portends the 'end of the world' or the dawn of 'a new age' found even greater optimism, with only 8 per cent holding the former view and 64 per cent the latter. These figures are all the more noteworthy given cultural historian L.B. Kuffert's finding that post-war Canada 'had not fully accepted science as part of its defining tradition.'[35]

Had these surprisingly positive Canadian attitudes toward the nuclear age been forged to any significant degree by the assurances of American atomic 'experts,' or did they simply reflect Canadians' nascent self-image – reinforced relentlessly by their own government and journalists – as a vital member of the nuclear vanguard? Britain shared the latter distinction but lacked both the inundation of U.S. narratives about the atomic age and, perhaps not entirely coincidentally, the degree of optimism expressed by Americans and Canadians: the multi-nation poll on atomic energy cited above found only 28 per cent of Britons believed nuclear technology would do more good than harm, while 46 per cent maintained the opposite.

In this instance, it seems evident that some credit must be given the U.S. press in the construction of Canadian opinion; had the above poll of Canadian attitudes been conducted in the hypothetical context in which residents spent one dollar on American magazines for every $100 spent on their British counterparts, it is not difficult to imagine that the percentages would more closely resemble those of Britain. Furthermore – and this is an issue I will draw out below – there appears to be little at stake with respect to Canadian identity in the embrace of an American view on this particular issue. On other occasions, as I will demonstrate, pro-American expressions were construed as effecting net losses to Canadian autonomy and ideals, and in these cases could provoke a backlash.

Prophecies surrounding the atomic future strayed well beyond the realm of science and warfare to lay claim to all manner of public policy. Many American and Canadian commentators were quick to associate the unlocking of the atomic secret with the supremacy of the democratic governments and capitalist economies of the Bomb's founding countries. Other analysts, particularly in Canada, countered that the state control and secrecy surrounding the affair highlighted the benefits of government regulation, and that it was capitalism's 'competitive spirit of economic war' itself that lay at the heart of the recent global conflicts. Writing for *Saturday Night*, Stuart Armour pointed to the atom's destructive potential as the basis for complete government control over all nuclear technologies. Since these technologies, it was believed, would soon become the prevailing source of energy the world over, Armour posed a solemn question: '… is it going too far to suggest that the days of free enterprise are over? As a corollary of the fore-going is the further question – have we yet reached such a stage of political maturity that we shall be able to reconcile the loss of free enterprise with the continuance of personal freedom?' Even leaders of Canada's largest corporations, who might expect to profit most from access to atomic power, called for 'rigid government control' over the technology in a survey conducted by the *Financial Post*. Co-operative Commonwealth Federation (CCF) leader M.J. Coldwell, perhaps floating his socialist party's first atomic-age election platform, promised that nuclear energy would finish off the twin banes of the Canadian citizenry: capitalist exploitation – since 'this wonderful discovery cannot be left to the profit-making motive of any individuals' – *and* Gulag-like winters. [36] Clearly, the uncertainty over what truly lay ahead rendered the narrative of the atomic future open to seemingly limitless exploitation.

Perhaps the most frequent point of analysis in the United States and Canada after the bombing related to the manner in which the atom would affect the post-war international order. Even before the possibility of near instantaneous global annihilation, the chaos of the global war and rapid advances in air power had virtually eliminated traditional isolationist sentiment in both countries. Further, many held that patently devastating hatreds based on narrow nationalism and racial hierarchy be replaced by notions of the essential unity of the species, a unity that would be guaranteed by the extension of so-called 'universal' values. Both of these themes fed into and built upon an international movement toward some form of global federation, and found a slogan when in 1943 former Republican presidential candidate Wendell Willkie published *One World*. A best-selling plea for world government widely serialized in Canadian and American newspapers, *One World* provided considerable momentum to public endorsement of the embryonic United Nations; fears raised by the Bomb ensured that these sentiments became a groundswell. When world leaders moved toward practical implementation of world federalism, it also became clear that the popularity of the concept owed a great deal to its connotative instability: 'One World' could be employed by speakers representing profoundly differing agendas, even those invested in the project of empire.

Struggles over the definition of foundational concepts like universalism and liberalism lay at the heart of these disputes over the meaning of 'One World.' Since its Enlightenment-era origins, Western liberalism – or the organization of society around principles of individual freedoms, representative government, the rule of law, and the free market – had been depicted by its advocates as the wave of the future, a redemptive, civilizing, and universally applicable entity to be promoted throughout the world (thus the frequent pairing of the terms 'liberal' and 'internationalism'). In theory, a liberal world is a prosperous and peaceful world, one that relies on cooperation, compromise, and international agreements and agencies – as opposed to mere power balancing – in order to maintain a stable international order.

When post-war American policy-makers moved toward practical application of these ideals, however, complications arose. In his appraisal of

American involvement in the Third World, Robert Packenham points to the ethnocentricity inherent in assuming that the Western European and American experience should serve as an immutable blueprint for the rest of the world, and that American ideals and institutions could be grafted with little difficulty onto developing countries, which would in turn embrace them enthusiastically. Drawing on the work of mid-century American intellectual Louis Hartz, Packenham suggests that the unique conditions under which U.S. liberalism developed furnished the nation with a rather circumscribed, conservative, and sometimes intolerant liberalism, one that came to view legitimate freedom struggles in foreign contexts as dangerously radical, and that favoured an imposition of stability from the outside that was often at odds with professed ideals of liberal democracy. Thus, to liberalism's intrinsic proselytizing spirit was added a high degree of suspicion toward anything that deviated from its particular American variant. In the words of Hartz, 'An absolute national morality is inspired either to withdraw from "alien" things or to transform them: it cannot live in comfort constantly by their side.'[37] In this view, the terms 'liberal' and 'American' are not precisely congruent, a distinction lost on many U.S. policy-makers and analysts.

Characteristics unique to America's domestic politics have also played a role in constraining the range of alternatives available to the makers of the nation's foreign policy. Diplomatic historian Fredrik Logevall points out that the wide dispersion of power and relative weakness of political parties, features that distinguish the American political system from its parliamentary counterparts, diminish executive control over foreign policy. Accordingly, leaders must generate broad popular and Congressional support for their positions, and success frequently hinges on base appeals to nationalism, excessive moralism, and exaggerations of national security threats. Having sold their initiatives through such means, many U.S. leaders find that they 'have backed themselves into a corner, severely constricting the range of policy options.' What's more, the pragmatism that has marked much European diplomacy has, through generations of two-party wrangling within the aforementioned parameters, become equated with weakness and moral laxity in the American political imagination.[38]

Frederick Dolan notes that the Cold War amplified these tendencies: as Americans became fixated on a paranoid crusade to uproot internal enemies, narratives of a stable, confident national project fell prey to self-doubt and ambiguity. 'Driven by the need to resolve doubt, to sift through phantasms and shadows,' the conflict served to figure the state itself 'as a subject, in particular, as an epistemological subject committed to guaranteeing the objectivity of the world' (fashioning what Louis Hartz termed America's 'totalitarian' liberalism).[39] The contours of the 'American way of life' contracted even as its advocates grew more vocal about its universality.

In the months following the Second World War, however, the nature of this universality was still open for debate. That debate turned on whether that universalism would be defined as an extension of a rather monolithic 'America' throughout the globe – publishing magnate Henry Luce's imperialist, 'civilizing' conception of the 'American Century' – or by more idealist models forwarded by such U.S. progressives as Henry Wallace and Carey McWilliams that underscored liberty and equality, rather than the interests of the American state, as first principles. African-American intellectuals like W.E.B. Du Bois, Ralph Ellison, and, later, Martin Luther King, Jr., seized upon the latter, explicitly linking the economic and political ascendance of the West to racial subjugation – be it under fascism, colonialism, or capitalism. To many black leaders, true universalism meant the forging of an internationalist ethos that sought to liberate people of colour by advocating full citizenship and/or true self-determination; moreover, ideals like freedom could mean different things to different peoples. In this schema, ideas of universalism and multiculturalism were closely allied and served valuable functions in the critique of what cultural historian Nikhil Pal Singh calls 'a political project in which a racial animus and an imperial ambition remained paramount.'[40]

Attempts by the U.S. mass media to make sense of the Bomb's geopolitical impact reveal these tensions over the international role and responsibilities of the United States. *Life* editors praised Truman for his refusal to employ 'the atomic bomb as a diplomatic weapon against Russia,' urging the administration to 'keep world peace on a genuinely Allied basis.' Yet the same editorial concluded by declaring that the United States could now unilaterally 'abolish warfare, and mitigate man's inhumanity to man' (adding rather portentously, for those alarmed by the crusading spirit of U.S. internationalism, 'But all this will take some doing'). Fousek argues that the looming Cold War was waged 'not primarily in the name of capitalism or Western civilization (neither of which would have united the American people behind the cause), but in the name of America – in the name, that is, of the nation,' tropes that emerged in the immediate aftermath of Hiroshima. This orientation built upon centuries-old ideals of chosen-ness and moral leadership that now, due in no small part to the atomic monopoly, could express global, not merely national, ambitions. As the mainstream media frequently implied – when they did not say so explicitly – 'One World' meant that the interests of other nations were at once indistinguishable from, and subordinated to, those of the United States; as such, expressions of U.S. unilateralism did not represent the polar opposite of expressions of internationalism. Still other observers rejected any kind of world-statist subordination of U.S. prerogatives, arguing that 'One World' advocates did not represent the majority of Americans, had played upon the 'hysteria' of Hiroshima in order to advance their agenda, and were fostering a global context in which the interests of Third World peoples and religions would domi-nate (leading directly, noted an alarmed analyst, to a possible 'worldwide ban on beef and pork').[41]

Canadians would be drawn in many directions on this issue. Some, like *Calgary Herald* columnist Richard J. Needham, embraced the dawning of American primacy ushered in by the nuclear monopoly because, he insisted, the United States could be trusted to use its power wisely. Free peoples are 'incapable of waging aggressive wars,' as these wars require, assured Needham (and inadvertently anticipating Noam Chomsky), 'a docile people' and 'a chained press.'[42]

Others in Canada hoped to piggyback off the post-war expansion of U.S. authority, while at the same time seeking to extend notions of 'the universal' beyond an exclusively 'American' and toward a more broadly defined 'Anglo-Saxon' world view. English-speaking nations, not merely the Americans, would rule the planet. This was a complicated bargain for Canadians, given that historically, British loyalism and anti-Americanism were often two sides of the same coin; further, any variety of Anglo-Saxon pre-eminence necessarily excluded many citizens, including the third of the population of francophone descent. 'At last,' noted *Globe and Mail* reader J.F. Boland in a letter to the editor, 'the Anglo-Saxon world has perfected a weapon which will make war impossible if they preserve and maintain the secrecy of the atomic bomb'; anything less would 'hasten the end of the Christian civilization.'[43]

Saturday Night contributor Stuart Armour advised that, as Canada's uranium deposits now render it the geographic epicentre of the global balance of power, and as the nation does not possess the military might to protect those deposits, Canadians should abandon 'past tub-thumping on the subject of the sacredness of sovereignty' and embrace an exclusive 'Pax Anglo-Saxonia.' This alliance would go so far as to oversee the estab-lishment of a common Anglo-Saxon citizenship, and would eschew the world federalism of the UN in favour of a preponderant English-speaking bloc, one that would expand to include only those applicants who demonstrated themselves 'moral in outlook, humanitarian in practice, and of proved willingness to fight and die for the freedom of mankind.'[44] Whether mandatory ESL seminars would follow successful applications for honorary 'Anglo-Saxonia' Armour did not say; ensuring a monopoly over the Bomb would, of course, be the linchpin of such a strategy.

Such opinions were exceedingly rare. In the main, Canadians exhibited a greater ecumenicalism when depicting the world that would or should emerge after the war, with many advocating a milieu in which individual and national self-determination trumped the monolithic dictates of any single nation or ideology (though provided, many made clear, that this agency was expressed within the general rubric of Western liberalism). The sources of this more multilateralist rhetoric are diverse, not the least being Canada's status as a 'second-tier' power (at best) that resented being taken for granted in international affairs, coupled with the nation's experience as a subservient member of a significant multilateral body – the British Commonwealth – in which a certain degree of give and take was expected. Moreover, Canada's particular history of relations with its dominant and sometimes insensitive southern neighbour – in the words of international relations analyst John Warnock, as 'partner to behemoth' – undoubtedly fuelled some of the calls for greater 'multivocality' in the administration of a post-war world order in which the United States appeared to be taking command. In this regard, the high-minded rhetoric employed by Canadian elites about the desirability of 'international cooperation' and 'multilateralism' owes as much to self-interest as it does to idealistic notions of global equity and justice.[45]

Media theorist Ann McKinnon goes further, arguing that Canada's legacy as a 'triply colonized space,' first by Britain and France and later by the United States, as well as its legacy of bilingualism and multiculturalism, provide Canadians with at least the possibility of embracing 'alterity and heterotopia over [America's mythic] homogeneity and utopia.' Such hypotheses should not be employed without a good deal of caution, caveats, and exceptions. Lumping Canada into the post-colonial camp could be, and has been, challenged by those who consider the nation an imperial actor from its inception, both with respect to the Third World (especially Latin America) and to internally colonized Indigenous Peoples. Too, efforts to extend Canada's present commitment to multiculturalism backward to an era of profound Euro-centrism, particularly among its leadership, would constitute an oversimplification of some magnitude. *Pace* the mid-century emergence of a social science literature that contrasted America's coercive 'melting pot' with Canada's harmonious 'cultural mosaic,' subaltern populations on either side of the border could be forgiven for failing to grasp the nuances of these supposed national discrepancies. In 1945, for example, federal cabinet ministers debated strenuously whether to deport all Canadians of Japanese descent, a proposal which received especially strong support on the West Coast.[46]

It is true that the horrors of fascism served to discredit some of the most overt forms of racism in Canada, leading to the post-war introduction of laws – generally in advance of similar measures in the United States – banning discrimination in such areas as hiring, accommodation, and home ownership. Still, as Indigenous Peoples, African Canadians, Asian Canadians, and other aggrieved groups found (and as numerous studies confirmed), structural and informal exclusions often provided insurmountable barriers to economic and social equality analogous to any that existed in the United States, particularly in the realm of education and employment. To cite one example: African-Canadian women were not permitted to enrol in Ontario's nurse-training programs until the early 1950s, and were barred from Quebec's until a decade later. The latter victory was roughly contemporaneous with James Meredith's successful and widely celebrated effort to desegregate the University of Mississippi. As for Canada's commitment to free and open debate, a recent study of this period argues that in many instances, 'Canada outdid the Americans in placing national security above individual rights,' and that from the mid-1930s through the late 1950s, the government of Quebec's repression of the left rendered that province 'one of the jurisdictions most inimical to civil liberties in the Western world.' The federal parliament banned the Communist Party for the duration of the Second World War, making Canada the only Western nation to outlaw the party while allied with the Soviets.[47]

How can we account for this apparent gulf between stated ideals and lived experience? To a very great extent, it must be viewed as a function of the ignorance of the Canadian people regarding the activities of their own government. Much wartime and post-war state repression of undesirables was so secretive that only its victims knew, allowing Canadians to persist in the illusion that their society stood above the excesses and intolerance of its southern neighbour; this sentiment would only increase when television broadcasts of the McCarthy hearings were beamed into Canada.[48]

At the same time, according to novelist and essayist John Ralston Saul, there may be some validity to Canadians' purported ability to accommodate difference, born in large measure from the multi-ethnic and -linguistic origins of the nation. The perpetual English–French–First Nations negotiation that defines Canadian society forecloses, he writes, efforts to enforce 'a reality which could produce a centralized mythology,' one that would be analogous to 'the standard monolithic mythology of other nation-states.' At its best, argues Saul, this failure to conform to the standard theoretical paradigm of Western nation-states allows for 'acceptance of complexity' and the ability to live 'with balance and doubt.' Other observers express greater degrees of pessimism about the origins of these supposed national traits: recent work on the history of Canadian multiculturalism finds that the policy was crafted in order to manage a hybrid and geographically diffuse population, and only after efforts to promote a singular, fixed national identity met significant resistance among those whom it excluded. Further, even after such a posture became enshrined in official bureaucratic policy, it most often amounted to a willingness to accommodate the voices of other *Europeans*. In his recent study of English-Canadian identity formation, Daniel Coleman traces the nineteenth- and twentieth-century project of naturalizing 'a specific form of whiteness based on a British model of civility' for all citizens, regardless of ethnic makeup, a fictive identity he terms 'white civility.' Even in its most generous renderings, however, this project was aimed primarily at immigrants from southern and eastern Europe; those outside this broad rubric of whiteness were habitually dismissed as 'inassimilable.'[49]

It may also be the case that by employing the language of tolerance, openness, and heterogeneity to define their society, by upholding authentic multilateralism and self-determination in international matters as somehow fundamentally Canadian, and by utilizing the language of victimization when discussing their nation's relation to the United States, Canadian elites unwittingly provided spaces for the truly marginalized in Canada to point to the contradictions and hypocrisy inherent to their country at mid-century. This dynamic between habitually iterated ideals and lived experience may go far in explaining the development, in the decades that followed, of what some analysts consider a more authentic multiculturalism.[50]

For all these reasons – domestic and international, idealistic and self-interested – there exists in many sectors of mainstream Canadian post-war opinion a resonance with the universalism of Wallace and McWilliams, with its emphasis on liberty and equality rather than the interests of the

American state. A sometimes heated resistance to the idea that the interests of other nations were at once identical and subordinate to those of the United States comprised a corollary to this view. By way of example, even before the war, many leading Canadian dailies carried regular, lengthy columns on news and perspectives from, not merely about, the world beyond national borders. I suggest that this sampling of worldwide opinion – with a particular eye, to be sure, on London and Washington – reflects not *merely* budgetary constraints or oft-cited Canadian insecurity and deference, but an interest in multiple viewpoints based on the orientation identified above. Indeed, this practice could be considered an informal application of atomic scientist and world federation advocate Leo Szilard's 1947 proposal that, in order to strengthen public loyalty to a supranational government, 'one page of every newspaper in the world' be given over to a non-aligned international information agency.[51]

Stories from the United Kingdom reprinted in the Canadian press on the post-war world order would reinforce these internationalist leanings, as they exhibited near unanimity on the choice before humankind: in the words of a *New Statesman* editorial reprinted in the *Ottawa Citizen*, 'world destruction or world government,' with control of the atomic weaponry handed over to the UN. Asking 'who owns omnipotence?' the *New Statesman* argued that withholding the secret of the Bomb would only encourage other nations to develop their own, and using the weapon to extract concessions from Moscow would engender a global rift which would mean catastrophe when the Soviets discover the secret, as they inevitably would.[52]

Many of these prophetic estimations formed a cornerstone of Canadian revisionings of geopolitics after the Bomb: Canadian analysts predicted that since the 'atomic secret' would not remain hidden for long, a political-realist reliance on power balancing had become an anachronism in a context where even a small nation could wreak global havoc; too, an arms race and MAD-like scenarios (though not yet defined as such) would develop if the Allied monopoly was maintained. Moreover, they admonished, sincere attention must be paid to the root causes of war – intolerance, ethnic and religious hatred, and, especially, nationalism and inequitable distribution of resources – for future war was now unthinkable. Again, these themes, especially the links between want and war, were not absent in the U.S. press, but in Canada the sheer force and repetition of these utterances points to a national constituency for whom multilateralism and world cooperation provided the starting point for all discussions of post-war international relations.

Above all, maintained the Canadian media, the Bomb had rendered notions of national sovereignty obsolete. 'Can we keep the peace,' asked Canada's most popular domestically produced magazine, *Maclean's*, in a characteristic take, 'in a world in which each competing national sovereignty possesses, to use as it likes, the power to destroy all others? The answer is: No.' Some took pains to advocate that in its stead, a kind of unity-in-diversity should carry the day, as opposed to the particularly American version of liberalism that many in the U.S. government and mainstream press endeavoured to extend. Arguing that humanity's survival depends on a greater tolerance for non-Western religious traditions and that these traditions themselves may also contain a blueprint for global peace, a *Saturday Night* reader maintained that 'stripped of institutional dogma the teachings of Christ and of Buddha are essentially the same, that man has within himself all knowledge and wisdom necessary' to live 'in harmony with the rhythm of the universe.' 'Will the Americans be able to reconcile themselves,' questioned foreign affairs specialist Willson Woodside in *Saturday Night*, 'to the idea of giving up their great navy, the Russians giving up their great army, the British, French and Dutch their empires? Will social democrats be ready to lie down with communists, monarchists with republicans, Jew with Arab, Moslem with Hindu ...?'[53] In the totalizing atmosphere that would follow, such willingness to suffer 'otherness' was frequently cast as vice rather than virtue, one orchestrated and disseminated by the communist enemy itself.

Still, the embrace of difference had limits. The 'Very Reverend W.R. Inge,' while rejecting nationalism, nonetheless framed that renunciation in the language of racial and religious distinction: 'Together with war,' Inge admonished, 'we must get rid of the insane worship of the God-nation which makes it impossible for us to be good Europeans or good Christians.' Similarly, columnist Percy Price advocated the cultivation of a 'world patriotism' based, not on outmoded conceptions of blood and heritage, but on the worldwide extension of justice and liberty – though not necessarily democracy, as colonial tutelage would still be required in many instances.[54] Despite these circumscriptions, it is important to note that the very notion on which Truman built support for American globalism – that is, nationalism – was viewed by many Canadians as the crux of recent global violence and the overriding threat to future peace.

It was along similar lines that many Canadian analysts and citizens called for a rapid end to the nuclear monopoly. In their front page item entitled 'Sharing the Secret,' *Saturday Night* editors maintained that, since 'our scientists ... cannot contemplate a future in which they will become the closely guarded servants, in effect prisoners, of the state,' atomic secrets must be shared – though this exchange should take place under the supervision of an international body. One day after Hiroshima, the *Toronto Star* somewhat optimistically presented international control as a *fait accompli,* writing, 'Now the United Nations have an atomic bomb of a destruction which passes imagination.' Canadian syndicated columnist Elmore Philpott was unequivocal about Washington's obligations: 'It seems to me that the announcement by President Truman of the intention to try to keep the atomic bomb an exclusive monopoly, was one of the greatest blunders of all these years,' he charged in an August 8 piece, warning that holding to this position would result in a crippling arms race.[55]

Another *Saturday Night* editorial titled 'Too Much Power' takes no comfort in the fact that Canada's two closest allies control the nuclear secret, suggesting that the United States and Britain may now be tempted to replay the horrors of Hiroshima and Nagasaki in Russia. In truth, it cautioned, the mere possession of such a weapon under the current arrangement would have debilitating geopolitical outcomes, since 'it could not fail to be ruinous to the character of both these nations which possess this absolute power and of those nations which feel themselves victims of it.' Ottawa's francophone *Le Droit* likewise cautioned its readers that 'countries without the atomic bomb would be at the mercy of those with it,' a reminder that Canada was on the outside of the atomic secret and the nation might therefore have reason to fear its wartime allies. In a *Winnipeg Tribune* survey of prominent Canadian women's attitudes to the Bomb, Women's Christian Temperance Union president, 'Mrs. George McNeill,' maintained that 'the invention would not be so terrifying if we could be convinced that the world is fighting for the social welfare of all peoples, for a freedom that does not mean license to do what one likes.'[56] As noted above, this contestation over the meaning of 'One World' – away from the subtext of a remaking of America everywhere or of U.S. control of post-war restructuring and toward connotations of a true coalition of international equals – represents a re-inscription in keeping with the broader arc of pre–Cold War Canadian internationalism.

It is important to point out that these debates were framed in the context of a wartime alliance with the Soviets that, for many average Canadians (like many in the United States), went deeper than a mere marriage of convenience. Whitaker and Marcuse argue that 'the continuity of anti-Communism throughout the twentieth century is more striking than any sudden oscillations' of Canadian opinion, but this statement best applies to elected officials, foreign affairs bureaucrats, and business elites. In hindsight, given the impending chill in East-West relations, the degree of goodwill afforded the Soviets by many Canadian journalists and readers alike, even as post-war negotiations begin to unravel, is rather striking. Time and again the Soviets were presented merely as 'tough bargainers' – like the United States and Britain – not nefarious ideologues; likewise, British and especially U.S. motives and tactics were often as likely to be condemned (and feared) as the Soviets'. In a September 22 piece, *Saturday Night* editors maintained that emerging post-war divisions over occupied territory, the role and makeup of the UN, and the like were driven, not by ideological discord, but by power politics and personality clashes among leading diplomats. One commentator, in a variation on a familiar theme, held that the Soviet demand for naval bases in the Mediterranean 'is no more reprehensible than the recently made American claim for a wide ring of Atlantic and Pacific bases, or the long-established British claim to a string of bases from Gibraltar through the Middle East and on out to Singapore and Hong Kong.'[57]

This is not to say that Canada was uniformly charitable toward communism or its particular Russian variant, or that Canadians trusted or mistrusted the Americans and Soviets equally; certainly, the closer neighbour remained the closer ally. Further, especially in Quebec, where the Catholic Church exerted considerable influence, and among recent immigrants from Europe, many of whom had direct experience with Stalin's brutality, virulent anti-communism remained a constant. Many fundamentalist Protestant denominations, as well as demagogic newspapers like the *Toronto Telegram*, could also be counted on to insist upon the malevolence of all varieties of socialism. In general, however, these more immoderate voices did not exert a great deal of influence over public discourse in English-speaking Canada, and even Whitaker and Marcuse acknowledge 'a leftward trend evident in Canadian public opinion during the latter war years,' one that 'contrasted sharply with a rightward trend evident in the United States at the same time.'[58] Certainly, older misgivings and fears regarding Russia and communism were never completely eradicated, providing a reservoir of anti-Soviet and -communist sentiment that could be tapped once the Cold War was under way. Nonetheless, in the months following the Second World War, the prevailing opinion in Canada held that no single nation – not the Russians, Britain, or the United States – should dictate the peace.

Greatest resistance, naturally, to expressions of U.S. hegemony would arise when Canada itself became the object of imperial ambition, as when the *New York Daily News* editorialized that 'enough patriotic Americans can probably be found to see to it that Canada does the right thing by us and by itself with its uranium.' The notion that the clear and present danger to the security of Canada's much-vaunted uranium supplies, and, by extension, the nation's sovereignty, came not from the Soviets but from the United States would not have seemed far-fetched to many Canadians, particularly those aware of previous American rhetoric and action in the name of Canadian territorial and resource procurement. The anglophone, business-oriented *Montreal Gazette*, in an editorial just days after the *Daily News* story, went so far as to advise Canadians to seek help in developing their resources, not from the United States, but from the Russians, since the latter are 'faced with nearly identical questions of economic geography.'[59]

In truth, Canadians had legitimate cause for concern regarding U.S. control over uranium deposits, situated as those deposits were in the nation's sparsely populated northern environs. Science historian Edward Jones-Imhotep writes that throughout this period U.S. officials frequently challenged Canada's claims to much of its northern territory, arguing that ownership be determined according to the principle of 'effective occupation': that is, the presence of public and private citizens and organizations, including policing and defence agencies. 'Invoking this principle throughout the early Cold War,' Jones-Imhotep writes, 'the United States made it clear that, in defence of their own interests, they would not hesitate to occupy the North if Canada could not secure it.'[60]

The fact that the Second World War witnessed the introduction of an estimated 43,000 U.S. military personnel in northern Canada, and that these troops had constructed numerous airfields, weather stations, supply roads, and military bases, suggested the threat to the nation's sovereignty was real. Nor did the *Daily News* editors or their Canadian counterparts realize that the proposed uranium seizure had already occurred under the top secret Murray Hill Area Project, which locked up all known Canadian uranium through long-term contracts between suppliers and private companies acting, covertly, on behalf of the U.S. military.[61]

As in other instances of perceived U.S. bullying, the *Daily News* admonition that Canada's 'best interests' lay in acquiescing to American dictates inspired effects roughly the opposite of winning hearts and minds; to be sure, U.S. media saturation in Canada could extend *and* check pro-American attitudes. *Saturday Night* viewed 'with tolerant amusement the demands of various United States newspapers that their government should proceed to possess itself of this very important instrument for world peace or world domination as the case may be.' The national business weekly *Financial Post*, hardly a repository of rabid anti-Americanism, found the editorial 'reminiscent of Hitler's approach when he coveted his neighbors' property.'[62]

However, Canadian editorial responses to the proposed uranium grab reveal insecurities over the ability to face down threats from the south, combined with a decidedly limited vision of sovereignty and nationalism. Canada's autonomy in these and other matters, claimed *Saturday Night*, would ultimately be protected, not by its own government and citizenry, but by the still mighty British Commonwealth; further, in the end the uranium in question belonged to an international authority, as 'we are no more anxious to see Canadian uranium under the absolute control of Canada than under the absolute control of the United States.' The *Globe and Mail* concurred, noting that Canada's 'best interests' would be served, not by delivering its uranium over to the United States, but in the collective security promised by the UN.[63] Publications that just days earlier had proudly equated Canada's uranium with a heightened international standing now appeared similarly invested in distancing that uranium from any semblance of national custodianship.

The cross-border squabble over who controlled the nation's uranium would represent one of the earliest stirrings in the Canadian public realm of the gathering debate over where the nation's post-war loyalty ultimately resided. The idea that the UN might serve as a counterweight to American influence in Canada would hold considerable appeal to the country's nationalists, British loyalists, and world federalists alike. By July 1946, nearly two-thirds of respondents to a Canadian Institute of Public Opinion poll agreed that Canada should 'turn over control of all her armed forces and munitions, including atomic bomb materials, to a world parliament, providing other nations did the same,' a percentage Lawrence Wittner, perhaps the leading authority on the history of the global disarmament movement, terms 'remarkable.'[64]

The foregoing summary of post-war public culture makes clear that, aside from providing letters to the editor, few women were granted licence to participate in debates over such 'serious business' as high policy. Even so, it was Mary Lowrey Ross, writer of *Saturday Night*'s 'The Lighter Side' (the kind of lifestyle/society column to which women were typically relegated), who furnished one of the more prescient and sophisticated early takes on the Bomb's implications. Just two weeks after the war's end, Ross presents a conversation with an apocryphal 'Miss A.' a

Canadian companion who nonetheless embodies what Canadians would have read as a distinctively American approach toward post-war internationalism. Because Canada's uranium deposits will render the nation the geopolitical centre of gravity and true custodian of the Bomb, Miss A. boasts that 'within a generation ... Canadian standards, Canadian culture and civilization will have spread all over the planet. The Canadian National Anthem will be sung in Chinese, in Hindustani, in Russian and Icelandic.' Trade agreements with the United States will be revised in light of Canada's new international muscle, and grievances relating to undue American influence over the Canadian media, military, and politics will finally receive a fair hearing. 'Naturally,' Miss A. confided with fully intended irony, 'we must not misuse our power to infringe on American autonomy.' Canada would colonize Third World nations under the guise of liberation, and the atomic monopoly, rather than multilateral control, would be maintained and utilized 'as Providence intended us to, in order to free the Russian people from communism and teach Russia the democratic way of life.'[65]

Ross never names the object of her satire, but many of her readers would have had no trouble decoding her empire-posing-as-liberator. To be sure, the author's depiction of the archetypal American represents a crude caricature that serves to elide the lively and productive debates engaged in by a wide variety of Americans after the Second World War. This raises a series of important issues that bear upon U.S. cultural expansion (both privately funded and state engineered) and audience response in the post-war era. In the majority of areas of apparent or perceived national difference cited above, Canadians were able to demarcate a distinctive and sometimes oppositional national identity based, not on their authentic reading of the multi-vocal American conversation (in all its complexity, contradiction, and contestation), but on the decidedly fragmentary and mediated rendering of that conversation presented by the U.S. communications industry and governmental 'information' bureaus.

In reality, and contrary to what Canadians were led to believe, arguments over the ethics of the bombing raged in the United States, though largely outside the mainstream publications, radio addresses, or political speeches that reached Canadian audiences. Scientists working in the United States were at the forefront of the post-war disarmament movement, and many sought not to comfort the public but alarm them toward action, yet their direst warnings were often available only in public meetings, activist publications, and conferences. 'One World' and multilateralist ideals that did not take U.S. domination or culture as a prerequisite resonated with religious, scientific, labour, and racial advocacy groups considered unrepresentative by the largest U.S. media conglomerates. In every case, Canadians accustomed to initiating their search for identity with the phrase 'not American' would find solace in the messages conveyed from the south, as these messages would enable a sometimes facile movement toward a contrary site (one that nonetheless inhabited, or was contained by, the basic framework of Western liberalism). Canadian narratives of heterogeneity, born in part by the nation's experience with two 'official' languages and cultures and as a 'triply colonized space,' also owe much to this eternal quest to differentiate themselves from their (imagined) 'homogeneous' neighbour.[66]

This being the case, I offer the following conjectures on the correlation between cross-border dialogue and national identities, musings which have both specific and general application. First, such a study says much about the nature of the U.S. media abroad, particularly the types of views available from a highly concentrated communications establishment. Was America's international image best served by the narrow range of opinion expressed by its corporate media, a set of messages that faced further constriction in the Cold War's global 'battle for hearts and minds'? Would a more representative portrayal of a broad range of sometimes critical perspectives render some simplistic anti-Americanisms untenable, or lead foreign peoples facing similar issues and exclusions toward a closer identification with the American people? In sum, would greater degrees of heterogeneity from the mass communications industry serve to more fully 'humanize' Americans for foreign audiences? That one of the nation's most reliable allies, with whom it shares 'the world's longest undefended border' as well as language and a large measure of culture and heritage, had little difficulty imagining a monolithic and not always admirable neighbour is, I think, instructive on this question.

Second, in articulating their national identity against the *dominant* culture in the United States, it could be argued that Canadians were in fact moving their society toward a more accurate reflection of what truly existed south of their border: that is, toward the embrace of a multiplicity of ideals, visions, and pragmatisms that were sublimated but never fully contained by dominant 'master narratives,' and away from still powerful vestiges of European right of birth and deference to authority operant in Canada. Not all of these American perspectives were equal in terms of audience size or access to power, and many would have been as invisible to mainstream Americans as they were to Canadians; nevertheless, these alternative views did provoke responses from and re-shapings of dominant discourse – that is, they were real and they mattered. Fretful Canadian nationalists might resist the implication that their society provided a more faithful representation of that of the United States than they had imagined; alternatively, interpretations from post-nationalist frameworks could celebrate the inability of ruling elites in either country to fully secure or contain a stable nation-based narrative that would serve their own interests.

Finally, the attitudes expressed by many Canadians toward the Bomb would appear incongruous with the looming U.S.-led, anti-Soviet consensus that emerged in Canadian society by mid-century. Most prominent of these include a willingness to question the tactics of even the 'right' side in a global conflict; the desire for an independent international voice and a genuinely multilateral administration of global security; and the necessity of international control of atomic weaponry. For differing reasons – and there is little to suggest a dialogue at this stage – Canadians sometimes articulated positions resembling those of marginalized Americans; significant numbers in both communities, it appears, felt themselves to be losers in the face of an American liberalism that was expanding geographically even as it contracted ideologically.

2 Espionage: 'Soviet Method Revealed!'

Canada's contribution to the Allied victory in the Second World War, along with its considerable uranium reserves and its role in the development of the atomic bomb, seemed to portend greater international significance following the conflict. However, it was an unexpected – though related – circumstance that, for a short time, placed the nation at the centre of the emerging Cold War. In February 1946, Canadian officials, tipped off by defecting Soviet embassy clerk Igor Gouzenko in Ottawa, revealed the existence of an espionage operation in Canada that targeted the Canadian civil service and, many feared, the nation's 'atomic secrets.' At once Canadians who craved greater international notice were provided much more than they had bargained for, with a surfeit of attention radiating not only from a prying Russian 'diplomatic' corps, but also from subsequent counsel provided by the British and American governments, as well as what a particularly testy *Ottawa Citizen* termed a 'sneering campaign of "advice"' offered by the foreign press.[1]

Though now largely forgotten in the United States, Gouzenko would become an iconic, enduring, and polarizing figure in Canadian culture. Revered by strident anti-communists, he was reviled by civil libertarians and progressives as an opportunist who produced a recklessly embellished account of Soviet information-gathering operations in order to secure permanent refuge and monetary gain in Canada. Indeed, though Gouzenko lived underground until his death in 1982 because he feared Soviet reprisals, he would surface intermittently in order to pursue the celebrity and revenue he believed his service to the West warranted. In the decades following his defection, Gouzenko would level increasingly implausible accusations regarding communist infiltration in a series of contexts, including 1953 testimony before representatives of the U.S.

House Committee on Un-American Activities. He would also appear – hooded – on Canadian news and current affairs television programs, produce a best-selling autobiography with the assistance of a Canadian sports journalist, and pen a predictably dystopian novel about life in the Soviet Union. The latter won a Governor General's Prize for fiction, an award that speaks more 'to the Cold War politics of the 1950s,' observe Whitaker and Hewitt, 'than to its literary merits.'[2]

In ways that mirror the wider Canadian-American relationship, Gouzenko's own strenuous efforts to profit from his experience would be trumped by those of Hollywood's Twentieth Century Fox, which generated the most widely circulated account of the Canadian espionage incident. In May 1948, the studio released *The Iron Curtain*, one of the earliest candidly anti-communist Hollywood productions. Shot on location in Ottawa, the film opened simultaneously in five hundred theatres throughout North America. As many early reviews of the film pointed out, such widespread release was extraordinary, and speaks to the degree of receptivity the studio anticipated in light of the increasingly anti-Soviet atmosphere evident by this juncture in both countries.

In spite of this growing consensus, a variety of leftist, peace, and world federalist organizations in both the United States and Canada, branded monolithically as 'Communist-led' and 'Red-front' groups by *Saturday Night* and *Time*, respectively, conducted demonstrations against the film outside theatres on the grounds that it would further damage international relations. Some Canadians resented, in particular, that what remained of their country's friendship with Russia could be impaired by a third party and, worse yet, in the name of economic gain. The Winnipeg Council for Canadian-Soviet Friendship, for one, circulated a letter charging that '20th Century-Fox is exploiting a delicate Canadian domestic situation in a way that will make our diplomatic relations with the USSR more difficult.' The widespread protests appear to have triggered the seemingly inevitable boomerang, boosting public interest in the film and box-office receipts for the studio. According to a Vancouver columnist, 'the left-wingers have made a serious tactical error in giving it so much publicity,' as the film 'just happens to be one of the dullest movies you ever saw in your life.'[3]

Not many in either country rose to defend the film on artistic grounds, but opinion was divided as to the propriety of its unreserved anti-Soviet message. *Time* held that *The Iron Curtain*'s 'imperfections hardly lessen the impact of the picture as a whole,' which constitutes 'topnotch anti-Communist propaganda,' an opinion espoused nearly verbatim by a *Sat-*

urday Night reviewer. Neither could the *Canadian Forum* miss the film's bruising didacticism: namely, 'that the Russians as a nation are unprincipled and vicious and that any attempt to deal with them in non-military terms is foolish and ultimately suicidal.' Yet this magazine would not applaud such a view, writing: 'It does not seem to have occurred to the peddlers of this notion that to accept it is equally disastrous, and an essential denial not only of democracy but of humanity itself.' The editor of the *Canadian Moving Picture Digest* did not identify *The Iron Curtain* by name, but produced a scathing piece on the eve of the film's release that opposed Hollywood's burgeoning anti-communism, charging that 'what this Industry does not know about Communism would fill an Encyclopedia,' and reminding American filmmakers that 'other countries may not desire Hollywood propaganda films, any more than the United States or Canada desires any other country's propaganda films.' The *New York Times* film reviewer concurred, condemning, in particular, the film's insinuation that all domestic groups advocating '"rights" and "freedom"' should be considered suspect.[4] By mid-1948, these represented increasingly lonely stands.

On one point, *The Iron Curtain*'s advocates and detractors could agree: the picture did not merely malign communist ideology, it denigrated Russian ethnicity itself to a degree that made even the film's supporters wince. All Russians, save the Gouzenkos, were represented as 'blatant fiends' noted the otherwise laudatory *Time*, and as 'obvious villains ... who invite investigation on sight,' observed *Saturday Night*. Here were the troubling 'old-fashioned villain stereotypes' according to the *New York Times*, a publication which, like the *Canadian Forum*, lamented the ease with which the Russian had replaced the Nazi as Hollywood's, and the West's, archetypal bogeyman (though the 'chunky, bull-necked actors' who made their living portraying the enemies of freedom remained constant).[5]

It was virtually compulsory, given the chauvinism embedded in the film, that *The Iron Curtain* portray Igor Gouzenko as a sincere, amiable 'American college-student type,' and his wife Svetlana as a 'sweet and domestic ...Western idealization' of femininity. While their ostensible compatriots converse in heavy (and variable) accents, the Gouzenkos speak in the flat, 'accent-less' tones of Middle America.[6] Casting more 'authentic' Russians as cinematic heroes would have undermined the Russo-phobia that otherwise oozed from the production, and could well have cut into box-office receipts. Fitting, then, that it was the scandal set in motion by the real Gouzenko two years earlier which had served for many in North America as the tipping point in the perception of the Russians, the episode that most clearly marked the latter's transformation from wartime ally to 'fiend' and 'villain.' Subsequent fractures in the East-West relationship would only confirm the essential depravity of their eastern adversaries; by 1948, the courage and principle that cinematic Gouzenko demonstrates by turning on his countrymen would be nearly inconceivable had it been realized by a bona fide Russian, who by this point had been demonized to a degree which foreclosed the possibility of redemption.

The meanings attached to the so-called Gouzenko Affair of 1946 would amplify and harden a growing hostility not only toward communism and the Soviets, but also to the left in general. Clearly, the scandal grew out of a series of provocative and rather clumsy actions on the part of the USSR in Canada; at the same time (and in a pattern that would be repeated in many Cold War contexts), political and cultural elites throughout the West carefully managed the linguistic and visual symbols employed to make sense of the event in ways that discredited all those who challenged the continental drift toward arch-conservatism.

The affair would also reveal the limits (and, indeed, provoked the contraction) of Canadians' purported commitment to liberal values and tolerance at home, as well as multilateralism abroad. In short order, the high-minded rhetoric of 'One World,' global cooperation, and collective security gave considerable ground to ideas that had recently been declared anachronistic, even suicidal: nationalism, power balancing, counter-subversion, and regional defence arrangements. Further, the quasi-dictatorial handling of the case provided something of a blueprint for the illiberal measures taken by other Western states in their battles against real and imagined insurgents and fifth columnists. In this latter respect, Canada provided a less-than-laudable example for its southern neighbour, and thus bears some responsibility for the shaping and regulation of an increasingly fervent anti-communism in the United States. The cross-border 'information highway' could, on occasion, facilitate travel in both directions.

For our purposes, however, three questions remain paramount: How did Canadian readings of the incident differ from those emanating from the United States? What role did U.S. voices play in shaping Canadians' understanding of Gouzenko? How did discourses surrounding the incident affect larger debates about the proper domestic and international responses to communism and the post-war order? I argue the affair provides a vivid illustration of the degree to which U.S. journalism, domestic politics, and popular culture could impinge upon Canadian public policy and opinion. In this case, that influence took two general forms: (1) U.S. views adopted more-or-less wholesale by Canadians, or those which find reasonably precise correlates in Canada (as I demonstrate, these attitudes represent a range of political orientations and geopolitical imaginings – American influence, though undeniable, does not always lead in a straight line toward Red-baiting or the advance of U.S. global hegemony); (2) Canadian responses posited as direct and deliberate counterchecks to U.S. views. While drawing on and enlarging an emergent Canadian nationalism, these contrapuntal positions frequently represented simplistic reversals of perceived American dogma; moreover, these responses fed into a pre-existing current of social democratic discourse in Canada that shared these deficiencies and would prove a ready target for nascent Cold Warriors. To a degree, then, opponents of bipolarity, the national security state, and nuclear monopoly served as architects of their own demise.

Attempts to make sense of the incident, and to employ Gouzenko in service of a variety of political agendas, also reveal the ambiguities inherent in defining a national character in opposition to both the American republic – with its 'mobocracy,' individualism, materialism, and racial diversity – and communism (as well as milder manifestations of socialism). Both orientations imperilled the status of Canadian elites, as well as the conservative tradition of 'peace, order, and good government' – the nation's more cautious and paternalistic antidote to 'life, liberty, and happiness.' Now, however, the nation-states that most clearly exemplified values associated with un-Canadianism were emerging as global rivals to one another. Could antipathy to both be maintained simultaneously? Or would the ostensibly unparalleled menace posed by Soviet communism temper, or supplant, fears of American influence? The rhetoric from the United States regarding the true threat to Canadians was, of course, mostly unequivocal on this matter; the espionage affair would lead many Canadian elites to articulate similar conclusions.

Before moving to a cross-cultural assessment of the ways in which the Gouzenko incident was represented, a brief summary of events is in order. In September 1945, Gouzenko, a cipher clerk from the Soviet embassy in Ottawa, defected to Canada, carrying with him documentation about a Soviet espionage ring that utilized Canadian civil servants as informants. Gouzenko and his family were granted asylum, but anxious Canadian officials, preparing for a Council of Foreign Ministers meeting in London which would discuss vital post-war issues, were loath to impair these delicate negotiations with allegations of Soviet malfeasance. Thus, while the Canadian government – in concert with that of the United States and Britain – began investigations of alleged espionage activities and discussions about how best to manage the incident, officials did not divulge the defection or subsequent investigation to the public, hoping instead to deal with the issue quietly through diplomatic channels. However, in February 1946 an American journalist acting on a leak from a U.S. government source broke the story. As I discuss in greater detail below, this leak required a reluctant Canadian administration to verify (and seek to establish control over) the narrative being generated south of the border, and to hastily round up suspects who would now know the jig was up.[7]

Once the affair became known, the Liberal government of Mackenzie King set into motion a plan devised months earlier and vetted by both Britain and the United States: using the extraordinary powers of the War Measures Act (which had been extended in September 1945 specifically for this purpose), the Liberals established a royal commission headed by Supreme Court justices Roy Kellock and Robert Taschereau to interrogate the Canadians fingered by Gouzenko. The so-called Kellock-Taschereau Commission was charged with identifying the nature and scope of the alleged spy ring and determining whether criminal charges should be laid. The six-week hearings were held in secret, and thirteen suspects detained incommunicado and without access to legal counsel. Witnesses were compelled to testify or be charged for refusing, even if the evidence they provided proved self-incriminating. Rather predictably, once enough evidence had been gathered to lay charges, the suspects were released by the commission and immediately arrested by the RCMP for violations of Canada's Official Secrets Act (OSA) and the Criminal Code, jailed, and later brought before a criminal tribunal.[8]

In the end, the Canadian 'espionage ring' – though existent – proved far less sensational or ruinous than many in government or the media suggested. Of the thirteen Canadians detained and eight others identified as spies by the commission, ten were convicted of violating the OSA (a rather underwhelming record given that the act required the accused to prove their innocence, rather than the prosecutor to prove guilt). Most of those charged were low-level bureaucrats, with the exception of Canadian Association of Scientific Workers president Raymond Boyer, the Canadian Parliament's only communist representative, the Labour-Progressive (formerly 'Canadian Communist') Party's Fred Rose, and one of the party's top organizers, Sam Carr. The information in question had been passed during the war to a nation allied with Canada. Accordingly, the accused could not be charged with treason or espionage, as those charges implied communication with a foreign enemy; instead, they stood accused of communicating classified information to a foreign government (a distinction lost on many reporters, whose headlines charted the progress of the 'treason trials').[9]

While some of the accused appear to have been motivated by a long-standing allegiance to Stalin's international directives, other detainees merely expressed a desire to assist the USSR in its war against Nazi aggression – at a time, they reasoned, when their own government's anti-Soviet bias prevented an appropriate level of official support. Others were convicted for discussing information they believed, in some cases correctly, already belonged to the public domain. Still others were convicted for communicating with an 'agent of a foreign power' (with 'agents' including those already convicted – in some cases, spuriously – as a result of the probe), however innocuous the conversation or unsuspecting the participants may have been. The information divulged by the Canadians involved, according to the Crown prosecutor himself, was of minimal importance. Still, the sentences handed down were surprisingly heavy, ranging from two to six years in prison, penalties based not on the value of the information but on the fact the accused had violated their oath of secrecy. Historians Whitaker and Marcuse argue that the stiff sentences served additional purposes, serving as a caveat to 'other left-leaning civil servants' and as a wider public warning about 'the aggressive nature of the Soviets as demonstrated by their espionage.' Unstated in the report, though certainly known to high-ranking Canadian officials involved in the case, was the fact that the RCMP conducted its own espionage operations against the Soviet diplomats in Canada even after the USSR had joined the Allies in the Second World War.[10]

Existing historiography concerning the episode emphasizes its impact on the Canadian government's domestic and international policy, as well as the nation's judicial traditions and practices. Denis Smith writes that the polarized atmosphere generated by the official narrative of the Gouzenko Affair 'narrow[ed] the range of speculation and enquiry about Russian intentions, and progressively limit[ed] the margins for diplomatic manoeuvre in relations with the USSR.' Historian Mark Kristmanson goes so far as to suggest that Gouzenko worked covertly for Britain, which orchestrated the defection to promote a unified, hardline response toward the Soviets among Western powers. 'Canada's "in-between" status as a junior partner in the Anglo-American alliance,' Kristmanson argues, 'along with its full integration in that alliance's media and propaganda circuits, would have recommended Ottawa as an appropriate setting for such an operation.'[11] Though Kristmanson's provocative claims require further substantiation, the ensuing climate certainly played to interests of British leaders seeking steadfast allies in their increasingly bitter post-war feud with Stalin. Canadian writer and filmmaker Merrily Weisbord takes stock of the domestic and international bearing of the episode:

> Red-baiting destroys the popular-front groups and the lobby for the international control of atomic weapons. It destroys the militant unions and is used to discredit the Canadian attempt to keep its unions independent of the American Internationals. The trials are the basis for a tidal wave of anti-Russian propaganda. They prepare the way for the North Atlantic Treaty Organization (NATO) and the era of atomic diplomacy. They justify the growth of secret security services.[12]

Whitaker and Marcuse, along with Amy Knight, the most recent contributor to Gouzenko scholarship, provide an especially thorough account of the damage done to the rule of law: for these authors, the handling of the 'espionage ring' constitutes the first example of the extreme violations of civil liberties that would characterize the looming Cold War – including guilt by association, character assassination, and judicial extremism in defence of liberty. Among the more egregious practices: Kellock and Taschereau found three witnesses treasonous who, in the commission's own words, 'did not so far as the evidence discloses take any active part in the subversive activities but would have done so if required.' Establishing that a suspect would practise subversion 'if required' rested largely on the ability of the justices to prove an affinity between the individual and often loosely defined communist organizations, individuals, or ideas. As Weisbord notes, the accused were tried 'not for what they did, but for who they were'; in some cases, bureaucrats who also appear to have violated the OSA but could not be linked to the 'Communist conspiracy' were not brought before the commission.[13]

Moreover, suspects interrogated by the commission were not permitted to confront their accusers or discover the full extent of the evidence and charges against them. And although the commission's final report was published after many of the accused had been exonerated in criminal court, in that report Kellock and Taschereau maintained that their original judgments were indeed correct, and that the courts would have agreed had they been granted access to the secret testimony provided to, and still known only by, the commission. Thus, while many of the accused had been declared innocent in court, they were now branded once more as culpable, with no further opportunity to clear their name. Such illiberal measures lead Whitaker and Marcuse to suggest that a procedure akin to McCarthyism emerged in Canada four years before McCarthy began his stateside crusade. As Weisbord notes, Canada's spy trials represent 'the first big show trials in the West.' The title of Knight's account, *How the Cold War Began,* may embellish the global reach of the affair, but the author provides ample evidence that the West's management of the defection 'produced an overreaction that polarized Western society and diverted Western governments from a more reasoned and productive response to Soviet espionage.'[14]

Analysts are divided in their assessments of the degree to which Canadians contested the government's secrecy and abridgment of standard judicial practices in the prosecution of the case. Whitaker and Marcuse are largely unimpressed by the public's timidity, and argue that any denunciations were severely constrained by the fact that those involved were suspected communists. Legal historian Dominique Clément challenges this notion of collective complacency, revealing instead a vigorous 'public backlash' against the proceedings witnessed in the press, opposition parties, professional legal organizations, and opinion polls. Despite the Red-baiting of proponents of civil liberties, Clément finds that the commission spurred public awareness of the issue of civil liberties, leading to the 1960 passage of Canada's first Bill of Rights.[15] That this long-overdue legislation was modelled on its American counterpart should be noted at the outset; as is evident in the following, the U.S. influence on Canadians' commitment to liberalism could pull in several directions at once.

That being said, it is possible that the 'spy scandal' would not have materialized at all were it not for the deliberate and coordinated intervention of a combination of U.S. interests. Americans did not fabricate the notion that a Soviet intelligence-gathering operation existed in Canada; furthermore, Americans do not appear to have played a part in Gouzenko's defection or in the workings of the Kellock-Taschereau Commission and subsequent legal proceedings against accused spies (though U.S. and British intelligence agencies assisted and sometimes drove the RCMP investigation). Still, the U.S. imprint upon this vital moment in the coalescence of anti-Soviet attitudes in Canada is substantial. Had the ruling Liberal Party managed the incident without outside intervention and in the manner it favoured, the result may have merely been the expulsion of Soviet diplomats and the quiet dismissal of a handful of civil servants.[16] While such clandestine machinations do not speak well of the degree of openness operant in a purported liberal democracy, they would be in keeping with the way the Canadian government preferred to do business, abetted by a public that was often unduly trusting of authority.

This more restrained course of action was rendered unworkable when Drew Pearson, a conservative U.S. radio and print commentator, divulged information from a confidential source about Gouzenko's defection. Certain U.S. interests had much to gain from Pearson's revelations. While the source of the leak has never been disclosed, scholars agree that the likely culprit was the FBI, which released the information in an effort to advance its broader anti-communist campaign, and did so at direct variance with the wishes of the State Department. Pearson's scoop, carried widely in both the U.S. and Canadian dailies on February 16, suggested as much: 'Serious secret differences inside the United States Government resulted from these revelations,' Pearson claimed, 'with the State Department anxious not to disrupt Russian relations, but the Justice Department anxious to arrest and prosecute.' A domestic bureaucratic squabble in the United States, it seems, could have serious ramifications for Canadians. (Pearson, however, appears to forget rather abruptly that the espionage ring was outed in Canada; after the second paragraph of a fourteen-paragraph column, no further mention is made of Canada. Instead, he reports that the incident 'confronts the U.S.A. with the most serious foreign-relations crisis since Pearl Harbor,' with the Soviets 'caught attempting to steal military secrets and undermine American officials.')[17]

There were other stateside winners in the Gouzenko fallout, some of whom took an active role in the release and shaping of the story. U.S. general Leslie Groves, a firm advocate of the U.S. nuclear monopoly and military, rather than civilian, control of atomic energy, proved the most voluble 'confidential source' behind a particularly unsettling component of the story: that 'atomic secrets' had been divulged to Russian agents (the implication being that the continuation of both the monopoly and military control were more important than ever). Groves passed the allegation on to U.S. journalist Frank McNaughton, who added it to the burgeoning hopper of charges. Believing that Truman himself had ultimately authorized the leaks, Canadian syndicated columnist Elmore Philpott offered up an observation that he dryly termed 'purely coincidental': 'It will be a lot easier for President Truman to hold the Democratic nomination now that Henry A. Wallace, the CIO political action committee and other avowed friends of Russia will be kept on the defensive by the calculated repercussions of the Ottawa spy scare.'[18]

Though Pearson's report appears to have provided reliable information on the bureaucratic tug-of-war over the disclosure, his other 'facts' appeared to rely on less dependable sources, if any at all. Indeed, his initial dispatch remains one of the most sensational accounts of a highly sensationalized affair, and to a great degree established the idioms and symbols through which subsequent reports were required to manoeuvre. Among his revelations: that the handful of persons seized constituted merely the initial traces of a massive fifth column operating in both the United States and Canada (with Pearson citing no less than '1,700 other Russian agents' currently working in both countries, including 'major' government officials); that those involved disclosed that a host of recent labour and protest activities outside the Soviet Union were in fact manufactured and/or manipulated by Russian operatives (including recent harbour-employee strikes 'involved in paralyzing' New York); that efforts to accommodate Stalin have led the West to let its collective guard down, and should now be considered naïve; and, perhaps most alarming of all, that the spies had been allowed to leave the United States toting 'plans of the atomic bomb … [and] samples of the metal from which the bomb is made.' (Pearson's assertion that the FBI was prevented from intercepting this transaction by an effete State Department unwilling to upset 'the diplomatic applecart with Russia' lends additional credence to the idea that the latter agency was not, in fact, the source of the leak:)[19] All the while, and like the high-ranking U.S. officials, the American press corps simultaneously manipulated the Gouzenko narrative and referred to it as an 'external matter' over which the United States had little influence.

Pearson did not manufacture the overall climate that lent credibility to many of these assertions – instead, he built upon, and certainly enhanced, themes already in circulation. Since the end of the war, aversion toward the Soviet Union had grown in both countries, as fears of an atomic arms race, the division of the globe into antagonistic spheres of influence, and seemingly intractable disputes over the structure and role of the United Nations encouraged a climate of hostility and distrust between the Soviets and the West.

Through sheer coincidence, on the very day that the RCMP rounded up Canadian civil servants implicated in the affair, the Canadian military launched a three-month northern excursion known as 'Operation Musk-Ox' in order to test the limits of military equipment in frigid climates.

The manoeuvres, which received technical and logistical support from the U.S. military, garnered considerable attention on both sides of the border and reinforced the idea that the Canadian Arctic constituted the first line of defence against an invasion of North America – should that invasion be launched by the Soviets. In fact, in its March 11 coverage of the operation, *Life* magazine provided its clearest signal yet that former ally Russia should now be considered America's foe, rendering a map of the trek that centred on the North Pole and revealed the unnerving proximity of the USSR to Canada and the United States. 'Canada's Exercise Musk Ox is the first big Allied peacetime military maneuver held in North America since the war's end,' *Life* explained. 'It is taking place on the great snow-driven northern wastes of Canada, around Hudson Bay, a region where some people think a future war may be held.'[20] For several weeks beginning in mid-February, reports on the infiltration of the Canadian and U.S. security apparatus ran alongside stories about the militarization of Canada's North in preparation for a possible Soviet military assault on the continent.

Many trusted voices who had been gravitating toward such a strategic reorientation found in Gouzenko's revelations their 'smoking gun.' By way of example, two widely read foreign affairs columnists who in the months immediately following the war were noted for their unflagging support of world government and their criticism of the West's insensitivity to the Soviet Union's post-war concerns – American Dorothy Thompson and Canadian Willson Woodside – now took the tone of something approaching hardened Cold Warriors. In a February column carried widely in both countries, Thompson argued that 'One World' was also Hitler's objective, and that the survival of the free world was more important than a unified world under potential Soviet domination. Woodside, who had previously held that global peace required that the West be willing to 'lie down with Communists,' was by this juncture equating the sharing of atomic secrets with 'freedom committing suicide.'[21] Particularly in this instance, however, analysts can be forgiven for alarm: as respected authorities had assured them, the spy ring had succeeded in obtaining atomic secrets, and as all knew by now, atomic issues were central not only to current great power negotiations, but to the survival of humanity itself.

As noted in the previous chapter, Canada did not possess, nor did its government covet, the 'atomic secret,' a circumstance firmly established by its elected leaders, scientists, and news media in the weeks following Hiroshima. Six months later, however, those same media outlets appear to have forgotten or dismissed their own bomb-related reportage in the rush for a gripping narrative. 'Atom Secret Leaks to Soviet,' headlined the generally reserved *Globe and Mail* in its first report on the incident. The less restrained *Toronto Telegram*, meanwhile, responded with a series of predictably lurid reports and editorials, the first of which identified the Bomb as the espionage ring's objective in the title, and went on to utilize the terms 'atomic bomb' or 'atomic energy' seven times (before concluding by cautioning readers not to be swayed by 'the flood of rumours and gossip'). Since the Russians had undoubtedly stolen the atomic secret, the *Telegram*'s editors concluded that what might otherwise be considered a rather conventional diplomatic dalliance was in fact 'fraught with more terrible possibilities than any that have yet faced the human race.' Other reports declared that the Russians had already infiltrated Canada's uranium procurement apparatus and/or were planning to discharge paratroopers over Canada's North in order to secure the vital ingredient for the cataclysmic weapon they now knew how to assemble. While historians now agree that espionage did hasten the Soviet development of the Bomb, these spying operations correctly focused on U.S. targets; Canada did not, nor could it, churn out 'atomic spies.' As the president of Canada's National Research Council assured U.S. officials, 'There has never been at any time any information about the bomb in Canada, and no information could possibly have been obtained from this country.'[22]

Speculation of this type seemed to know no bounds, and, given the stakes, it should not be surprising that it tended to feed upon itself. In a *New York Times* 'special' run by dailies in both countries, reporter P.J. Philip unwittingly summed up the circular nature of press logic on Gouzenko and the Bomb: 'Despite the half denial of Minister C.D. Howe that the secrets involved regarded atomic energy,' Philip wrote, 'the general consensus is that it could not have been anything else as there are no other developments which rank anywhere as high.' Given that the story's 'high ranking' owed a great deal to journalists' own specious and repeated connections between spies and atoms – while the governments of Canada, the United States, Britain, and the USSR took pains to minimize the importance of the dispute and insisted that the 'atomic secret' had not been surrendered – Philip's reasoning provides a lesson in circular logic. (A translation might read: 'Because the Bomb is involved, this is a big story. Because this story is so big, the Bomb must be involved.') The 'atom' charge likewise dominated U.S. headlines and reports; British commentators, on the other hand, underscored their own nation's vital wartime contribution, emphasizing (quite correctly) that the spies sought 'Empire' radar.[23]

Columnists in both the United States and Canada were quick, too, to build upon another of Pearson's claims: that the Soviets were solely responsible for the emerging global rift, that they were not rational actors engaged in traditional power-balancing contests, but rather, by their very nature, were mysterious, manipulative, even evil. Expressions of sympathy for the USSR's geopolitical concerns or its atomic deficit, sentiments already fading in light of heightened international tensions, were for many dealt a fatal blow. By the same token, the wartime alliance between liberal democracies and communism was depicted as anomalous to the 'normal' aversion the West should exhibit toward Russia. 'Soviet Method Revealed,' trumpeted the *Toronto Telegram* headline the day Pearson's story appeared, implying that the paper had always known that the USSR was a preordained saboteur, that only the *mode* of duplicity had, until now, lain hidden. Referring to the Popular Front, Soviet friendship societies, and seemingly genuine, grassroots identification with the Russian people that emerged during the war, editors at Toronto's *Globe and Mail* argued that a reversal of Canadian benevolence (and artlessness) was now in order. Employing terms that underscored the fundamentally alien character of their erstwhile ally, they wrote: 'Unquestionably the fact that an unceasing propaganda has been going on, building up the nobility of this strange ideology has had some effect in breaking down the natural barriers of restraint in personal and official relationships. A false conception of the other party's sincerity and good faith has been built up, now to be rudely disillusioned.'[24] In editorials and cartoons, Stalin became a simple re-embodiment of Hitler, and communism of Nazism.

Nor did Pearson's allegations of an extensive fifth column escape notice. Though the thirteen Canadians apprehended in mid-February represent the sum total of all suspects brought before the Kellock-Taschereau Commission, journalists repeatedly implied that these arrests represented merely 'the tip of the iceberg.' 'Twenty-two persons are now held by the RCMP,' claimed the *Toronto Telegram* on February 16, citing an apparently confused government source who went on to peg the total number of civil servants known to be involved at '40 to 50.' 'Scores Still Face Arrest,' headlined the *Vancouver Sun* in its first Gouzenko report, while *Saturday Night* took as given the existence of a 'far-reaching fifth column' in its initial editorial. Many reporters in both countries reiterated without corroboration the initial claim that 1,700 Russian agents haunted the United States and Canada; it was left to an *Ottawa Citizen* reader to question why 'the authorities did nothing to deny' such rumours, yet two weeks later had arrested only thirteen. 'The alleged spy ring has been reduced by over 99 per cent,' he noted, 'and against the remaining 1 per cent no charges can as yet be made. No scientist would be impressed by data of this sort.'[25] Nevertheless, time and again in the weeks following the first arrests, journalists citing 'reliable sources' predicted that the scale of the operation would 'snowball' and reveal a continent-wide insurgency as the commission interrogated and broke down the initial pool of turncoats.

How to account for insurgency on such a scale? Like their U.S. counterparts, many in the Canadian government and media moved with remarkable ease to the conclusion that virtually all leftist organizations, activities, and sympathies served as recruiting grounds – if not out-and-out fronts – for Russian intelligence operations. In this, they were in large measure simply reviving an attack on the left (in both countries) that had been sublimated by wartime alliances. With proof of subversion, however, their campaign reached new heights, and was augmented when the commission report cited 'adherence to communist ideology' as the motivation for spying. A story from Montreal noted that the city police force's 'Red Squad' had compiled files on every known communist in the district, and estimated the number of card-carrying party members and fellow travellers at 12,000 to 18,000 in that city alone; it went without saying that all should now be deemed potential conspirators. And detecting a Soviet mole was easier than one might think: the Canadian Press revealed that books left in one detainee's room included the rabble-rousing *War and Peace* and, more ominous still, 'a Russian-English Dictionary.' The reliably anti-union *Calgary Herald*'s subhead to the initial Drew Pearson dispatch, meanwhile, exulted that in his 'confession,' Gouzenko had 'name[d] some labour leaders.'[26]

The *Toronto Telegram* was quick to connect the spy activities to long-standing efforts to organize Canada's northern mine workers. 'Ottawa's disclosure of suspected Russian espionage in Canada,' it noted, 'made the average Northern Ontario citizen weigh the significance of the intensive pro-Soviet propaganda campaign which has been waged throughout the gold mining areas for the past five years.' 'Average' (presumed definition: 'non-unionized') citizens were further, and grimly, informed that the pro-labour *Northern Citizen* received weekly envelopes 'bearing the label "Soviet Embassy, Washington."' Almost at once, all local, national, and global threats to peace, order, democracy, free enterprise, and Western hegemony could be grasped according to a simple master narrative. How, queried *Calgary Herald* editors, can we account for the post-war 'strike epidemic' in the United States, which, incidentally, has 'crippled postwar production' while the Soviet economy 'is going ahead full steam?' According to that paper, it could be linked directly to 'Communist inspiration and encouragement.' Rioting in Bombay against more than three centuries of British colonial rule? To *Toronto Telegram* editors, it clearly 'stems from a similar source' to that of recent 'strikes among Canadian and United States forces.'[27] Under this reductionist schema, the unsettling muddle of the post-war globe, while perhaps no less unsettling, could at the very least be comprehended.

Quebec premier Maurice Duplessis, a long-time anti-communist reactionary who would come to embody French Canada's nearest answer to Joseph McCarthy, was an old hand at generating political opportunity from such a state of affairs. In a press conference held three days after Gouzenko's defection, the premier assured reporters that the province 'will not tolerate communistic propaganda within its boundaries' and pledged immediate cooperation with 'federal authorities in uncovering the plot and the guilt.' Such a rush to judgment may have seemed improper for a provincial leader who also served as the province's attorney general. It would not have come as news to Quebecers involved in leftist and labour organizations, who were subjected to the province's suffocating Padlock Law – which permitted the province to close any premises used to advance 'communism or bolshevism by any means whatever' – as well as to what Whitaker and Hewitt consider some of the most repressive anti-labour laws in North America during the era.[28]

English Canada's most notorious right-wing demagogue, Ontario premier George Drew of the Progressive Conservative Party, also sensed blood. 'There never was a time,' he warned in a speech covered by several dailies across the country, 'when it was more necessary that there be a vigorous and effective organization of Canada's political and democratic forces against the Communist menace to our democratic form of government.' Drew then widened the scope of suspicion beyond the detained civil servants to encompass nearly everything to his left (that is, nearly everything), including organized labour, progressive, big city politicos, and those who would oppose 'Bible teaching' in the province's public schools. Drew's panacea to the unequivocal Red peril was as straightforward as it was predictable: mobilization of his PC Party's members – whom he now cast as the solitary 'guardians of democracy' in Canada – in anticipation of a looming federal election against the ruling Liberals.[29]

It was neither the first nor last time that a wildly exaggerated communist threat was utilized in service of political ambition, but the Ontario premier employed the spy scare to discredit the nation's ruling, and thoroughly anti-communist, party even before such tactics had become standard Republican Party practice in the United States. Drew's serial Red-baiting was successful, to a degree. The publicity gained through such tactics helped him secure the national leadership of the Progressive Conservative Party in 1948, but he failed in two successive attempts to achieve the nation's highest office. This failure owes a great deal to Drew's thoroughgoing British chauvinism and its attendant distaste for Catholicism and the French language, which naturally won few supporters in vote-rich Quebec. That such sentiments were common among the more conservative of English-Canadian Protestants also impeded the emergence of a more dynamic McCarthyite atmosphere in Canada; the nation's two most dependable reservoirs of anti-communism could not, and would not, be conjoined.[30]

As is evident from the foregoing, the mere betrayal of state secrets by Canadian bureaucrats cannot account for the venom directed toward the espionage activities. The fact that communist Russia sought and obtained the information lay at the heart of the collective resentment. Hostility on the part of governmental, business, and religious leaders toward a system which sought to subvert their authority should come as no surprise; however, reactions to the incident were also rooted in a particular moment in the nationalist discourses of the United States and Canada.

Not only was communism an 'alien ideology' with respect to politics, economics, and social and religious values, its emphasis on international working-class solidarity would, according to many of its advocates and detractors, diminish allegiance to the nation-state. Communism, as theologian Reinhold Niebuhr pointed out in a 1946 *Life* article, was 'universalist, rather than nationalist' (and, not incidentally, 'evil'), an orientation that for Niebuhr formed the basis of both Soviet designs for world conquest and of the rationale for containment. *Globe and Mail* editors made a similar point in their initial comment on the Gouzenko Affair, instructing readers that Canadian communists, 'though in many cases technically Canadian citizens, habitually put loyalty to their party above loyalty to their country,' sentiments reprised nearly verbatim in the Kellock-Taschereau Commission's initial report.[31]

In post-war Canada, as in the United States, such transnational political identifications were greeted with increasing hostility (the same *Globe* editorial called this internationalist orientation 'a moral fungus which corrupts the national integrity'). Both nations were experiencing an upsurge in nationalist sentiment during this period, and from some of the same sources: victory in war, coupled with the emergence of a powerful and potentially threatening adversary in the form of the Soviets. In Canada, these trends were augmented by the fact that the global influence of Britain, the nation's traditional benefactor and the primary locus of identity for many Anglo Canadians, was on the wane. As a result, Canada's very existence might now require a more assertive and independent sense of collective identity – though many nationalists still maintained that the threat to the state's survival was just as likely to arise from U.S. cultural and economic incursions as it was from Soviet invasion or communist fifth columnists. 'Is Canada a nation, and if not, should she be?' queried a 1946 article in the *Canadian Forum*, posing 'the 79-year-old question' – and answering the latter in the affirmative in order 'to create the harmony and unity needed for dealing with problems of domestic development and international cooperation.'[32]

To complicate these matters, the country faced a labour shortage at the same time that immigration from western and northern Europe was drying up, a prospect that long troubled even the most dedicated champions of Canadian tolerance and diversity. While Kate Foster's influential 1926 publication, *Our Canadian Mosaic*, lauded 'the incorporating into our national life of all people within our borders for their common well being' with 'each race contributing something of value' (in contrast to the coercion and racial exclusion attributed to the American melting pot), the author made it clear that some newcomers were more welcome than others:

> We can surely learn a lesson from our great neighbour to the South for there is such thing as a country being swamped by unemployable and undesirable immigrants. Thus Limited Selective Immigration is Canada's great need today. Prospective immigrants should be selected preferably from British stock or from among the more readily assimilable peoples of Europe.[33]

As sociologist Richard Day observes, though the war had effected a transformation in the language of identity and difference from *race* to *culture* and/or *ethnicity*, 'other axes of discourse' concerning identity remained intact: the notions that culture (heretofore 'race') *defined* character, and that an evolutionary hierarchy of cultures existed. If permitted a place in the mosaic, immigrants of non-canoncial identities – neither British nor French – would require tutelage in order to grasp and fulfil the requirements of the Canadian nation-state. Opinion polls confirmed that these attitudes toward prospective immigrants held considerable sway among average Canadians.[34]

Tutelage would be particularly important for new arrivals from nations with communist regimes and/or traditions of labour radicalism – at least, for those prospective immigrants who managed to permeate the increasingly stringent and top-secret screening protocol, overseen by the RCMP and intended to intercept 'Reds.' As Mark Kristmanson points out, the unavoidable broadening of Canada's immigrant base went hand-in-hand with an intensification of the nation's national security apparatus: 'multicultural states are, intrinsically, *security states*,' he argues, and demonstrates how the state sanctioning of 'tolerance' was accompanied by a marked intensification in the RCMP's distrust and surveillance of non-traditional immigrant communities. Historian Gregory Kealey concurs, identifying the formative 'ideological logic' of Canada's security system as 'nativist, anti-Semetic, and, above all, anti-communist.'[35]

Unsurprising, then, that the moulding of a patriotic, harmonious, and productive citizenry in Canada was taken on as a core post-war governmental project, one that would be fostered through significant public expenditures. Historian Franca Iacovetta sums up the stakes involved in these efforts: '... the process of making "New Canadians" or moulding "Model Citizens" out of Holocaust survivors, former Fascists, anti-Soviet refugees, and other immigrants became urgent moral campaigns for democratic decency and test cases for proving the greater good of Western liberal democracies.' Evidence for the emergence of what Richard Day calls the Canadian bureaucracy's 'citizenship machine' can be found in the 1946 passage of the Canadian Citizenship Act, which for the first time legally defined citizens as primarily Canadian, rather than British, subjects, in the 1949 creation of the Department of Citizenship and Immigration, and in the post-war establishment of a series of prominent government inquiries aimed at defining and safeguarding an essential (in both senses) Canadian culture and identity. The most influential of these, the 1949 Royal Commission on National Development in the Arts, Letters and Sciences, or Massey Commission, championed an elitist, anglophilic nationalism. More clandestine efforts to construct and manage national identity included attempts by the RCMP to enhance the standing of stridently anti-communist members of ethnic communities.[36]

The virulence of anti-communism emanating from many sectors of the Canadian populace, then, owes much to the fact that communist internationalism (and to a lesser, though important, extent, world-statism) was directly antithetical to what elites had constructed as the proper – and for a nation then lacking even its own flag and anthem, a relatively novel – attitude toward citizenship and the nation-state both during and after the war. Anthropologist Eva Mackey's remarks on contemporary anxiety over the inability to locate an authentic, singular national Canadian culture are also apposite here: 'national identity is not so much in a constant state of crisis,' she argues; rather, 'the reproduction of "crisis" allows the nation to be a site of constantly regulated politics of identity.'[37] The real and imagined transnational allegiances ferreted out by justices Taschereau and Kellock flew in the face of, and at the same time would serve to spur, vigorous government efforts to consolidate citizen loyalty to the project of nation-building following the Second World War.

What made these post-war efforts to locate and define a fixed, unique national character both ironic and thorny is that the United States had traditionally functioned, for Anglo-Canadian elites, in particular, as the primary foil for Canadian identity; supercilious Tory Canadians were often 'gratifyingly appalled,' in the words of historian S.F. Wise, by the perceived excesses of their southern neighbours. Attitudes to the United States had been shaped by Loyalist refugees, acrimonious border disputes, fear of annexation, actual invasion, and an elitist scorn for the ruinous cultural, economic, and spiritual influences of American 'mobocracy.' These circumstances contributed to a reservoir of anti-Americanism that served as a consistent rallying point for a disparate and sparsely populated (and, some held, artificial) nation.[38]

In the twentieth century, this posture was not so much jettisoned as it was compounded and delimited by the growth of international communism. The era's elites continued to caution against the 'decadence' of American mass culture; indeed, the impetus for the landmark Massey Commission lay in anxieties over the threats posed by American influence to Canada's post-colonial identity – and, just as importantly, to the status of privileged anglophilic Canadians.[39] Now, however, a more fundamental menace emerged to trump these customary concerns. Thus, in the same manner that '100 per cent Americanism' implied a rejection of everything redolent of collectivist ideology in Cold War America, 'bolshevism' was offered up by many 'opinion-makers' as the *final* antithesis of a true Canadian; a nation struggling to define its particular identity for recent arrivals and long-time residents alike had identified a truly sinister 'Other' against which it could map out its own character. This hierarchization of 'Other-ness' would serve as a necessary prerequisite to the Cold War realignment of Canadian alliances *toward* the entity that had heretofore provoked the bulk of national anxieties.

The existence of a communist spy ring – including some Canadian co-conspirators of East-European, Jewish, and Russian ancestry – only accelerated this project. As Quebec premier Duplessis made clear in his February 19 press conference, communism was not merely the ideology of a potentially hostile international adversary, it was a sinister internal threat, 'an enemy of our dearest traditions, an enemy of our system of social life, family and national.' In his diary entries concerning the spy case, Mackenzie King mused repeatedly on an apparently biological affinity among Jews for leftist sedition, concluding that 'in a large percentage of the race there are tendencies and trends which are dangerous indeed.' Editorials about the lessons of Gouzenko, like the aforementioned *Globe* reference to 'this strange ideology,' took on the air of government manuals on what it means to be Canadian. On this score, the *Halifax Chronicle-Herald* led the way, lecturing its readers that 'the very word traitor, like espionage, has a foreign sound. It reeks of balkanistic activities unknown in this country.'[40]

The same issue of the *Herald* contained a report by the paper's editor-in-chief, Edgar Kelley, who hammered home this line of thinking in yet starker terms: 'Here is none of the clean, straightforward, honest wholesomeness of the Canadian way of life. Here is something dark and mysterious, something sinister and ugly and slimy, something utterly foreign to the Canadian character and the Canadian conscience.' Montreal's *Le Devoir*, too, equated communism with 'an alien nationalist party.' A *Calgary Herald* cartoon featuring bearded, ragged, and impish Bolsheviks rummaging through a bedroom that represented the Canadian state made the same point: spies and communists were an alien virus; those Canadians involved, having fallen under this 'dark and mysterious' spell, had been rendered un-Canadian; newcomers take note. The *New York Times'* Ottawa correspondent, P.J. Philip, was particularly discerning on this matter, writing that questions of 'alien loyalty ... profoundly moved this country, in which national consciousness and loyalty are relatively new developments .... Now suddenly and alarmingly there has developed evidence of a loyalty to a political doctrine and foreign national system that has nothing in common with Canadian liberty.'[41] Unsurprising, too, that the francophone press, which exhibited considerably less investment in a monolithic and state-defined 'Canadian way of life,' would largely ignore the spy scandal.

Historian Keith Walden's study of dime-store novels featuring Canadian Mounties defending the Canadian frontier reveals that by mid-century, communist insurgents had replaced American fortune-hunters as the principal threat to national sovereignty; in this abrupt about-face, the Mounties were now depicted as 'part of a continental defence system in which the interests of Canada and the United States were identical.'[42] Clearly, journalists and politicians had done their part in preparing readers for this shift. Somewhat paradoxically, those assailing communist internationalism as the primary threat to an incipient Canadian nationalism had also abetted a third option, one that also imperilled a clear sense of national identity: continentalism, or greater integration with the United States.

All told, the above responses to Gouzenko, though set in motion by American officials and journalists, were neither exotic nor outlandish to many in Canada; I have provided a sampling of similar readings from Canadians to demonstrate the degree to which these highly provocative appraisals 'made sense' to, and were driven by, Canadians. It is also worthwhile to point out the functions and effects of these reiterations, particularly as they related to the construction of an anti-Soviet consensus. That the clandestine pursuit of the 'atomic secret' by an irrational state bent on world domination would provoke fear and antagonism is the most obvious of these.

Less apparent but still noteworthy are the consequences of emphasizing the far-reaching, bilateral character of the infiltration – a theme most frequently noted by various U.S. officials and commentators (who were, after all, pitching the story to their own domestic audience).[43] This consistent avowal served to further amalgamate in the public mind the security, interests, and identity of Canadians and Americans in important ways. For one, a cross-border insurgency would be best met with a united defence. What's more, allegations of the simultaneous targeting of both the United States and Canada was proof that smaller, less hostile nations were as likely to be the objects of Soviet desire as those more powerful and 'hard line'; no nation could expect to remain neutral in the emerging global standoff. Finally, speaking of the United States and Canada as a unitary entity whose 'way of life' was now threatened served to solidify the image of their former Russian ally, its government, economic system, and people, as fundamentally alien and inimical to the two Western states' security and shared values. Canadians who still hoped to stake

out a more independent position in global affairs or who clung to aspirations of an effective world government and international control of
atomic weaponry had more to fear from the spy scare than the loss of
state secrets.

The above interpretations by Canadians of the causes and implications
of the Gouzenko Affair are nearly indistinguishable from increasingly
doctrinaire U.S. mass media views of the Soviets, communist ideology,
and the left, in general, and of the espionage revelations, in particular.
Yet a comparison of the communications and public opinion landscape
in both countries does reveal several significant discrepancies. The first
of these involves the role of influential U.S. voices in not only intensify-
ing panic over the incident, but in seeking to contain the surge in anti-
communist hysteria. As such, the specific attitudes exported from
the south defy straightforward characterization. Rather than a one-
dimensional campaign to smear the Russians as the converse of the moral statesmanship embodied by the United States, American responses to
the espionage ring sometimes represented the most ardent calls for moderation, toleration, and perspective available to the Canadian public.

Political commentator and former U.S. ambassador to Moscow Joseph
Davies produced the most prominent of these appeals for calm. In a
February 18 dispatch carried or summarized in nearly every major daily
in the United States and Canada, Davies noted that all powerful nations
employ espionage. If the Soviets had developed the Bomb and withheld it from its allies, he argued, the United States would certainly have
sought to obtain information on the weapon through every means at
its disposal. Gainsaying General Groves, who used the spy ring to justify a continued U.S. monopoly, Davies argued that only UN control of
the Bomb would prevent an escalation of spying and a terrifying arms
race. Canadian newspapers known for their progressive editorial stances,
which had to this point expressed a mixture of shock and silence over the
incident, now adopted many of these arguments wholesale. This led the
decisively anti-communist *Calgary Herald* to wonder whether this simili-
tude was simply further evidence of Soviet infiltration and control: 'This
explanation,' it noted, 'is being so generally used that one may suspect
that it emanates from an identical source.' Montreal's *Le Devoir*, while
no advocate of Stalinist Russia, utilized Davies' argument to reinforce its
ongoing call to ban nuclear weapons. 'It is for Russia,' wrote Paul Sauriol
in the daily, 'a question of legitimate defence to investigate the secrets of
the atomic bomb and she has an absolute moral right to do so.'[44]

New York Herald Tribune and CBS military analyst George Fielding Eliot made similar arguments to Davies' for readers in both countries, providing a laundry list of suspicious and provocative actions by the United States, Canada, and Britain that could provide a rationale for Russian spying. Shortly thereafter, the *Globe and Mail* reprinted an editorial from the same American newspaper that called espionage 'inevitable' in the atomic age, and urged both those spying and those spied upon 'to conduct the dual process as efficiently and painlessly as possible.' After the Kellock-Taschereau Commission released its first interim report in early May, the *New York Times* concluded that most of the information sought 'could have been obtained by any military attaché by request,' and that 'there is no indication in the report that any of this secret information was obtained or communicated.'[45]

While these opinions were not representative of *dominant* U.S. attitudes, they constituted an essential ingredient in Canadians' ability to make sense of the espionage activities. The idea that they were at the centre of an acrimonious international incident was something new for the country, and it is not surprising that many in Canada would overstate its significance or, in the absence of credible government information about the true scope and nature of the spy operations, call for immediate and sweeping reprisals against anything that hinted of the adversary. As a rule, such misfortunes afflicted *others*, and as a rule, Canadians could offer their opinions and analyses about these matters free from the messy pragmatics of making and carrying out decisions, or from the anxieties inherent in being preyed upon. Now, American commentators and politicians turned a sometimes critical gaze toward the actions of Canadians; now, it was the Americans who in some cases urged restraint, patience, and perspective – or reacted with amusement – while many Canadians succumbed to near-panic.[46] It is worth being mindful of this reversal when assessing the degree to which more extreme manifestations of anti-communism were able to gain a foothold in the United States – a nation whose international and domestic interests represented the more frequent targets of Soviet 'attention'; the above responses suggest that adherence to stated ideals, appeals for calm, and occasionally sanctimonious moralizing become more difficult when troubling events impact a nation's citizens directly.

The kinship expressed by many Canadians toward the stance articulated by Davies and Eliot points to a second cross-border distinction: namely, the degree to which such views were considered constructive or, at the very least, sufferable. Even as late as the winter of 1946, there remained in Canada a significant constituency which vigorously defended world government, international control of the Bomb, and the Soviets' international grievances. These views were not absent from American public discourse when Drew Pearson went public, but were in the process of being pushed to the margins: increasingly, such sentiments represented the sole province of African-American and labour organizations, and, in government circles, an increasingly disparaged and isolated U.S. State Department (an atmosphere McCarthy would exploit so proficiently).

In the months following the war, President Truman's pronouncements had moved away from a privileging of multilateralism and toward – utilizing strongly nationalist language – a world order defined and arbitrated by a preponderant United States. At the same time, Republican foreign policy advisor John Foster Dulles and others began to argue that the Soviets threatened America's 'core values' as opposed to the nation's global, capitalist ambitions. A series of highly publicized speeches that addressed and broadened the growing rift, all of which were drafted with an eye toward the Gouzenko Affair, appeared in short order: on February 9, Stalin delivered a belligerent address on international relations in Moscow; at month's end, Pennsylvania senator Arthur Vandenberg and U.S. secretary of state James Byrnes presented what an approving *New York Times* called 'the most forthright speeches thus far' about the need for American moral leadership and toughness vis-à-vis the Soviets; Churchill's 'Iron Curtain' speech would be delivered one week later.[47]

With the fissures in international relations increasingly framed in the context of a battle between 'good and evil,' it was becoming more difficult to maintain an alternative view in the United States without being branded disloyal. 'In such discourse,' observes John Fousek, 'all attributes of U.S. policy that might be seen as meddlesome, provocative, or overreaching were effectively projected onto the image of the adversary. This ideological emphasis served to obfuscate the global reach of U.S. economic and security interests.' Accordingly, defenders of Russian intelligence gathering like Davies and Eliot were, in the main, received more favourably in Canada, despite that nation's position as the recipient of the sabotage. Davies, in particular, faced a torrent of editorial and governmental rebuke in the United States for conveying empathy regarding Soviet motives, with New York Republican congressman Ralph Gwinn going so far as to accuse the former ambassador of 'moral treason' over the remarks.[48]

Canada, while by no means a disinterested third party when it came to the emerging international polarization, could nonetheless – as a 'middle power' – observe the fractiousness with a greater degree of remove (the Gouzenko Affair excepted). This luxury, coupled with a political climate that tolerated and occasionally elected provincial and national politicians who called themselves socialist, an embryonic and unstable idea of national sovereignty, and still fluid and oft-times contradictory notions of appropriate international allegiances (Would closer ties to the United States represent or require an attenuation of loyalty to Britain? Was the USSR truly a greater threat to Canadian sovereignty than the United States?) created spaces for a less homogenous analysis of international affairs. This is not to say that all points of view received an equal airing, or that the debates over the post-war order and the nation's proper position in that order were not bitterly contested. In fact, the nation had been undergoing something of a 'culture war' since the end of the Second World War over this very issue, an increasingly polarized *internal* clash over Canada's proper role, priorities, and allegiances.

As evidenced above, many of Canada's newspapers and magazines had, by early 1946, adopted a rather dark view of the Soviets and, as a corollary, an effective world government. Some, like the *Toronto Telegram* and the French-language press in general, had sustained their attacks on Russia even while the USSR was Canada's wartime ally. Many average Canadians, on the other hand, expressed misgivings about the reliability and the implications of such views, a notion borne out by Canadian public opinion polls from the era. A Gallup poll conducted near war's end determined that while 44 per cent of Canadians believed the Russian government had not changed substantially in the past five years, nearly one-third held that it had, believing that Russia had grown more tolerant, democratic, and cooperative during that period. Post-war polls revealed that Canadians consistently displayed more faith in the United Nations and international control of the Bomb than did Americans. A survey of public opinion in the United States, France, Australia, and Canada found that residents of the latter country were *least* likely to believe that any single country 'wants to dominate the world' – this despite the fact that polling in Canada was conducted immediately *following* the disclosure of the spy scandal, and in the other nations, just before it. Similar surveys suggested that while Canadians' mistrust of the Russians increased after Gouzenko, anti-Soviet sentiment held greater sway in the United States during the same period. And as late as September 1946, Stalin himself tied for sixth in a list of living individuals most admired by Canadians (two percentage points below President Truman and just one behind the apparently fused 'King and Queen').[49]

Letters protesting the growing anti-Soviet climate reached Canadian publications of all regions and political orientations; in a sense, the Gouzenko incident represented merely the latest round in a discursive contest over the mutable meanings of loyalty, duty, and international obligations. Given recent tidal shifts in official and often rigidly policed attitudes toward the USSR, citizens could be forgiven for lacking confidence in their leaders' most recent directives, or for believing that elites were once again raising the alarm in order to further their own ulterior agendas. A *Calgary Herald* reader, in defiance of that paper's editorial assault against Russia and the left following Gouzenko, observed that 'before the war Russia was painted to us as being everything a nation should not be, but when her help was needed it was a different story we read. British imperialism has called the tune for so long it comes hard to have to dance for a change.' A letter in the same publication fumed that 'for the past twenty-five years we have had "bolshevik bogey" propaganda shoved at us,' noting with some prescience that if present trends continue, 'the future generation in our capitalist countries is bound to have an unfriendly attitude towards the USSR, our supposed enemy.' 'We have listened and read propaganda against the Russians for over 20 years and are sick of it,' proclaimed an *Ottawa Citizen* reader, while another asked whether 'we have to have these Fascist "red scares" again as we had in 1919, or have we learned from the slaughter of 100 million people in ten years by Fascism in all parts of the world?'[50] If the twists and turns of official policy seemed confusing and erratic, they were (though no more volatile than similar oscillations in official Communist Party attitudes toward the New Deal, democratic socialism, Hitler, the war, etc. – these were puzzling times for partisans of many stripes).

Other letters echoed the charge that the state's obsessive pre-war campaign against communism had obscured the more pressing dangers from the right, contending that post-war attacks on leftist individuals, states, and organizations merely represented a return to business as usual for government, media, and business leaders. 'May I remind your readers,' declared a letter in the *Ottawa Citizen*, 'that during the 1930's many proven Fascist agents of Hitler and Mussolini worked openly in all parts of Canada without interference from the RCMP, or without such public concern, except in progressive circles.' Raising a common argument, a Second World War veteran and *Vancouver Sun* reader pointed to the tremendous losses suffered by the Soviets in order to defeat Nazism, and the fact that Russia was an ally at the time of the alleged spying activities. In an effort to make sense out of the recent reversal in attitudes, he came to the distressing conclusion that 'our "would-be leaders"' might be 'trying to talk "us" into another war.' The Canadian Seamen's Union expressed similar suspicions, passing a post-Gouzenko resolution asking the government to 'immediately take steps to halt the malicious anti-Soviet and anti-labour campaign being conducted in the press and on the radio' on the grounds that their members 'suffered in one war and ... don't intend to suffer in another.'[51] In sum, while their 'opinion-makers' warned that the post-war tactics and objectives of Soviets and their sympathizers in the West represented an unprecedented threat, for many average citizens, the reprise of ideas, phrases, and symbols associated with 'Red scares,' 'bolshevism,' and the like served to diminish the potency of these concepts and leave them open for destabilization. Used by the same speakers who had employed similar fear-mongering for unscrupulous objectives in the past – in particular, demagogic politicians, the RCMP, business leaders, and the right-wing press – the language of Red-baiting had been stripped of some of its efficacy.

Such opinions were not absent in letters to editors of U.S. newspapers, but they no longer appeared with the frequency seen north of the border. What truly separated the Canadian communications terrain from that of the United States, however, was the fact that the editorial boards of several Canadian dailies retained solid, war-forged affinities toward the Soviet Union. These attitudes ranged from a *realpolitik*-centred empathy for Russian geopolitical concerns to unabashed Soviet cheerleading. As antagonism between the United States and the USSR intensified, a sometimes vigorous opposition to U.S. unilateralism and global ambition also became a component of this stance. It was, to be sure, becoming unwieldy to remain supportive of both emerging superpowers simultaneously, a fact which explains the lack of corresponding Soviet-friendly editorial positions in the mainstream U.S. press. The Gouzenko incident, more than any other, was successfully utilized as a cudgel against those expressing Russian sympathies in Canada, a circumstance that owes as much to the limits of these alternative visions as it does to the 'realities' exposed by the espionage activities.

Again, faulty logic provided momentum for the largely successful attempts to vanquish those still favouring international cooperation: How could average citizens make sense of the frequently invoked first premise that tens of thousands of domestic Soviet partisans were actively cooperating with Stalin, that communist fronts masquerading as progressive organizations could with little effort convince so many Canadians to turn on their own, liberal-democratic state in the name of a repressive government? Why did Canadian citizens allegedly constitute the 'weak link' in the Anglo-American intelligence and security apparatus? It was here that many commentators pointed to a discrepancy between the public discourses of the United States and Canada, and framed that discrepancy in increasingly disapproving terms: Canada's supposedly greater tolerance for differing political views, its traditional apprehensions about close ties with the United States, its unwillingness to frame growing international tensions in moral terms rather than as the product of traditional power balancing, had engendered an atmosphere in which legions of the weak could be swayed by communist agitation. The primary architects of this collective 'softening,' according to exponents of this view, included the CBC, the National Film Board, Soviet friendship societies, and, in particular, progressive newspapers.

Not coincidentally, many of the publications now on the defensive for abetting Stalin's international objectives were clustered in the Canadian West. Long a hub of agrarian populism (a good deal of it brought northward by migrating American farmers), by the early twentieth century the growth of resource extraction industries in the West had contributed to intense battles between capital and labour, as well as some of the nation's most successful union-organizing efforts. The region also served as a refuge and/or repository for Canadians of non-canonical identities, including Indigenous Peoples, the Métis, as well as Asian and East-European immigrants. The latter carried with them a tradition of labour radicalism when they arrived in Canada; all of these groups became increasingly politicized as they confronted the persistent exclusions of dominant, 'British stock' Canadians. These factors contributed to an atmosphere of Canadian patriotism 'so weak that successive prime ministers up to the time of Mackenzie King had worried that the region might try to secede and join the United States.'[52]

Some western editors reflected this more radical tradition as they sought to make sense of Gouzenko. From British Columbia – identified by the *Financial Post* as the 'no. 1 hotbed' of communist labour organizing in Canada – the *Vancouver Sun* expressed hope that the spy scare would not impair the goodwill that had always characterized relations between the two nations, save for when 1930s Conservative prime minister R.B. Bennett's 'piety got the best of him.' The *Winnipeg Tribune*, published in a city that had witnessed a landmark general strike in 1919 and still possessed a powerful labour movement, withheld editorial comment on the issue for ten days before urging calm, and recommending that any enmity be directed not at the Soviets but at those Canadians who betrayed their country. In Regina, capital of a province which at the time featured the nation's first socialist provincial government, the *Leader-Post* reminded readers that there exists 'a legitimate field of activity which goes under the name of foreign intelligence,' also noting for the sake of comparison 'the very wide scope of British intelligence activities before and during the war.' For the *Hamilton Spectator* and other Canadians who didn't appreciate such fusions of international politics and nuance (or the slighting of the beloved Empire), these opinions represented the rantings of 'Canadian Russo-maniacs.'[53]

Though the 'Russo-maniacs' were concentrated in the West, the debates between those advocating friendship with the Soviets and those talking 'toughness' in light of the spy scare played out most dramatically in the competing newspapers of what was then Canada's second largest city, Toronto. On one side of the issue stood the Tory *Globe and Mail*, along with the equally conservative but generally more demagogic *Toronto Telegram*; on the other, the aforementioned *Toronto Star*, a relatively steadfast advocate of labour, civil liberties, racial equality, and Stalinist Russia (the last of which the paper frequently championed as the fullest embodiment of the preceding). While the competing dailies habitually denigrated the positions of one another on such issues as the domestic left, the USSR, and post-war great power claims, the Gouzenko revelations provided the *Globe* and *Telegram* with what they considered the *coup de grace*. Commenting on the fact that the alleged spies did not appear to have received money for passing information, the *Globe* pointed to the 'uncomfortable suspicion that the agents from abroad did not have to spend money because here in Canada they found, and probably not to their amazement, an organization of spiritual handservants.' Who was responsible for amassing this working pool of lackeys and dupes? For the *Globe*, certain (at this point unnamed) 'newspapers which have lent themselves to this unhappy opportunism must assume much of the burden of responsibility' for moulding traitorous citizens.[54]

The *Telegram* likewise laid the blame squarely – and in its refusal to identify the offending publication by name, just as coyly – at the feet of 'one Ontario daily newspaper and organizations styling themselves friends of the Soviet Union, who have been so Russophile that in their eyes Moscow could do no wrong no matter how out of tune with the Atlantic charter its attitudes and actions have been.' 'Falsehood was propagated in the press, in the pulpit, and in the university,' its editors fumed. On the same page as the latter charge, the paper featured a cartoon depicting an apparently Japanese male in a straightjacket glaring at the '"Tely" [or *Telegram*] Bulletin Board.' The board reads: 'Re Russia: Excuse Us if We

Say, "We Told You So!"[55] The Gouzenko story had emerged in the midst of a public and parliamentary debate over whether to forcibly repatriate residents of Japanese descent, and the *Telegram*, an unreserved supporter of both repatriation and 'toughness' toward the Soviets, was making a tenuous linkage indeed: namely, that its now proven 'reliability' about the Russian threat should be taken as a confirmation that it was also correct about the need to evict the Japanese. Canadian security, it seems, would require a rollback of existing tolerance toward the USSR, the domestic left, and non–Anglo-Saxon immigrants, among others. Again, the spy scandal could be readily employed as a stalking horse for a host of long-standing enemies and grievances, and, again, some analysts on the right advanced the paradox that patently illiberal measures might be the only way to preserve liberty.

By February 21, the *Globe* was finally ready to name names, running an editorial cartoon featuring a human figure with an enormous star-shaped head standing atop a soapbox and clutching a pamphlet entitled 'Soviet Friendship Campaign'; for those still perplexed about the star-figure's intended denotation, the cartoonist was considerate enough to emblazon the caricature's forehead with the designation 'Daily Star.' In the frame, Starman's pro-Soviet hucksterism is interrupted when he catches sight of a sandwich board bearing the headline 'Russian Spy Ring in Canada Revealed.' A pipe-smoking, moustached man in a fedora (unambiguous emblems of respectability and judiciousness these!), his hat labelled 'Toronto,' gazes expectantly toward the figure. 'Well?' the representative Torontonian inquires, waiting for a response to the damning exposé. Starman blushes acutely, and sweats so ferociously that pools have formed at the base of his soapbox. His mouth is agape and his finger raised as if to make a point, but though the cartoonist has provided a large word bubble (again, featuring the helpful, if superfluous, label 'Editorial Comment'), the bubble remains blank. The overall message of the image, titled 'Suspended Animation,' is as unequivocal and didactic as its constituent parts: even permanent and desperately naïve Soviet apologists have been rendered utterly mute by the espionage revelations.[56]

The cartoonist got at least one thing right: in the immediate aftermath of Gouzenko's defection, the *Star*'s editors, never ones to shy away from an opportunity to promote goodwill toward the Russians and the necessity of international cooperation, were suddenly speechless. Of course, the paper could not deny the existence of the spy scandal, and provided what are in retrospect some of the more prudent and even-handed reports of the circumstances surrounding the affair. Unlike many other Canadian and U.S. dailies, the paper avoided both the 'atomic' allegations in its initial headlines and overly sensational language in its stories; its own reporters and the articles it culled from wire services emphasized the relative worthlessness of the information exchanged, the fact that all great powers spy, and that the Soviets have reason to be suspicious of a series of provocative acts on the part of the West. One *Star* reporter conducted 'a personal survey of 50 persons in ordinary walks of life' ('none of them in any way pro-Soviet and none connected with the Labour-Progressive party,' he assured, overlooking the fact that citizens with these affiliations had recently been seized and were now held incommunicado, and as a result, such self-identification might have fallen rather abruptly out of favour). The reporter's 'personal survey' determined that average Canadians were far more worried that the incident 'may set back the tempo of international co-operation,' than they were 'about any military or scientific data which Russia may have succeeded in getting from Canada,' a finding that conformed closely – perhaps too closely – to the *Star*'s own orientation on matters of this nature.[57]

Yet while the paper's editorial stance could be reasonably inferred by surveying the stories they assigned their own reporters and culled from other publications, the editors themselves were unwilling or unable to provide a response to the Gouzenko incident for nearly one week. Even as newspapers the world over provided editorial assessments of the progression of events in Canada on a daily basis, *Star* editors ignored the issue altogether, instead warning that a global fascist movement was reorganizing in Argentina and denouncing calls for the deportation of Japanese residents – along with addressing a host of other, more mundane concerns. It is unlikely that the foregrounding of such matters in the wake of Pearson's revelations is coincidental: the true threat, the increasingly isolated *Star* editors held, remained the totalitarianism of the *right*. On February 20, for instance, they quoted approvingly a CIO resolution which denounced the post-war reappearance of 'those who place profits before people, who believe the Negro "should be kept in his place," who seek a scapegoat in the Jew and who seek to crush labour.'[58] That such viruses could and did also plague communist regimes did not seem to occur to the *Star*. Fascism alone remained the root of all evil.

Fully one week after the government roundup of conspirators, *Star* editors were finally prepared to speak. In concise, matter-of-fact prose, they provided a summary of the past week's most momentous incident, giving roughly equal space to Prime Minister Mackenzie King's initial espionage accusations and to the Soviets' rebuttal. While not denying that Canadian citizens had provided 'insignificant secret data' to Soviet diplomats – who were subsequently recalled for participating in such 'unauthorized' interactions – the Russians had accused the Canadian leader and the nation's press of conspiring to foment an atmosphere 'hostile to the Soviet Union' in Canada. The *Star* editorial found reason to defend King against such accusations, pointing to his previous constructive relations with the Russians, which, the editors believed, he would not imperil without cause; at the same time, they called for further 'explanation from Mr. King' as to whether his handling of the case 'was compatible with friendly relations between the two countries.' Tellingly, the *Star* offered no parallel rebuttal to the charges of anti-Soviet hostility in the Canadian media.

The piece concluded by asserting that 'public opinion in Canada will finally be formed when the report of the judges is published'; in light of the collective rush to judgment evidenced in other public forums throughout the country, such claims of collective prudence were informed by a good dose of wishful thinking. It is also noteworthy that alongside its initial editorial measurement of the spy scandal, the paper ran the lengthy justification – cited above – of Soviet information-gathering in Canada written by the *New York Herald Tribune*'s George Fielding Eliot. Two weeks later, the 'explanation' demanded by the *Star* had apparently been furnished, as the editors produced the sort of *mea culpa* generally voiced by doomed detainees at a show trial: Prime Minister King's investigation, they noted meekly, 'was the only action he and his government could possibly take and its justification cannot be questioned.'[59]

In the weeks that followed, the *Star* would begin to regain its nerve, emerging as a spirited defender of the civil liberties of the accused and a harsh critic of both government secrecy and the 'dictatorial course' of the investigation – a welcome antidote to the rather tepid stances on these issues taken up by many of Canada's leading publications.[60] Nevertheless, after Gouzenko, the *Star* began to tone down its determined defence of the USSR, and diluted perceptibly its calls for an effective world government and the sharing of nuclear secrets. This, I believe, speaks to the limits of leftist discourse in Canada in the years before the formal declaration of Cold War, a matter to which I return below.

The views of the *Globe* and *Telegram* would not have been out of place alongside any number of leading U.S. dailies. Still, as several Canadian journalists and readers noted after the spy accusations emerged, the degree of anti-Soviet rhetoric propagated in Canada paled in comparison to that in the United States. In their survey of U.S. coverage of the Gouzenko revelations, the Canadian Press determined that notoriously anti-Soviet U.S. papers 'were having a field day' over the incident, which was being exploited in service of their 'continued campaign directed at Russia.' An *Ottawa Citizen* reader and apparent U.S. media cartel-watch-dog blamed the ferocious rumour-mongering on 'the Hearst-McCormick-Gannett-Paterson Fascist news axis in the US,' abetted by 'their Canadian quislings.' After Soviet officials protested that the alleged spy ring was part and parcel of a wider Canadian propaganda campaign against Russia, a Canadian Press journalist based in Washington, DC, reported that 'the feeling among observers here is that the charge of hostility to Russia in Canada's press and other circles could be multiplied many times in respect of the United States as measured by the volume of that sort of argument published and spoken in the two countries.' Given these widely noted national disparities in attitudes toward Russia, it is not implausible to conceive that the FBI leaked the Gouzenko story to serve the double function of discrediting the Soviet 'appeasers' in the State Department and striking at that department's 'fellow travellers' in Canada, a nation whose uranium, shared border, and proximity to the USSR made it an indispensable partner in any U.S.-led anti-Soviet alliance.[61]

The *Ottawa Citizen* found the degree to which American politicians, bureaucrats, and especially journalists appeared to be interpreting the lessons of Gouzenko for Canadians particularly galling. The paper published a series of increasingly irate editorials concerning the 'highly-colored melodrama' crafted by U.S. columnists that, in the eyes of its editors, served to occlude the views of the citizens of both countries and could only 'drive Russia back into isolation and foment a new race in armaments.' Nor was such a campaign unprecedented: 'All the signs of the "parlor Bolshevism" mania which made [the United States] the laughing-stock of the rest of the world in the years after the First World War are reappearing,' the *Citizen* noted. The editors held that the patently 'anti-Soviet press across the international boundary' does not represent 'all the people in Canada who are not blinded by religious and political feeling against Soviet ideology,' nor does it reflect 'sane and sober American opinion, which realizes how "psychological warfare" of such sort, can readily lead to war.'[62] To this point, a well-reasoned and suitably historicized appraisal of the intersecting dynamics of media, public opinion, and international borders; it is also worth noting that the *Citizen* retained a healthy dose of skepticism about the totalizing and simplistic claims of strident anti-communists in both countries throughout the Cold War.

However, the clamour raised by *Citizen* editors over the influence of the U.S. media in Canada was of such intensity and duration (with almost daily condemnations provided in the two-week period following Pearson's initial column) that the generally more insular American press began to take notice of, and provide rebuttals to, the Canadian paper's charges. Perhaps intoxicated by the rare display of American attention and overreaching themselves in hopes of a knockout punch, *Citizen* editors concluded a particularly bristly attack on the anti-Soviet bias of the U.S. press with a paean to Stalin that could have (indeed, may have) been lifted directly from *Pravda*: 'Peace is Stalin's ambition and his dream,' they resounded. 'He desires ardently to leave as his memorial to the Russian people a peaceable, prosperous, Socialist economy, powerful, respected and, above all, secure.' When several U.S. dailies reprinted the passage, bracketed with barely contained – and largely deserved – editorial ridicule, the *Citizen* dug itself in yet deeper, rejoining: '*The Citizen*'s statement … having been questioned and a couple of United States newspaper correspondents quoted against it, the fact may now be disclosed that *The Citizen*'s authority is President Benes, of Czechoslovakia, who knows more about Stalin and Russia than probably any other man in Europe.'[63] Precisely what Czech nationalist Eduard Benes knew or said, and in what context, the paper did not divulge, but Benes would learn a great deal more about Stalin's ambitions and dreams just two years later, when his coalition government would be forced from office by a Soviet-rigged communist takeover.

The *Citizen*'s alarm over the degree of influence exercised by the U.S. media in Canada was echoed by other journalists, government officials, and average citizens (and who, in a familiar pattern, seized upon the most lurid U.S. reports as if they represented the sum total of American reportage). While by no means new, these sentiments appear to have experienced a 'spike' over coverage of the Gouzenko Affair. No doubt this is owing in large measure to the fact that a Canadian incident was receiving an unprecedented degree of international, and especially American, attention; Canadians were accustomed to having events *beyond* their borders explained to them by U.S. analysts, but were less so to being given advice on happenings within their own country. This growing concern about foreign manipulation must also be framed within the emerging sense of Canadian nationalism. When national sovereignty and identity are not highly developed or valued – as when individuals consider themselves British subjects who happen to reside in Canada – citizens may have the luxury of dismissing as vaguely bothersome the views of their

American neighbours; there remains, after all, the vaunted opinion of the British homeland to serve as a bulwark against foreign influences. When Canadians begin to conceive of themselves as a sovereign people with an independent identity and global role, the American presence may strike some in new ways; namely, as hampering or rendering impossible true autonomy.

Several additional issues arise from the foregoing debates between the *Ottawa Citizen* and the U.S. press, as well as those involving the competing Toronto dailies, issues which point to the specificities – and limitations – of Canadian post-war progressivism. First, the *Citizen*'s rather one-dimensional Stalinist apologia is emblematic of a more general myopia that seemed to plague many Canadian readings of the post-war landscape: that is, aiming to strike a contrapuntal posture in an increasingly U.S.-dominated hemisphere and globe, some in Canada resorted to merely extolling the Americans' adversary rather than staking out a truly autonomous position, one that could speak to the vices and virtues of both emerging superpowers. Clearly, a measure of this often simplistic Russian championing must be viewed in functional terms as a rhetorical strategy; namely, as a part of a calculated campaign to offset the frequently one-dimensional American perspectives – those framing the global rift as a contest between good and evil – that reached Canadians from the south. It is also true that many of the pieces that at points lavished praise on the USSR also contained caveats that leavened their overall 'Russophilia.' Nevertheless, it was discursive indiscretions like the ones cited above (calling Stalin a man of peace, for instance) that stood out and became fodder for the anti-Soviet constituencies in both countries. As the international rift hardened and as the Soviet experiment's more egregious excesses became widely acknowledged, past praise for the Generalissimo and his government was affixed to, and became an albatross for, progressives throughout the West.

In a similar vein, and like the Labour-Progressive Party and the Canadian-Soviet Friendship Society, the *Toronto Star* had so closely linked the Soviets to all manner of progressive politics, often portraying the Russian experiment as something approaching humanity's best hope in the realms of racial and gender equality, equitable distribution of wealth, international peace (and so on), that it could offer little in the way of defence of Soviet espionage activities without appearing disingenuous; thus, its protracted silence. A tradition of simplistic Soviet advocacy made it difficult for the *Star* and its ilk to suggest that the USSR was simply behaving like other great powers (since the Soviets were not supposed to

behave like the other degenerate, duplicitous, and imperialistic international powers), or that the conspicuous defects of the Russian variant of
socialism did not necessarily tar the idea in theory.

It was perhaps even more difficult in this context to suggest that spy
revelations, coupled with Soviet land grabs and mounting evidence of
Stalin's brutality, did not obviate the need for effective world government and international control of the Bomb; in other words, to hold that
negotiation and cooperation with the Soviet leaders did not require or
signify that one felt affection for them. Instead, voices like the *Star* and
the *Citizen* had insinuated that, freed from the conservative bias of much
of the North American media, not only the Russian people but its Bolshevik rulers would be understood as trustworthy, affable, even noble,
and it was for these reasons that the West should consent to open diplomatic channels and multilateralism. This line of reasoning collapsed
along with the false attributes of Soviet benevolence. Again, the lack of
nuance on the domestic left rendered it an easier target for its enemies,
since mounting evidence of Soviet deficiencies could be translated with
little effort into a discrediting of that country's defenders in Canada.

In the fall of 1947, internationally read and respected American journalist Walter Lippmann lamented his nation's disinclination to engage
in good-faith dialogue with the Soviets. 'For a diplomat to think that
rival and unfriendly powers cannot be brought to a settlement is to forget what diplomacy is all about,' he wrote. 'There would be little for
diplomats to do if the world consisted of partners, enjoying political intimacy, and responding to common appeals.'[64] Lippmann's reasoning –
that affection for the Soviets need not be a prerequisite for constructive
engagement – inhabits a discursive space that is able to withstand shifts
in public perceptions of a nation's international rivals, even reprehensible behaviour on the part of those rivals. While such a position would
have served Canadian critics of Cold War bellicosity well, it was wholly
absent from mainstream public debate in Canada.

Whitaker and Marcuse have argued that during the first years of the
Cold War in Canada, 'any resistance to mobilization for war under American leadership was forced into the camp of Soviet apologetics, or into
silence.'[65] As the foregoing study suggests, these coercive processes were
accelerated markedly by the Gouzenko Affair and were engineered by
forces on the right in *both* countries, which had much to gain as a result.
This survey also suggests that the 'camp of Soviet apologetics' served
as a popular retreat even before the revival of intensive Red-baiting in
Canada, and included some of the nation's most visible exponents of

social democracy. Because of the deficiencies embedded in their critique of emergent bipolarity, they, too, bear some responsibility for the effectiveness of the era's crackdown on the left.

In the end, through all the contests over the meaning of Gouzenko, at least two truths held constant: where spies and atoms were concerned, sensationalism remained the order of the day, and in a polarizing global contest for hearts and minds – and for Canadians beholden to an asymmetrical communications landscape – the struggle over the narrative of the spy scandal could not be contained within national boundaries.

3 The Cold War and the Third World: 'Time to Lay Bogey of British Imperialism'

On 26 October 1942, following a worldwide fact-finding tour to determine the origins of the crisis then gripping the globe, former Republican presidential nominee Wendell Willkie broadcast a radio message on the progress of his mission. Carried on all four U.S. radio networks as well as the CBC, Willkie's 'Report to the People' assigned the roots of the world conflagration to the inequities generated by all forms of coercive governance. Resisting the simplistic binaries between 'Allied freedom' and 'Axis tyranny,' America's self-declared 'trouble-shooter in a troubled world' concluded that colonialism, and particularly the imperial holdings of Britain and France, constituted a grave threat to both the Allied war effort and the future peace. Particularly galling to Third World peoples, argued Willkie, was the rhetoric of Western leaders, who voiced stirring appeals to freedom while suppressing advances toward autonomy among their own subject peoples – most notably, at that time, in India. 'Our Western World with its presumed supremacy is on trial,' he warned. 'Our boasting and our big talk leave Asia cold.'[1]

Willkie's message was heard by an estimated 36 million Americans, and received an enthusiastic response in that nation's press. So favourable, in fact, was the reaction that Willkie decided to expand his reflections into a short treatise on the need for international unity and equity. Published in April 1943, Willkie's *One World* became an instant bestseller and generated increased public support for the idea of the United Nations. The author's standing among Canadians, however, was somewhat more complicated; in fact, many influential voices found his views impudent and naïve. *Saturday Night* magazine's F. Fraser Hunter provided a typical response: 'What a pity Mr. Willkie did not go to India!' he wrote after hearing Willkie's radio address, noting that the fact-finding trip did not include a stop on the subcontinent. 'A few hours in India, to such a brilliant mind, might have convinced him not only of the competence and sincerity of Great Britain, but that to use his own generality statement, "India is indeed one of the world's toughest problems."' Hunter concluded by coldly informing 'Mr. Willkie and his kind that India never was, is not now, and never will be, America's problem.'[2]

As a world war developed into a Cold War, the basic contours of these national discrepancies held firm: many in Canada continued to defend the practice of colonialism, while American popular discourses adhered to traditional republican critiques of foreign domination. This state of affairs points to a number of rather acute contradictions, which I expand upon in the pages that follow. For one, polls conducted in the years immediately following the Second World War indicate that Canadians consistently expressed greater support than Americans for the UN, in particular, and multilateral liberal internationalism, in general; endorsements of imperialism would appear incongruous alongside this apparent preference for a democratic global order composed of sovereign nation-states. Second, even as many post-war Americans continued to condemn colonial practices and uphold their nation as the foremost international advocate of self-government, aspects of the emerging U.S. anti-communist foreign policy took on a decidedly imperial aura. Finally, Canada itself was not spared the effects of the growth of U.S. hegemony, and by the late 1950s, increasing numbers of Canadians denounced the perceived American domination of their nation's internal and external affairs. These critics of 'Yankee Imperialism' were quick to blame the self-interested and expansionist character of the United States, as well as that nation's irrational anti-communism, for Canada's loss of autonomy.

The conclusion reached by these resurgent Canadian nationalists represents a significant oversimplification, as well as a measure of hypocrisy. In fact, imperial defenders like F. Fraser Hunter had done much to ready the Canadian public for a new kind of global 'burden' and a new form of empire. In their attempts to shield British imperialism from American admonitions, Canadian anglophiles posited a world where certain varieties of foreign control were defensible and even advisable, where intrinsic cultural and racial hierarchies marked the rulers and the ruled, and where the withdrawal of Western authority would invite a more sinister form of domination. Ironically – for Canada's anglophiles traditionally served as the nation's most steadfast anti-Americans – each of these assumptions could also be marshalled in support of U.S. management of the globe. Historians Reg Whitaker and Gary Marcuse have outlined the role Canada's politicians and diplomats played in spurring their formerly isolationist neighbour toward global leadership; only later did Canadian officials become alarmed at how seriously U.S. leaders took up the cause – 'once,' as these authors write, 'the spirit had entered them.'[3] A comparison of Canadian and American debates over colonialism finds that public opinion and popular discourse also helped lay the groundwork for this development.

To state that all Canadians supported imperialism while Americans opposed it would be to endorse a further oversimplification. While many Canadian anglophiles had long resented stateside reproofs of colonialism, by the early twentieth century Canadian progressives – in particular, those associated with the social democratic CCF Party and the *Canadian Forum* – had become increasingly cognizant and appreciative of this republican critique of foreign domination. By interweaving these discourses with local and British strains of anti-colonialism, Canadian progressives were able to recognize, in advance of many of their U.S. counterparts, some of the correlations between post-war American internationalism and more traditional expressions of empire. In some cases, these Canadian critics employed Americans' anti-imperial ideals and rhetoric directly and pointedly, hoping to reignite seemingly dormant stateside opposition to U.S. expansionism.

Post-war debates over imperialism and decolonization, then, provide another angle of vision into the emerging Cold War consensus in the United States and Canada. A number of interrelated questions form the basis of this inquiry: How firm were citizens' commitments to applying the principles outlined in the Four Freedoms, Atlantic Charter, and United Nations accord to the peoples of the Third World? Were the rights of colonized peoples framed as inimical to Western economic and security interests in a bipolar world? As a corollary, to what extent did citizens label anti-colonial struggles 'communist-inspired,' thus providing the pretext for dismissing these issues altogether (and for advancing status quo agendas)? As always, these issues are filtered through the overarching themes: How did national identity affect these responses? Did U.S. views of these matters influence Canadians, and vice versa? How did these debates encourage or constrain the movement toward an American-led anti-communist consensus in Canada?

In an effort to excavate these phenomena, this chapter surveys appraisals of post-war freedom struggles in the Philippines and India, colonies selected first and foremost because their independence was achieved during the formative period of the Cold War. Moreover, I focus on these geographies because departing imperial powers – the United States and Britain – comprise Canada's closest allies and, for English Canada, primary bases of preoccupation and identity formation; debates over decolonization in Canada show both supporters and detractors of Western rule accentuating or undermining aspects of American and British influences and ideals in an effort to advance their positions. To a great extent, I also selected these geographies by default: other independence movements gaining momentum at war's end, most notably in Burma, Indonesia, and Indochina, were largely ignored in U.S. and Canadian public discourses. This erasure owes much to enormous problems facing post-war Europe that diverted attention from those of the Third World, and to a more long-standing Western disregard for peoples of non-European origin.

At first glance, Canadian and American national contexts would suggest a relatively analogous response to race and colonialism. Both nation-states began as British 'settler' colonies before gaining independence, conducted violent campaigns against indigenous peoples as they expanded to the Pacific, and though comprised of multi-ethnic populations, remained dominated by citizens of European – especially West-European – descent. Yet significant elements of each nation's experiences and self-conceptions could produce widely divergent responses to imperialism and its relationship to the post-war order. Because these contextual differences are at once subtle and profound, it is worth beginning by sketching some mediating factors in national responses to race and colonialism before drawing out those responses through close readings of mid-century anti-colonial struggles.

In 1960 the United Nations asked the Canadian government to supply bilingual peacekeeping troops to the newly independent Belgian Congo, where decolonization efforts threatened to descend into chaos. When Canadian officials countered with a largely token offer of a few aircraft, newspaper editors and their readers were quick to express their dissatisfaction. The *Globe and Mail* scoffed at the 'meagre' contribution, while the *Ottawa Journal* maintained that Canadians expected an 'imaginative and wide-visioned and generous response.' In the days that followed, the government abruptly reversed its decision and provided a large contingent of soldiers for the duration of a four-year UN operation. Note historians Norman Hillmer and J.L. Granatstein: 'Ottawa had been virtually forced into major participation by public opinion';[4] offering assistance to Third World sovereignty efforts had, it appears, come to function as an important element of the nation's self-image. However, this commitment to international dispute resolution and self-determination for formerly colonized peoples was apparent only in embryo at the conclusion of the Second World War, and a number of factors mitigated against its emergence as a dominant collective aspiration.

First, though mid-century Canada represented a former colony which might be expected to sympathize with other peoples who had yet to achieve independence, the nation's sovereignty was limited by its 'Dominion' status within the Commonwealth. This *semi*-autonomous position acknowledged the continuing primacy of Britain (both politically and as a trading partner); further, it had been attained through negotiation rather revolt. The aversion to foreign rule that fuelled the American Revolution and inspired the culture and institutions of republicanism had few corollaries in Canada – at least, in English Canada.

Second, the nation remained a settler society dominated by British- and French-stock whites with strong affinities toward their homelands (which were themselves the modern era's 'greatest' colonizers). Restrictive immigration guidelines operant until the mid-1950s sought to maintain the 'Nordic' character of the nation's citizenry, a character often framed in direct contradistinction to the perceived chaos and decadence engendered by the more 'liberal' immigration policies of the United States. As anthropologist Eva Mackey notes, Canadian immigration practices enshrined 'an environmental racism' that excluded 'Blacks and Asians on the grounds that they were unsuited to the cold climate of Canada.' The underlying fear, however, was that admission of 'weaker southern races' would 'contaminate' the nation's homogeneous racial makeup and dilute its British character – precisely the qualities, according to the nation's ruling elites, that made the Canadian experiment preferable to that of the United States.[5]

That these national myths appeared to cancel out another font of Canadian superiority – its greater tolerance – did not trouble the architects of immigration policies. The nation's tolerance could be verified by observing English forbearance toward the French, a people who exhibited enough similarity in character to Anglo-Saxons to construct a cohesive national project. Inclusion of peoples of greater dissimilarity, meanwhile, would only usher in the decay observable to the south. The fact that U.S. policy-makers of the interwar period substantially reworked their nation's immigration quotas in accordance with many of these same prejudices would only lend credence to the notion that Canada had established a more reasoned approach from the beginning. As Canadian prime minister Mackenzie King argued as late as 1947, post-war immigration guidelines must take into account the 'absorptive capacity' of potential newcomers, since 'the people of Canada do not wish to make a fundamental alteration in the character of their population through mass migration.'[6]

These policies and attitudes directly impacted Canadian perceptions of decolonization in important ways. As a result of immigration restrictions, post-war Canada contained only a small, dispersed, and largely unacknowledged minority population from which to seek alternative visions of issues relating to race, the Third World, and so on. It is also true that the structural racism embedded in state-sponsored conceptions of national identity was frequently projected beyond national borders. That is, Canada's progression from colony to nation did not, in the minds of many of its citizens, serve as a model for colonial subjects elsewhere. Rather, post-colonial status represented an ideal more suitable for some societies than others: namely, those administered by 'enlightened' peoples – a classification, for prominent turn-of-the-century Canadian author and educator George Parkin, which was synonymous with the 'sturdy races' of the North. Significantly, in addition to characterizing Southern peoples as inferior, weak, and, in Eva Mackey's words, 'essentially female,' opponents of more liberal immigration policies also suggested that ideas of democracy had been forged by the northern, 'masculine virtues' of vigour and self-reliance. Southerners, by contrast (and to again quote Parkin), were 'unaccustomed to political freedom, unaccustomed to self-government.'[7] Under this schema, efforts toward decolonization were ill-advised, even potentially catastrophic to global peace and stability.

In fact, as Carl Berger, Daniel Coleman, and Philip Massolin have demonstrated, significant numbers of early twentieth-century English-Canadian nationalists like Parkin proudly called themselves 'Imperialists' whose primary identity lay in their British heritage and their own nation's continued, and leading, status within the Commonwealth. Though technically subservient to Britain, these Canadian imperialists considered themselves partners, rather than subjects, in the colonial project. In fact, many held that Canada's vast territory and resources would allow their nation to replace a decaying Britain as the imperial metropolis. In Coleman's words, Canada was 'the loyal son who would reinvigorate the aging empire by producing a strengthened and improved character in the hinterland.' Naturally, such champions of empire were rarely found on the frontlines of the anti-colonial struggle. These anglophiles' 'contempt for democracy and their respect for the role of privilege,' and their espousal of 'organic, evolutionary change' over revolution, would also represent affiliations antithetical to the interests of the Third World. Not incidentally, these attitudes added to Canadian imperialists' distaste for the United States itself, and ardent British loyalists had always comprised the most consistently anti-American demographic in Canada. These Tory Canadians could simultaneously enhance support for British imperialism and aversion to the United States by pointing to the *quid pro quo* implied by their nation's support for the Empire, especially in war: it would, they argued, 'purchase' a renewed British commitment to protect Canada from a frequently exaggerated American expansionism.[8]

I do not wish to conflate these ideas with those of Canadians as a whole: emphasis on Canada's British heritage was strongest in Ontario, less so in areas of more heterogeneous ethnic makeup, and non-existent among francophones. Furthermore, this conservative nationalism faced significant challenges by the mid-twentieth century, first from a liberal nationalism that hoped to moderate ties with Britain – often through expanded connections to the United States – and later from a social democratic variant that rebuked both 'imperial' centres.[9] At the same time, however, staunch anglophilia remained one of the surest avenues to success in post-war English Canada, be it in the public or private realm. To a great extent, proponents of decolonization were required to argue against this venerable and still powerful discursive tradition in Canada if they hoped to move the public toward a more progressive outlook on the issue of Third World sovereignty.

Despite these constraints against the emergence of a dynamic anti-imperialism, certain elements of the nation's makeup and experience provided a framework for challenging the colonial status quo. Foremost among these was the historically large and, especially after the Second World War, growing non-British presence in Canada. For obvious reasons, French Canadians were hardly fond of British imperial exploits. Francophone distaste for the Empire, and Canada's perceived servility to it, would increase dramatically as the result of the nation's participation in the Boer War and the First and Second World Wars, conflicts aimed, to varying degrees, at shoring up British imperialism. The federal government's imposition of conscription in support of the First World War led to riots and near secession in Quebec; a 1942 referendum on conscription found that three-quarters in the province opposed the measure (which was eventually implemented), while overwhelming majorities outside Quebec supported it. As an aggregate, the wars served to intensify French-Canadian nationalism and the movement for a sovereign Quebec.[10]

Since the turn of the century, francophone anti-imperialists also found allies in growing numbers of residents of non-British ethnicity (and in 'anglophobes' of Irish and German descent, in particular), as well as in labour, leftist, pacifist, and liberal individuals and organizations, many of whom forged strong links with like-minded citizens in the United States and Britain. Reassessments of the Boer War and the First World War, as well as the growth of the left during the Popular Front era, raised the profile of the anti-colonial cause in the 1920s and 1930s. Proponents of the cause would find a political home with the 1932 creation of the social democratic CCF party, whose founding manifesto included a pledge to 'refuse to be entangled in any more wars fought to make the world safe for capitalism' – a direct rebuke of Britain and its Canadian loyalists.[11]

That said, outside of Quebec, impassioned critics of imperialism remained rare in the first half of the twentieth century. As James Naylor's study of the CCF's response to the Second World War has shown, this absence can be accounted for, in part, by the fact that activists on this issue could be easily Red-baited; Naylor also points out that the Second World War had complicated the conclusion among leftists that all war was essentially an outgrowth of class conflict and competing imperial systems. While the CCF continued to speak out against imperialism following the war, its overriding foreign policy concerns centred on building support for the liberal internationalism exemplified by the United Nations. It should also be noted that, like their counterparts in French Canada, anti-imperialists from English Canada frequently confined their focus to issues surrounding Canadian sovereignty in the face of British and U.S. hegemony. Their opposition to foreign domination did not, in other words, necessarily constitute a critique of imperialism in general, particularly where non-white peoples were concerned.[12] Still, through these avenues, anti-imperial sentiment was able to gain greater purchase among the Canadian polity by mid-century than had existed in 1900.

A second opportunity for challenging colonialism lay in Canada's so-called non-imperial past. While European settlers of Canada had replicated some of imperialism's more egregious practices of racial violence against indigenous – and now internally colonized – communities, and while the British conduct toward the French frequently assumed elements of a *de facto* colonial relationship, the nation had no history of overseas territorial acquisition. The roots of this refusal were more practical than principled: the thinly populated and often cash-strapped nation had difficulty enough maintaining centralized control over its own geography and inhabitants; further, as willing partners in the project of British imperialism, a Canadian variant would represent both redundancy and unwanted competition. To a great extent, membership in the Commonwealth allowed Canadians to reap the economic benefits of empire without suffering the stigma of 'colonizer.'

By the early twentieth century, however, this 'non-imperial' past served to furnish Canadian critics of colonialism with at least a measure of moral authority, just as it would later provide the nation greater credibility as an 'honest broker' in mediating disputes that involved the Third World. And while the advent of the Cold War meant that Canadian leaders, like those in the United States, would weigh carefully the origins and trajectories of independence movements for signs of communist influence, the reordering of the globe under U.S. leadership also provided Canadian critics of imperialism with new sources of leverage. That is, while some of the impetus for supporting freedom for the colonized doubtless arose from sympathy for their plight, this stance could also serve national interests in a bipolar world. Even before the Second World War, Canadian opponents of continental integration had begun advancing the notion that, having only recently gained autonomy from Britain, Canada was being manoeuvred toward a colonial relationship with the United States. In the words of mid-century historian Harold Innis (themselves a play on the title of A.R.M. Lower's 1946 history of Canada, *Colony to Nation*), the country had progressed 'from colony to nation to colony.'[13] Though one-to-one comparisons between Canadians' own experience of foreign domination and that of Third World peoples were and are problematic on many levels, their own perceptions of dependence led some in Canada to internationalize their critique of imperialism.

At the very least, promoting a cooperative world order made up of equal *and* autonomous international actors – through support of self-government, multilateral institutions, and, later, peacekeeping – offered the nation a 'third way' out of the blind alley and transparent deference of superpower alignment. Namely, this general orientation would serve the double function of confirming a more independent foreign policy and constraining U.S. unilateralism. As political scientist and Canadian diplomat John Holmes writes: 'There is nothing particularly high-minded or unselfish about a strong internationalist policy on the part of a country that so obviously cannot protect its people and its interest except in collaboration with others.'[14]

Finally, as we have already seen, national discourses surrounding multiculturalism, tolerance, 'the mosaic,' etc., gained increasing currency during this period, motivated by a series of internal and external stimuli. Domestically, anxious Canadian elites hoped that state-mediated pluralism would serve to manage the increasingly diversified and politicized national community engendered by post-war immigration and Quebec separatism. In addition, these discourses represented the persistent desire among some Canadians to separate their national experience from that of the United States – a task that appeared both more urgent and more feasible in light of the increasingly publicized struggle for civil rights in the United States following the Second World War.[15] People of colour within and beyond Canada's borders rightly wished to know what these utterances (in Canada) were worth.

Anti-imperialism has a longer and more intrinsic connection to the American past. Though the United States, like Canada, was a settler society, the former gained independence through an anti-colonial revolution rather than the 'organic and evolutionary change' preferred by Canadian Tories (and Burkean Conservatism in general). After independence, the nation established a constitution and bill of rights which, in accordance with liberal and republican principles and in highly idealistic tones, took direct aim at various manifestations of foreign tyranny. Accordingly, many within and beyond U.S. borders came to view the nation as a friend of anti-imperial struggles everywhere, as a model for the establishment and preservation of autonomous states; these sentiments would be strengthened when presidents such as Woodrow Wilson and Franklin Roosevelt pressured European societies to divest themselves of colonies. Moreover, people of colour in the United States – who linked their own experience of racial subjugation to that of the world's colonized peoples – formed the core of a critique of empire that began in the late nineteenth century.[16] These various fonts of anti-colonialist sentiment account for the fact that when official state policies did not align with principles of self-determination (as with the seizure of territory during the Spanish-American War), vigorous resistance often followed (in this case, through the Anti-Imperialist League). By contrast, Canada lacked a revolutionary challenge to foreign rule, its own constitution and bill of rights, and the degree of racial diversity present in the United States; largely as a consequence, it also lacked an established legacy of organized resistance to imperialism.

Yet important elements of U.S. ideals and experiences moderated the nation's anti-colonialism – and, indeed, could serve to sustain and defend the practice. For one, by this juncture the United States was itself

a traditional imperial power with overseas holdings – though one, in
the words of Michael Ignatieff, that generally lacked (and for Ignatieff,
continues to lack) 'consciousness of itself as such.' Diplomatic historian
Frank Ninkovich finds that the nation's late-nineteenth-century acquisition of colonies was construed by its advocates, not as a deviation from
U.S. liberal values, but an attempt, on the part of a self-styled 'redeemer' nation, to internationalize those values through the introduction of
purportedly universal liberal institutions in foreign lands. Colonization,
then, was upheld as one method of creating a cooperative, like-minded
'world civilization' based on liberal ideals, and as a logical extension of
the nation's perceived mission of uplift.[17]

Of course, American proponents of imperialism also hoped to realize
economic benefits for a rapidly expanding industrial economy through
this formal extension of American hegemony. In this sense, they shared
a basic objective with those who employed classical liberal economic
theories to espouse 'open door' policies, rather than the spheres of
influence and closed mercantilist economies fashioned by empires.
Though theoretically at odds, the effects of both formal colonial control and open door strategies were frequently indistinguishable to the
indigenous populations involved, as were the means of achieving those
effects (including, if necessary, military coercions). These claims are not
new, having achieved near-canonical status among critics of American
empire after the publication of William Appleman Williams's 1959 study,
The Tragedy of American Diplomacy. Still, as Amy Kaplan's oft-cited introduction to *Cultures of United States Imperialism* points out, analysts of U.S.
history and culture have only recently begun to fully acknowledge the
centrality of imperialism to their field (a redress which owes a considerable debt to this same volume). Particularly in the immediate aftermath
of the Second World War, these interpretations remained under-
appreciated in American public discourse, adding another layer of complexity to Ignatieff's representation of an empire that does not imagine itself as one, and explaining why many mid-century U.S. analysts
could malign European colonialism without acknowledging its American counterpart. Assumptions of U.S. support for decolonization must
also be tempered by the particular and narrow variety of U.S. liberalism, a variant that viewed legitimate liberal movements in foreign contexts as dangerously radical, and that favoured the imposition of stability
from the outside that was often at odds with professed ideals of liberal
democracy.[18]

As with all significant issues of the day, the Cold War muddied considerably these established lines of thinking about colonialism. Post-war claims of moral leadership – as 'leader of free world' – meant that the U.S. commitment to freedom and democracy at home and abroad, not merely its security concerns and economic interests, would require consideration. Yet the Second World War witnessed the United States aligning itself with the leading imperialist powers of the day, and the emerging geopolitical bipolarity led the nation's leaders to mute or reverse their criticism of their reliable, and anti-Soviet, European allies. As cultural historian Andrew Rotter explains, American officials extended this forbearance not merely because they wished to maintain cordiality with Western Europe, but because they feared that rapid decolonization would 'undermine the economy of the noncommunist world,' in the emerging contest for global dominance. This shift in state responses to colonialism began even before war's end, with the Office of Strategic Services maintaining as early as April 1945 that U.S. interests lay in 'the maintenance of the British, French and Dutch colonial empires' as a check against growing Soviet influence.[19]

The intersection of the Cold War and the global movement toward decolonization provided other dilemmas for the United States. The dismantling of empires would produce new nations which might opt for neutrality or alliance with the USSR; on the other hand, U.S. opposition to sovereignty for Third World peoples might *guarantee* this gravitation toward the Soviet bloc. What is more, communism, like economic liberalism, provided a widely known theoretical basis for opposing colonization. While proponents of both systems found it more difficult to resist domination of foreign peoples in practice, the Soviets and later the Chinese became ardent supporters of national liberation movements beyond their own 'spheres of influence,' especially in Asia and Africa, in large part to counter the pre-existing dominance of Western capital in those regions.[20] Supporters of the colonial status quo in the West could therefore effectively tar liberation movements in general as 'communist-inspired' (and in many cases be at least partially correct); communist nations, on the other hand, could point to Western intransigence regarding Third World sovereignty (and domestic civil rights) as proof of the racism they believed to underlie the capitalist world system.

U.S. leaders were required to negotiate this complex interplay of liberal principles, national security, global anti-communism, domestic politics, and economic self-interest when deciding whether to support independence movements or to defer calls for decolonization. Over time, post-colonial historian Robert Young argues, a rather simplistic formula emerged: namely, 'supporting independence movements while at the same time attempting to suppress them if they showed leftist leanings.' Though useful as a general orientation, Young's synopsis flattens the multifarious American governmental attitudes and responses to Third World independence, even in the years after the ascendance of a rather monolithic anti-communist orthodoxy ossified the thinking of policy-makers. Nor does this characterization accommodate the full range of U.S. public opinion on the issue, with members of the African-American community, in particular, continuing to press their government on the matter throughout the Cold War.[21] And especially in the period under study – before the more thoroughgoing constraints on discourse that marked the McCarthyite era – public and governmental responses were still under sometimes intensive negotiation. It should not be surprising, then, that U.S. public reactions to the decolonization process (like those in Canada, for differing reasons) varied considerably, and exhibited a great deal of internal contradiction. In the following case studies of reactions to decolonization, I also show that American responses suggest many citizens held firm to traditional liberal and republican ideals regarding self-government even after their own elected officials and foreign policy bureaucrats concluded that Cold War exigencies trumped those same ideals.

Many of the earliest North American post-war representations of decolonization that appeared in the popular press were framed as a counterpoint to past Nazi domination of foreign peoples, as confirmation that right had prevailed in the Second World War. At the same time, post-war readers would have experienced little difficulty in extracting the more immediate moral imperatives implicit – and sometimes explicit – in steady and adamant references to newly independent peoples as 'freedom-' and 'democracy-loving,' to departing Western imperial powers as unrivalled champions of the Four Freedoms, the Atlantic Charter, and UN principles, to the new nations as devotees and replicas of 'our way of life.' On the other side of these various divides lay Soviet communism, and the relentless evocation of these stark binaries served not merely as a reminder to domestic and post-colonial audiences of their good fortune as citizens of the 'free world'; these near-mantric reiterations exposed the profound anxieties surrounding the decolonization process, functioning as strenuous attempts to foreclose alternate outcomes, to will that which was enunciated into existence. That is, these newly autonomous international actors *would indeed* remain satellites for Western interests and exemplars of Western values, and would not, having relinquished the economic and military security afforded by their colonial status, be enticed or forcibly absorbed into the Russian orbit. Readers of these independence narratives might have been surprised to learn that decolonization was in fact proceeding slowly, that colonial powers were actively resisting it on many fronts, that 'sovereignty' could still entail a high degree of foreign control, and that communists of many guises had toiled longer and more strenuously against colonialism than many advocates of capitalism. These calculated omissions characterized the analysis of even the earliest post-war decolonization event – that of the celebration on 4 July 1946 of Philippine independence.

While many U.S. commentators had previously questioned whether Filipinos were truly 'ready' for self-government, by the summer of 1946, the dominant attitude had moved toward veneration for the beneficence and moral leadership exemplified by the United States. Improvements in the educational, legal, political, and economic realms since the U.S. takeover were duly noted by the press, and in many cases, warranted. However, the brutality required to subdue the islands after the Spanish ouster, the vigorous and principled objections to this imperial acquisition advanced by many influential Americans, the ensuing half-century of fundamentally self-interested rule, and the patently limited autonomy stipulated by the terms of 'independence' were erased from Filipino history in the American mass media's independence narrative. 'Philippine Republic Is Born as U.S. Rule Ends in Glory,' proclaimed the *New York Times* on July 4, and in an editorial in the same edition extolled the U.S. government for enacting a 'colonial policy such as the world has not seen before.' The emerging geopolitical bifurcation and Soviet moves to establish puppet governments in territories they occupied were not cited expressly, but these events provided the tacit frame of reference for the *Times'* welcoming of the Philippines into 'the Parliament of Free and Independent nations *at a critical time in the world's history*,' a 'precedent ... set[ting]' episode 'that may have more far-reaching consequences than we can now foresee' (italics added).[22]

Representing the United States as the moral converse of the USSR, and portraying the granting of autonomy as proof that the United States was best suited for global leadership in the face of a growing communist threat, served as a leitmotif of other mainstream accounts of Philippine independence. *Life* called independence 'an event without real precedent in the history of nations,' while *Collier's* ran a lengthy article by U.S. high commissioner to the Philippines, Paul C. McNutt, which cited 4 July 1946 as 'a day of history not only for the Philippines ... [and]

the United States,' but 'for the entire world.' Employing terms that implicitly maligned the Soviets, and that underscored starkly nationalist conceptions of liberal universalism, McNutt held that the United States had 'enabled a democracy-loving people to preserve and extend their freedom and to perpetuate the existence in the Orient of a miniature version of our own way of life.' And anticipating the basic idioms of the Truman Doctrine, McNutt noted that the episode exemplified 'the first principle' of post-war U.S. foreign policy, namely: 'that American power is to be used for the preservation of peace and the support of democracy wherever possible in the world.'[23]

Such a global mandate was not without complexities, in that newly autonomous states might gravitate toward (or be swallowed up by) the Soviet bloc. U.S. policy-makers did not ignore these concerns in drawing up their plans for a sovereign Philippines. In truth, the islands passed on July 4th from colony to *de facto* military protectorate, with the United States retaining considerable jurisdiction over the Philippine economy and resources, and securing exclusive rights to construct twenty-three military bases throughout the republic. As Frank Ninkovich makes clear, this thoroughly constrained sovereignty had been necessitated, in the minds of U.S. officials, by the strategic importance of the islands in view of the emerging bipolar globe.[24] Simultaneously, the Filipino people had become archetypes for, and victims of, Cold War realignments.

The manifest tensions between ideals of self-determination and the imperatives of the post-war containment of perceived Soviet expansionism go far in explaining why, with the exception of Philippine independence celebrations, neither U.S. leaders nor the mainstream media paid a great deal of attention to the anti-colonialist cause in the years immediately following the war.[25] The fact that the Philippines had been a U.S. possession accounts for the disproportionate attention paid to Filipino independence, but not for the near total silence regarding similar independence struggles – particularly in light of claims that the events of 4 July 1946 had provided a model for the implementation of UN principles, and should now be emulated by all imperial powers. As suggested above, this disregard fit a broader, pre-existing pattern of slighting non-Western peoples, an oversight that was unlikely to be reversed amidst heightened Cold War concerns about national security and Soviet expansion in Eastern Europe.

These issues were not ignored outright: In August 1946, recently ousted Secretary of the Interior Harold Ickes published an article in *Collier's*, unsubtly titled 'The Navy at Its Worst,' which contrasted American rhetoric about self-determination to the wartime acquisition of territory in the Pacific (not merely 'points of geography' or 'strategic bases,' noted Ickes, but 'areas inhabited by human beings'). The African-American press, for their part, made the disparity between the professed ideals of the Western democracies and the lived experience of Third World peoples a regular feature of their post-war reportage. The *Pittsburgh Courier*'s George Schuyler was among the most consistent and acerbic of these critics, providing case after case of colonized peoples who, 'in their naïve way, took the Atlantic Charter seriously,' and who continued to suffer 'under the heels of the "democracies."'[26] Importantly, the views of marginalized populations reached only a limited audience within U.S. borders, and were virtually invisible beyond them; in the main, Canadians and the rest of the world saw merely the triumphalism, pageantry, and self-congratulation (and, to some, hypocrisy) of the American liberation narrative.

It should not be surprising that Canadian commentary on Philippine independence lacked the exultant tones characteristic of U.S. coverage. More remarkable, given that a majority of Canadians purportedly shared with their American counterparts aspirations for a sovereign and liberal post-war order, is the formers' general disregard for the event and its broader implications. Most Canadian dailies carried only abbreviated Associated Press reports of the independence celebrations in the Philippines – some on the front page (generally near the bottom), others in their international pages, surrounded by minutia about miscellaneous diplomatic legations and unremarkable speeches. The Canadian Press did not file a report from the Philippines, and editorial boards chose to address a host of other matters on July 4 (all the more noteworthy considering the date provided an obvious incentive for discussing things American); readers neither addressed the event nor protested the slighting of the story in letters to the editor. This silence was symptomatic of a broader pattern in the Canadian press: an index of leading Canadian periodicals reveals a near blackout when it came to Canadian stories about the Philippines in the years surrounding that nation's independence.[27]

This absence can be accounted for, I believe, by parsing the overlapping and often mutually reinforcing identities and interests that characterized Canada's journalistic class. The Tory elites among them had traditionally cast the United States as an expansionist, predatory force intent on swallowing the entire continent – and, admittedly, could reference real events to support their claims. By the early twentieth century, they were joined by a burgeoning intellectual elite to their left, many of whom recast the object of American desire as the globe itself – again, a stance that was not entirely lacking in material evidence. Such articles of faith did not square well with this voluntary contraction of territory in the Pacific. It is hard to imagine, on the other hand, this degree of indifference had the event occurred a few years later, when apprehensions regarding American domination had for many been eclipsed by fears of a presumably more sinister expansionist power in the Russians. The failure to seize upon the story as an object lesson in the comparative ethical superiority of anti-communist nations, in general, and the United States, in particular, points to the still-tentative nature of the anti-Soviet consensus in Canada in the summer of 1946.

Anxieties about growing U.S. international influence are, however, only part of the story. Perhaps more importantly, white, professional-class Canadians of all political stripes exhibited a rather mechanical tendency to fall back on and overstate their nation's 'British character' as the decisive marker of distinction from their more heterogeneous American neighbours, a stance that implied varying degrees of toleration for Britain's imperial project.[28] The granting of independence by a sovereign to a subject people was thus doubly challenging, as the act amounted to an undeniable censure of Britannia: while the Empire had granted practical autonomy to realms dominated by British-stock settlers (who, again, thereafter considered themselves imperial partners rather than subject-peoples), it had yet to do so for its Third World wards. Better, then, to let this story languish – and to lash out against American criticism of British imperialism, as we will see below.

Admittedly, both of the above explanations for the slighting of Philippine independence rely on a measure of conjecture. No editorial boards provided justifications for their omissions, nor should explanations that constitute *mea culpas* or that might lay bare illogic or pettiness be expected. The above analysis, can be situated, however, within a broad pattern of Canadian responses to matters that touch on the intersection of Britain, the United States, and imperialism discussed below. Historian Robert Young notes that immediately after co-authoring the Atlantic Charter with Franklin Roosevelt, Winston Churchill denied that the document applied to his own nation's colonial subjects.[29] Apparently, many Canadians, who in other contexts presented themselves as staunch defenders of the principles of self-determination outlined in the Four Freedoms, the Atlantic Charter, and UN principles, could exhibit a similar relativism in the earliest years of the Cold War.

When India and Pakistan attained independence from Britain just one year later, the Canadian response differed dramatically in both scope and tenor, an about-face that had less to do with the passage of time than with the identities of the principal actors involved. Notable, too (and not a little ironic), is the degree to which dominant Canadian readings of the event echoed American mass media reports about the significance of *Philippine* independence: the British, Canadian writers maintained, had always intended for Indians to govern themselves, and centuries of European rule – or, rather, 'uplift' – were necessary prerequisites for 'home rule'; while other colonizers exploited their subjects, the British variant of imperialism implied a singularly altruistic governance for which all members of the Commonwealth should be proud; all 'progress' and 'improvement' in South Asia, including independence itself, was by and large a British achievement, and was recognized as such by a grateful subject people; having so thoroughly and properly set Indians and Pakistanis on the road to democracy, all current and future problems would belong to the newly sovereign states alone. Like U.S. accounts of Filipino independence, the hardening great-power rivalry shaped all of these claims, though now – in the wake of the Truman Doctrine – the relationship between decolonization and the bipolar balance of power was, in general, made more explicit. A final analogy: as with American voices critical of their own nation's interactions with the Third World, not all Canadian analysts read the events as a case study in Western-power greatness.

In the years leading up to Indian and Pakistani independence, opinion in Canada was divided as to the nature of the British legacy in the region, whether Britain would or should depart South Asia, and whether indigenous inhabitants (particularly of this number and religious and ethnic variation) could be expected to govern themselves. These issues became much more than academic when wartime unrest in India threatened to divert British attentions from Europe, a phenomenon that, for the conspicuously anglophile *Saturday Night* in particular, became a regular – if somewhat repetitive – rallying point for the prolongation of the Raj. Some of the magazine's analysts spoke of the 'problem' of India from largely practical rather than moral perspectives (Was the region a drain or boon to the Empire's finances? Would its 'teeming masses' assist or inhibit the war effort?). Most were unequivocal in their support for continued British control of the subcontinent, either because they considered Britain's rule benign, the local population incapable, or both – or because a British departure would lead directly to Axis takeover, perhaps, conjectured one, even turning the global tide toward Hitler.[30] As many Canadian publications and *Saturday Night*, in particular, relied heavily on British 'experts' who had worked in military or civilian capacities in India, the overall tenor of the coverage was largely foreordained.

That India already suffered under foreign rule proved a tricky matter for those who simultaneously denounced their Axis enemies' undemocratic global expansionism, but piece after piece in *Saturday Night* made clear that Nazi domination was of a different character altogether, and that India was an exceptional and extraordinarily complex case that required and even embraced foreign stewardship, and that actually 'fears freedom.' 'Democratic Self-Government Impossible in India,' proclaimed the title of a Sir Richard Clifford Tute article in the October 1942 edition, highlighting the alleged intractability of India's religious and ethnic divisions. In the off chance that their subscribers found Sir Richard's hypothesis excessively opaque, the magazine followed a month later with a piece entitled 'India Is Not a Nation, and Cannot Become One.'[31] In both cases, readers who bothered to move beyond these unambiguous headlines were in for few surprises.

As Canadian Institute of Public Opinion polling suggested, these authors spoke to and bolstered a strong current of public opinion: in April 1946, as Britain negotiated the future of India with indigenous leaders, just 18 per cent of Canadians believed India was ready 'for the same amount of self-government as Canada has'; 46 per cent answered in the negative. Just as telling, fully one-third of the respondents admitted they did not know enough about the most populous imperial holding in the Commonwealth to render judgment. Not surprisingly, opposition to Indian self-government was highest among Progressive Conservative voters, a party still dominated by 'Empire Loyalists.' Residents of Quebec, who could point to a substantively different encounter with British imperialism, were of a different mind altogether. In fact, the majority of those who expressed an opinion held that Indians were indeed prepared to rule themselves. While CIPO pollsters expressed surprise at the high level of public ignorance regarding the issue, they themselves were symptomatic of, and accessories to, that ignorance: this 1946 survey constitutes the only measure of public attitudes to colonization or even to issues specific to the Third World taken by the agency during the years 1945–50.[32]

Once the British formally announced their intentions to 'quit' India, the terms of debate in Canada's mass media shifted from frequently reactionary defences of foreign rule to frequently platitudinous celebrations of the British legacy on the subcontinent. As with U.S. accounts of Filipino independence, (oppressive) Soviet domination of foreign peoples provided the counterpoint to (beneficent) English domination. The evidence? For one, Britain seized foreign lands not merely for economic or strategic benefit, but with the primary aim of 'rais[ing] the natives' standard of living and open[ing] up opportunities for education and self-betterment,' wrote Margaret Kirkland for *Saturday Night*.[33]

In a similar story just prior to independence, the aptly named David England heaped praise on Britain for a century of public works projects that brought unprecedented prosperity to what the author seemed to imply was a formerly barren land. Like many other apologists for imperialism, England failed to interrogate precisely who benefited from this upsurge in prosperity, or to acknowledge the coercion of labour behind the construction of dams, bridges, and canals that made possible this economic transformation (crediting instead only the 'patient labor' of 'British engineering'). Likewise, centuries of violence associated with European conquest and rule, as well as the omnipresence of indigenous resistance, were vanquished from the imperial record as journalists took stock of the British legacy. James McCook of the Canadian Press noted without irony that the protracted British occupation had 'protected India from invasion,' while the editors of the *Halifax Chronicle-Herald* argued that true 'oppressors' could not have provided an allegedly trouble-free 'peace and law and order for these teeming millions' for so long.[34] Strategic requirements – along with habitual assumptions of racial and cultural superiority – lay behind many of these upbeat revisionings, just as they did for assessments produced during the war; the Soviets had merely replaced the Nazis as the justification for British hegemony. Time and again, attitudes toward decolonization and the Third World in general would be determined by, and subordinated to, the alleged strategic needs of the West.

If British rule itself had been, for Canadian anglophiles, ultimately a good thing, the act of bestowing independence on the peoples of South Asia constituted an even clearer indication of the Empire's magnanimity. Again, the growing East-West divide is important here. By establishing the supremacy of British statesmanship and the benevolence of British governance, the event verified the nation's continued suitability for global leadership, even in an emerging post-colonial context: as the Soviets moved to enslave the world, history's most storied imperial ruler was taking steps to free it. The *Globe and Mail* called Indian sovereignty 'a triumph in the readjustment of relations between Europe and Asia, based

firmly on the principles of the UN charter'; at least the West was upholding its end of the 'One World' bargain. Further, while many writers
praised Nehru and especially Gandhi for effective and prudent leadership, they made it clear that an autonomous India and Pakistan was largely a Britain accomplishment. Independence had been willingly 'granted'
rather than demanded and seized by a long-suffering people. Reporter
James McCook exemplified this pattern – and unwittingly verified that
more attention should have been paid in Canada to recent events in the
Philippines – when he exulted that 'history had no parallel for the voluntary decision of a great power' to 'free' one of its subject peoples.[35]

More a-historical still were declarations that the centuries-long project
of British conquest and domination was actually a calculated exercise
in liberation. Toronto's *Globe and Mail*, in particular, strained to impart
a unified and laudable teleology to the project of British imperialism.
Where observers sympathetic to the colonized might see an indigenous
resistance leading first to grudging ameliorations of repression and
finally to the expulsion of foreign rulers, the *Globe* delineated a markedly different trajectory: 'The long series of political reforms in India,
giving Indians an increasing share in the direction of affairs, is sufficient
proof that independence is the fulfillment, not the wreck, of British
intentions.' Ottawa correspondent for the *London Times* Alexander Inglis made similar claims, and stressed the immeasurable and thankless
sacrifices made by 'a great host of British civil servants [who] have given
the best years of their lives to the service of India.' The *Regina Leader-
Post* seemed intent on deflating the near-mythic status of Gandhi among
Third World peoples and their sympathizers, arguing that independence
was not achieved 'by any one man,' but through 'wise and statesman-like
moves all down through the years of British rule and guidance.'[36]

For some, the notion that Britain's work was both beneficial and primarily altruistic was evidenced by the fact that a subcontinent formerly
riven with linguistic variance was now unified in its adoption of the English language. Further evidence could be found, according to reporter
James McCook, in the fact that where the Europeans had first encountered 'princes in jeweled turbans,' they now leave 'men in business suits'
who have been cured of 'many savage customs.' Though these post-Hol-
ocaust analyses took pains to avoid the language of racial hierarchy, the
shift to the discourse of ethnicity, culture, and 'development' carried
forward many of the same evolutionary and essentialist assumptions
regarding individual and societal character.[37]

How effective was this massive and protracted exercise in cultural and political tutelage? Despite more than three hundred years of various manifestations of European rule, and nearly a century of direct British governance under the Raj (whose ostensible goal, to repeat, was assiduous preparation for self-rule), considerable questions remained regarding the 'ability' of these indigenous populations to govern themselves. Few observers seemed to grasp the paradox in the apparent gulf between the intentions and effects of the extended imperial mission. In fact, the most pessimistic assessments of the Indian and Pakistani future could appear in articles that went to considerable lengths extolling the work Britain had done in grooming them for that future. 'For more than a century, the deliberate aim of British policy has been to equip the Indians for full self-government,' the *Globe and Mail* maintained, and in the very next paragraph lamented that the new nation's leaders 'can hardly be said to have the backing of an alert and informed public opinion because the great mass of Indians know nothing of politics.'[38] Perhaps another century was needed? The *Globe* did not say.

This apparent incongruity between goals and results could be explained away by a myriad of circumstances, but the most likely would appear to involve any combination of incapable students, ineffective teachers, and an imperial objective that was perhaps less motivated by selfless pedagogical exertions than its supporters claimed. Not surprisingly, inferences tended toward the first of these: the *Winnipeg Tribune* ran an editorial cartoon depicting new leaders Nehru and Jinnah holding turbaned, unruly children representing India's princes, while a matronly woman wearing an apron (and war helmet) and carrying Union Jack–decorated suitcases prepares to leave. Its caption, 'Your Babies Now,' suggested that this long-suffering nanny had done all she could with such hapless pupils. As Andrew Rotter notes, this colonial subject-as-child motif was ubiquitous in depictions of India and of colonized peoples in general, and had decidedly functional aims: 'Children,' he observes 'were naïve, impetuous, quarrelsome, physically and emotionally immature, and unable to manage tasks (like trade) requiring numbers, because their thinking was not linear and they failed to understand time.' Further, the child motif provided yet another opportunity for Canadian imperialists to divorce their post-colonial experience from that of South Asians: Canada, in their view, had achieved national manhood. As Daniel Francis writes, early twentieth-century Canadians frequently utilized the metaphor of 'the maturation of a child to responsible adulthood' to characterize their own nation's development from colony to partner in the British Empire.[39]

In a similar manner, the factional violence that plagued the region both before and after independence received extensive coverage throughout the West; however, the explanation offered for this unrest – that inhabitants of the subcontinent were essentially irrational, passion-driven, and immature – was decidedly less developed, and elided centuries of foreign divide-and-rule tactics. Accordingly, *Halifax Chronicle-Herald* editors held little hope for this experiment in Third World sovereignty, predicting 'internal chaos' that will 'make Pax Britannica something to be looked back upon with yearning by India's millions.'[40]

What made questions of 'readiness' increasingly vital was the prospect that the failure of democracy and, more importantly, pro-Western sentiment could deliver one-fifth of the world's population to the Soviet camp. Just months after the end of the Second World War, *Saturday Night* contributor Margaret Kirkland defended British imperialism on the grounds that it thwarted Russian imperialism. At the height of the Gouzenko spy scare, the *Toronto Telegram* found 'communist inspiration' in a host of domestic and worldwide events, the most ominous being the 'Quit India' movement that sought to hand India over to Russia. The *Globe and Mail*, foreshadowing the rationale for the twenty-first-century Bush Doctrine, held that utilizing far-flung British colonies and troop deployments to check communists abroad meant not having to face them at home. 'Britain,' it argued, '...is helping to save this country, among others, from the necessity of offering a direct military challenge to the Russians.' For the *Globe*, those who suggest 'that the British should throw off the responsibilities of a major Power' were succumbing to an 'ideological fad' that would only bolster 'militant Communism.'[41] In this manner, the *Globe*, like many other Canadian voices, saw Indian independence as an exceptional case; broader calls for the decolonization of Western subjects were viewed with a mixture of indifference and, in the face of an expansionist Soviet empire, growing alarm.

Not all Canadians fell back upon this reflexive defence of British imperialism, in general, or the Raj, in particular. J.A. Stevenson of the *Dalhousie Review*, while agreeing that the Soviets likely had designs on the region, argued that decolonization would in fact deter Russian meddling. If Britain fails to broker a negotiated sovereignty, he cautioned, a violent revolt might ensue which 'could rely upon encouragement and even some practical help from Russia.' In Stevenson's schema, self-determination would serve, rather than impair, the global interests of a pro-U.S. consensus. The leftist *Toronto Star*'s independence day editorial heralded the end of 'alien rule' in India; elsewhere, editors called for a more widespread curtailment of both British imperial holdings and of the country's 'delusions of national grandeur.'[42]

Syndicated columnist Elmore Philpott provided a rare intervention into the chorus of praise for Britain's tutelage and uplift, holding that Indian independence had been achieved, not by emulating the freedom struggles of West liberal nation-states, but by providing a morally superior model for liberation. 'Suppose,' he conjectured, 'Gandhi had torn another leaf from the Western book of history. Suppose, just after the first world war, he had decided to go after freedom as the English themselves did in 1688, the Americans did in 1776, the French did in 1789, the Canadians did in 1837, or the Irish did in 1919?' If so, Philpott argued, India would still have achieved independence, though one drenched with blood that would deprive Britons of the accolades of 'nobility' and 'honour' ascribed to their departure.[43]

Philpott's themes were mirrored – and enhanced considerably – in one of the only letters-to-the-editor about Indian/Pakistani independence that appeared in Canadian publications in the weeks surrounding the event. Perhaps not surprisingly, this rare reader response to the epochal moment came from a self-identified Indian national, a *Globe and Mail* subscriber by the name of N. Dharmarajan. Unsurprising, too, is the fact that one of the few people of colour allowed to weigh in on the matter disrupts the main currents of established wisdom. In a sophisticated laying-out of positions aimed directly at press spin, Dharmarajan disputes notions 'that the spirit of psychological freedom is essentially a British product, and that the Orientals are perennially wont to create despots to rule over them.' S/he counters that Britain, too, has experienced cyclical episodes of despotic rule followed by popular resistance against it, and holds that while tyranny did exist in India at times before European conquest, British rule constituted the most 'vociferous and spectacular form' of despotism Indians had yet encountered.

Dharmarajan goes on to question why the most acute forms of much-referenced factional violence occur in industrialized cities, while rural Indians of great diversity coexist in much greater harmony than 'the labor and capital division in the West, to speak only of one form of Occidental diversities.' The divide-and-rule requirements of both capitalism and imperial domination, the writer argues, contributed greatly to the current factional strife. 'It must be admitted,' Dharmarajan contends, 'that British institutions, however mobile, have not brought about a millennium in this world,' before concluding that a non-hierarchical appreciation for all cultures is necessary 'to ward off the doomed day of the human race.'[44] Later, many of these positions would be termed 'post-colonial' by the academic establishment.

Not surprisingly, francophone publications also called into question the mobility and salvific capacities of British institutions. Here, emergent Quebec nationalism provided the backdrop for representations of independence in South Asia. 'August 14 and 15, 1947 mark a great date in world history,' observed *Le Devoir*, though the paper maintained that the glory of the event was not Britain's; rather, Indian and Pakistani sovereignty signified the end of 'the domination of the rulers over the ruled' and a fatal (and welcome) blow to the economic sustainability of the British Empire.[45]

The most unrelenting challenge to the narrative of British beneficence in India would emerge from the editors and contributors at the *Canadian Forum*. In fact, the publication – which, like the *Dalhousie Review* and *Queen's Quarterly*, catered to a progressive, urban (and relatively small) audience – had for many years chipped away at the basic assumptions of colonial rule. Established in 1920, the journal served as a candid intervention into the traditional scholarly and popular analyses of Canadian politics and society, analyses which the *Forum* castigated as overly positivistic, statist, rooted in superficial notions of British superiority, and dismissive of links between the Canadian and American experience.

In actual fact, those links were profound. As Carl Berger's survey of Canadian historiography demonstrates, leading contributors to the *Forum*, such as historian Frank Underhill, drew consciously and heavily upon the progressive or 'new' history emerging from the United States that emphasized materialism, class conflict, the 'common man,' and authorial subjectivity – orientations almost wholly absent in mainstream Canadian social sciences at the turn of the century. Moreover, by employing these fresh analytical tools, Canadian proponents of the new history arrived at the conclusion so dreaded by the nation's conservative Anglo elite: that in many respects, in Underhill's words, 'the United States is simply Canada writ large.'[46] That is, Canada, too, constituted a site of intensive class conflict, racial animosity, corporate-governmental collusion, and so on.

Many of the new history's leading American exponents, including Charles Beard, James Harvey Robinson, and Vernon Parrington, aimed to reinvigorate ideals they believed their nation had lost during the Gilded Age and the imperialistic fervour of the late nineteenth century; as such, their work frequently included condemnations of colonial practices at home and abroad. In Canada, practitioners of this largely imported progressive orientation shared with their American progenitors a thoroughgoing critique of manifestations of foreign control – including, for the *Forum*, British colonization, Soviet puppet regimes, and U.S. economic imperialism. To the largely marginalized and dispersed currents of anticolonialism in Canada (heretofore largely associated with ethnic minorities, radical labour, and pacifist groups) was added a forceful new voice; it borrowed heavily and consciously from American progressivism and, by proxy, from that nation's republican and liberal ideals. (Nor was this the first instance of Canadian anti-imperialism relying on the American tradition for inspiration: turn-of-the-century Canadian publisher Goldwin Smith, the era's most noted English-speaking critic of colonialism, was so fond of republican ideals that he made American annexation of Canada his life mission.) Contemporary historian Michael Fellman, a self-described 'American-Canadian,' finds that Canadians' 'mythic self-constructions' prevent them from appreciating 'that they have learned anything progressive from Americans.'[47] The growing influence of anti-colonialism in Canadian popular consciousness during the interwar era gives the lie to that collective denial.

Even during the war, when cross-examinations of British colonialism – near-treasonous at the best of times – were tantamount to providing 'aid and comfort' to the enemy, the *Canadian Forum* refused to reign in its condemnation of the Empire. In a 1944 article titled 'Equatorial Conflict – a Study in Black and White,' Bruce Woodsworth maintained that citizens of Western powers must press their governments to implement the Four Freedoms in areas currently languishing under foreign domination – and, specifically, in British colonies. In measured and reserved tones, and employing extensive material evidence, Woodsworth argued that while Britain was among the most 'enlightened' of colonial rulers, even that nation's conduct toward 'colored folk living in its colonies' could only be considered appalling: indigenous labourers toiled as virtual slaves, while the much-vaunted colonial educational system eschewed true 'uplift' for a dead-end curriculum of 'personal cleanliness' and 'gardening.' (Woodsworth also anticipated a significant later-century historiographical turn in pointing out that 'unorganized passive resistance and feigned stupidity are constantly employed to hamper and frustrate the white man.') The author concluded that the Allies' professed revulsion for Nazism's white supremacy does not square with the colonial practices of the West. 'While native troops die in Africa and Asia so that the western democracies may be ensured freedom of speech and religion, freedom from want and fear, it is well to know that these same natives enjoy few rights of any description.'[48]

The *Canadian Forum*'s critical scrutiny of British imperial rhetoric and action (and frequently the wide chasm separating the two) did not turn to uncritical applause once the Crown announced plans to negotiate Indian independence. Challenging the frequently voiced notion that India's ethnic/religious diversity was solely to blame for the divisions that imperilled sovereignty negotiations, the journal instead found the roots of much of the factionalism in the divisive rule of the British. When India and Pakistan finally achieved sovereignty, *Forum* editors decried Western reporters' fixation with ethnic and religious unrest, and suggested a specific motive: 'The present disturbances have been put out of focus,' they wrote, 'by what appears to be a deliberate campaign' to discredit indigenous rule. In the following issue, they returned to the same matter, arguing 'the vague impression, that the native governments cannot control the situation only because the guiding hand of Britain has been withdrawn is misleading.' As a point of comparison, the *Forum* reminded readers that a much greater administrative failure – the wartime Bengal Famine, which killed between 1.5 and 3 million people and owed much to callous and ineffective British colonial policies – was barely reported in the West. Along these same lines, editors credited the indigenous insurgency and leaders like Nehru (an individual 'immeasurably superior, both morally and intellectually, to most of the recent representatives of British imperialism in India,' *Forum* editors maintained) as the true architects of independence.[49]

In this manner, anti-imperialist intellectual currents characteristic to the American milieu were introduced to Canadian political discourse. Further, U.S. analysts did not merely provide their northern neighbours some of the tools to challenge imperialism; where the colonialism of European nations was concerned – and to the dismay of many Canadians – Americans did so directly. An October 1942 *Life* editorial took stock of U.S. public opinion and concluded that 'one thing we are *not* fighting for is to hold the British Empire together' (emphasis in original). Writes Mary Ann Heiss: 'As the American public saw things, the war was being fought for the ideas set for in the Atlantic Charter – freedom, self-determination, anticolonialism, global cooperation. It was not being waged to defend the old order but to create a new one, founded on principles that had long been accepted in the United States.' Particular attention was paid, both during and after the war, to India. In the October 1942 radio broadcast cited above, Wendell Willkie pointed to

India as 'a symbol throughout the whole of Asia' for the hollowness of Allied talk of freedom. The following day, M.J. Coldwell, national leader of the CCF Party (an organization with strong links to writers and readers of the *Canadian Forum*), urged Prime Minister Mackenzie King to pressure Britain to reopen negotiations with the Indian Congress Party, a call that was echoed by 'a host of others' in Canada.[50]

American condemnation of British imperialism was not limited to progressives like Willkie. *Time* magazine's summary of the transition to self-rule carried little of the exaltation for Britain that served as a prerequisite for mainstream Canadian reports; rather, lassitude and retreat marked the terminus of British rule. 'History, sloppy as usual, had decreed a fade-out rather than a blackout of the British Raj,' *Time* eulogized bleakly, noting that citizens of the new republics set out almost immediately to recover their own sense of self by 'erasing the memory of British rule from the very place names.' While crediting the Europeans for modernizing India's infrastructure and judicial system, *Time* argued that the 'debits' left by Britain were also 'enormous.' As the Raj ended, '... Indians were still among the world's poorest people ...; seventy-five percent hovered perpetually between hunger and outright starvation.' Life expectancy, meanwhile, remained 'the world's lowest – 27 years.'[51] Such disheartening statistics were doubtless also available to Canadian editorial boards, but would have done little to serve the narrative of 'uplift.'

American syndicated columnist Dorothy Thompson, too, deflated the aura of imperial grandeur, pointing to an obvious truth that many in Canada seemed to argue against, even as they refused to name it openly: that the British had been driven from South Asia despite their vigorous and protracted attempt to hold it through violence. While the *Globe and Mail* hailed independence as the 'fulfillment ... of British intentions,' Thompson pointed out that the British 'withdraw before a movement led by a man who taught that all weapons break on the absolutely non-aggressive, resistant spirit.' Robert Trumbull of the *New York Times* expressed surprise at the 'outpouring of joy' witnessed during independence celebrations, as 'Indian nature ... is not given to joy – Indians have had so little of it in their long history.' *Time*'s correspondent in Pakistan raised questions about the much-lauded transformation of the subcontinent's economy and infrastructure under European rule, making note of the poverty and squalor in the city of Karachi, perhaps the most industrialized and westernized urban centre in all of Pakistan and India. The editors of the *New York Times* praised Britain's establishment of peace and unity in 'that seething land of many races,' as well as the introduction of liberal-democratic ideals to 'Oriental' minds previously captive (uniquely, it would seem) to 'patriarchal traditions.' At the same time, the paper heralded the fact that the British 'captains and kings that strutted across the scene of India's history depart, one hopes, never to return.' With somewhat premature optimism, the *Times* argued that 'the real significance of the day … is that it marks the twilight of colonialism everywhere.'[52] For the indigenous citizens of Indochina, Africa, and elsewhere, the imperial 'fade-out' would, of course, prove lengthy and frequently brutal.

This is not to say that American reports were unrelentingly critical of British colonial practices. Many insisted that, as far as foreign domination goes, Britain's variant remained comparatively temperate – a claim that could easily be translated into a condemnation of current Soviet expansionism. However, the critiques of imperialism emerging from the United States appeared in that nation's mainstream media. In Canada, by contrast, the subtle and overt condemnations of colonial practices arose largely from the margins: *Canadian Forum* catered to left-leaning urban elites; voices like Elmore Philpott and the *Toronto Star*, meanwhile, were largely isolated, and were frequently disparaged in dominant Canadian publications.

The perceived irrelevance of, and disdain for, the anti-colonial posture in Canada can be witnessed by the *Globe and Mail*'s response to the *Toronto Star*'s call for more widespread British decolonization: 'Consider the Source,' they titled their rejoinder, and compared the *Star*'s 'astonishing' and 'contemptible' reprimand of British imperialism to 'a street arab blowing peas at Mount Everest' (and thereby revealing perhaps more than they wished about their own attitudes toward Third World inhabitants). The most widespread condemnation, however, was reserved for the much more vocal American critics of British colonial holdings, and of imperialism generally. The *Globe* bristled that some 'American friends' could not resist 'ironic comments about Britain's "graceful exit," [or] remarking that India's continuing Commonwealth link is what Britain has "salvaged" from "the demise of British power."' The *Globe*'s rebuttal came in the form of the now well-worn tune that Britain had worked and planned for Indian sovereignty from the beginning.[53]

Canadian remonstrations against American 'meddling' in the Indian 'problem,' or against 'enlightened' imperialism in general, were nothing new. For many years, a great deal of the Canadian celebration of

Avenging Genii

For *Globe and Mail* cartoonist Jack Boothe, the bombing of Hiroshima finds its justification in Japan's surprise attack at Pearl Harbor. Though Canadians appeared more likely to consider the morality of the bombings a legitimate topic of debate, most Canadian analysts, like their American counterparts, ultimately defended the act. ('Avenging Genii,' *Globe and Mail*, 9 August 1945 – reprinted with permission from the *Globe and Mail*)

Pity the Poor Cartoonist

Here Boothe addresses the optimism surrounding the potential peacetime applications of nuclear technology, an optimism shared by higher percentages of American and Canadian residents than those of any other nation surveyed at the dawn of the atomic age. While the fictional cartoonist is clearly distressed over the creative challenge posed by Hiroshima, Boothe may also be reflecting wider anxieties about more sinister 'atomic possibilities.' ('Pity the Poor Cartoonist,' *Globe and Mail*, 11 August 1945 – reprinted with permission from the *Globe and Mail*)

Operation Musk-Ox, February–May 1946. Canadian forces making the trek from Fort Churchill, Manitoba, to Edmonton depended on aircraft – here, a U.S. Air Force glider – for supplies. The operation, which began on the same day that the RCMP rounded up Canadian suspects in the Gouzenko Affair, reinforced the notion that the Soviets were the most tangible threat to North American security. (Library and Archives Canada/Department of National Defence collection/PA196940)

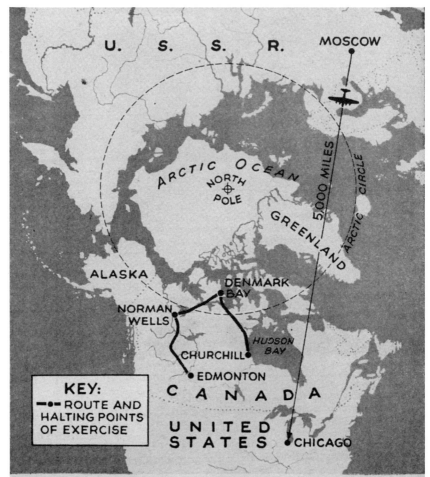

THE 3,130-MILE ROUTE, Churchill to Edmonton, goes 350 miles past Arctic Circle, with ten stops. Only four snowmobiles will go to northernmost point, Denmark Bay.

In its 11 March 1946 edition, Henry Luce's *Life* magazine offered its clearest signal to date that the Soviets had shifted from ally to foe, providing a map of Operation Musk-Ox that reveals the unnerving proximity – via the Arctic – of Moscow to North America. The silhouette of what could easily pass as a Soviet heavy bomber en route to Chicago adds a particularly transparent subtext. ('Exercise Musk Ox,' *Life*, 11 March 1946, 40)

Suspended Animation

The Tory *Globe and Mail* utilizes the Gouzenko Affair to discredit Canada's Soviet friends and, more pointedly, the paper's largest rival in Toronto's newspaper circulation wars. (Jack Boothe, 'Suspended Animation,' *Globe and Mail*, 21 February 1946 – reprinted with permission from the *Globe and Mail*)

Igor and Svetlana Gouzenko are reinvented as Middle Americans by Dana Andrews and Gene Tierney in 20th Century-Fox's version of the Gouzenko Affair. Despite its apparent standing as 'the most amazing plot in 3300 years of recorded espionage,' the incident has been largely forgotten in American history. (*The Iron Curtain* © 1948 Twentieth Century Fox, all rights reserved)

" YOUR BABIES NOW "

Jinnah and Nehru are left to contend with infantile princes by a long-suffering British nanny in a *Winnipeg Tribune* cartoon marking Indian-Pakistani independence. At the outset of the Cold War, Canadian anglophiles took pains to emphasize the contrast between Britain's 'beneficent' global conquests and the post-war takeovers initiated by Stalin, and called for the perpetuation of British imperialism as a check against the spread of communism. ('Your Babies Now,' *Winnipeg Tribune*, 16 August 1947)

"THE GOOD RIGHT ARM"

THE DEMOCRATIC WORLD

COOPERATION WITH OTHER DEMOCRATIC NATIONS

While Canadians emphasized the multilateral character of the North Atlantic Treaty, U.S. officials and media representatives – here, noted labour cartoonist Bernard Seaman – viewed the pact as America's coronation as global leader, and as a means of realizing America's international objectives. ('The Good Right Arm,' *New York Times*, 3 April 1949)

YES, WE MUST BE STRONG!

For *Saturday Night*, Canadians questioning the North Atlantic Treaty served the Kremlin's interests – either unwittingly or, more likely, because they were Stalin's operatives. Note, too, that Canada's guardians appear strangely quiescent regarding the threat in comparison to their more dynamic southern neighbour. (Jacques, 'Yes, We Must Be Strong!' *Saturday Night*, 17 May 1949, 5)

LOS ANGELES' "CRUSADE AGAINST COMMUNISM"
Sock and then ask.

The outbreak of the Korean War heightened an already acute contempt for those associated with the left. Here a group of Second World War veterans attack and 'badly maul' three unionized workers emerging from a Los Angeles auto plant (only to discover that two of their 'unpatriotic' victims were also veterans). Corresponding attitudes led the *Vancouver Sun* to urge essential-industries' workers 'to be on guard against disloyal elements secretly planning destruction in their midst.' (AP photo, *Time*, 31 July 1950, 13).

FINALLY, A LEADER AND A RALLYING POINT.

As the neophyte UN possessed few symbols around which to rally support for the Korean War, several Canadian cartoonists relied upon American iconography. Uncle Sam, frequently an object of derision in previous Canadian representations, is here reconfigured in heroic idioms. Such images did little to dispel the notion that the war was primarily a U.S., rather than a UN, operation. (Les Callan, 'Finally, a Leader and a Rallying Point,' *Toronto Star*, 29 June 1950 – reprinted with permission from Torstar Syndication Services)

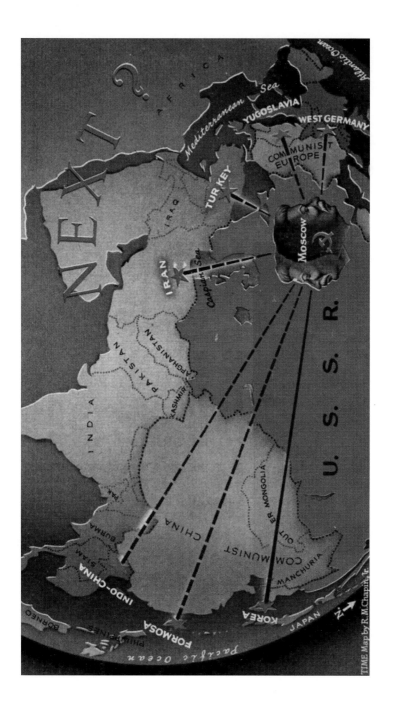

As U.S. forces lose ground in South Korea at an alarming rate, *Time*'s interpretation of Stalin's grand strategy reinforces fears of a unitary, expansionist enemy that appears to be dominating the global battle. (*Time*, 17 July 1950, 24)

empire was generated as a direct response to U.S. criticisms of the practice. Sir Richard Tute's 'Democratic Self-Government Impossible in India,' published in *Saturday Night* on the eve of Willkie's 1942 radio address, suggested that the American anti-imperialist lobby had been duped by the sham 'holy men' who controlled the Indian Congress Party (and who, while touring North America, practised 'their home industry of religious mendicancy'). In a dress rehearsal for Cold War era pretexts for foreign domination, Tute claimed that the 'Quit India' lobby and other Third World independence movements were an Axis plot, and that the truth would be revealed only after 'it is realized in America that the Indian Congress is not a group of high-minded ascetics, but a camarilla of cunning and exceedingly unscrupulous traitors to their country.' Following Willkie's broadcast, F.F. Hunter noted that the American's opinions were shared by none other than Canadian communists – at a time, it should be added, when the Soviets were Canada's allies in a war against fascism.[54]

In a *Saturday Night* commentary, London lawyer and 'advisory member of the Council of the Empire Press Union' H.S.L. Polak (like Tute's 'holy men,' also touring North America, though truly, it appears, a manipulator of facts) angrily rebuked *Life* magazine for suggesting, quite correctly, that wartime India 'is on the verge of revolt' and that only its inhabitants' greater disdain for fascism prevented more widespread resistance. Even Willson Woodside, a considerably less enthusiastic champion of the Crown, paternalistically chided the 'many well-intentioned American publicists' and 'progressives' insisting on complete Indian freedom, which he believed should not be granted either 'now or in the future.' The basis for Woodside's denial was equally patronizing, and in the context of a people simply asking for the same treatment afforded other former colonies in the Commonwealth, more than a little abstruse: 'Complete freedom – freedom from all obligations whatsoever to other members of the society – is no longer possible in this world, if it ever was.'[55]

This counterattack against U.S. anti-colonial discourse did not abate with war's end – it merely switched nemeses. The title of Margaret Kirkland's March 1946 *Saturday Night* article, 'Time to Lay Bogey of British Imperialism,' was aimed squarely at the moralizing American anti-colonial rhetoric employed by U.S. senators, which the author believed imperilled a vigorous Anglo-American alliance against 'totalitarian aggression' (now of the *Soviet* variety). Much of Kirkland's reasoning and marshalling of evidence was both specious and internally contradictory: British holdings had been acquired, not by 'strong-arm methods of seizure, but [by] peaceful trade penetration ... which invariably raised the natives' standard of living'; having established British imperialism as a self-evident good, Kirkland simultaneously makes the hedging claim that 'even here in North America we can't point to our treatment of native Indians with any pride'; and, she asks, 'Which kind of Imperialism does our neighbour to the South prefer – the British or the Russian kind?' as if colonialism was somehow a natural or unavoidable political arrangement, or that one could not logically oppose all national variants. Too, this last assertion simply reoriented the 'lesser-of-two-evils' defence of British domination away from Hitler and toward Stalin.

Kirkland was on surer footing, however, in underscoring the analogies between British colonialism and 'any type of financial imperialism which operates whenever foreign capital, including American, is invested in resources, plants, and equipment in a foreign country.' Similar concerns about growing post-war American hegemony and its resemblance to older manifestations of colonialism appeared in other Canadian analyses from the era, some of which posited Canada itself as an object of imperial desire. Though these anxieties had been a feature in intellectual circles even before the war, they were given new credence by the confluence of a series of notable readjustments in U.S.-Canada relations: the 1940 Ogdensburg Agreement, which established a coordinated bilateral defence of North America – and, to historians R.D. Cuff and J.L. Granatstein, 'marked the shift from Canada as a British dominion to Canada as an American protectorate'; the 1944 Bretton Woods Agreement, which enshrined a global, economic liberal order administered and dominated by the United States; and the post-war emergence of the United States as Canada's largest trading partner and foreign investor (replacing, agonizingly for some, Britain). Roughly coterminous with Indian independence celebrations, the Canadian Parliament passed a bill allowing those American soldiers on Canadian soil (concern enough for Canadian nationalists, especially given that the war was over) to police themselves according to U.S. law. Debate over the bill's passage was heated, with members of the CCF Party predicting that the measure presaged nothing less than formal annexation to the United States. 'Are the Yanks Invading Canada?' asked the title of a September 1947 *Maclean's* story on the bill's passage.[56] The article concluded the negative, but its title attested to the pervasive existence of those fears.

The *Canadian Forum*, with its penchant for materialist analysis, was particularly attuned to the degree to which American economic imperatives necessitated a very specific reordering of the post-war world. More than one year before the end of the Second World War, the journal's editors predicted that the stateside return of the 'big business' agenda meant that Canadians had no reason to fear the revival of American isolationism following the war. On the other hand, according to the *Forum*, readers should be alarmed at the *nature* of the internationalism that was taking shape. Rather than the cooperative multilateralism of 'Mr. Willkie,' the *Forum* held that the rollback of the New Deal and the reascendance of '"free enterprise" means an aggressively nationalistic policy in world affairs, of which the beginnings can already be seen in activities about oil in the Middle East ...' In September 1947, the *Forum* chastised the U.S. State Department ('that great champion of democracy,' they noted sardonically) for supporting attempts by the Netherlands to reassert control over Indonesia. U.S. ideals regarding self-determination, held the journal, had been sabotaged, not by the demands of global power balancing, but by the dictates of 'Western private enterprise' and its efforts 'to stampede governments into trying to hold down the vast movements toward independence' throughout the Third World. With eerie clairvoyance, the *Forum* warned that, 'if carried out all over Asia,' the type of guerrilla insurgency aimed at exhausting Dutch resolve and finances 'could ruin bigger countries than Holland.' 'It would be fantastic,' editors concluded, 'if the United States, which owes its existence as a nation to having blown up the mercantilist theory of empire, should be dragged into this appallingly futile effort to force the same theory on others.'[57]

Just two months after Indian/Pakistani independence, the *Canadian Forum* believed that the struggle for true sovereignty in Asia was being lost – and that both emerging superpowers were to blame. A November editorial, employing a term coined by George Orwell in 1945 but that Bernard Baruch had introduced to the lexicon surrounding international bipolarity just that spring, pointed glumly to signs that the two new Dominions appeared to be developing into neo-colonial pawns constituting 'another battleground of the Russo-American cold war.' At the same time, the notion that post-war U.S. internationalism was taking on a decidedly imperial character was under-appreciated by the stateside media, according to John Fousek. He finds that in the first years of the Cold War, 'the white-controlled press ... generally suggested that the United States stood apart from, and above, the traditions of European imperialism and colonialism.' 'Even in the African American press,' he writes, 'European colonialism received scorn and vilification that US foreign policy was largely spared.'[58]

As the foregoing analysis suggests, in the years that followed the war but preceded the establishment of a relatively stable anti-communist orthodoxy in the West, Canadians produced and consumed widely divergent narratives surrounding decolonization. At the risk of oversimplification, the narratives generated in Canada can be grouped into two broad classes: (1) imperial apologists, many of whom claimed kinship ties to Britain, if not direct experience as agents of British colonial regimes; (2) anti-imperialists, who directed their critique at the traditional oversees holdings of the West, as well as a suspected creeping neo-imperialism that they cast as an emerging threat to Canadian sovereignty. Both of these orientations say a great deal about attitudes toward Russia, the emerging pro-U.S. Cold War consensus in Canada, and, in particular, the ways in which Cold War discourses could be employed in both Western nations.

The more powerful of these narratives, reiterated with little variation among mainstream, English-speaking analysts, simultaneously praised an exceptional (in both senses) British colonialism and rebuked Americans for their 'well-intentioned' but naïve anti-imperialism. The specific basis for that rebuke is important for our purposes, since, when juxtaposed to nation-based narratives associated with the Gouzenko Affair, it constitutes a rather remarkable reversal of positions vis-à-vis the growing international bifurcation. Where Gouzenko was concerned, many mainstream U.S. analysts resorted to lecturing well-meaning but ingenuous Canadians about the depraved nature of communist Russia as verified by its espionage operations, while some Canadians took considerable exception to the re-emergence of the 'bolshevik bogey' of the interwar years. In the case of Indian/Pakistani independence, and of British imperialism generally, those north of the border appeared far more apt to cite the strategic concerns of the West and the undeniable menace posed by communism as grounds for rejecting decolonization. In articles produced in direct response to U.S. challenges to colonial practices, they instructed Americans that both domestic and international communists also supported independence movements, that departing Western colonial regimes would be immediately replaced by those of the Soviet variety, and so on.

There is nothing particularly novel in suggesting that anti-communism could be employed to forward a vast array of domestic and international agendas, many of which lacked even the thinnest connections to communism *per se*. Here, however, we have an especially instructive set of comparative scenarios which expose some of the more important interests of leading constituencies in both countries. For U.S. citizens, Soviet espionage in Canada could be employed to advance the cause of American global hegemony, including the atomic monopoly, to neighbouring citizens who expressed a greater measure of doubt about emerging Cold War fundamentals and greater fears about the prospect of continental integration.

In the United States, those same hegemonic ambitions were seen to be inhibited by the persistence of closed, mercantilist empires, in general, and the potential revival of British international dominance, in particular; what is more, empires comprised an affront to stated U.S. values that had recently been reinvigorated by wartime rhetoric. Thus the renewed U.S. calls for decolonization following the war. Meanwhile, some Canadian imperialists, to be sure, feared that rapid decolonization would leave Britain vulnerable in the face of growing Russian influence in Europe, and considered American moralizing over the issue insensitive and untimely. Others had simply located a post–Second World War rationale for the perpetuation of colonialism, a practice that, in the wake of the bold claims of the Four Freedoms and Atlantic Charter, provided an increasingly difficult challenge to their notions of the superiority of British institutions. Such justifications of imperialism rendered a critique of emerging U.S. global hegemony, predicated as it was on precisely the same grounds extolled by many English-speaking Canadians vis-à-vis the British variety, a particularly delicate manoeuvre. Canada's anglophiles should not be ascribed sole credit for their nation's endorsement of American preponderance as a check against Soviet expansion, but they helped construct the ideological framework for public consent in this development.

Such opportunistic deployments of the 'communist menace' render a reliable measuring of a Cold War consensus in either country exceedingly difficult. Certainly, 'true believers' inhabited both nations and maintained a vigorous anti-communist posture regardless of the issue at hand. However, the degree of aversion to communism in either country tended to ebb and flow according to issues that had as much to do with an array of national identities and interests as they did straightforward assessments of national security. At the very least, this survey of attitudes toward imperialism demonstrates that frequently reckless and opportunistic Red-baiting of individuals and issues was not something exclusive to, or always most acute in, the American context. Keeping in mind such repeated manipulation of public discourses relating to communism and the left, it is little wonder that a wide-ranging public hysteria over these issues would emerge, one that would obstruct productive analysis of a host of vital issues.

I have also introduced a second broad current of Canadian interpretations of imperialism and its relationship to the post-war world order, one that drew upon and expanded republican, liberal, and progressive oppositions to the practice that were historically more common to the American experience. These intellectual borrowings enabled an initially small cadre of Canadians to disrupt acclamations of colonialism, and especially its British variant, that had characterized English-Canadian public discourse from the beginning.

Further, following the war, some Canadian progressive voices employing this same theoretical framework began to distinguish an increasingly pronounced gulf between the rhetoric of the American anti-colonial tradition and the current overseas operations of the Truman administration. To be sure, the 'empire without consciousness of itself as such' lived on, but its progressive tradition had abetted a challenge to a more conscious and deeply rooted tradition of imperialism in Canada.

4 NATO: 'Our Only Present Means of Salvation'

On 4 April 1949 ten Western European nations, along with the United States and Canada, convened in Washington, DC, to sign the North Atlantic Treaty, forming a coalition that would come to be known as the North Atlantic Treaty Organization (NATO); this anti-communist alliance built upon the five-nation Brussels Pact established the previous year to defend against any attempted Russian takeover of member states. Prominent U.S. and Canadian voices from across the (conspicuously contracting) political spectrum offered enthusiastic praise for the formal establishment of a U.S.-led anti-communist alliance, including the *Canadian Forum*, a journal known previously as a consistent critic of U.S. foreign policy and its perceived imperial drift following the Second World War. Now, in its editorials surrounding the signing of the Atlantic pact, the publication moved from castigating containment strategies as neo-colonial to ridiculing the U.S. government for not insinuating itself into *more* areas of the globe, including Asia, Palestine, and Berlin. (The badgering of the Truman administration, at least, remained consistent.) The United States, the *Forum* decreed in February 1949, must 'accept the responsibility and the odium which power brings.'[1]

Regarding the Atlantic treaty itself, the *Forum* couched its unbridled acclaim in what were, for a socialist organ, unexpectedly spiritual timbres: the alliance, it held, represented 'our only present means of salvation.' Moreover, the journal viewed the pact as the only possible response to the 'uncompromising attitude of the Soviet Union both in and outside of the UN.' Finally, public scrutiny and potential criticism of the treaty document itself – one hammered out in intense secrecy – was considered unnecessary and unwelcome, as this might bog down or torpedo enactment of the pact. Accordingly, the *Forum* withheld all reservations until its April issue, when its editors declared that cross-examinations were now permissible: 'Now that the pact is a reality and is likely to be signed within a few days,' they wrote, 'it is well to examine its weaknesses ...' These shortcomings included the undoubted escalation of the arms race that would follow, a circumstance which would intensify public fears of global war and divert funds from badly needed rebuilding efforts in Europe.[2] These were no mean deficiencies, nor were they of the variety those on the left habitually ignored.

The *Forum* was not the only erstwhile skeptic of Cold War certainties to cross the floor in the late 1940s, but was among the more unexpected. Its editors had also mirrored or anticipated many of the chief premises employed by Canadian and American treaty supporters in their efforts to build public assent for the alliance: a regional, U.S.-led military alliance was the only recourse if Western civilization were to be preserved; international relations had taken on the trappings of a 'spiritual' battle between the forces of darkness and light; the Soviets alone bore the blame for global tensions; transparency and public input on such matters was needless and unwise. In its own way, each assumption served to chip away at the very liberal-internationalist ideals the Atlantic alliance was said to preserve.

While scholars have since debated (after debate was once again welcome) the motivations behind and the consequences of NATO's founding, they generally agree that this was an epochal moment in the Cold War. The principle of universality implicit in the idea of the United Nations was scuttled – or, at least, diminished – by the establishment of a parallel and decidedly circumscribed association of 'like-minded' nations. Collective security had been eschewed for regional defence, and a severely weakened UN was made to embark upon its seemingly perennial battle with 'irrelevance.' The division of Europe was formalized, leading the Soviets to announce their own, largely perfunctory 'multinational' defence agreement in the Warsaw Pact. Armaments spending and fears of another global war rose precipitously, phenomena that would only increase after the Soviets detonated their first atomic bomb in August 1949. For all but the most ardent idealists, 'One World' was now, irrevocably, two.

The specific implications for the two nations on which this study focuses were no less profound. By signing on to NATO, the United States, while clearly no longer isolationist in any real sense, had officially overcome its anxiety regarding 'entangling alliances' and received its formal coronation from other Western nations as 'leader of the free world' – thus obtaining from the West political capital it intended to spend. And official Canadian policy, though never truly neutral in the post-war standoff, abandoned all semblance of objectivity regarding the U.S.-Soviet bifurcation, binding itself to a U.S.-led anti-communist bloc. Moreover, in signing the treaty, the Canadian state had turned over a great deal of its sovereignty in foreign affairs to a U.S.-led (and predominantly military) alliance, a move that signalled the death knell for the forces of idealism, universal internationalism, UN control of the Bomb, and cooperation with communist nations that had appeared so powerful in 1945.

The effects on Canadian sovereignty were therefore substantial, as the nation's foreign policy and defence spending were expected to conform to NATO prerogatives. To a great degree, Canadian autonomy had been exchanged for security, and the nation had 'dutifully' fallen into line as a U.S. satellite. As such, 'policy regarding China, Korea, the Middle East and North American air defence between 1949 and 1957 was that of the United States, rather than of a country with separate interests, independently pursued.'[3] Nor was this merely a shift in state policy. The NATO question provided the most intensive post-war measure to date of citizen loyalty to the Canadian state, an ironic litmus test given that the pact represented the nation's formal submission to the dictates of a foreign power and, to a great extent, the purging of national identity differentiations.

For both the United States and Canada, then, NATO constitutes a rather significant break from tradition. On the other hand, a series of events had laid the groundwork for what would be a *relatively* quiescent acceptance of the treaty in both countries – though the degree of quiescence was overstated and indeed manufactured by the press, especially in Canada. Though disparate in origin and prompted by a variety of domestic and international stimuli, all fed a growing sense of emergency regarding communist expansion and domestic subversion. In March 1947, shortly before Indian/Pakistani independence discussed in the previous chapter, the Truman Doctrine was announced; in June of that year, the European Recovery Program, or Marshall Plan, was proposed. Both programs sought to check perceived Soviet expansionism and safeguard U.S. economic interests – though the latter plan was couched as a straightforward act of foreign assistance. Meanwhile, George Kennan had expanded his 'long telegram' into the influential and ominous article for *Foreign Affairs* titled 'The Sources of Soviet Conduct.' This piece, which appeared in July 1947, outlined the strategy of containment on which both the Truman Doctrine and Marshall Plan were based; significantly, it also held that the Russians bowed only to firmness in word and deed. Fredrik Logevall summarizes the underlying assumptions that linked (and constrained) the approaches of Kennan, the Truman Doctrine, and the Marshall Plan: 'Soviet-American friction ... did not result from clashing national interests, but from the moral shortcomings of Kremlin leaders, which in turn meant that negotiations were pointless until such a time as the regime underwent a transformation and abandoned its ideology.'[4]

In retrospect, the Marshall Plan seems a particularly vital ingredient in Canadians' later acceptance of the idea of NATO. In consultations over the scope and character of the program, Canadian officials convinced their American counterparts that Marshall dollars could be utilized to purchase both American *and* Canadian products, a genuine negotiations coup according to the latter nation's politicians and press (and many subsequent historians). As Canadian economic fortunes were now closely intertwined with those of Western Europe, further communist expansion in Europe would directly threaten Canadians' material well-being, an idea not lost on the nation's commentators. And since the plan enshrined the notion that the United States served as the guarantor of Western European – and therefore Canadian – economic security, it served as a precursor to the idea of a formal Atlantic alliance under American leadership. The means of achieving public consent for the plan would also establish important precedents for the later debates over NATO: in addition to forwarding economic rationales for the program, its supporters also relied on a good dose of anti-communism to silence critics; this was the case even among the social democratic leaders of trade unions and the CCF. As a result, prospective opponents of NATO would have been well aware of the treatment reserved for them.[5]

Certain activities of the Soviets, meanwhile, seemed nearly choreographed to corroborate the underlying assumptions of these influential U.S. repositionings: in February 1948, the Soviet-directed communist coup in Czechoslovakia terminated the only remaining liberal government in Eastern Europe, while the Berlin Blockade established in June of the same year sought to establish exclusive Soviet control over the German capital. Those requiring further evidence that global communism was 'on the march' could look to gains achieved by the Red Army in China, which was generally acknowledged to be on the cusp of victory in the spring of 1949, when the North Atlantic Treaty went before the legislative bodies of its respective signatories for final approval. Domestic developments in the United States also contributed to the mounting anxiety, including the 1948 allegations brought before the U.S. House Un-American Activities Committee hearings that communists had infiltrated both Hollywood and, with the investigation of Alger Hiss, the State Department.

Likewise, events in Canada immediately surrounding the formal initiation of the NATO pact seemed to corroborate the wider aura of communist conspiracy. In the days leading up to the April 4 signing of the treaty, the Canadian Seamen's Union – an organization known to contain communist members and leaders, and one that would soon be purged from its parent Trades and Labour Congress – began a turbulent strike. (The TLC was the Canadian affiliate of the American Federation of Labor; the latter would place intensive pressure on its Canadian associates to expel the CSU and other suspected communist unions and members.) Three days after the signing, Sam Carr, the last of the Gouzenko Affair defendants, was sentenced to six years in prison. Coming on the heels of the Czech coup – which relied on insurgents and political machinations rather than invading armies – Carr's case reminded the public just why, in Kennan's words, 'the adroit and vigilant application of counterforce at a series of constantly shifting geographical and political points' (at home and abroad) would be vital to the preservation of freedom.[6] As never before, ideas, words, and beliefs that hinted at subversion were viewed as an immediate danger to the liberal-democratic order, and any erring in battles between civil liberties and state security would be undertaken on the side of the latter. In hindsight, the outcome of the 'debate' surrounding the prudence of an anti-communist Western alliance was largely a foregone conclusion.

Historians and political scientists on both sides of the border have written extensively on the political and diplomatic reasoning behind the North American nations' decision to join a Western alliance against communism and have concluded that, among policy-makers at least, the decision was not a particularly onerous one. For the United States, NATO 'made sense' for a number of reasons. For one, the United States had already made firm commitments to the preservation of anti-communist governments and investor-friendly economies in Europe; NATO merely provided the permanent architecture to what had formerly been an ad hoc U.S. internationalism following the war. The agreement would also permit greater authority over the militaries and economies of Western Europe, both of which were perceived as vital to holding communist expansion in check. Beneath these conclusions lay the mutually reinforcing beliefs that oceans no longer guaranteed American security, that the Soviets were bent on world conquest, and that Russians, in accordance with Kennan's warnings, responded only to force or the threat of force. In other words, relying on negotiation and diplomacy alone (or at all) would accomplish little. As Kennan advised, 'Soviet pressure against the free institutions of the western world ... cannot be charmed or talked out of existence.'[7]

In light of these largely unchallenged orthodoxies, the interrelated concepts that had framed traditional American apprehensions about joining such organizations – isolationism, 'hemispheric solidarity,' the decadence of European civilization, and the like – appeared petty and outmoded. Meanwhile, more recent objections to such a treaty – those based on the call for arms reduction and the abolition of war in the atomic age, the need to strengthen rather than undermine the UN, the potentially suicidal consequences of nationalism and military alliances, and fears that the organization would become a tool of U.S. imperialism – were often framed as alien viruses planted in the body politic by international communism. Canadians were not immune to such Red-baiting discourse regarding critics of NATO. In truth, as I will demonstrate below, this approach to silencing opponents of the treaty was more prevalent north of the border, largely because Canadian critics tended to be clustered on the left, whereas the most visible American opponents were Republican U.S. senators who adhered to the traditional arguments for avoiding European affairs.

For the Canadian diplomatic corps, at least, the need to sign on to the treaty was as patently self-evident as it was for their colleagues in the United States – in fact, Canadian officials favoured such an alliance before their American counterparts, and expended a good deal of effort winning the United States over to the cause. As with the United States, the foundational assumptions driving Canadian policy also included the convictions that isolationism was now imprudent and that Russian territorial ambitions were boundless; after the Czech coup, even many traditional defenders of Russian security interests provided no counter-argument to the idea that the Soviets coveted nothing less than the entire planet.

Other Canadian motivations, however, differed considerably from those of the United States. Since Canada could not be expected to repel a Soviet attack alone, some sort of assistance was required, and a clearly enfeebled Britain could no longer guarantee Canadian security. Accordingly, a multilateral treaty incorporating a number of nations of various strengths was perceived as preferable to a bilateral arrangement with the United States, under which Canadian interests would be perpetually sacrificed to those of the Americans. Similarly, Canadians hoped that bringing the traditionally unilateralist United States into an ostensibly democratic alliance of nations would provide some leverage over the behaviour of an ally who might act rashly otherwise (and still possessed an atomic monopoly), or who might once again retreat into isolationism in Europe's hour of need.

Further, traditional Canadian policy had focused on maintaining sovereignty by balancing Britain against the United States; now, the international moves of both potential threats to Canadian autonomy would be 'contained' by NATO, and Canadian participation as an equal member within the body might allow the nation to influence, or at least monitor, the actions of both. Little wonder, then, that Canadian diplomats chafed at initial suggestions that Britain solely represent, and speak for, the Commonwealth within the Atlantic alliance.[8] Finally, economic considerations required consideration. The Canadian economy had become reliant on the European purchasing power enabled by Marshall Plan dollars. The further spread of communism in Europe was thus perceived as a direct threat to national well-being.

In the ensuing analysis, my primary concern is not to break down the reasoning behind official policy-makers' decisions to support or oppose the treaty, nor to assess whether NATO was the best or, as many held, the only choice for the North American nations involved – these questions having been addressed in great detail by analysts of both countries. Instead, in accordance with the primary objectives of this study, I provide a broad outline of the public discourses surrounding the issue in both nations, and the ways in which these discourses drew upon and transformed attitudes to the early Cold War era.

A few preliminary guideposts: One, while both societies came up with the same answer regarding the alliance – that is, the preponderance of public opinion in the United States and Canada came down on the side of NATO – the routes to achieving this relatively stable consensus were more divergent than one might expect from purportedly 'like-minded' nations that exhibited a 'common heritage' and 'shared values.' I draw attention to this point because the language of commonality was utilized repeatedly by elites in order to demonstrate the logic of an Atlantic alliance. In this instance, the two nations that arguably displayed the greatest cultural congruence among member states required sometimes widely divergent justifications for joining the organization. In other words, the idea of a cohesive 'Atlantic community' may have been oversold in an effort to gain public consent.

Two, at the micro level at least – that is, when examining only the rhetoric directly related to the NATO issue – there is very little evidence to support the notion that U.S. voices sought to manoeuvre their northern neighbours toward supporting an American-led military alliance. In fact, the reverse is more apparent: many Canadians, fearing the U.S. might opt out of the organization, took pains to admonish their neighbours for shirking past responsibilities, and (sometimes smugly) applauded the fact that Americans now appeared ready to assume the mantle of global leadership. Of course, it could be argued that the relentless and generally unparalleled anti-Soviet campaign that had characterized elements of U.S. society and culture since war's end had contributed to a level of fear in Canada which led Canadians to set aside traditional concerns regarding American hegemony. In this sense, the anti-communist consensus American popular and public culture helped to construct both domestically and internationally was now being employed to prod U.S. leaders into the uncharacteristic terrain of peacetime multilateralism.

Finally, if elements of both societies were still apprehensive about the rectitude and/or the intensity of the anti-communist campaign at home and abroad, it is clear that by this point, members of the mainstream media had made up their minds. In fact, journalists from both nations consciously and candidly initiated a crusade to sell the idea of the treaty to a public they frequently considered ignorant of foreign affairs and soft on the communist menace, and lashed out at any doubters, regardless of the basis of that hesitation. Indeed, the unanimity exhibited by the journalistic class over NATO – and importantly, the congruity between press and state articulations surrounding the issue – is without parallel in the era covered by this study. However, if this acquiescence to the prerogatives of the state among the U.S. press served to bolster American nationalism, the outcome of that process in Canada was somewhat more complicated.

One of the basic premises employed by supporters of an Atlantic alliance was that the UN, due in large part to the impasse created by the Great Power veto, had proven an abject failure, and that all informed and clear-thinking free peoples understood this. 'The North Atlantic pact confirmed on paper what most people knew in their hearts,' declared *Time*. Namely: that the world was divided beyond repair, and that the 'high hopes of San Francisco' had been replaced in the public imagination by 'the bitter lesson learned in Munich in 1938.'[9] *Time*'s reference to the Munich Conference was not coincidental. Not only did this meeting between Hitler and other Western leaders represent the 'high point of appeasement,' a mistake that the West would not repeat, it also involved Czechoslovakia, a nation whose more recent takeover by Stalin had been one of the main catalysts of the negotiations for a Western alliance. In *Time*'s view, the blame for the divided world lay solely with the Russians, who were, it appeared, walking quite literally in Hitler's footsteps.

It is hard to overestimate the chilling effect the Czechoslovakian coup of February 1948 had on commentators in both the United States and Canada. *Saturday Night* columnist Willson Woodside was characteristic when he decried the 'second seizure of Czechoslovakia' as 'so much the same as the first,' an assault which had set in motion 'the great and terrible events that have tumbled on top of each other and on top of us in the past nine years.' In a series of polemical articles, Woodside warned that this was merely the re-engagement of Soviet plans for indefinite expansion, that war was not coming but was already here in a new, gradualist, subversion-oriented format, and that Italy would be next (followed in rapid succession by the remainder of non-communist nations of Europe, Asia, and the Middle East, all of which Woodside, like a doomsday prophet, called out by name and in the order in which they would fall).[10]

Woodside claimed that 'Canadians have felt as deeply affected as I have been' by events in Czechoslovakia, and there is little doubt that citizens attuned to foreign affairs on *both* sides of the border would have been troubled by the Soviet action against a sovereign, democratic nation. In fact, virtually no one outside the North American communist parties countered the notion that the Czech coup marked the re-emergence of Russian designs on all of Europe – though it is also true that the airing of independent opinions on these matters was becoming increasingly perilous. What is less clear is whether these concerns led the public to the same panacea to Soviet aggression as the one tabled by Woodside. 'There is only one answer,' he informed readers immediately after the coup, 'the Union of Western Europe, with a solid military guarantee from the U.S.' The idea that an anti-Soviet (and largely anti-UN) alliance of Western nations was the *only* choice for Europe, democracy, and even humanity itself would become a fixture of the NATO-booster's tool kit, as would Woodside's contention that 'the overwhelming majority of Canadians support such a policy as the best means of averting war.'[11] It is beyond the scope of this analysis to assess the soundness of the first of these assumptions, but I do wish to complicate the latter, as even the methods used by the boosters themselves to secure public approval for the treaty seem to contradict the claims of public unanimity.

It is a truism of Cold War studies that public opinion becomes more difficult to assess as dissent becomes more costly. By the time the Western powers began their discussions about an Atlantic alliance, citizens in both countries had witnessed sensational trials of suspected communists, as well as extensive purges of unions, political parties, and other leftist and/or progressive organizations. As studies of African-American internationalism in this period have shown, even organizations that had traditionally exhibited a good deal of independence from state coercion, such as the NAACP, began turning out members who were open or suspected communists in an effort to retain the ear of the federal government on domestic civil rights issues – an approach that in the NAACP's case brought little tangible success.[12] Questioning the solidifying consensus about the need for 'toughness' toward the Soviets could, by this point, invite personal ruin.

Still, elements of both U.S. and Canadian society exhibited opinions at variance with the 'bulletproof' case for a military alliance outside the purview of the UN. Opinion polls from both nations do show increasing distrust of the Russians, their global designs, and their desire for peace, a trend that owes as much to Soviet blunders, aggression, and tactlessness as it does to a burgeoning culture of demonization of the regime evident in Western nations. By way of example, a March 1946 poll conducted in various Western nations asked if respondents believed 'any nation wants to dominate the world.' Fifty-eight per cent of Canadians, and 59 per cent of Americans, answered in the affirmative. (And while half of all Canadians who believed the statement true identified Russia as the covetous nation, only one-quarter of their American counterparts agreed, as the latter also displayed significant concerns about Britain, Germany, and Japan.) By August 1947, an identical 71 per cent in both the United States and Canada believed that one nation sought world domination, and nearly two-thirds of those named Russia – although those identifying the United States also rose in all nations polled, including the United States. One year later, and following the Czech coup, affirmative respondents totalled 82 per cent in Canada and 76 per cent in the United States, though for the first time, a higher percentage of Americans (84 per cent) than Canadians (80 per cent) cited Russia as the nation bent on domination.[13]

However, the other pillar of the case for NATO – the conclusion that the UN was now considered a failure – does not find corroboration in polling data. As with surveys of public opinion in general from this period, analysis is hampered by the fact that questions asked by polling agencies are frequently too divergent to allow for an analysis across time and among various geographies. That said, while residents of both countries exhibited a degree of pessimism about the UN's ability to keep the peace even at the organization's inception, faith in the UN held relatively steady between 1945 and 1949 – and throughout the period, Canadians and Americans reported virtually identical rates of satisfaction with the progress made by the organization.

In April 1946, about one-third of Canadians expressed satisfaction with the work done by the UN and believed the agency would prevent another world war during the next twenty-five years, figures that remained consistent in subsequent polls over the next several years. Levels of dissatisfaction were generally, though marginally, higher, with those undecided ranging between 25 and 39 per cent. Numbers from the United States were similar, with levels of satisfaction actually exceeding those of dissatisfaction in a January 1947 poll (39 per cent versus 33 per cent). These figures did not experience radical shifts over the next several years. By February 1949, Canadian pollsters expressed surprise at the results of a six-nation survey of opinions regarding the UN, which showed levels of satisfaction virtually identical to those of September 1947 for all nations involved, despite a recent UN session which observers considered a 'virtual failure.' For Canada, the 1949 numbers for 'satisfied,' 'dissatisfied,' and 'undecided' were 26 per cent (unchanged since the autumn of 1947), 35 per cent, and 39 per cent, respectively; for the United States, the rates stood at 28 per cent satisfied (down from 33 percent), 47 percent unsatisfied, and 25 percent undecided. Levels of optimism recorded in the United States in this 1949 survey were actually slightly higher than those registered in the first ever of such polls, conducted in July 1946, during what might be considered the UN's 'honeymoon' period (26 percent, 49 percent, and 25 percent, respectively).[14]

In July 1948, while diplomats engaged in intensive debate over the makeup and mandate of the North Atlantic Treaty, a majority of Canadians – 52 per cent - felt that 'the work done so far by the United Nations' had been either largely or partly successful; only 9 per cent considered the body 'completely unsuccessful' to that point (and even this verdict does not necessarily indicate a desire to write off the organization). When asked in a follow-up question 'What do you think is the chief reason for its failures?' a leading 34 per cent blamed factors related to nationalism, greed, and power politics – phenomena a North Atlantic military alliance was unlikely to redress. The specific actions of the two superpowers were next on the list, garnering 18 per cent of the blame, while the third highest group (though receiving only 3 per cent of the total) felt that the UN needed to be strengthened. Curiously, the UN failing touted over and over by supporters of NATO – the right of veto – was named by only 2 per cent of Canadians.[15] The narrative that the public had grown increasingly weary of the UN, and especially the much maligned veto, and was now demanding an alternative approach to the management of international affairs, is not borne out by the polling numbers.

NATO advocates had other reasons for concern as they sought to gain public consent for this radical shift in post-war foreign policy. In the United States, the most powerful, and by this point most notorious, obstacle to a peacetime military alliance lay in the isolationism of old guard Republican senators. This group, which had exercised such influence over U.S. foreign policy – and, by extension, the global balance of power – in the 1920s and '30s, had by this point achieved something of a pariah status midst the upsurge in internationalism that followed the Second World War. For the new internationalists, events of the past two decades had verified the limits of several key foundations of isolationism: that the United States was invulnerable from foreign attack, that totalitarian dictators abroad did not constitute a threat to U.S. interests and objectives, and that Great Powers had no moral responsibility to safeguard the lives and liberty of all humanity. As Thomas McCormick argues, the right's own obsession with anti-communism and national security could easily be turned against them by opportunistic Democrats, with the momentum toward internationalism already firmly established before the outset of the Atlantic treaty negotiations. He observes: 'Having acquiesced in the Truman Doctrine and the Marshall Plan, [conservatives] were easily bought off with perfunctory and unpersuasive promises that NATO would not require substantial numbers of American troops in Europe, nor would it require remilitarization of Germany.'[16]

Still, one maxim left over from the isolationist philosophy – that Congress alone had the authority to declare war – was protected in the final version of the North Atlantic Treaty at the insistence of U.S. negotiators, who feared a Senate veto of the agreement. Thus, while pure isolationism was in its death throes in the United States, and in truth the Atlantic alliance was never in danger of Congressional rejection, old-line Republican thinking exerted a considerable and perhaps disproportionate degree of influence over the final shape of the agreement. Fears of Senate rejection would animate not only U.S. negotiators, but also a great deal of journalistic advocacy in favour of NATO in both the United States and Canada.

As the dominant discourse would have it, the only other stateside opponents to the treaty were communists and fellow travellers, whose sometimes cogent critiques of the alliance as a dangerous departure in global relations and an invitation to U.S. imperialism were nullified by their consonance with the Kremlin's own denunciations (the direct source of many of these critiques, after all). However, other constituencies also expressed pointed concerns. As numerous studies demonstrate, African Americans comprised some of the more committed internationalists in the United States. in the years surrounding the war. Brenda Gayle Plummer's work, in particular, points to the solid black affinities for, and influence on, the establishment of the UN; many African-American activists expressed hopes that the supranational organization would take a forceful stand on the pressing issues of international colonialism and domestic segregation.[17]

The diversion of resources and attention toward an anti-Soviet military alliance thus met a great deal of resistance from black leaders and organizations. The most prominent critics included W.E.B. Du Bois, Fisk University president Charles S. Johnson, and the Annual Conference of NAACP Branches, local chapters of the organization which defied the national directorate's official endorsement of the Atlantic treaty. The basis of much African-American condemnation of the alliance rested less on the potentially harmful effects on U.S.-Soviet relations than on the rectitude of U.S. arms and aid to the world's largest colonial powers. In 1949, the NAACP branches produced a resolution that foreign assistance schemes 'which permit the European nations to continue to hold their empires and help finance the armies which continue the oppression of the African people and other colonials, are not the real way to secure peace in the world.' As Plummer notes, NAACP headquarters had forbidden local branches from passing resolutions on international affairs two years earlier in an effort to avoid such embarrassments, and the organization's leadership habitually stated that such 'branch militancy showed communism at work.' Fearful of alienating both their grassroots support and the White House, NAACP officials neither 'explicitly opposed' nor 'endorsed' NATO. Perhaps in a nod to branch agitation, however, the organization issued a statement in March 1949 that 'urged that the treaty be amended to preclude NATO's use against colonial liberation movements.'[18]

A handful of religious and peace organizations also joined the condemnation of NATO, one of the more outspoken being the Chicago-based *Christian Century*. In a series of editorials that appeared both before and after the signing of the pact, the non-denominational, mainline Protestant serial roundly and repeatedly castigated U.S. treaty proponents for weakening the UN, redirecting funds from the rebuilding to the rearming of Europe, placing American foreign policy in the hands of military leaders rather than diplomats, and inviting a Third World War. In truth, editors maintained, the 'failure' of the UN was something of a conspiracy hatched by opponents of universal internationalism: 'The caustic speeches in the United Nations,' they wrote, 'were in reality a maneuver to establish the uselessness of further negotiations.' If the proposed alliance becomes a reality, they cautioned, 'the foreign policy of the United States will be controlled in the Pentagon building' by 'generals, admirals and the secretary of defense,' notions that evidently could still raise eyebrows in 1949. In another prophetic swipe, they predicted that inevitable U.S. domination of the supposedly multilateral organization, and the arms race and fears of a European war the alliance would generate, would make average citizens of the European continent 'actively anti-American.'[19]

Other potential sources of opposition to NATO in the United States – those associated with the progressive left – were uncharacteristically silent. As McCormick notes, this constituency 'had been disheartened by [Henry] Wallace's poor showing in the 1948 presidential race'; moreover, 'the post election repression of the left quickened pace in both organized labor and the Democratic party.'[20] Voices that had expressed concerns over the provocative and imperialist nature of both the Truman Doctrine and Marshall Plan had been excised from progressive organizations, or chose restraint and self-preservation over frankness.

Though the isolationism that had characterized much of Canada's foreign affairs before the Second World War was no longer a factor, there were still Canadian doubters when it came to NATO (beyond the requisite condemnations from the Communist Party). Francophones were traditionally some of the nation's strongest critics of internationalism, in the main because that internationalism had been focused on providing assistance to Britain and had resulted in the drafting, and sacrificing, of young francophone men. These concerns did not vanish as a result of the proposed anti-Soviet alliance, but were tempered by the militant anti-communism overdetermined by the Catholic Church and Quebec's provincial government under Maurice Duplessis.

Still, some French-language newspapers expressed nuanced misgivings

about the alliance that went beyond the simple 'NATO or tyranny' binary that marked the preponderance of Canadian and American analysis.
Several francophone commentators worried about the monetary commitments that this new world order would entail, and what this would
mean for social programs in a largely rural province characterized by
large families and, in many regions, high rates of poverty. The populist
Le Canada wanted to know 'what the gigantic peace-saving enterprise
was going to cost us in hard cash' and praised a recent federal budget
for 'giving priority to the social question in spite of the heavy military
demands' entailed by the alliance. *Le Devoir* expressed a less sanguine
view of the same budget, asking whether it was merely 'calculated to sug-
ar the pill of the Atlantic Pact, a pact likely to cause automatically a new
world war?' The day after the treaty was signed, the same daily featured
a front-page mock, though prophetic, news story on the signing of a
Moscow-led 'defensive' pact in Mexico City, one uniting all nations who
espouse 'peace' and oppose 'the manoeuvres of bloodthirsty capitalism.'
Here, ersatz statesmen 'Churchillovsky,' 'Bevinin,' and 'Schumannski'
make a case for the need for a pact to protect their citizens against
(unnamed) nations who possess the Bomb and have already deployed
it against their enemies. The piece concludes with the question, 'What
would you say?'[21]

Canadian peace groups and certain church organizations, most notably the Anglican Church, also warned that the treaty would hasten, rather
than prevent, another global war. The CCF party, meanwhile, experienced a rift not unlike that of the NAACP over the issue. Its national
leadership officially endorsed the pact, part of a broader commitment
to line up with the forces of anti-communism in an effort to avoid being
Red-baited; the party had officially endorsed the 1947 Marshall Plan for
much the same reason. As with the NAACP, the CCF received little in
return for its bargain, and faced a grassroots revolt among members in
British Columbia and Manitoba over its assent to an American-led crusade against communism.[22]

One of the more even-handed assessments of the pact's implications
for Canada appeared in the pages of *International Journal*, a scholarly
publication founded in 1946 amidst the upbeat atmosphere surrounding Canada's support for internationalism and the UN. The journal's
summer 1949 edition featured a report authored by 'A Winnipeg Study
Group' entitled 'Canada and the North Atlantic Treaty.' The seven-mem-
ber study group was less a grassroots assemblage than a collection of local
foreign policy specialists, who, in the wake of the North Atlantic Treaty

signing, provided a kind of post-mortem on Canadian representations of the alliance. The group included prominent western-Canadian historian W.L. Morton, a scholar who, as Carl Berger observes, 'possessed an exceptional feeling for the integrity and legitimacy of the western region and its localities,' and for the 'plurality of Canadian life.'[23] The report, in other words, would not simply reiterate the monolithic platitudes purveyed by the so-called eastern establishment.

The document begins with a declaration largely absent from the unequivocal interpretations that characterized most analysis: that the treaty can be interpreted in a number of ways, that its meaning(s) might be fluid rather than fixed. In their words, the pact can be seen

> as an outgrowth of anti-communist imperialism on the part of American or Anglo-American capitalists; as a device to restore the balance of power in world affairs by forming a military alliance against the Soviet Union and her satellites; as a defensive security association to be classed as a regional arrangement under the United Nations; or as a substitute league for the present United Nations.

Rather than designate the 'authentic' view, the group finds a certain degree of validity in each conception. The authors do identify, however, what they consider to be a rather unitary Canadian perspective on each of these representations. Though they fear Soviet ambitions, 'the sober sense of Canadians will not permit them to indulge in a military crusade against Communism, and would warn them of the dangers of being swept into imperialist adventures by American pressure.' Further, average citizens have no desire to abandon the UN and return to the old 'game of power politics [in which] a small or middle state is disqualified by the very fact of lesser status.'

In the group's own opinion, the alliance neither assists nor adheres to UN policy, despite claims that the UN Charter permits the establishment of regional defence agreements. According to the Charter, the authors note, such an agreement must be created in consultation with the Security Council and must be considered a temporary arrangement 'until the Security Council and collective security are fully operational under the United Nations – and not as a substitute of semi-permanent or permanent nature.' The report concludes that while an argument could be made for the temporary need for an Atlantic alliance, NATO is a poor 'long-range programme for lasting world peace' and a 'disappointment as an international instrument.'[24]

Were these truly, as the authors' claim, opinions shared by the Canadian public, or were they merely the conclusions of a progressive intellectual elite? Government officials seemed to believe at least one aspect of the foregoing critique: that the public had little use for a purely military alliance based on the old power politics of balancing and counterbalancing. Precisely for this reason, Canadian negotiators pushed for the inclusion of Article 2 into the treaty – the so-called Canadian article – which called for member countries to 'make every effort, individually and collectively, to promote the economic well-being of their peoples and to achieve social justice.'[25]

In other words, NATO would not be a military alliance like those of the past, its members having committed to an agenda that would not have sounded out of place within the UN Charter. In fact, as Tom Keating notes in his study of the Canadian multilaterlist tradition, the article was included to demonstrate to Canadians that NATO 'was in no way inconsistent with their support for the UN. The alliance would instead become a way station until other members of the UN were willing to support collective security and Western values.' At the time, U.S. secretary of state Dean Acheson called Article 2 'the least essential article,' an appraisal that most analysts of NATO's history now share.[26]

Perhaps Article 2 did do a great deal to assuage Canadians' fears of an anti-Soviet military alliance led by the United States, as in the end, public opinion polls indicated an overwhelming support for Canada's participation in NATO. On the other hand, a productive and lively debate that would wrestle with the issues presented by the Winnipeg Study Group or the *Christian Century* never occurred in either country. More than that, the debate was not permitted; opponents were silenced, ridiculed, and threatened by a press corps that had come to resemble an arm of the federal bureaucracy.

It is noteworthy, given the vitriol that would mark the campaign, that while criticisms emerged from a variety of quarters in both countries – from peace activists, racial and ethnic minorities, Prairie study groups, and a few of members of a waning socialist political party – these dissenters were united in their distance from centres of power. In other words, these treaty opponents could not be considered to possess a liberal measure of the public's ear on this or any other matter. The handful of isolationist senators are the notable exception, though they, too, were largely dismissed by a U.S. public that had repudiated isolationism. The intensity of the attack on NATO opponents thus seems incongruous, and must be viewed as a measure of the palpable fears associated with permitting 'subversive' ideas a quarter in the public sphere, where they could take root and multiply. Only aggressive containment of these voices, it was believed, would ensure the perpetuation of freedom. Especially where Canada is concerned, the opposition to open deliberation also pointed to the fact that the logic of the treaty as presented to the public was perhaps not as indisputable as supporters claimed.

As the preceding chapters of this study make clear, dominant media organizations in both the United States and Canada had for some time been gravitating away from one-world idealism, universal internationalism, and collective security, and toward unmitigated support of anti-communism at home and abroad. Press support for NATO, then, is not unexpected. Less expected, to the point of being remarkable, is the intensity and sheer nakedness of the campaign undertaken in both countries to sell the alliance to the public. Commentators made absolutely clear not only their position on the Atlantic treaty (roughly, faultless), but that they had taken it upon themselves to more or less bully their readers into capitulation over the matter.

To a great extent, the anti-democratic character of the 'discussions' surrounding the treaty was enshrined by its architects; this was, in the truest sense, a 'top-down' affair. In both the United States and Canada, legislative bodies were not consulted and the public was not apprised of the details of the discussions until negotiations had been completed. Instead, citizens and their representatives were simultaneously presented with a *fait accompli* and a barrage of official speeches and press releases that would verify the probity of the treaty. 'Seldom since the war had a diplomatic document been drafted in greater secrecy,' noted *Time* in January 1949; once these star-chamber negotiations were over, 'the State Department started a sales campaign to tell the US what its general form would be.' However, *Time* did not object to the idea of a government sales job over the issue: the remainder of the article is rendered in wholly flattering tones ('experts of seven nations, like diligent sculptors, had chipped away' at the document), and future issues of the publication failed to raise a single objection to the idea of an alliance.[27] For all intents and purposes, *Time* had signed on as an underwriter to the campaign, and made no apologies for doing so.

For historian Don Cook, the bureaucratic stealth cited in the above piece was essential to the process, as it 'allowed diplomats to move forward carefully behind the scenes, below the surface, while postwar events in Europe – particularly the Berlin blockade – steadily propelled political and public acceptance in the United States of the wisdom and necessity of an entangling alliance to keep the peace.' Those expecting less subsurface activity and more transparency from representative governments were not as eulogistic. The *Nation*, noting with alarm the absence of public discussion over the treaty, dedicated its issue of 19 March 1949 to an appraisal of the North Atlantic pact by a variety of domestic and international supporters and opponents. However, the final draft of the treaty was released to the public on March 18 (and again, signed, April 4). This forced the *Nation*'s commentators, like those 'in every country,' to base their assessments exclusively on 'broad outlines of the pact as revealed in the various foreign offices,' as the editors explained in a testy introduction to their special issue. 'To facilitate negotiation, secrecy may have seemed useful,' they granted. 'In terms of an informed public opinion it was deplorable, and the uneasiness it created was intensified by the air of desperate urgency in Washington' – urgency, namely, to complete the negotiations and to pressure Scandinavian countries to join. To the *Nation*, these blunders only served to give credence to Soviet propaganda that NATO was an instrument of imperialism and a precursor to a preventative war.[28]

In Canada, Minister of Foreign Affairs Lester Pearson and Prime Minister Louis St Laurent directed their own 'sales campaign' in support of the pact and against those who hoped to preserve a more neutral posture. Again, *Time* was unambiguous about the oligarchic character of the process in Canada, writing that though the ruling Liberal Party was 'hazy' in the fall of 1948 about the costs of the plan for the nation, 'clearly the government was preparing the public for its role in North Atlantic defense.' St Laurent began by assuring that NATO was the nation's only hope – and that public attitudes meant very little under the circumstances – coldly informing the electorate that 'Canada cannot possibly remain neutral in a third world war even if 11,999,999 out of 12,000,000 Canadians want to stay out.'[29]

Such bluster and oversimplification on the part of politicians is to be expected. Many in the media, however, were equally disdainful of popular will and open debate regarding the treaty, and were frank about their own perceived task as NATO cheerleaders. Willson Woodside, who opened an October 1948 celebration of the proposed alliance with the assertion that the 'overwhelming proportion of Canadians support' the proposed security system, nonetheless advised that 'there is a big job of pubic information to be carried out' in order to gain citizen approval. The precise character of this 'information' campaign is explicitly outlined later on in the article, when Woodside speaks of the methods

required to assure passage of the treaty: 'Once again one is reminded
of the apt remark,' wrote Woodside in a paraphrase of Senator Arthur
Vandenberg, 'that to intimidate the Soviets we will have to take measures
which will scare our own people.' That levels of anxiety were already
approaching fever pitch, and had begun to generate outcomes that out-
stripped officials' ability to control them, did not seem to trouble the
author. *Maclean's* saluted the Members of Parliament from Quebec who
'solemnly accept and endorse' the idea of an anti-communist alliance,
advising: 'That is, it seems to us, the way all Canadians should – and
probably do – regard the pact.'[30]

Saturday Night editors derided the Anglican Peace Council's warning
that citizens were being 'conditioned' for war by the alliance, complain-
ing instead that citizens of liberal democracies had not been 'conditioned' enough in the run-up to the Second World War. In their words,
'it is deeply to be regretted that all these nations were not conditioned
much more effectively and much earlier, in which event the Hitler War
might very easily have been unnecessary.' The magazine's steady diet
of editorials and articles celebrating NATO and flaying treaty critics
betrayed its belief that the press bore a primary responsibility for this
conditioning, and placed *Saturday Night* firmly in the vanguard of the
anti-communist re-education curriculum. The *Vancouver Sun* applauded
the paucity of debate, suggesting that this demonstrated the nation's
maturity: 'Through this solidarity Canada is able to present the same
unified front on foreign affairs that is apparent in the United States and
Britain and in every other country that signed the treaty.' The *Regina
Leader-Post* made the same point in an editorial bearing the Orwellian
title 'In Unity Is Strength,' praising the 'fundamental unity' of Canadians on this issue. In light of these views, *Le Devoir*'s assessment of journalists' response to the pact – that 'to a certain degree,' they had been
taken by 'the influence of official propaganda'– represents a marked
understatement.[31]

Most mainstream U.S. publications were similarly laudatory about the
pact and blunt in their perceived role as NATO spokespersons. As *Time*
correctly noted in its survey of leading dailies, 'most of the nation's edi-
torialists gave their sober approval.' The *Saturday Evening Post* concurred
and seemed intent on making doubters feel odd, claiming that 'the
basic necessity to shore up the economies and defense equipment of the
western democracies is questioned by almost nobody.' Even progressive
journals like the *Nation* and *New Republic,* while critical of the Truman
administration's handling of the negotiations, generally supported the

notion of an alliance; for the latter publication, 'the essential question' was 'what the US will do if the cold war goes the way of the phony war of 1940.'[32] In other words, was the United States truly committed, as it should be, to an immediate military response to aggression in Europe? Those who raised more substantial questions – about the wisdom of such an alliance in the first place – would be in for a rough ride.

It was clear, then, that the press would support NATO and would encourage the public to do the same. Clearly, by the end of the 1940s, dominant media establishments in both countries believed themselves to be less forums for unfettered debate than spokespersons for the national interests in the battle for hearts and minds. Again, this relinquishment of journalistic responsibilities must be contextualized: it was based, in part, on the success of insurgent-oriented communist movements in Europe and Asia, movements which relied on indoctrination in conjunction with brute force in order to 'soften' potential targets. Ambiguity and doubt, it was believed, only served the purposes of the enemy.

Analysis of the specifics of the press campaign to sell NATO in both countries makes these processes plain. The lines between freedom and tyranny were made explicit, and those inhabiting the borderlands between these two realms were called upon to make their allegiances known. Yet NATO apologetics were not precisely congruent in the United States and Canada. Canadian supporters were more likely to paint the agreement in idealistic terms – as a companion organization to the UN – while those in the United States tended to view the agreement as a return to realism and power politics in international relations. Where Canadians saw a partnership whose costs and benefits, as well as its overall direction, would be shared equally (or at least proportionately), American commentators observed a U.S. hegemon extending its protection and influence over a vulnerable Western bloc. In the end, the U.S. understandings – which implied net losses for Canadian sovereignty – proved closer to the truth, and many in Canada came to regret the uncritical endorsement of the pact. Ironically, this circumscription of national authority under the aegis of a U.S.-led coalition had not come at the prodding of the Americans; rather, more so than any other issue addressed in this study, this public accession was largely a homegrown product.

On one important point – what was ultimately at stake in the postwar conflict between East and West – the press in both countries largely agreed: the formation of an alliance binding 'like-minded' nations would be the linchpin in the battle to ensure the continued existence of the West's shared, and superior, cultural values and institutions. The alliance, wrote *New York Times'* editors in language echoed repeatedly in both the United States and Canada, makes the 'Atlantic community ... stand together in defense of their ways of life and of Western civilization.' The metaphor of a harmonious community of states that shared core values would be a prerequisite to knitting together (and glossing over) rather disparate national myths, values, institutions, and the like. For example, before this moment Canadians, like Americans, had rarely spoken of their kinship with the Portuguese or the Italians; in fact, official constructions of national identity were often framed in direct contrast to those of southern European and/or non-Protestant geographies. The image of regional symmetry would also be crucial in encouraging the public to reconsider, and temper, contemporaneous attempts to delineate a *universal* humanity – undertaken, for example, by the Kinsey reports, Wendell Willkie's *One World*, and Edward Steichen's photography exhibition *The Family of Man*.[33] Before discussions of an Atlantic alliance had been initiated, this broader universalist project had frequently been touted as humanity's only hope in the aftermath of the extreme nationalism and racism that drove the Second World War, and had found its fullest political expression in the UN.

For the second time in the space of a few short years, then, citizens were encouraged to conceptualize their identities in new ways, still bounded beyond the nation-state yet, now, short of the human species itself. The idea of an 'Atlantic community' would draw explicitly on perceived commonalties in the realms of religion, language, ethnicity, and political and economic institutions. Over and over journalists pointed to the dichotomies – certainly real, though hardly as absolute as advertised – between nations that upheld democracy, individualism, and human rights, and those that did not. Willson Woodside expressed relief at this evolving public disavowal of universal internationalism, apparently preferring even nuclear annihilation to communist rule. 'No World,' he counselled, 'is preferable to a slave world.'[34] Better dead than Red indeed.

Here, too, were elements of the 'Pax Anglo-Saxonia' prescribed four years earlier by *Saturday Night* contributor Stuart Armour. True, other ethno-linguistic groups had been permitted entry into the alliance, but the pact's two dominant members were the great English-speaking powers, and Canada was one of the alliance's principal catalysts. Other member nations, meanwhile, were marked by differences less fundamental than those exhibited by non-Western societies. The vast majority of Canadians, in fact, could trace their national and ethnic origin to one of the alliance member countries (the nation's immigration policies having long been oriented toward the 'Nordic' peoples of Europe). A smaller proportion, though still a majority, of Americans could make similar claims. And roughly coterminous with the coalescence of an Atlantic community internationally, the domestic racial landscape was being remapped to bring non–Anglo-Saxon European ethnics under the rubric of 'Whiteness,' a project which would broaden the ability of WASP Canadians and Americans to include a wider range of Europeans in definitions of 'us.'[35] Whether the Atlantic alliance abetted this process in either country is an intriguing, though open, question.

For Canadians, an Atlantic alliance would also serve to reduce the tensions between national identity myths, heightened international responsibilities, and racist assumptions. As suggested previously, notions of a cultural mosaic, multilateralism, and – after the Second World War – vigorous internationalism were foundational to Canadians' sense of self (and often drawn in opposition to perceptions of the United States). Partnership within an Atlantic community would allow Canadians to persist with positive self-conceptions in this regard, while also permitting citizens to carry forward commonly held assumptions of racial hierarchy. A 1946 poll, conducted at what might be considered the apex of universal internationalism in Canada, asked which 'nationalities,' if any, respondents 'would like to keep out'; that the less inflammatory 'nationalities' served as a stand-in for 'race' in the eyes of many of those asked is evident by their responses. Sixty per cent cited the Japanese, 49 per cent Jews (just one year after the defeat of the Nazis), and nearly one-third mentioned Germans, Russians, and/or 'Negroes'; prospective Chinese and South- and East-European immigrants would also have been turned away by significant percentages of Canadians. Totals were well in excess of 100 per cent because many respondents offered up multiple categories of 'undesirable' immigrants, while only 18 per cent declined the opportunity to ban at least one 'nationality.'[36] In light of these findings, and of paternalistic attitudes toward prospects for Third World sovereignty discussed in the previous chapter, NATO constituted a commitment to foreign peoples that would appear to align with domestic preferences.

The 'community' metaphor would also rely upon a characterization of member nations as essentially and exclusively Christian. Though clearly foundational to prior understandings of Canadian and U.S. society, the global struggle against a formally atheistic adversary provided foreign policy architects (of indisputably wide-ranging spiritual commitments) unprecedented opportunities to underscore religious identity as they sought to gain public assent for their temporal strategies. When Western leaders began to formulate plans for an alliance, many spoke of the treaty as fulfilling an unambiguous, divinely ordained mandate – even as some of the treaty's harshest critics also utilized Christian discourses to *oppose* the pact. In his earliest communiqués to fellow Commonwealth leaders on the need for a pact, British prime minister Clement Attlee wrote: 'If we are to stem further encroachment of Soviet ties, we should organize the ethical and spiritual forces of Western Europe backed by the power and resources of the Commonwealth and the Americas, thus creating a solid foundation for the advance of western civilization in the widest sense.' Terms like 'spiritual,' 'ethical forces,' and 'Christian civilization' abound in the communications between and within states involved in the early negotiations. Undersecretary of State Lester Pearson, for his part, seemed intent on evoking the idioms of an earlier crusade in his memorandum of 14 March 1948 to Prime Minister King on the progress of the talks. 'Here it is essential to remember,' noted Pearson, 'that the purpose of the pact is to rally the spiritual as well as the military and economic resources of Western Christendom against Soviet totalitarianism.'[37]

In the fall of 1948, Willson Woodside pointed to the efficacy of drawing out the religious components of the ideological struggle in an attempt to bring isolationist-minded Quebecers into the NATO camp, noting that 'defence against atheistic Communism might find a response in that province.' Pearson and Louis St Laurent, by that point minister of external affairs and prime minister, respectively, appeared to be listening; their speeches in Quebec stressed the 'spiritual' dimensions of the global struggle, as well as Communist Party suppression of Christianity in Eastern Europe. Significant numbers of Canadians appeared amenable to such views, with a Gallup poll conducted in the summer of 1948 identifying 'religion' as 'the greatest force for peace in the world.' One-third of all respondents agreed with the claim (though pollsters seemed to be interested in certain branches of religion, relegating answers like 'Jehovah's Witnesses' to the category 'Other'). More worldly forces did not fare as well: the UN finished second at 25 per cent, while the British Commonwealth and the Marshall Plan each polled 10 per cent.[38]

During his speech at the April 4 signing ceremony, Dean Acheson applied the words of Christ himself to the treaty, suggesting that alliance nations were nothing less than an arm of divine justice. Paraphrasing Matthew 18:7, he cautioned: 'For those who set their feet upon the path of aggression, it [the pact] is a warning that if it must needs be that offenses come, then woe unto them by whom the offense cometh.' The generally secular *New York Times'* editorial from the same day utilized lyricism redolent of a biblical prophet ('The fear of war sweeps the world and bends down men's hearts like a wind among the reeds') before calling for a future in which, 'by God's grace,' war will be abolished. Likewise, *Saturday Night* heralded that global stability would now depend on the fortitude of 'the great Christian nations.'[39]

In all, treaty advocates drew upon and enhanced the idea that member nations comprised an association of 'kin' – another frequent descriptor in assessments of the alliance. 'The whole feeling,' Woodside wrote of the treaty signing ceremony, 'was of a family affair,' a characterization still utilized without complication by some contemporary analysts.[40] NATO's Article 2, the 'Canadian article,' which promoted 'better understanding of the principles upon which these [free] institutions are founded,' also had the effect of reinforcing the cultural cohesiveness and 'natural bonds' of member nations – some of whom, it should be remembered, had dropped bombs on one another in the not-so-distant past.

Through such efforts, advocates of the Atlantic alliance helped to construct a 'collective identity,' a phrase, according to political scientist Alexander Wendt, which connotes 'positive identification with the welfare of another, such that the other is seen as a cognitive extension of Self rather than as an independent.' The *New York Times*, for instance, explicitly encouraged readers to redefine 'Otherness' by enlarging the notion of 'Us' to include citizens of NATO nations. 'Even the word "foreign" has taken on a new meaning,' it noted. 'Nothing is foreign to us if it concerns the fate of the civilization we cherish and which we are called upon to maintain, perfect and defend.'[41] For Canada, positing a collective identity which linked national characteristics to those of a wider European, as opposed to merely British, community would provide obvious benefits in gaining assent in Quebec. It would also enshrine the erstwhile counterpoint to Canadian identity – the United States – as a component of 'Self.'

Obviously, Soviet communism was the foil to this remapping of Western identities, raising a number of issues germane to this discussion. For one, political theorists employing constructivist models of transnational identity formation hold that nations do not form alliances and foster a sense of kinship because they first feel threatened by aggressors; rather, the sense of community precedes and *creates* the sense of threat by outsiders. As Thomas Risse observes of the so-called democratic peace, 'the collective identity led to the threat perception, not the other way around,' a notion of Western culpability that mid-century anti-communists would have considered baseless (and, of course, 'communist-inspired').[42]

Furthermore, like the Truman Doctrine, which depicted a simple world of slave and free, this collective identity relied on an East-West binary that largely erased the non-white world. 'We' meant Western Europe and its North American 'kin'; 'they' referred to the Soviet Union and its satellites. Was the 'Third World,' still largely colonized, on the side of freedom by virtue of its Western governance? Or, in this life-and-death struggle, should resources and energies be devoted primarily or even exclusively to the defence of the West? The language of 'One World' at least provided spaces for the articulation of Third World concerns and for the conceptualization of a truly universalist internationalism; remapping the world order according to the East-West dispute served to occlude the South. Three years after the treaty's founding, NAACP leader Walter White would complain that 'most areas under the rule of major powers can receive assistance only in connection with plans for defense of the North Atlantic Area. This means that the colonial people in Africa and Asia come in solely as fifth wheels to the European war machine.'[43]

In 1949, few NATO exponents in either the United States or Canada attempted to wade into this quagmire – that is, to delineate, in specific geographical and human terms, what was meant by 'our civilization,' and precisely what and who was worth saving (a dilemma that became apparent in the inconsistent responses to communism in Asia). When analysts did, the tensions inherent in utilizing Western collective identity to inspire sacrifices in the name of anti-communism became apparent. In a direct challenge to leftist calls for smaller, weaker nations to remain neutral in the superpower standoff, the *Vancouver Sun* held that in the case of NATO, 'culture' (a category, as their subsequent discussion revealed, that had much to do with race) had trumped class. 'In the case of the West,' they argued, 'a common cultural inheritance which far transcends differences of economic and social ideology has been the [rallying] cause.' But the exact dimensions of a call for a campaign against global communism, on the one hand, and one based on a defence of 'our civilization,' on the other, were unclear to *Sun* editors. 'We may yet in this great cause find need to establish a Pacific Security Treaty to extend a helping hand to our brothers in Australia and New Zealand,' they maintained, then added, 'if not to those of other races farther afield.' Would the security club be organized around freedom or whiteness? In 1949, these matters remained unclear. *New York Times* editors wrestled with the same question in more cryptic terms: 'A fog of uncertainty hangs over many areas in which we would like to draw boundaries,' they wrote. 'In many of these areas we are not yet able to say, thus far and no further.'[44]

This reduction of the international arena into two camps, one good and the other evil, also had domestic correlates. Despite the sometimes judicious and carefully articulated criticisms of the pact from various individuals and groups outlined above, NATO advocates frequently declared all treaty opponents communists – a charge that gained credibility when Stalin emerged as the pact's most visible critic. Those making the simple equation of NATO opposition with communism did little to clarify the yawning gulf between the percentages of those who opposed the treaty and those who belonged to or voted for the Communist Party, except to claim that committed communists bred fellow travellers and unwitting dupes. To illustrate this apparent illogic: polls from both countries conducted in 1948 showed significant percentages of citizens did not endorse the idea of an Atlantic alliance, with one-quarter of Canadians and one-third of Americans expressing opposition or uncertainty regarding the treaty. In the June 1949 Canadian federal election, the communist Labour-Progressive Party polled just over 0.5 per cent of the vote. As Stephen Whitfield notes, Communist Party membership in the United States stood at 43,000 in 1950 – about the same total, in a nation of 150 million, as 'the Finnish Evangelical Lutheran church (Suomi Synod).'[45] Apparently, this tiny fraction of the public could exert an inordinate and hypnotic effect over the wider citizenry.

The line of reasoning that connected opposition to the Atlantic alliance with communist subversion was nearly ubiquitous, at least in Canada: according to the *Hamilton Spectator*, 'Moscow is the horned property man in the wings' that coordinates opposition to the pact and to all other 'sincere endeavours of Canada's Parliament to safeguard our Christian civilization.' As the Winnipeg Study Group lamented, communists did indeed oppose the pact, leading treaty advocates to emphasize this fact to the exclusion of all others. 'The consequence,' they noted, 'is that the Pact has been carried through with more propaganda than discussion and with more enthusiasm than knowledge.' The *Regina Leader-Post* broadened (marginally) the basis of anti-NATO opposition, while at the same time setting back English-French relations a generation. 'In 1939 only two groups in the country opposed participation,' they recalled: namely, Quebecers and communists. 'Again in 1949 protest is limited to these same groups, neither of them Canadian in any true sense of the term.'[46]

The indiscriminate smear directed at all those who would question the alignment of U.S. and Canadian international interests or who called for a more conciliatory tone was too much for some average citizens. A *Vancouver Sun* reader shot back that many of her/his 'fellow Canadians' felt that the communist witch hunt was going too far, and that the United States bore *some* responsibility for 'this cold war of nerves.' Knowing such claims would raise the habitual suspicions, and could thus be dismissed at once, the writer felt obliged to pledge, 'I am not a Communist. I never will be,' before enumerating why other 'ordinary citizens,' who were, he noted, also 'not communists,' might have motivations other than communism for preferring peace to war. For those who may have missed it, the letter is signed 'Not a Communist.' Fears of being publicly identified with the 'dangerous' desire for peace may also have inspired this desire for anonymity.[47]

Saturday Night editors would give 'Not a Communist,' along with communists, world federalists, advocates of neutrality, pacifists, anti-imperialists, isolationists, and any other NATO doubters, solid justifications for their fears. As the news weekly would have it, all of these designations were merely smokescreens for minds constrained by slavish adherence to the Kremlin. Voices still advocating global cooperation over confrontation, they maintained, were 'either deceived by others, deceived by themselves, or busy trying to do some deceiving – usually the last one of the three.'[48] It would be easy to forget, in surveying the publication's increasingly McCarthyite tone in the late 1940s, that during and after the war, *Saturday Night* editors had been relatively stalwart defenders of civil liberties. They provided, for example, a sustained and principled indictment of the government's internment of Japanese residents – at a time when many others remained silent, expressed their approval, or called for even harsher measures.

By the time that an Atlantic alliance had been proposed, however, the time for debate, questioning governmental policy, and upholding civil liberties was over. When a dispute emerged from the ranks of the socialist, though anti-communist, CCF over its leaders' support for the pact, editors warned that local party members were 'engaging in a peace campaign indistinguishable from that of the Communist party,' and one that would doom upcoming CCF election prospects. When (extremely limited) protests against NATO continued in the months after the treaty was signed, *Saturday Night* was furious. Questioning the pact was nothing less than 'anti-democratic, an assertion of a right of the individual to contract out of the decisions which have been arrived at by the democratic process and which we regard as binding on all the citizens.'[49]

The relationship between this view and the magazine's earlier stand against Japanese internment, a policy decision also 'arrived at by the democratic process,' or between the editors' current position on civil liberties and those of fascist corporatism or Soviet collectivism, seemed to provide openings for further discussion. But unfettered discussion, like the 'right of the individual,' apparently constituted luxuries the nation could not at present afford. The same editorial concluded that mere questioning of the pact clearly equalled disloyalty; editors then considered whether such disloyalty amounted to treason, and whether 'opponents of the Pact should not be permitted to do their opposing in public.' On both points, the publication provided a hesitant 'no,' conceding 'that the campaign [against NATO] is not in itself illegal, and that participation in it is not of itself a proof of membership in the Communist party' – the insinuation being that if either of these criteria were met, the editors would have no qualms about rounding up NATO opponents.[50] Clearly, *Saturday Night* had lost a good degree of perspective: citizens merely questioning a peacetime military alliance were being discussed in terms that had historically, at least, been reserved for those actively colluding with an enemy in time of war.

Conversely, *Saturday Night* may have shared with Willson Woodside the assumption that 'war is not near, it is on now … the war of ideas and political systems, by which whole countries are being captured before our eyes with scarcely a pistol shot fired.' A cartoon run two weeks later seemed to confirm that communist-backed anti-NATO forces had the Canadian state on the verge of total collapse. In the illustration, a scientist, an 'essential industries' worker, and members of the nation's armed services are shown on the front lines of a wall designated 'North Atlantic Defense: Canadian Section.' Across the ocean, behind another wall labelled 'Iron Curtain,' Stalin looms, expectantly. The immediate danger, however, emerges from behind these sentries, from within Canadian society itself. Here, shadowy figures utter 'communistic & other subversive & selfish ideas' in an attempt to divert the sentries' attention from their task. Notably, these insurgents wear the same uniforms as those they seek to corrupt – that is, they have infiltrated the organizations most vital to national security. The scientist is offered cash for 'the secret formula,' while the others are told to strike, to refuse to fight, and to take note of 'class distinction.' Stalin shouts encouragement to his Canadian minions, while a soldier in the 'US Section' of the North American wall is shown (happily) giving the boot to the insurgent behind him; the cartoonist clearly endorsed the more dynamic U.S. approach to dealing with the Red menace. The title of the image – 'Yes, We Must Be Strong!' – would not be out of place on a mural in a Soviet factory.[51] And while one might expect the nation's press corps might also be depicted as a target for fifth columnists, the illustrator may have understood that by this point any suggestion that the media harboured contrary views would have been considered farcical – among *Saturday Night* readers, at least.

It is true, as the cartoon suggests, that communist opposition to NATO was less palpable in the United States. This was in part a testament to the more advanced state of the campaign of counter-subversion being waged in that country, which had by this point intimidated the left and eviscerated the Communist Party to degrees that made Canadian Cold Warriors envious; it was also based on the fact that the bulk of media attention was paid to opponents on the right. Serials such as *Time*, *Newsweek*, and *Life* did make frequent connections between treaty critics and Soviet communism when discussing the prospects for ratification in foreign countries – in Denmark, France, Norway, and especially Italy, where communists still held a high percentage of parliamentary seats. *Time*, for instance, determined that all protestors marching against the pact in Italy were 'Marxists,' as if they were a phenotype that could be identified on sight.[52] American journals did not take this line, however, in discussions of Canada. There, despite the anxieties raised by *Saturday Night*, passage seemed so assured that close analysis of the sources of opposition may have appeared unwarranted.

Still, domestic American treaty opponents of the conservative variety were often afforded nearly as much disdain as the Canadian media directed at its own 'communist' NATO opponents. This ran counter to the wider trend in both countries, one that saw the press forsake its role as a watchdog of the government, and generally adopt fawning tones when discussing political elites. (This approach would serve the double function of not providing fodder for communist propaganda and not soliciting a HUAC subpoena.) The handling of Republican senators' opposition under this wider atmosphere of obsequiousness stands out. The following are excerpts from *Time*'s coverage of the Senate debate over NATO, a piece, it should be added, that was not an editorial but a weekly report presented within the magazine's regular 'National Affairs' column. Doubting senators, *Time* began, had revisited upon Europe

the sickening sensation of being left in the lurch. The Senate was droning through the day's business when Missouri's plodding Republican Forrest Donnell rose [to ask whether the pact would obligate a U.S. military response to aggression] ... Old Tom Connally, chairman of the Foreign Relations Committee, reacted like a punch-drunk fighter at the sound of a dinner bell. 'Texas Tawm' was none too clear on what the Atlantic pact was supposed to do, but he yielded to no man in his jealousy of congressional prerogatives. Swinging wildly, he charged through the work of careful months of negotiation.[53]

And on and on. *Time* expressed some sound reasons for rejecting the old isolationist philosophy, but the effect of this and other reports about NATO detractors was the same as the campaign conducted in Canada against treaty critics: namely, to render opponents simpletons (in this case, Texas hayseeds, who by definition could not comprehend complex international matters), to make it clear that there was little here to debate, to cause those with doubts to question their political acumen – if not their loyalty. By way of comparison, NATO negotiators and spokespersons were granted a near-regal character by the media. According to *Time*, Dean Acheson delivered a radio broadcast justifying the alliance 'with a Shakespearian actor's measured resonance.' *Newsweek* commended Acheson's 'surgical precision' at the press conference unveiling the text of the treaty. In Canada, too, government pronouncements about the pact went unchallenged, and the officials delivering them were accorded a respect that bordered on veneration; Woodside seemed to fetishize even the 'stiff and gold-edged and beautifully bound' document signed at the April 4 ceremony.[54]

In these regards, NATO discourse in both the United States and Canada exhibited a great deal of consonance. Other aspects of the 'debate,' however, were marked by greater divergence. I have outlined previously one of the primary means of securing solid francophone support for a commitment to the defence of foreign nations: that is, playing upon the 'spiritual' character of the Cold War standoff. Two other constituencies that might be expected to express alarm over Canada's inclusion in a U.S.-led military alliance, the nation's loyal anglophiles and its fervent nationalists, found their own ways to justify their assent. Though historically some of the nation's most consistent and acerbic sources of anti-Americanism, Canadian Tories and nationalists alike found they could stomach such an arrangement by virtue of a series of interrelated arguments, some of which were highly contestable: (1) the very idea of an Atlantic pact was the product of British genius, Canadian genius, or both – these national divisions being largely irrelevant, for anglophiles at least; (2) Britain and Canada, by impelling a reluctant United States into the agreement, were tutoring the powerful but adolescent nation in its global responsibilities; (3) this being an association of equals, the organization would constrain rather than encourage U.S. imperial ambitions; (4) NATO would enhance rather than stifle the overall objectives of the UN. I will briefly address each of these in turn, and the manner in which they related to U.S. versions of these same themes.

On 1 April 1949, Winston Churchill made a speech in Boston praising the toughness and resolve exhibited by the West toward the Soviets. Coming only three days before the signing of the North Atlantic Treaty, the speech provided a reminder, at least to Canadian audiences, of the prime mover behind the organization. Canadian editorials and stories covering the speech pointed out that it was Churchill who, three years earlier in his last major North American appearance, had called for an Anglo-American alliance against Soviet aggression. This so-called Iron Curtain Speech, the Tory *Globe and Mail* noted with obvious satisfaction, had been 'greeted with shocked surprise or howls of rage ... Yet precisely what he suggested has come to pass.' Churchill had foreseen the danger, and proposed the panacea, long before those in the United States, Canada, and even Britain (a nation, according to Canadian Tories, currently afflicted by a supine Labour government). For the Atlantic pact, then, 'the honor of paternity belongs to Mr. Churchill more than to any other individual.'[55]

More than any other figure, Churchill exuded, for many Canadian anglophones, an air of infallibility. Two post-war polls found him the most admired man in Canada by wide margins, a feeling only compounded when his predictions of Russian malfeasance and Western coalescence proved accurate. As Woodside observed, '[Churchill] would be the last to claim omniscience. But surely there is no one else whose opinion so many value so highly.' However, for many subsequent Cold War analysts, Churchill did much more than merely reflect these Cold War phenomena – his rancorous talk helped foster aggression and distrust among Russians, and exaggerated fears of the Soviets in the West. As political scientist David Haglund notes in summarizing constructivist models of international tensions, 'enmity, as well as amity, is socially constructed in that words and deeds, and not theoretical postulates, provide the inspiration for states' regarding themselves to be either threatened or assured.' The *Globe* inadvertently lent credence to this notion by claiming that 'in the free world there is no one with a firmer hold on men's minds ... than Mr. Winston Churchill.'[56] Nonetheless, citing Churchill as the architect of the plan would go a long way to stilling fears that NATO constituted a U.S. conspiracy to dominate the post-war globe.

Fears would also be ameliorated, and national pride enhanced, by the fact that the Canadian government played 'a leading part in urging the formation of a North Atlantic security system,' as *Saturday Night* observed. Prime Minister St Laurent was accurately portrayed as one of NATO's earliest and most committed advocates, and the pact was often depicted as a kind of extension of Canadian values (the mosaic on a grand scale) to the wider international community.[57] Canada was the first member nation to ratify the treaty. None of these phenomena suggested a docile or weak nation coerced into an alliance led by the United States.

Indeed, the negotiation process was frequently depicted, with a certain degree of accuracy, in opposite terms. Canadian journalists raised serious questions from the beginning as to whether the United States would agree to a peacetime alliance, and whether it would live up to that agreement if the situation demanded. *Saturday Night* bemoaned the weakening of the pact's language to allow for greater Congressional influence over the use of force, noting that the new and vague language 'spread dismay in the chancelleries [*sic*] of the Western Union powers.' 'We should know from experience,' the publication maintained, 'that dictators seize upon every such encouragement to fool themselves that their adversaries "don't really mean it."'[58] The reference to 'experience,' echoed in many reports, was based on the charge that the United States had dithered while Hitler ran amuck, and that Canada and Britain (to name but two nations) had shouldered their burden from the start. Some insinuated, while others stated plainly, that the Second World War would have been avoided had the United States lived up to its global responsibilities.

When it appeared that the U.S. Senate would not, as feared, be an obstacle to a pact with true muscle, the Canadian media expressed relief – and assigned their own nation some of the credit. The paternalistic tone of this *Saturday Night* post-mortem is typical: In passing the Neutrality Acts of the 1930s, 'the American people, or at least its Congress, thus declared it just didn't live in this world. The nation seemed determined to learn the hard way ... Finally, but only when it was forced on them, the Americans accepted their part in the war.' Now, at long last, the one-time 'irresponsible nation' was 'soberly taking up the burden of leading the free world.' Again, these are hardly the words of those resistant to U.S. global leadership. Significantly, a similar process was taking place behind the scenes at the diplomatic level: Canadian officials, fearing a U.S. reversion to 'Fortress America' after the Second World War, worked strenuously to move the Truman administration toward active participation in the post-war world – and, later, were more than a little alarmed about how seriously U.S. leaders took up the cause.[59] The NATO debate represents the clearest example of the workings of this process at the public level.

Analysts in the United States did not deny that they had to be coaxed into a posture of global leadership, but many framed the process in decidedly different terms. Elements of the Canadian Tory line of reasoning – that the United States had let down the liberal-democratic order twice before, and would do well to assume its duties in an age of Soviet aggression – were also present in American narratives regarding NATO, especially in the pages of the *Nation* and *New Republic*. Other reports drew upon older American myths of national chosen-ness and of the depravity of European civilization to argue that only a committed and powerful United States could end the European will toward violence; that is, Europe was largely liable for its past and current 'troubles' and required the oversight of a benevolent hegemon. While these same arguments about the United States as a redeemer nation and the 'Old World' as infirm and decaying had also served as the basis for isolationism, the idea that European war did not adversely impact the Western Hemisphere was now considered obsolete. Thus, while the United States bore no particular blame for the outbreak of previous global wars, it would now respond to Europe's invitation to, quite literally, save the continent from itself. As a *New York Times* editorial on NATO put it, 'We are the first nation in all history to have thrust upon us a power which we did not plan for and did not desire ... Now we must create, in cooperation with other peoples, a world-wide climate of democracy or the chilling winds from the north will sweep us into everlasting desolation.'[60]

Along these same lines, several U.S. cartoonists depicted Europe as female, delicate, and in need of, alternately, Uncle Sam or a chivalrous American knight. Whether feminine Europe was a medieval damsel tied to a tree waiting for Sir Galahad (as in *Newsweek*), or a licentious Jezebel luring yet again a naïve and weak-willed 'Uncle Sap' across the ocean with the plea 'Save me, Sam, from myself' (in the isolationist holdout *New York Daily News*), the message was the same: the maiden had found herself in trouble again. *New York Times* reporter James Reston likened Senate ratification of NATO to 'a grumpy father [who] consents to the marriage of his beautiful daughter to the wily foreigner ... The old man is reluctantly willing to agree that he can't very well oppose the facts of life and maturity ... but he's bridling a little about paying the whole bill.' *New Republic* editors provided a rare dissenting voice to the notion that the problem lay exclusively with Europe and that the United States had resolved, out of sheer altruism, to deliver them. 'The essential point,' they argued in their assessment of Senate opposition to the pact, 'is that Western Europeans, now on the terrain of the cold war, see that war as America's far more than it is theirs ... [T]his time, when they want desperately to be spared the pre-liberation phases of a world war, they are forced to face the possibility that, after all, the US has *not* changed' (italics in original).[61] In this view, the United States bore significant responsibility for Europe's past subjugation and its current fears.

If the United States had required a good deal of persuasion in order to sign on to the idea of an Atlantic alliance, many reports in that country made it explicitly clear that, once the decision to join had been made, the United States would exercise firm if not exclusive control over NATO's direction. A *New York Times* cartoon on the eve of the pact's signing depicted a brawny Uncle Sam single-handedly hoisting the entire 'democratic world' on 'the good right arm' (no need for the left here!). Those fearing that the agreement would become an instrument of U.S. imperialism would not have been heartened by the *New York Time*'s eschatological claim that 'it is the very genius of our history that ... our efforts over a century and a half to perfect our democracy at home should lead us across the seas and continents.' The idea that the pact might be less a partnership than an extension of the State Department was not merely the perception of the U.S. media: once convinced that a pact was necessary by their European allies, U.S. officials took the lead in negotiations, rewriting basic components and pressuring uncommitted nations to join. Noted *Time*: 'Denmark's Foreign Minister Gustav Rasmussen arrived in Washington, and was closeted with Secretary of State Dean Acheson, who told him the facts of life as related to peace for the Atlantic community.' Historians Stephen Ambrose and Douglas Brinkley find no basis to 'the claim that NATO represented a pact between equals, for the United States had no intention of sharing the control of its atomic weapons with its NATO partners, and the bomb was the only weapon that gave NATO's military posture validity.'[62]

Many of Canada's NATO proponents, meanwhile, alternately skirted or denied the fact that the pact would be dominated by its most powerful member. In a response to local CCF Party members who claimed that U.S. interests would eclipse those of its alliance partners, the *Vancouver Sun* simply assured that 'it is nonsense to argue that the people of the United States or their government are the enemies of the freedom we cherish.' The *Regina Leader-Post* negated the same CCF argument by pointing to the fact that the United States was invited into the alliance by anxious West Europeans. Peter Inglis of *Saturday Night* trotted out a reliable discursive checkmate, arguing that those Europeans taken by the notion that 'the United States is domineering and does have ambitions of world power,' served as proof that 'Russian propaganda has had its victories in Europe.' The *Halifax Chronicle-Herald* followed the same tack: since the Soviets also level the charge of imperialism, it must have no basis in fact.[63]

Conversely, Willson Woodside clearly and repeatedly pointed out that the United States 'is heading the show' and was the 'king-pin of this new grouping.' For Woodside, this was an acceptable bargain, as the alternate king-pin was unthinkable – even more unthinkable than 'No World' at all. Even less Strangelovean analysts found merit in this argument. Though NATO might enshrine an apparatus whereby the United States could exercise formal control over the foreign policies and military spending of 'partner' nations, an unfettered, unilateralist, and adventurist United States was potentially deadly. As U.S. commentator Walter Lippmann wrote in a piece serialized in both countries, the pact will ensure that 'no one will on his own motion go off the deep end ... [or] settle great affairs with a loud bang.'[64] In this sense, the pact would simultaneously enhance and constrain American power.

Surprisingly, the economic components of an alliance, or the financial penalties associated with opting out, received scant attention. The *Calgary Herald* produced one of the few economic rationales for NATO membership, pointing out that Canada needs a stable and capitalist Europe in order to prosper. The Winnipeg Study Group took stock of what they considered the collective national vibe: 'With some reservations, perhaps, there seems to be a basic confidence that American policy is not one of uninhibited expansionism.' At the same time, they cautioned that 'the suspicion that Canada's economic dependence on the United States might make her a tool of American dominance in world affairs cannot be dismissed lightly.' Still, if participation in NATO would mean a net loss for Canadian autonomy, these fears were partially offset by 'self-congratulation at taking a part among the great powers.'[65] In other words, while Canada would never lead the free world, joining the alliance proved that it had cracked the top twelve. And in the end, the UN would remain the pre-eminent world body, safeguarding Canadian autonomy and providing a forum for the nation's concerns.

As noted previously, Canadian negotiators insisted on the inclusion of Article 2 in an attempt to assure domestic audiences that NATO would not be a solely military alliance, and that it would seek to uphold the same noble aims as the UN. The nation's media establishment, too, tended to play up this more quixotic take on the pact – to a greater degree, at least, than their American counterparts. This was not, they assured, a betrayal of post-war ideals and a return to power politics (which would, as the Winnipeg Study Group pointed out, again relegate 'middle powers' to the margins). At the heart of many proponents' arguments was the mostly spurious idea that the alliance was fully compatible with, even encouraged by, the charter *and* spirit of the UN. The *Winnipeg Tribune* promised, without further explanation, that 'the Pact may well prove in the light of history to be a bulwark for the United Nations itself,' and stressed the 'positive social, economic and political measures' that proved this was more than a military alliance. The *Halifax Chronicle-Herald* believed NATO to be the second coming of One-Worldism, calling the pact 'a real UN on the smaller scale, but one with teeth,' that would soon expand to recreate 'a full UN' – though one, it is assumed, without the Russians.[66] Time and again, the military alliance was characterized as a peace organization, one directed at 'aggression' rather than any particular nation.

Others acknowledged that the alliance undercut the authority and the spirit of the UN to varying degrees, but maintained that the organization's charter did not forbid such ancillary, power-balancing international bodies. *Saturday Night* was most consistent on this point (if not always intelligible), 'clarifying' in one editorial the quadruply negative axiom that 'there is nothing discreditable about power politics when used by those who have not accepted an obligation not to use them, and nobody in the United Nations has accepted any such obligation.' Many publications on the right, conversely, welcomed the abandonment of the frivolous dalliance with collective security and the return of realism and power politics – along with the concomitant build-up of military 'preparedness' – to international affairs. The UN, in other words, was dead; long live NATO. *Maclean's* editors expressed what could be considered the median view, calling the pact a necessity, but one that should be mourned as a loss: '… it is a second best,' they conceded, 'a poor substitute for the one-world dream of the end of the war.' *Le Devoir* concurred, stating, 'If one believes what was said at Lake Success, it seems that, despite the pact's preamble, this alliance relegates the UN to second place …'[67]

While a few publications from the United States, especially the *New York Times*, attempted to reconcile the idealism of the UN with the new Atlantic treaty, efforts on this front were less zealous; after all, the pact amounted to the replacing of a combative, stalemated body with an organization through which the nation might finally implement its post-war vision. Canadians' fears of a return to second-tier status in the 'old game' of power balancing, or of being a quiescent partner in a multilateral organization dominated by the nation's most durable antagonist, had no correlates south of the border. Article 2 received little attention in the United States; this was an unabashed military alliance intended to intimidate, and possibly strike at, the Soviets. In fact, the combative language used by the U.S. media to depict NATO – for example, that it 'represents a smashing military defeat for Soviet Russia' and will permit, through U.S. access to overseas air bases, U.S. bombers to 'carry the atomic bomb straight to the heart of the Soviet Union' – was so ubiquitous that *Saturday Evening Post* editors felt compelled to call for a moderation in rhetoric. 'The important thing,' they admonished, 'is to avoid providing raw material for the Soviet propaganda machine,' which casts the alliance as fundamentally imperialist, and a prelude to war.[68]

In sum, analysts in both countries put forward various representations of NATO, some of which were widely divergent and mutually contradictory. Further, many depictions in Canada were clearly aimed at 'sugaring the pill of the Atlantic pact' for Tories, nationalists, internationalists, and francophones – groups that might have been expected to raise more significant opposition to the alliance (and certainly would in the future). For the purposes of this study, it is important to note that these NATO apologias emerged, not from the United States, but from within Canada itself, and were forwarded by some of the nation's more forceful opponents of continentalism. In fact, closer attention to much of the media analysis imported from the United States, which conceived of the pact as a U.S.-led and -dominated military alliance intended to replace the failed UN, might have led to more realistic appraisals in Canada. Finally, although (tame) arguments emerged among Canadians over the meaning of the pact, almost no one questioned the basic necessity of such an arrangement.

It would be tempting for past and present Canadian opponents of NATO to view their nation's support for an American-led anti-communist military alliance as the consummation of a conspiracy, or at least a steady campaign, overseen by the forces of the far right and continentalist integration in Canada and the United States since 1945. Doubts regarding the straightforward acceptance of this thesis are cast by the conclusions drawn by three of the most outspoken and independent Canadian publications on matters concerning the emerging Cold War. The *Ottawa Citizen* had regularly framed its editorial posture as a direct counterpoint to positions adopted by the U.S. administration and to views the *Citizen* believed characterized the U.S. media. Now, though the paper continued to contextualize and justify Russian anxieties toward the West, though it argued that the UN was still 'of primary importance as an agency for peace,' and though it upheld the right and obligation of the CCF to openly debate the treaty, the *Citizen* did not oppose this formal pledge of allegiance to the anti-communist cause. The *Toronto Star*, formerly the Soviet Union's most dedicated champion in Canadian mainstream journalism, now blamed the breakdown in relations entirely on the Russians, and looked forward to a Soviet withdrawal from the UN that 'would permit cooperative members of the United Nations a freer hand to get on with their task of building a better world.'[69] Most surprising, as described at the outset of this chapter, was the about-face at the *Canadian Forum.*

Had these characteristically bold and independent-minded publications grown timid in a climate of intimidation, or weary of their increasingly isolated stand, or did they truly believe that the Russian threat trumped their more traditional concerns? All of these motivations may have been operational to varying degrees. For this group, at least, a fourth explanation seems unconvincing: that they had been convinced to abandon post-war idealism by a bellicose anti-Soviet campaign emerging from the United States. All were careful watchers and frequently strident critics of the United States; all, it seems, found reasons to support the alliance based on their own perceptions of costs and benefits.

After the April 4 signing ceremony, the treaty was put before the legislative bodies of all twelve nations for ratification. Canada was the first to do so, its Parliament registering only two dissenting votes; the U.S. Congress endorsed the treaty by an overwhelming 6–1 margin – ratios not unlike those generally produced by what *Time* dubbed 'Russia's rubber-stamp parliament.' A U.S. survey conducted prior to the vote determined that more than three-quarters of respondents endorsed the idea of the treaty, while a similar Canadian poll found that roughly 90 per cent of 'informed' citizens – those who could, according to pollsters, correctly identify the basic contours of the treaty – supported Canadian participation.[70]

Media organizations in both countries heralded the nearly universal acceptance of the pact (and certainly had reason to, given their prominent role in building public consent). In fact, the treaty endorsement was presented in terms bordering on, or hurdling past, grandiloquence. 'The most fateful peacetime step in US diplomatic history since the Monroe Doctrine,' proclaimed *Time*; 'the most remarkable treaty of modern times, if not, indeed, in all history,' declared the *Calgary Herald* – language similar, in fact, to that employed at the UN's formation four years earlier. Yet journalists seemed confused, even saddened, by the seeming lack of public enthusiasm surrounding this momentous achievement. *Time* reported that the American public greeted the pact with 'almost a disinterested silence ... The State Department, which gets bushels of letters when Palestine, China, or Spain is involved, had gotten only a trickle in the weeks the North Atlantic pact was being negotiated. Did this indicate apathy or agreement?' Willson Woodside, the treaty's earliest and most committed supporter among Canadian journalists, likewise wondered why 'our people did not become excited over the Atlantic pact.'[71] These characterizations appear to accurately reflect public attitudes: no marches for or against the pact occurred in North America (as they did in Europe); letters-to-the-editor largely ignored the issue, in stark contrast to matters such as the Bomb and Soviet espionage.

Both Woodside and *Time* conjectured that public silence proved public assent. As with other aspects of the relationship between NATO and the popular consciousness, this view has merit but oversimplifies a more complex set of circumstances. In this case, public silence may also connote lack of public information. The survey of Canadian public opinion taken on the eve of the signing ceremony found that less than half of Canadians asked 'knew what the treaty meant.'[72] This figure seems to verify concerns raised by the *Nation* that the public was expected to give unequivocal support to a treaty whose details were kept from them until the last minute. It is also likely that the percentage of 'informed Canadians' would have been higher had the press taken it upon themselves to provide a thorough dissection of, and debate over, specific treaty components, rather than a superficial 'conditioning' campaign to promote the general idea of an Atlantic alliance.

The press campaign itself provides another answer: Canadian doubters were mercilessly Red-baited and/or rendered un-Canadian; in the United States, leading opponents were ridiculed as slow-talking, wheezing 'Texas Tawms'; citizens could join the derision or leave themselves open to suspicion. Finally, the authentic excitement that greeted the formation of the UN, with its attendant optimism that humanity had perhaps turned a corner and would now eschew war as an instrument of diplomacy, could not be accorded a treaty that placed armies and alliances back in control of international affairs. To all but its most naïve supporters, NATO served as an acknowledgment (to be sure, one that a majority considered warranted, given widespread acceptance of the 'fact' of Soviet expansionism) that the old and troubled 'balance of power' schema for keeping peace had returned. In this sense, *Maclean's* assessment of the treaty as 'a poor substitute for the one-world dream' seems an apt gauge of the public mood.

For Canada, NATO represented an unambiguous victory for those endorsing a U.S.-led anti-communist consensus. Almost immediately after joining the alliance, however, concerns were raised about the agreement. Some Canadians seemed surprised at the alarming rise in armaments budgets, the strictures placed on an autonomous foreign policy, and the expectation that they would follow the United States into far-flung military exploits. Ironically, these matters would have been expected had *greater* attention been paid to the U.S. media; that is, if American reportage on this issue exerted more influence in Canada. By contrast, the 'sales campaign' conducted in Canada would depend upon an almost wilful denial of the predictable outcomes widely acknowledged in the U.S. press. Conceived by Canadian diplomats as a method of constraining the United States, the alliance instead led to greater U.S. control over Canadian diplomacy, a heightened U.S. military presence in Canada, and, as historian Kenneth McNaught writes, 'acquiescence [to] Washington's ideological anti-communism.'[73] With apologies to both McNaught and the Winnipeg Study Group (which claimed 'the sober sense of Canadians' immunized them from an anti-communist crusade), the foregoing survey suggests that 'ideological anti-communism' was not an outlook bounded by the Beltway or by international borders.

5 Korea: 'From an Imperial Frying Pan into an American Fire'

In December 1950, nearly six months into the Korean War, *Maclean's* magazine sent its veteran Ottawa correspondent and senior editor Blair Fraser on an extended visit to the peninsula; his mission was to gauge the progress of the fight for which the Canadian government had recently pledged ground troops. Fraser would find much that he considered unsettling, including a South Korean government so corrupt and reactionary that many of its citizens welcomed totalitarian invaders as liberators, a pattern of deliberate misinformation on the part of U.S. officials seeking to compel greater contributions from their UN allies, and a decidedly 'chilly' relationship between Western soldiers and the South Korean people those soldiers had come to save.[1]

The Canadian journalist managed to find one exception to the latter pattern, however, in the Pusan office of the U.S. armed forces newspaper, *Stars and Stripes*. While Fraser considered the situation 'heart-warming,' the relationship he went on to describe served as an apt reflection of the paternalism and chauvinism that had long characterized the Western encounter with 'the Orient,' and would also mark important aspects of the UN intervention in Korea. Fraser reported that the journalists at the *Stars and Stripes* had 'jointly become a foster father' to a two-and-a-half-year-old boy separated from his parents as a result of the conflict. Rather than investigate the fate of the boy's parents and, if they could not be found, place the child with relatives or an orphanage, the journalists 'adopted him as a mascot,' fattened him up with army rations, and dressed him in the uniform of a U.S. corporal. Though the toddler 'couldn't talk intelligibly in any language' upon arrival, his accidental guardians had begun to teach him their native tongue. 'He still can't talk much English,' Fraser noted, 'but he salutes beautifully.' The project of Westernizing the child, of raising him to comprehend only a foreigner's language, diet, and military loyalties, would appear a reckless endeavour on the part of those whose posting in Korea was temporary. 'Nobody seems to have figured out what's to become of him when the US Army moves out,' granted Fraser, 'but that's a detail.'[2] Such 'details' appeared small indeed to those who considered their way of life universal. Yet while Fraser himself commended the actions of his fellow journalists in this instance, participation in an American-led war would lead many Canadians to the conclusion that defining a monolithic Western 'way of life' proved more challenging than anticipated.

Though by 1950 the West could hardly be described as complacent regarding the threat of communist expansion, the North Korean invasion of the South in June of that year caught the United States and its allies unawares. The U.S. and UN response was devised and implemented on the fly, and debated and revised continuously as the battle descended into a brutal stalemate. In the main, the policies that emerged adhered to the basic structure of Western anti-communist praxis as it stood at mid-century. At the same time, the conflict, by transforming the East-West clash from cold to hot war, served to crystallize what had previously been a relatively hazy understanding of the implications of containment: before Korea, the confrontational anti-communist posture adopted by the United States after the Second World War had not translated into an engagement with the communist enemy on the battlefield; Canada, having refused to participate in the 1948–9 Berlin airlift, stood at even greater remove from any tangible proof of its commitment to American Cold War strategy. Even the NATO agreement did not offer an ironclad guarantee of a military response on the part of member states to communist expansion, and many still doubted whether the West, and most importantly the United States, would provide vigorous assistance to foreign victims of aggression. Korea would remove all doubts – though in the end, of course, neither side could claim victory, and the issues that divided the two Koreas would remain unresolved.

The conflict did, on the other hand, bring a certain resolution to the question of how far U.S. allies were prepared to submit to the dictates of American global leadership. Even before the Korean War became an intractable quagmire, fissures appeared between various members of the UN 'police force,' including Canada and the United States. From the beginnings of their involvement in the conflict, Canadian officials made concerted efforts to separate elements of their foreign policy from that of the United States and to construct an image as both an international mediator and a partner – rather than a 'foster father' – to Third World peoples; following the war, Canada began to scale back its commitment to NATO.[3] The Canadian public, too, lost some of its appetite for automatic submission to the dictates of containment, and the ensuing years would see a resurgence of a Canadian nationalism predicated, in large part, on the desire to establish a more autonomous bearing in international affairs. The looming Vietnam War, in other words, would confirm and intensify, rather than create, the resistance toward U.S. foreign policy expressed from many quarters in Canada in the 1960s and 1970s.

Ironically, deliberations at the outset of the Korean conflict over the nature and scale of Canadian participation suggest that Ottawa had already developed misgivings about the direction and scope of the U.S.-led anti-communist campaign in advance of average citizens. While Parliament endorsed the UN Security Council resolution committing a UN force to the peninsula, the Liberal government's reservations about the strategic threat posed by Korea led to a largely tokenist commitment to that force: three destroyers, and no ground troops. Only in September did they reverse this policy, setting in motion the process that would see ground forces sent by February 1951. For their initial hesitations, Canadian officials received upbraidings from all directions – from the Truman administration, the U.S. State Department, the American media, and from UN secretary general Trygve Lie. The most consistent and vehement criticisms, however, arose from Canadian citizens themselves, who had evidently taken to heart, and now angrily recited, their leaders' earlier warnings concerning the perils posed by global communism. Indeed, at the outset of the war, U.S. and Canadian public discourse on Korea revealed a shared interpretation of the war's origins and wider significance, and, as a result, a broad consensus of support for both the initial U.S. intervention and subsequent UN resolutions on the matter. Even so, differing understandings of what Korea meant for their respective nations and the world, and of the appropriate means of addressing the crisis, were apparent from the start; many of these points of disagreement would become sites of open hostility as the costs and limitations of containment strategy became apparent.

In this chapter, I concentrate on the factors mediating each nation's decision to go to war, and on the ways various American and Canadian actors saw the stakes, methods, aims, and wider meaning surrounding the conflict. I focus, therefore, on the first months of the conflict, after the United States had joined the fight but before Ottawa's acquiescence to appeals for Canadian ground forces. This period would witness passionate debates in both nations regarding the communist threat, the nature of liberal internationalism, and their country's responsibilities to

NATO, the UN, and each other. National identity informed a good measure of these responses to Korea, although American nationalism seemed to grow in significance and self-assurance at the same time that Canada's became more convoluted and, for some, less relevant. Furthermore, because the war involved people of colour in an era of decolonization, issues of imperialism, race, and the West's responsibility to the Third World formed a central theme in collective understandings of the crisis. Here a legacy of anti-Asian bias collided with the open-ended guarantees of the Truman Doctrine, leading many of the war's Canadian and American supporters to emphasize national security, rather than altruism and the rule of law, as the basis of Western intervention. In many accounts, Korea and Koreans were less fellow humans sharing a common humanity than they were a firewall against communist expansion, a metaphor whose suitability is confirmed by the willingness among key architects of the battle to obliterate the peninsula and its inhabitants rather than resort to diplomatic compromise, and by calls to subject the enemy to extensive atomic bombing.

While Korea was a distant and largely unknown territory to most Westerners, the region served as a continual source of friction between the United States and the USSR, and to a lesser extent between the United States and Canada, following the Second World War. Abiding by a prior agreement, in 1945 American and Russian liberating armies met in Korea at the 38th parallel, a division regarded as temporary by both the foreign occupiers and the region's inhabitants, and one never recognized as an international border by the UN. When the seemingly inevitable clash over the reunification process emerged, the superpowers established rival governments in the northern (Soviet) and southern (U.S.) zones; each government subsequently claimed sovereignty over all of Korea.

Canada's involvement in the Korean affair began in 1947, when Canadian delegates to the UN accepted a U.S. invitation to join the United Nations Temporary Commission on Korea (UNTCOK). The commission's task involved assessing the feasibility for peninsula-wide UN-supervised elections, a plan that, as political scientist Tom Keating notes, the United States assumed the Soviets would oppose. In fact, he writes, 'the Americans were anxious to force the Soviets to reject American *qua* UN proposals for elections and to proceed with their own American-run elections in South Korea.' Canadian prime minister Mackenzie King was so appalled by the Canadian delegation's decision to join the commission – which was made without his cabinet's approval – that he threatened to resign if the action was not reversed; members of King's cabinet made a similar pledge if the prime minister did not reverse *his* opposition. To King, the U.S. manoeuvrings in UNTCOK proved that the Americans 'were seeking to make the United Nations a political arm of the State Department.' Moreover, the prime minister feared that intensive Canadian involvement in the volatile and polarized region might draw his nation into participating in armed conflict in Asia, an area he considered outside of Canada's security interests and expertise. Finally, King worried that elections would render the temporary division permanent. Following a direct appeal from President Truman, King backed down from his threat to quit, but instructed his delegation to hold the position that UN-sponsored elections would be valid only if both the United States and the USSR consented. UNTCOK representatives ultimately rejected this view and organized elections solely for the South. In May 1948 this plebiscite made arch-conservative Syngman Rhee president of the newly established Republic of Korea, despite continued protestations from the Canadian, Australian, and Syrian UN delegations.[4]

Though by the spring of 1949 the American and Soviet armies had withdrawn, both Rhee's regime and the North Korean communist government of Kim Il Sung threatened one another with invasion, and North and South carried on a low-intensity conflict that between 1946 and 1950 had claimed 100,000 lives. The United States clearly believed Rhee's threats of forcible reunion, and disapproved of them, supplying him with only enough arms for defence. The North Koreans, then, enjoyed the advantage of surprise and superior weaponry when they launched a large-scale attack on the South on June 25th. In response, the Truman administration decided to oppose the aggression by force, and asked the UN Security Council to support this decision. With the Soviets boycotting the Security Council, the motion passed, and over the next few months the United States convinced twenty other nations, including Canada, to join the UN force. While the UN coalition successfully drove the North Koreans back across the 38th parallel by October, the decision to opt for a total victory that would destroy the Northern army and government and reunite the peninsula under Southern leadership brought the People's Republic of China to North Korea's defence. As a result, the war continued until the July 1953 signing of an armistice that recognized both Koreas and established a demilitarized zone near the old 38th parallel boundary. More than two million people died in the fighting, the vast majority of whom were Koreans. The United States, which contributed nearly 90 per cent of all foreign troops to the UN force, lost 33,000 lives. Nearly 27,000 Canadians participated in the war, and 406 died as a result of the conflict.[5]

Such an ambiguous and costly outcome stands in sharp contrast to the conviction and confidence that marked the West's initial response to the war. By June 1950, the Cold War consensus had engendered such a climate of Western righteousness and Soviet malevolence (and territorial voraciousness) that a number of matters germane to the Korean conflict emerged as dead certainties. The notion that Stalin had ordered the invasion as a component of his wider plan for world conquest stands as perhaps the firmest of these. 'It is patently more than a civil war among the Koreans themselves,' assured a June 27 editorial in the *Halifax Chronicle-Herald* in a typical phrase, and like most other proponents of this view, offered no supporting evidence for allegations of the invasion's ultimate provenance. The next day, the same paper printed a cartoon depicting a giant, brawny Stalin smashing a diminutive figure labelled 'South Korea' with a similar individual identified as 'North Korea,' whom the Generalissimo brandished like a sledgehammer. One week later, the same cartoonist had Stalin scooping up tiny, faceless Chinese hordes and stuffing them into a pail destined for the 'Korean Front.' Not only was Stalin the puppet-master, but in populous Asian allies he possessed, as the cartoon's title noted, 'an inexhaustible supply' of sycophantic warriors.[6]

Canadian audiences displayed a decided readiness to accept these assumptions. A poll conducted just prior to the North Korean offensive found that 80 per cent of respondents believed the Soviet regime was predicated upon a desire for world supremacy and/or expansionist war. This figure had increased by 22 per cent since 1946 and marked a sharp reversal from a survey taken in 1942, which concluded that a 'decisive majority' believed the Russians would cooperate with the West in promoting representative governments after Germany's defeat. Canadian officials and their American counterparts expressed similar convictions about the Korean conflict's origins – in part based on repeated and exaggerated CIA reports leading up to the war that North Korea was 'completely under Soviet control.' Once the war began, the CIA (which had failed to detect the slightest hint of the impending attack) concluded that the invasion 'was undoubtedly undertaken at Soviet direction.'[7]

U.S. media reports were equally adamant, and equally unsubstantiated. The *New York Times* maintained that the 'final outcome of this struggle' will not be decided in Korea, but 'in the Kremlin, which prepared, instigated and directed this war in furtherance of its own purposes.' *Newsweek* spoke of the 'Kremlin-controlled armies of North Korea' and, like innumerable publications over the coming months, produced a map of the entire globe (this one titled 'What We're Up Against') showing blackened 'communist dominated' regions radiating arrows outward in all directions to demonstrate 'threatened areas.' *Time* held that Soviet ambassador to North Korea, Terenty Shtykov, was in reality 'Stalin's pro-consul,' and then reminded readers of the spiritual stakes bound up in this global standoff: Shtykov, the magazine noted, commanded his Soviet colony 'from his roomy, three story mansion, built on the site of the old Presbyterian Mission compound in Pyongyang.' The *Christian Century* provided an atypical dose of discretion to the notion that the attack was ordered by Moscow, arguing that 'no move of this kind would have been made without the *consent* of the Kremlin' (italics added). Soviet archival evidence confirms this more tempered view, revealing that Stalin permit-ted the offensive only after repeated pleas from Kim, who assured the Soviet leader of a quick and convincing victory.[8]

The *Ottawa Citizen* produced a rare effort to actually verify the Soviet directive behind the invasion, citing a recent fact-finding trip to Asia by 'the leading foreign affairs expert of the Republican party in the United States,' one John Foster Dulles. According to the *Citizen*, Dulles, at the time a State Department advisor, claimed that unspecified 'progress' made by the South had begun to embarrass foreign communist officials; those same officials also realized that a Korea united under Soviet domi-nation would place Japan 'between the upper and lower jaws of the Rus-sian bear.' In sum, Dulles warned, the attack was clearly 'part of the world strategy of international Communism.' Historian Stephen Whitfield has pointed to the air of infallibility afforded high-ranking foreign-policy specialists, and particularly Dulles, by the era's U.S. news media, which frequently eschewed field reporting from Asia in favour of uncritical reiteration of official government statements (an approach replicated in the first years of the Vietnam War, before revelations of a 'credibility gap' rendered the practice untenable). In instances such as these, Cana-dians faced a double-remove from the facts on the ground in Asia, as they often possessed neither field reporters nor their own 'experts' on the region. In short, the Canadian press simply replicated the opinions expressed by figures such as Dulles, as those opinions were understood and represented by their American counterparts; such closed, self-refer-ential reportage was bound to breed imbalanced and monolithic analysis. Later in the war, when it became clear that a good deal of misinforma-tion and censorship plagued reports from Korea, the *Canadian Forum* raised objections to the fact that the Canadian Press assigned only two reporters to all of the Far East. In consequence, they complained, Cana-dians 'obtain all but a fraction of our Korean news from American wire services. The decision in respect to what will continue to pass as news for public consumption is likely to remain therefore in other hands.'[9]

Impugning Stalin for the latest international breach of justice should have required at least some corroborating data, if only because the North Korean offensive seemed to deviate substantially from the dictator's earlier moves: this was not Europe or the Middle East, the site of previous Soviet 'probes' of 'Western resolve,' nor was this blatant aggression in line with the multi-faceted and often clandestine manipulations that marked the seizure of the states that constituted Russia's *cordon sanitaire.* For those beholden to the verity of monolithic communism, however, the ur-'fact' that Stalin mandated the attack trumped the need to marshal other evidence in support of their thesis. In other words, the idea that the assault did not fit the usual Soviet methodology simply proved that the methodology had changed. Here, President Truman led the way, charging in his June 27 press statement that 'the attack upon Korea makes it plain beyond all doubt that Communism has passed beyond the use of subversion to conquer independent nations and will now use armed invasion and war.'[10]

Countless journalists followed, puzzling over why Stalin's *modus operandi* had shifted so suddenly and how the Soviets could have prepared themselves for war with the West so quickly (when most experts predicted that Russia would not be ready for the final showdown until the mid-1950s). The *Globe and Mail* is representative, marvelling that 'normally the expansion of the Soviet sphere of domination has been managed by such relatively subtle methods as infiltration, propaganda, terrorism and coup.' 'It is significant that Moscow,' observed the *Saturday Evening Post,* '... is exhibiting less timidity in Asia' than it had in other geographies. Ernest Lindley, political analyst for *Newsweek* agreed: 'Every previous act of Communist aggression,' he noted, 'has had some protective coloration' such as 'internal insurrection, or "elections"... This is naked aggression.' Wide-ranging hypotheses as to why the Russians had chosen Asia for their next move and where they might strike next usually followed. Sebastian Haffner, regular contributor to both the *London Observer* and *Saturday Night,* pointed to the 'queer logic' behind the Soviet action, one that was impenetrable to 'Western minds.'[11] Churchill's proverbial 'riddle wrapped in a mystery inside an enigma' had grown even more inscrutable.

Given that a powerful and depraved dictator had launched a war for global supremacy in defiance of world opinion and international law, and that his tactics included seizing small, weak nations in a piecemeal fashion while the West dithered, it made for quick work to connect the current crisis with the events leading to the Second World War. A *Calgary Herald* cartoon featured an automobile designated 'the Atlantic "Twelve'" at a forked road, and a female passenger pointing toward the highway labelled 'Route of the 30's / Wishing for Peace.' The more sensible male driver, however, has already chosen 'Route '50 / Working For It,' stating, 'we tried that way before.' 'This might be a good time to go back to the history books,' began a June 28 editorial in the *Regina Leader-Post*, which then provided a sombre, methodical review of major international events between 1933 and 1939 before asking whether the West has the courage to halt Russian expansion now, or 'whether history is going to repeat itself.' Government officials, too, immediately linked Stalin's apparent probe of Western resolve to that of Hitler.[12]

Likewise, 'appeasement' and 'Munich' were invoked repeatedly in the reportage from both nations – though the *Toronto Telegram* found the slander of the British implicit in these terms too much, at least when they were uttered by Americans. U.S. leaders and journalists, *Telegram* editors fumed, 'would be wiser to forget Munich and consider their own record. The Munich agreement was merely one of the consequences of American isolationism, the most disastrous folly of modern times.' Still, in casting U.S. disengagement from global affairs as the ultimate invitation to expansionist nation-states, the paper reinforced the notion that the Korean situation was best viewed through the lens of the recent German aggression. Some of these the Second World War–Korea correlations appeared less compelling, as when *Newsweek* observed that 'like the Japanese bombing of Pearl Harbor on Dec. 7, 1941, the North Korean attack began around dawn on a Sunday morning.'[13] Nevertheless, with memories of the most devastating conflict in history still vivid, the incessant invocation of that conflict as the means of understanding the North Korean 'blitzkrieg' (another recurrent and loaded descriptor) would have obvious impact. If the analogy was sound, only a decisive, immediate counteraction would thwart another global war.

In fact, many believed that as a result of Kim Il Sung's invasion, the third global conflict in little more than a generation was either inevitable or already under way. Many analysts and officials interpreted the flare-up in Korea as Stalin's diversionary manoeuvre for a subsequent, all-out attack on Europe, Iran, or even North America. 'Whether the attack on Korea be called the Austria, the Ethiopia, or the Czechoslovakia of the third world war, its meaning is comparable to those preliminary Axis aggressions,' claimed *Newsweek*'s Ernest Lindley – again eliding the fact that the attack 'on Korea' had also been launched *by* Korea. Just before the invasion of South Korea, polls found that the 'threat of war' was the most significant concern of U.S. citizens; while Canadians rated it a close second – to unemployment – the number citing war (12 per cent) had more than tripled in just five months. An August 1950 survey of when Canadians believed the next world war would break out determined that 21 per cent thought another world war unlikely and 10 per cent expressed no opinion on the matter. The remaining 69 per cent believed another global conflict was inevitable, with the median time frame for the beginning of the 'real' battle estimated at ten months; 4 per cent held that the war was already on. By January 1951, the percentage of Canadians citing the 'threat of war' (presumably global war, as their nation *was* at war in Korea) as Canada's greatest problem had risen from the pre-war total of 12 to 53, and in February more than a third of those polled believed there was 'a chance' their own nation could be attacked by 'enemy forces' before the end of that year. One month later, when offered the hypothetical opportunity to ask one question of the prime minister, a leading 13 per cent posed the query 'Will there will be another war?' while questions about the possibility of conscription finished second.[14]

Predictably, the prospect of an all-out battle with an enemy that now possessed atomic weaponry produced widespread anxiety. Two weeks into the war, U.S. evangelist Billy Graham informed Truman that the U.S. public was seized by 'a fear you could almost call hysteria,' and petitioned the president (in vain) to declare a national day of prayer. A November survey of Canadians concluded that two-thirds of those polled held that the government was not adequately preparing citizens for 'enemy air attacks,' and that one-third had thought out a possible response to those attacks (preferred strategy: 'hide' – in cellar / under a table / under bed). Still, U.S. national weeklies like *Time* and *Newsweek*, which had assailed Truman continuously for his 'softness' toward communist expansion in Asia, seemed intent on proving that Americans, at least, were unafraid of, even eager for, the fight. *Newsweek*'s measure of public attitudes at the outset of the conflict determined that average Americans were 'tired of murky defeats, inconclusive victories, and faulty diplomatic footwork' associated with the seemingly passive strategy of containment. Instead, the public allegedly greeted the outbreak of authentic combat with 'relief.' '"If this is it, let it come," said taxi driver, farmer, factory worker, and businessman' in apparent unison. 'Rather than feeling alarm at the risks,' *Time* agreed, 'many seemed to be grateful for the end of an era of uncertainty.'[15]

Whether 'grateful' to be at war or not, the broad consensus of support for Truman's action was indisputable. All major American and

English-language Canadian daily newspapers supported Truman's decision to fight in Korea. Polls conducted in July determined that 81 percent of Americans and 75 per cent of Canadians approved of the immediate infusion of U.S. troops into the conflict. Canada's CCF Party, whose
founding manifesto pledged to 'refuse to be entangled in any more wars
fought to make the world safe for capitalism,' endorsed the decision.
Americans for Democratic Action, a liberal organization so disillusioned
with Truman's incumbency in 1948 that they petitioned Dwight Eisenhower to seek the Democratic nomination, now likened Truman to the
revered Franklin Roosevelt. In the U.S. press, opposition was limited to
the *National Guardian*, and in Canada, to the communist *Canadian Tribune* and a handful of Quebec publications.[16]

With core facets of the meaning of Korea largely agreed upon – that
it marked the 'next phase' of Soviet expansionism, and that immediate
use of force was the only panacea to the eruption of full-scale war – a
further conclusion appeared indisputable: that defence spending must
escalate dramatically. In the United States, a massive increase in military
expenditures was a key governmental objective even before the outbreak
of war, having been proposed in the April 1950 publication of NSC-68,
a joint State and Defense Department report. Public and Congressional
approval of that report, which proposed a nearly 300 per cent increase
in defence spending (from $13 billion to $50 billion) in order to meet
what its authors portrayed as Moscow's fanatical drive for world supremacy, appeared unlikely to many in the Truman administration. Then, in
the famed acknowledgment of Secretary of State Dean Acheson, 'Korea
came along and saved us.' As retired General Carl Spaatz noted in a special July 10 editorial of *Newsweek*, Korea demonstrated that the United
States 'must increase substantially the strength of our armed forces and
our munitions output,' and 'must start making the sacrifices our national
mission requires of us.' Ernest Lindley extended these same obligations
beyond American borders in a subsequent issue, warning that if the 'free
nations ... do not use every day of respite to expand their military power,
their ultimate penalty is only too likely to be annihilation.' Here, Lindley
was merely echoing sentiments expressed in NSC-68 itself, which cited
the need to press 'other like-minded nations' to commit themselves fully
to the global anti-communist struggle, with massive rearmament marking the clearest testimony to that commitment.[17]

Few in Canada disagreed. The *Vancouver Sun* felt that American citizens who had resisted a massive military buildup prior to Korea simply
did not understand the stakes. 'Even back in 1944 and 1945,' the *Sun*

pointed out, 'in the *less desperate struggle against Hitler*, the US was spending at a rate of $84 billion a year' (italics added). Michael Barkway of *Saturday Night* lamented what might also be cited as one of the hallmarks of a healthy democracy, pointing out that 'there are no giant standing armies on our side of the Iron Curtain.' Most rancour on this issue was reserved, however, for the condition of Canada's fighting forces. In the weeks following the outbreak of the war, Canadian publications repeatedly condemned the preparedness, weakness, and, in the words of the *Globe and Mail*, the generally 'sorry state' of the Canadian military – a condition best ameliorated by an immediate and substantial infusion of cash. 'An entirely new defence budget should be prepared,' counselled the *Winnipeg Free Press*, 'on the only safe assumption of possible outright war.' *Saturday Night* editors held that a September 1950 government proposal to more than double Canada's defence budget – from $425 million to $1 billion – was 'by no means extravagant' when compared to recent increases in military spending witnessed in the United States as a result of Korea (that is, in the Western nation which now boasted the largest per capita military expenditures). The *Ottawa Citizen* praised those same American increases, predicting somewhat optimistically that they 'will boost the United Nations [not the U.S.] flag higher than ever.' *Halifax Chronicle-Herald* editors noted that average citizens will certainly feel the burden of escalating military budgets. 'Very well then!' they wrote, '… we should pay gladly for it is our future and our children's future that is at stake.'[18]

A few observers were willing to sketch out in specific terms the costs of such increases. Shortly after the Second World War, Prime Minister Mackenzie King wrote privately of the need 'to decide whether we were going in for increased military expenditures or to seek to carry out our programme of social legislation.' After war broke out in Korea, *Saturday Night* offered an answer, advising that 'there must be a drastic reduction' in a wide range of government and private spending not related to military matters. At issue, then, was a model of state roles and responsibilities – as a buffer against the excesses of the fee market – that had long served as a core facet of national identity (juxtaposed, predictably, with the rampant individualism and unregulated economy ascribed to the United States). The *Calgary Herald* shared this call for a thorough revision of national priorities in light of Korea, noting that while the Canadian government spent $380 million on defence in 1949, it also dispensed $268 million in family allowances. 'Pretty soon,' the *Herald* lectured, '… Canada will have to decide between eating her cake and having it.'[19] The editors did not specify which expenditures should be sacrificed, nor did they need to. As a result of the conspicuous threat to Canada's very existence represented by Korea, the expanded welfare state that the newspaper vehemently opposed could now be framed as nothing less than a threat to national security.

Like-minded columnist Richard Needham joined the campaign, arguing in the same Alberta paper that social programs were merely superfluous 'schemes designed to make life more rich, more beautiful,' and to ensure job security for civil servants. 'So if we are going to pay cash for our war,' he advised, 'a great deal of the uplift will have to go, and a great many of the uplifters.' 'Parliament has been concerning itself with methods of providing further social security,' agreed the *Toronto Telegram*, 'but the country's greatest concern at this juncture should be with national security.' Nor would the 'costs' be solely financial. After exaggerating considerably the disparity between the number of Soviet and NATO armoured divisions, Willson Woodside admitted that closing the gap might cripple a thriving Canadian economy, degrade government services, and require the ultimate sacrifice of the nation's young men. 'But consider the alternatives,' he concluded – including the loss of all Asia, Europe, and the reversion of the United States into 'an armed camp facing an enemy controlling the greater part of the world.'[20]

As was the case in the United States, Korea proved to be the panacea for Canadians advocating increased military expenditures. The nation's defence budget, which stood at less than $200 million in 1947, had nearly doubled by 1949–50, largely as a result of Canada's new NATO-related obligations. It doubled again in 1950–1, to $780 million, in response to the outbreak of fighting in Korea. By the end of the Korean War, annual defence spending amounted to $2 billion, or 45 per cent of *all* federal spending, and the nation's defence-GDP ratio was fourth highest among NATO members. Some observers continue to view these skyrocketing budgets as a necessary corrective to what military historian David Bercuson deems the 'pitiful state' that characterized the Canadian military of the late 1940s. Such analysis raises questions as to whether Soviet desires for global domination were incontrovertible, whether communist victories in small, remote nations constituted a threat to Canadian security, and whether the interests of global stability might be better served by the creation of a permanent UN military force rather than a global arms race. These matters can be debated, but it must be acknowledged that one of the arguments for Canadian participation in NATO was that in allowing nations to pool military resources rather than requiring each to maintain a defence force robust enough to face the Soviets alone, military expenditures would actually decrease.[21]

While the need to deploy these reinvigorated military forces in defence of South Korea was generally taken as axiomatic, the specific rationale for doing so tilted heavily toward the threat the conflict posed to the West: monolithic, expansionist communism and the potential 'loss' of all Asia, with its strategic value and vast markets and natural resources, proved powerful arguments for galvanizing public opinion in favour of military intervention in Korea. Less apparent were voices that justified Western intervention on more altruistic grounds. Indeed, past U.S. and Canadian responses to Asia and Asians provided obstacles to promoting public affinities for the plight of South Korea.

As noted in the previous chapter, debates surrounding the formation of an anti-Soviet alliance of 'like-minded' nations raised questions in both the United States and Canada about who would or would not be protected from communist aggression – where, in common parlance, the 'line should be drawn.' Given the complicated and often troubling history of Canadian and American interactions with the Asian continent and its peoples, the idea that blood and treasure should be sacrificed in Korea on merely humanitarian grounds or to defend the rule of law would appear to hold little sway in the public mind.

In fact, the foreign and domestic policies of both nations reveal a mixed pattern of disdain, apathy, and, in the case of the United States, imperial aggression toward the Far East and its inhabitants. During the previous fifty years alone, the United States had suppressed the Filipino uprising against American takeover, assisted in quashing the Boxer Rebellion, and battled with Japan for hegemony in the Pacific – first commercially, then in a gruesome military confrontation that concluded with atomic bombings. The Chinese Exclusion Act, introduced by the U.S. Congress in 1882, remained in force until 1943, the Immigration Acts of the 1920s barred Asians outright, and during the Second World War, President Roosevelt authorized the internment of West Coast residents of Japanese ancestry. Following the war, the United States seized territory (inhabited by human beings, as Harold Ickes reminded) throughout the Pacific in service of strategic aims, and evacuated, then obliterated, the island of Bikini Atoll in a 1946 atomic test. Extreme racial bias served as a component, and sometimes a principal feature, of each of these episodes. Asking citizens to put their lives on the line solely in the interests of Korean freedom seemed like a tough sell.

Canada had less direct contact with Asia, and few of the nation's elites mourned this experiential deficit. The nation's political, commercial, and military ties were oriented largely toward the Western Hemisphere and Europe, verifying Prime Minister King's claims that Canada possessed few interests in (or interest about) the Far East. Like the United States, Canadian immigration policy sought to virtually eliminate newcomers from Asia once the bulk of the nation's railroad construction had been completed. Between 1885 and 1923, the federal government placed a 'head tax' on immigrants of Chinese ancestry, the only group so targeted in Canadian history. Initially set at $50, the fee had increased to an intentionally prohibitive $500 by 1903. The nation's own Chinese Exclusion Act arrived later (1923), though lasted longer (1947) than its American namesake (surviving even Canada's wartime alliance with China). Following Pearl Harbor and the U.S. lead, King's government interned Japanese residents and, after the war, barred them from returning to the British Columbia coast and encouraged the 'repatriation' of even Canadian-born internees to Japan – to the applause of many conservative newspaper editors. As mentioned in chapter 4, many of their readers echoed these sentiments, with a leading 60 per cent of respondents in a 1946 poll identifying the Japanese as the nationality they 'would like to keep out' of Canada. Wartime hostility is only part of the story here, as 24 per cent singled out prospective immigrants from wartime ally China for similar treatment. As a consequence of these policies and attitudes, residents of Asian descent made up only 0.5 per cent of the nation's population in 1950; official barriers to Asian immigrants remained until the late 1960s. (Today, by contrast, nearly 9 per cent of Canadians self-identify as ethnically Asian.) Finally, Canada's previous military experience in Asia was limited to a brief and catastrophic attempt to garrison Hong Kong on behalf of the British in 1941.[22] None of these experiences, policies, or attitudes suggest a nation now eager to throw itself into the breach in Asia.

Supporters of intervention in Korea from both countries were aware of the sense of estrangement many of their citizens felt toward Asia and the ways in which this alienation might hamper the desire to go to Korea. *Time* referred to the 'distant, strange little republic of Korea,' and admitted 'it was a rare US citizen who could pass a detailed quiz on the little piece of Asiatic peninsula he had just guaranteed with troops, planes, and ships' ('Were the people Indians or Japanese?' wondered one Dallas resident.) *Saturday Night* editors agreed with an unidentified Canadian official who conceded that most average Canadians 'don't even know where Korea is' – though the magazine still insisted that citizens supported intervening there, wherever 'there' was. War opponent *Le Devoir* wondered how many Canadians could find Korea on a map, conjecturing (rather generously), 'probably not 10 per cent.' A *Globe and Mail* cartoonist depicted even a Canadian politician inquiring: 'Korea! Where's that, in Quebec?'[23]

A host of analysts endeavoured to provide briefings on the land and people that had suddenly emerged as the focus of the entire globe. *Saturday Night*'s Willson Woodside appended a section captioned 'Timely Reading' to his report on the UN decision to send forces to Korea, offering a list of (hawkish) books on the appropriate Western response to communism, in general, and Asia, in particular – including *War or Peace* by the omnipresent Dulles. 'Americans are having difficulty saying what U.S. troops are fighting over,' conceded *Time*, though only in the most literal sense: the unintentionally provocative phrase led off a tutorial on pronunciation titled 'Those Korean Names.' 'Taejon rhymes with had fun,' they instructed. 'Pusan rhymes with shoes on ... Pyongyang rhymes (more or less) with strung young,' and so on. *Newsweek* interspersed its first field reports of U.S. fighting in Korea with a series of purported 'Korean proverbs,' all of which bespoke the insightful and contemplative 'Oriental' many Western readers of the immensely popular Pearl Buck would have come to expect (and all of which, though ostensibly ancient, seemed to anticipate and endorse the core components of the Truman Doctrine). Such attitudes served as a Korean variant of what Karen J. Leong calls the 'China mystique,' a romanticized view of that nation's inhabitants which emerged during China's alliance with the United States against Japanese aggression, and which replaced some of the more abject representations of Asians that had characterized previous American and Canadian discourse.[24]

Some of these early-war synopses of the land and its people, however, maintained the older, more disparaging stereotypes and caricatures that have been identified by many recent studies of Western perceptions of the East. Korea, to *Time*, was deeply primitive, 'a land where men had hardly caught up with Galileo.' Willson Woodside concurred, estimating that the West was 'perhaps a century or so ahead of [Asians'] development' in terms of political sophistication. Richard Needham of the *Calgary Herald* provided a brisk dash through the last 350 years of Korean history before concluding with a concise précis of the Korean character: 'Their chief aim in life,' he reported, 'is to have as many children as possible, preferably boys. The women are completely subject to the men, and spend most of their time washing.' The *Globe and Mail* reprinted a piece from O.M. Green of the *London Observer* called 'The People. of Korea,' which made similar claims. While Korea's girls 'are often very pretty,' Green observed that 'as in all Eastern countries the women are drudges accepting meekly their inferior position. But the men can and do work, if not intensively...' Despite their apparently incurable timidity, however, 'Korean women ... have their own prejudices and beliefs, from which apparently nothing can move them.' No further clarification or corroboration for this last and considerably opaque declaration is offered, and Green's exposition does little to alleviate what he calls 'the riddle of the Korean people, in many ways so attractive, in much so difficult.' As Indian prime minister Nehru stated in a speech on Korea to his nation's parliament, the West was implementing 'decisions affecting vast areas of Asia without understanding the real needs and mind of the people.'[25] In the context of a global battle for 'hearts and minds,' such words were both deliberate and prescient.

Having just emerged from a highly racialized conflict with the Japanese (and beholden to the still regressive attitudes expressed in media and popular culture), some fell rather effortlessly into old and particularly odious patterns of maligning Asians, even while the West was fighting *for* (some) Asians. After spending time at the Korean front, *Maclean's* editor Blair Fraser found that entrenched Western chauvinism was impeding the war effort, pointing to the 'chilly' relationship between UN troops and the local population those troops had been sent to save. And in this instance, the intolerance could not be ascribed solely to the Americans, with their notorious 'race problem.' 'It's true that the GI refers to all Koreans as "gooks," that he shows contempt for the native at every turn,' Fraser reported. 'But let's not be smug about it. Canadian troops developed some of the same prejudice within a week of their arrival.' Fraser's own publication did little to bolster readers' affinities for their Asian allies, pointing, for example, to the 'Oriental cunning of the Muscovite' as the font of all global flare-ups, including Korea. Saving Koreans from said cunning would, it appears, also require saving them from themselves. Others expressed frustration that simple dichotomies between 'us' and 'them' based on physical characteristics did not hold up under these circumstances. *Canadian Forum* editor Frank Underhill reported one U.S. soldier as grumbling: 'At least with the Japs we knew who the enemy was. He was anybody with slant eyes. Here everybody but us has got slant eyes. How're going to tell who's who?'[26]

One month after the U.S. intervention in Korea began, the *Toronto Star* devoted an editorial to the need for tolerance toward Koreans; though the paper did not identify offending publications or authors, the lengthy reprimand served as tangible evidence that disparaging Orientalist discourses ran rampant in the first weeks of the war. 'Koreans of both North and South,' instructed the *Star*, 'are proud people. They resent any assertion of race superiority by whites and rightly so ... It would be a tragic mistake,' they continued, 'if [UN forces] were ... to regard all Koreans as treacherous or untrustworthy. Koreans are a fine, intelligent, and courageous people. They should not be called "gooks"...' The publication considered such reminders vital to reinforcing the notion that foreign troops were not in Korea due to self-interest or as conquerors, but in order to uphold the international rule of law and to deliver fellow human beings 'from a bondage worse than death.' In other words, South Koreans should be viewed as friends, allies, and full-fledged members of the international community, and for these reasons alone they (like West Europeans) deserve our protection against communist 'enslavement.'[27] It is difficult to find similar arguments for Western involvement – that it was simply a just and honourable course of action taken to uphold the rule of law, regardless of any net benefits that 'we' might accrue – in the public discourses of either the United States or Canada.

In Korea, then, the bitter racial animus that had characterized previous East-West confrontations could not be utilized in service of strategic objectives without also impairing those objectives. Some analysts, including Truman himself, skirted this quandary altogether by referring to South Koreans simply as 'Koreans' and North Koreans as 'communists' or 'bandits and thugs.' These latter descriptors became commonplace in both countries – the *Globe and Mail*, for instance, deployed them faithfully and added the unnerving (and evidently durable) 'evil-doers' to the demonic fusion.[28] Another means of addressing the issue involved projecting the war's impetus entirely onto the Soviets, as we have seen, and representing all Koreans as victims of foreign communist aggression. Frequently, this tack required that its advocates present all Koreans as unsophisticated, susceptible to outside influence, and desirous of tutelage. If this was indeed the case, it became incumbent upon the West to ensure that this tutelage originated from liberal as opposed to communist masters.

According to these latter Orientalist projections, Asians' 'inherent' malleability and thirst for outside guidance led them to admire powerful leadership above any other considerations, such as political ideology, morality, or justice; as historian Mark Bradley has shown, such assumptions would plague the United States again in its formulation of strategy in Vietnam.[29] To Westerners, this attribute is what made the pitiless and fearsome Stalin such a dangerous figure in Asia, and why a spectacular and crushing military defeat of communism in Korea, even one that left the peninsula in tatters, would be preferable to a peace rendered through negotiation and compromise.

The leading spokesman for this school of thought was Douglas MacArthur, the American general selected – after he had already initiated military actions in Korea on behalf of the United States – to lead the UN command in Korea. According to the general, those foolish enough to pay heed to local and regional initiatives and concerns in an attempt to resolve the crisis were simply advocates of appeasement. What is more, they 'do not grasp Oriental psychology,' which 'respect[s] and follow[s] aggressive, resolute, and dynamic leadership' – embodied, for instance, in himself. Canadian colonel Wallace Goforth agreed, claiming that superficial feelings of 'nationalist fervor' currently expressed by Asians would wither under 'a display of ruthless force. Their respect for effective power tends always to overshadow understanding of – or attention to – moral issues.'[30] By 'moral issues,' the colonel meant the ethical superiority of liberalism over communism, obvious to Westerners but occluded by the Asian peasant mentality. No word on the relationship between the 'ruthless force' Goforth recommends as the cure for the region's nationalist and leftist tendencies and the 'moral issues' Asians (alone) did not appear to grasp. The matter ultimately haunting such lines of reasoning was whether the use of the Bomb, the most ruthless display of force available, would promote or impede the cause of freedom in Asia. I will return to this issue below.

It is important to take stock of these cultural attitudes not merely to demonstrate Western chauvinism; each of these assumptions would have a direct impact on the ability of the West to prosecute an effective campaign on the peninsula. A public that is asked to support an allegedly primitive, lazy, and contemptible people may be prone to waver in the face of difficulty, and soldiers who regard their South Korean allies in similar terms would face obstacles in forming a cohesive military force. It is also unsurprising that Westerners exposed to such views would believe they were in for an easy fight against the North Korean military. The initial and dramatic U.S. battlefield failures thus proved both shocking, and for analysts, difficult to rationalize. Some expressed a grudging appreciation for the fighting abilities of the North Koreans, while others emphasized the essentially Soviet makeup of the invasion or, in a reprise of Orientalist conceptions of Asian deceit, the 'dirty tricks' of an unprincipled enemy. *Time* voiced regret that a 'realistic appraisal of a really formidable enemy came after the fight and not before,' quoting a

U.S. officer who admitted his previous contemptuousness of the North Koreans. After encountering them in the field, the magazine noted that 'he lost his contempt.' Briton Sebastian Haffner, a regular contributor to *Saturday Night*, managed to maintain his contempt even as he gained a measure of respect for Asians' capacity to fight, reporting that 'weary US front line troops had learned the hard way not to underrate the cunning, savagery or persistence of the Communist "gooks."'[31]

Newsweek, like Haffner, pointed to unscrupulous fighting tactics, warning that it would take a while before 'American power could overcome … surprise, treachery, and totalitarian preparedness.' The *Halifax Chronicle-Herald* picked up on the last theme, attributing early successes to the training and equipment provided by the Soviets, which meant that the North Koreans were no longer 'just a horde of fanatical natives.' 'Those who have some experience with various Asiatic armies,' agreed Canadian Colonel Goforth, 'will be the first to credit the Russian officers [assisting the North Korean military] with a record-breaking performance.'[32] Asians, to Goforth, simply could not compete with the West on the battlefield without outside help. The recent and highly effective armies raised by Japan and the People's Republic of China, to name but two, should have given pause. One is also led to wonder how many lives were lost while the architects of Western military strategy in Asia were disabused of the notions that the region's indigenous fighters were naturally inferior and its people would quickly bend to the display of 'ruthless force' visited upon them by the UN coalition forces.

Orientalist assumptions may also help to explain a circumstance bemoaned by early observers of the war: an alleged unwillingness on the part of Western soldiers to fight with tenacity in defence of South Korea. This point should be prefaced by acknowledging that Korea was a new kind of conflict. It was fought under a UN, rather than a national, flag. It took place in a theatre on the opposite side of the globe and involved an enemy that had not attacked either North American nation. It was referred to as a 'police action,' and its objectives were unclear from the outset. All of these factors may have contributed to the perceived lack of enthusiasm among Allied troops. It is also true that popular representations of Asians as fundamentally alien, backward, incapable of understanding political complexities, charmed by naked displays of power, and so on, would do little to encourage a sense of 'collective identity' between Westerners and their imperilled South Korean allies.

Six weeks into the war, the *Halifax Chronicle-Herald* commented on allegations that early U.S. defeats in Korea could be explained, in part, because their troops lacked the 'stamina' born of an unyielding will to fight. Such lassitude arises, according to the daily, when a soldier fails to understand 'that his cause is just' and 'that he is fighting for his own family.' The *Herald*, like the preponderance of voices emanating from the West in support of intervention in Korea, went on to demonstrate the justice of the cause by pointing to the UN authorization of the mission. That the soldiers were fighting for kin could have been established by taking up the 'family-of-man' and 'One-World' arguments that had enjoyed a brief but widespread influence at the conclusion of the Second World War, ideas reprised by the *Toronto Star*, above. Instead the *Herald*, like many others, interpreted the concept literally: because global communist strategy had progressed from 'subversion' to 'conquest,' Western soldiers were in fact defending their own nations, communities, and nuclear families. Further, should Canadian ground troops join the fight, they must 'be thoroughly indoctrinated' with these facts if they are to fight with appropriate zeal.[33]

Similarly, North Korean aggression, to the *Globe and Mail*, constituted a 'challenge to *our* civilization' and a 'menace' to 'the Western family of nations' (italics added). The *Vancouver Sun*, whose readers made up the Canadian residents nearest the conflict, determined that 'the affair in Korea' verified the need for a 'Pacific Pact' of nations. The paper's notoriously anti-Asian editorial board proposed that such a pact would bind Canada, Britain, and the United States, as well as Australia and New Zealand, the latter nations 'comprising two small white communities' faced with an 'overhanging menace.' Koreans, North and South, seemed virtually incidental to the conflict – both in popular discourses and official policy. As George Kennan told a closed meeting of NATO leaders on June 27, Truman's decision 'was not dictated by any overpowering consideration of the strategic importance of Korea itself,' but by a desire to safeguard American international prestige.[34]

Calgary Herald editors were not afraid to say it aloud, admitting that they 'don't imagine that many Occidentals care very deeply about what happens to Korea and the Koreans.' Rather, it was time to be 'cold-blooded and admit that we are fighting for nothing more and nothing less' in Korea than ourselves and our very 'national survival.' A *Globe and Mail* reader's 'cold-bloodedness' to the fate of Asia led him in another direction – toward fortress 'Americas.' Claiming that not 'one Canadian in a hundred' supported the 'squandering' of 'men and materials' on Koreans, the reader maintained that 'what Canada should work for now is an integration of defense of the Americas, from Hudson Bay to the tip of Cape Horn, and leave to non-Communists in Asia the task of preserving peace there; or if they prefer it, the present chaos.' Writes Canadian Cold War historian Robert Bothwell: 'Canada did not participate in the UN expedition to Korea because of any intrinsic concern for Korea and Koreans, but because of an interest in the UN, first, and in relations with the United States, second.'[35] Evidence presented above suggests a third foundational motivation: authentic fears that the final, all-out battle with communism had begun. 'Intrinsic concern' for Koreans, on the other hand, was a rare commodity, one tempered by the racial and cultural biases endemic in the popular and public culture of both the United States and Canada.

As the conflict dragged on, signs emerged that members of the public felt the intensive labours to save Asia from communism were not worth the effort involved – a sentiment echoed by some soldiers themselves, according to Blair Fraser. A December 1950 Canadian survey determined that much higher per centages supported sending troops to defend Europe (where there was no war), than had called, the previous July, for the provision of troops to Korea (where a state of war undeniably existed). A U.S. poll conducted in January 1951 found that 50 per cent of those surveyed considered American intervention in Korea a mistake – up from 20 per cent in August 1950 – and that a strong and growing majority of those with an opinion believed that it was more important to halt Russian expansionism in Europe than in Asia. Significantly, these trends do not reflect ebbing fears of the global communist conspiracy; McCarthyism, for example, was ascendant at the time. Nor do they represent a reversal of the conviction that Korea was a component of Stalin's 'master plan' (pollsters asked whether it was more important to 'Stop Russia' – not 'communism' – in Asia or in Europe). Similarly, these results do not denote a challenge to the rectitude of containment itself: a greater number of respondents advocated stopping Soviet expansion in Europe in this poll than they did in a survey conducted the previous September.[36]   Rather, with the costs of containment higher than many anticipated, it was necessary to make choices about who and what was worth saving – from what many Westerners, it should be re-emphasized, still believed was 'a fate worse than death.'

At the outset of UN involvement in Korea, however, few in the United States or Canada questioned the rectitude of foreign intervention in the conflict. I have pointed above to areas of great synchronicity in national attitudes toward the conflict in Korea, including its origins, its potential to spawn or thwart the Third World War, and its implications for defence spending. Consonant, too, were renderings of the peoples of Asia that could either deflate enthusiasm for intervention or lead supporters of intervention to emphasize that participation in Korea was primarily a defence of the West rather than South Korea. In short, visions of the nature of the threat faced by the West were virtually synonymous. However, disparities between Canadians and Americans emerged, and would broaden over time, concerning questions of war aims, strategies, and wider implications. The most consistent of these differences was apparent at the outset: was this a U.S.- or UN-led battle?

The UN Security Council's decision to authorize a military response to the crises in Korea represents the only such episode in the organization's history between its creation in 1945 and the end of the Cold War. It was a patent anomaly, one made possible by the absence from Security Council proceedings of the Russian delegate over the UN's failure to seat a representative from the People's Republic of China. Nonetheless, the Korean 'police action' was cheered in both the United States and Canada as a marker of the international body's renewed, and apparently now permanent, relevance: though a poll conducted on the eve of the conflict found faith in the UN's ability to prevent a general war at an all-time low, an August 1950 survey revealed a sharp rebound in public satisfaction with the organization, with recent resolutions on Korea cited most frequently as the basis of this new confidence.[37]

A survey conducted in December of that year, however, determined that Canadians and Americans differed markedly on their visions for the future of the UN. Fifty per cent of those in the United States maintained that excluding communist countries from the organization would make it easier for the UN 'to maintain peace in the world,' while only 29 per cent held the opposing view. In Canada those numbers were roughly reversed: 21 per cent versus 49 per cent, respectively.[38] This discrepancy points to broader national differences over matters involving internationalism, global leadership, the appropriate use of force, and the role of negotiation in maintaining international stability. Were U.S. international interests, approaches, and values synonymous with those of the 'free world' as a whole? Would the UN be most effective as a truly democratic body or under U.S. direction? Korea brought these issues to the fore, and revealed a less united array of 'free nations' than had been suggested, for instance, by the drafters and advocates of NATO.

For those who had stubbornly defended the UN throughout the late 1940s despite growing frustrations over its effectiveness, Security Council resolutions calling for a cessation of hostilities (June 25) and authorizing a military response (June 27) seemed to represent a long-awaited redemption. In this sense, 'Korea came along and saved' them, too. Perhaps the most resilient American exponent of the UN and the wider concept of multilateral global governance was the *Christian Century*, which titled its editorial on the collective international response to Korea 'Out of Darkness, Hope!' and called the UN 'the instrument which could prove our salvation.' Syndicated columnist Walter Lippmann concurred, insisting that the United States 'need[s] a UN which works' if it hopes to maintain peace in the world.[39]

Many observers north of the border expressed similar measures of optimism and relief that multilateralism had not been totally eclipsed by bipolarity and power politics. In fact, the views of the *Christian Century* and Lippmann had many more correlates in Canada than in the United States. *Maclean's* editors confessed that they had paid a great deal of 'pious lip service to the UN in the past,' even when the organization did not fully warrant that praise (and to the consistent 'sneers' of UN detractors). Korea, however, had at last established 'one thing: The United Nations, with all its faults and failings, has been worth while.' The *Canadian Forum* agreed that recent UN actions indeed 'revived hopes' that the body would serve as an effective deterrent to war, but cautioned that the conditions which rendered it effective in this case may not be present in the future and called for the establishment of a permanent UN military force to respond to future aggression. Others emphasized that Korea did not prove past UN detractors wrong as much as the conflict generated a radical shift in the organization's fortitude. 'The United Nations has suddenly acquired new vigor and importance,' marvelled the *Globe and Mail*; it has 'suddenly found itself,' observed the *Calgary Herald*.[40]

Had the UN 'found itself' by aligning its aims behind those of the United States, which throughout the Korean affair directed and manoeuvred the world body down paths that the Truman administration had already chosen? Several U.S. reports adopted this view, and praised their nation's leaders for taking firm control of the organization. Was this, then, a strengthening or a subversion of international will? Did the United States need the UN, or vice-versa? Though these latter questions received cursory treatment in many U.S.-based analyses, the issue of what all of this meant for the future of the UN, and what the international body's next move might be, did not appear to be of paramount importance.

The relative inattention paid by U.S. observers to the UN's role in Korea points to a fundamental variance in the Canadian versus American relationship to post-war internationalism. Canadian officials *required* UN authorization and direction of any proposed international participation in Korea in order to refute charges of U.S. imperialism – both in Korea and, more importantly, over Canada's foreign policy. The Truman administration, however, faced a series of powerful inducements toward a unilateralist rendering of U.S. actions on the peninsula, at least for domestic audiences. For one, though the desire for isolation within 'Fortress America' had been rendered obsolete by the experiences of two global wars and the technological improvements that served to 'shrink' the globe, notions of exceptionalism that underlay the old isolationism remained. In other words, the need to act in concert with other states was diminished not only by American preponderance following the Second World War, but also by deep-rooted ideas of national destiny that favoured U.S. global leadership over more democratic approaches to collective security, and that viewed American values as universal. In this sense, the new American internationalism was the child of both American nationalism and isolationism – was still 'America-first.' In political scientist Mark Peceny's succinct observation, 'Cycles of international interventionism and isolationism in the history of American foreign policy both flow from the same cultural pathologies.' The escalating global confrontation with communism would only amplify this sense of national righteousness and chosen-ness. Those on the right, in particular, could maintain both the disregard for Europe that characterized their earlier isolationism and a strong internationalist bearing by identifying Asia as the proper focus of U.S. interests beyond the Western Hemisphere, an orientation known as 'Asia-first.'[41]

Since members of the Republican Party constituted some of the most committed proponents of this combination of 'America-first' and 'Asia-first' approach to post-war internationalism *and* the party's polling numbers were rising, the Democratic president was under pressure to emphasize decisiveness and leadership in Asia for domestic audiences – thus redoubling the long-standing U.S. tendency, outlined by Fredrik Logevall, to embellish the nationalistic and moralistic aspects of international policy-making. The Soviet detonation of the Bomb in August 1949, and associated claims that the United States was rife with atomic traitors and spies, had increased anxieties and calls for 'toughness' in the face of the communist threat. The 'loss' of China in that same year, affixed to Truman and the Democrats, only amplified these pressures. Indeed, the so-called China lobby in the United States, the most visible manifestation of 'Asia-first' school, remained powerful even after Mao's victory on the mainland. The lobby's members, including *Time*'s Henry Luce and the Hearst and McCormick newspaper chains, immediately connected the Korean situation to China, and called for a pan-Asian, U.S.-led response to the rise of communism in the Far East.[42]

The lobby also existed in Congress as the 'China bloc'; as international relations historian Rosemary Foot observes, 'Though the bloc was small, the infrequency of attempts to oppose its arguments led it to assume a position of influence far beyond its actual size.'[43] At the same time, McCarthyite attacks on the 'spy-infested' State Department provided further inducement for the rightward trend in U.S. foreign policy-making. In all, from the outset of the Korean crisis, it was incumbent upon the president to verify that he was resolute, that he was directing rather than consulting with his international partners, that he was acting first and foremost in the national interest, and that he cared for Asia.

On many of these issues, Truman himself needed little prodding. Arnold Offner's biography of the president finds Truman among the most parochial and nationalistic leaders in U.S. history, one who considered rather narrowly defined U.S. values at once superior to all others, universally applicable, easily transmitted, and openly desired by the majority of the globe. Like those associated with the China lobby, he considered Korea a metaphor for all Asia, a 'testing ground' for U.S. resolve and credibility in the region. Convinced of his mission as an agent of divine justice, the president sought neither Congressional nor foreign input into his response to North Korean aggression, and rendered the rivalry between competing Korean regimes in stark, moralistic, and apocalyptic terms.[44]

The fact that both Truman and Acheson admitted that they would have gone to Korea with or without the UN serves as evidence of the profoundly unilateralist character of the administration's foreign policy at the time.[45] It also points to the American regime's primary objective in gaining the critical mass necessary to go forward with their action: in order to wage war, they would need the backing primarily of the U.S. public, and only secondarily (and optionally) of the international community. U.S. participation in Korea, in other words, required the former and not the latter. Thus, Truman's representation of the conflict necessarily relied upon doctrinaire appeals to nationalism and uncompromising American global leadership, themes taken up enthusiastically by the press and public in the earliest days of the war. At the same time, and importantly for our purposes, these decidedly unilateralist renderings could deflate foreign support for the venture; this was particularly true for Canada, the anticipated coalition member with unrivalled proximity to American views and a legacy of sensitivity to U.S. influence. As we will see, influential U.S. voices simultaneously condemned the inadequacy of the Allied contribution and presented the conflict in ways that complicated profoundly the ability of foreign audiences to support the venture.

This unilateralist take on the war would emerge from many directions. The president's own terse, 350-word press statement of June 27 was candid about who was in control of the defence of South Korea, and indeed of all Asia. 'I have ordered United States Air and Sea forces' to assist the Koreans, declared Truman. 'I have ordered the Seventh Fleet' to defend Formosa; 'I am calling upon the Chinese government on Formosa' to cease attacks on the mainland; 'I have also directed' U.S. forces be strengthened in the Philippines; 'I have similarly directed acceleration' of military assistance to the French colonial regime in Indo-China; 'I have instructed' the U.S. ambassador to the UN to inform the Security Council of (rather than debate) these actions; and finally, a veiled warning to accede to U.S. authority: 'I know that all members of the United Nations will consider carefully the consequences of this latest aggression in Korea ... The United States [for one] will continue to uphold the rule of law.'[46] The American president, it appeared, possessed the capacity to direct the course of events on the other side of the globe and in a half-dozen geopolitical contexts, as well as in the UN itself, simply by fiat. More importantly, here was determined action undertaken by a single individual in consultation with no other within or beyond American borders, on behalf of his own nation but with the expectation that the global community would fall into line behind his dictates. Action had preceded, indeed precluded, debate; decisive U.S. military leadership had obviated the painstaking work of assembling a multinational force under UN command prior to engagement in battle. Old fears of sending U.S. troops to fight under the command of a weak-willed international body had been undercut. It was a speech that sited domestic political concerns at the fore.

Truman's tough and unilateral approach worked, at least at the beginning, as the public, press, and Congress rallied behind the formerly maligned leader. Even the president's harshest Republican critics, including Joseph McCarthy, voiced their approval. U.S. reports were similarly unambiguous about who was in the driver's seat in the region and the world. *Newsweek*'s Ernest Lindley credited Truman with 'saving' the UN, and spoke plainly about the fact that the State Department and the nation's diplomatic corps were shepherding predetermined U.S. policy through the international body 'with speed and sure-handed skill.' *Time* pointed out that it was Ernest Goss, U.S. deputy representative to the UN, who had awoken UN Secretary General Trygve Lie at 3 a.m. on June 25 with a request to assemble the Security Council, and that Goss had also tabled the resolution ultimately adopted. *New York Times'* Paris correspondent Anne O'Hare McCormick reported that French officials were pleased that the torch of global leadership had passed from Europe directly to the United States ('America has grown up,' noted one); no mention was made of the role of the supposedly supreme governing body of international affairs. The paper's editors, meanwhile, shared Secretary Acheson's satisfaction that that the 'free world' had come to embrace 'American policy' in Korea. *Time* provided an exhaustive, ten-page overview of the Korean situation in its July 10 edition, though readers would need to soldier on to the bottom of the ninth page to find an account of the UN debates over the appropriate response to North Korea's invasion. This discussion followed detailed analysis of Truman's conduct, Congressional deliberations, U.S. public attitudes, the first days of the battle itself, and MacArthur's overall strategy.[47] In short, this was a U.S. battle, initiated and directed by the president, and one in which American soldiers – at this point, alone among UN member nations – were fighting and dying.

These American renderings of the Korean conflict point to the persistent dilemma faced by U.S. leaders who seek to assemble both domestic and international consent for military action. In this instance, those in Canada who supported a vigorous rather than tokenist response by their own government could respond to the unilateralist and imperial tendencies in U.S. narratives about Korea by (1) seeking to reinscribe the U.S.-led response to Korea as a truly multilateral exercise, as an exemplar of liberal internationalism; (2) de-emphasizing the importance of Canadian nationalism and fears of American dominance in the face of a broader and more ominous threat to Western civilization / the free world; (3) representing the United States as simply a belated but welcome partner in the centuries-old project of Western European management of the globe; and (4) assuring Canadians that through participation in Korea, American unilateralism and imperialism would be attenuated and Canadian values would be represented on the international stage. I will address each of these approaches in turn.

Though the UN took a back seat in many U.S. accounts, to many Canadians the Security Council's sanctioning of a military response to North Korean aggression was *the* story, even though that sanctioning occurred after the United States had presented the UN with a *fait accompli* in Korea. UN authorization was imperative, noted *Maclean's*, so that Canada would not be seen 'as the tail to an American kite. As one External Affairs man put it, "We can't jump from an imperial frying pan into an American fire."' External affairs minister Lester Pearson informed the House of

Commons that the government supported 'the action taken by the Security Council because it represents collective action through the United Nations for peace.' Pearson then led the House through a labyrinthine dissection of the UN Charter as it applied to checking acts of aggression prior to Security Council authorization; he concluded that in an emergency, such unilateral actions were permissible among 'individual members of the Security Council, acting within the terms of the Charter, but on their own initiative,' a set of criteria that would appear rife for subjective interpretation by various Security Council members of diverse international agendas.[48]

This, at least, was the official line. In private, Pearson and the ruling Liberals expressed surprise that the United States had chosen to take a stand over South Korea, considered the 'UN intervention' in Korea a decidedly American initiative and a violation of the UN Charter, and endeavoured to commit as little to the fight as possible. In fact, Pearson initially labelled the conflict a civil war, one that did not call for a UN response.[49] The external affairs minister's true feelings are best summed up in a memorandum to the prime minister the day that news of the conflict reached the West:

> Surely if the United States wished to intervene in this way, it should be done after the matter had been discussed at the Security Council and appropriate action had been taken there through a resolution, which would bring such intervention within the terms of the Charter. As the Security Council was meeting this very afternoon, no delay would be involved in the United States bringing the matter before it. What the President was proposing was action which might mean U.S. intervention, but which would not be collective action as a result of any collective decision. This would mean that the U.S. would take the action and would expect other countries later to support and sanction it. I felt that this was the wrong way to proceed, even though I realized that the time element was so important.[50]

Such misgivings remained well hidden to *Saturday Night* editors, who guaranteed that if hesitant Quebec politicians 'or Pravda or anybody else says we're being blindly dragged along by the US, they know nothing of the feeling in Government.' The *Ottawa Citizen* simply reversed the timeline of events in order to maintain the semblance of international law, claiming that the United States had 'responded immediately' to the UN appeal for assistance to South Korea. The *Globe and Mail*'s earliest editorials called the unilateral U.S. action 'technically' illegal, though one justified by the circumstances.[51]

Other supporters of Canadian intervention in Korea offered perhaps too much protest against the notion that the defence of South Korea had taken on the air of an American war. The Security Council resolutions, noted the Department of External Affairs' monthly report, 'demonstrated clearly to the world that the action undertaken in Korea was, notwithstanding the preponderance of American forces, a United Nations undertaking.' The *Globe and Mail* held that as early as July 4th, as the United States fought alone alongside South Korean forces, 'a world government, or something nearly approaching it, is at this moment functioning in defence of Korea.' 'This is a UN war,' the *Vancouver Sun* noted plainly, a fact that Canadians, who are 'supposed to be most UN-minded, seem to be forgetting.' 'A U.N. Flag, a U.N. Commander,' headlined a *Regina Leader-Post* editorial, after the widely praised (especially in Canada) decision to have troops fight under the UN banner.[52]

Again, however, officials' off-the-record statements contradicted their public mantras to multilateralism. A June 28 memorandum to Pearson from Canada's ambassador to the United States, Hume Wrong, epitomized the PR conundrum faced by prospective coalition partners in Korea: while stressing the need to frame the defence of South Korea as a UN Security Council prerogative, Wrong pointed out that 'offers of assistance should not, in the view of the State Department, be addressed to the Security Council, which has no responsibility for directing the operations now in progress.' Two days later, Canada's permanent delegate to the UN assured Pearson that both the United States and Britain were 'bending as far as possible to give this all the characteristics of a United Nations project,' as 'there must be some United Nations cover for the operation.'[53]

The *Toronto Star* offered a way out of the current quandary of using U.S. power to defend purported UN interests, predicting a permanent UN army 'will be built up gradually into a formidable force, giving the United Nations prestige and authority that the old League of Nations never possessed.' CCF leader M.J. Coldwell urged the Liberal government to take the lead in organizing this permanent global force. In sum, if it was important to Canadian national identity and autonomy that the nation's foreign policy be determined by an international collective and not a single hegemon, it was vital to downplay the undeniable U.S. control over the current operation, or to present it as a provisional state of affairs. This *was* a truly multilateral endeavour, defenders insisted – at least, that is, until things went wrong. At that point, Canadians were apt to point fingers at a single and familiar culprit. When North Korean forces achieved surprising gains in the first weeks of the war, the *Globe and Mail* impugned only the 'bad management in Washington.' After the entry of China led to stalemate, Canadians searched for a scapegoat: 'more often than not it turned out to be US leadership,' wrote *Time*.[54] On the whole, however, the alleged UN direction of the Western coalition remained an important and consistent theme in Canada's early Korean War coverage.

A second general response to the dilemma posed by the unambiguous American primacy regarding Western policy-making was to admit this fact frankly, and to prepare Canadians for an increasingly Americanized future. Part of this desire for closer interaction between the two nations stemmed from the wartime need to integrate economic production. After an August 1950 U.S.-Canada summit generated a bilateral agreement to coordinate war supplies, a Canadian official assured that his nation will become 'a 49th state as far as war production is concerned.' A *Saturday Night* cartoonist heralded the agreement with a depiction of the U.S. Capitol and Canadian Parliament buildings united by a giant conveyer belt labelled 'cooperation'; the same publication called for further progress in arms standardization between the United States and Canada.[55]

Shortly after UN involvement in the Korean conflict began, the Canadian state itself sought to strengthen the feelings of kinship and gloss over traditional enmities between the North American neighbours. In a testament to anxieties surrounding the unprecedented act of following the United States rather than Britain into war, Canada's Department of External Affairs promptly issued a brochure entitled 'Canada and the United States.' The publication praised the close bilateral cooperation in defence, in industry and trade, and in resource management. It highlighted the presence of common multinational organizations, including labour unions and 'Ducks Unlimited,' and similarities in culture, standards of living, and ethnic makeup. Terms like 'cooperation,' 'coordination,' 'exchange,' 'equity,' and 'reciprocity' abound in the document; this was patently not a relationship involving unequals, domination, or any vestige of neo-colonialism (cultural parity, for example, was confirmed by the presence of '100 Canadian works' in a 1949 Boston art exhibition).[56]

Early in July, the *Halifax Chronicle-Herald* wrote that simply strengthening relations with the United States was not enough in the face of 'the unanimity and cohesion of totalitarian policy and action.' Corroborating a recent letter to the *London Times* by eminent British historian Arnold Toynbee, the *Herald* submitted that like other Western nations Canada may need to renounce national sovereignty if it wishes to survive the threat of global communism, though the editors at first favoured a broad union of 'the Democracies' over simple absorption into the United States. Later that month, they whittled their proposal down to a simple 'federation of ... this North American continent' (though they appeared to forget that Mexico also inhabited the land mass), one which would share a common foreign policy, military, and currency, and would permit the free exchange of goods and services. '[H]onoring the American flag' under the current circumstances 'is almost like honoring our own,' noted the *Herald* a few weeks later. 'Canada would surely throw her whole weight into the movement to federate,' syndicated columnist Elmore Philpott assured a U.S. audience.[57]

These were not simply the armchair musings of editorial boards: at the outset of the Korean War, members of both the American and Canadian Senates called for a convention to discuss the formal federation of interested NATO members. Not surprisingly, the chief difference between the Canadian and U.S. proposals lay in the geographic location of the proposed Atlantic federation capital; here, 'outmoded' nationalisms swiftly rematerialized. Talk of a formal continental and/or Atlantic federation was so ubiquitous in the first months of the war that Pearson felt it necessary to declare that the increasingly intimate relationship between Canada and the United States 'should not be misconstrued as meaning that Canada is moving inevitably and happily into union with the United States.'[58]

Tensions over the question of global leadership are also present in numerous Canadian political cartoons of the era, as commentators struggled to represent the new world order. Uncle Sam, often lampooned as a bullying, predatory, insensitive, and/or boorish figure in previous Canadian discourse, is in many of these illustrations reconfigured in heroic idioms, and as an icon of the UN rather than merely the United States. In one, Douglas MacArthur assumes the 'I-Want-You' pose traditionally struck by Uncle Sam in time of war, though the general stands before a UN flag, while his shirt collar bears the designation 'UN Commander MacArthur.' Other cartoons depict a hyper-masculine and righteously indignant Uncle Sam commanding a UN army, or at the head of a collection of other nations' personifications (John Bull, a Canadian Mountie, etc.). An illustration in the *Regina Leader-Post* shows a sun adorned with stars and stripes rising over 'the Orient,' its radiance dispelling 'skepticism, fear, hopelessness, cynicism, lack of faith, insecurity.' A later cartoon in the same paper shows determined U.S. troops holding a trench line in front of a flag bearing both 'United Nations' and 'US.' As a British and French soldier arrive on the scene, the former declares: 'U.S. – That also spells "Us."'[59] Still a neophyte organization, the UN lacked the identity and iconography through which these artists could depict a collective international response to Korea. Instead, U.S. symbols were simply reassigned to the world body, a practice that did little to dispel the notion that the United States controlled Korean operations, or that the values and aspirations of the American nation were synonymous with those of the globe.

A third interpretation of the interplay between U.S. and UN control over world affairs took the form of lauding Americans' submission to models of international stability and regulation developed by Europeans, particularly Britain. For all intents and purposes, this amounted to a celebration of imperialism as a civilizing and pacifying entity, and as a vehicle for the transmission of liberal rather than communist ideals. The flip side of these notions involved the assertion that Third World nationalism was simply a Trojan horse for international communism, and that even sincere nationalists amounted to Stalinist dupes. The irony inherent in this move was that American officials and political analysts took great pains to represent their actions in Korea as simple state-to-state assistance rather than another instance of Western manipulation in Asia. Canadian imperial apologists, as noted in chapter 3 a healthy constituency, did them few favours in this regard. To many Canadians, however, viewing the American-led mission in Korea in such terms would have lent a familiar and comforting air to the emergence of American global supremacy, while also serving as a reproof of long-standing American denunciations of European colonialism; the nascent American globalism was less the rising of a new empire than the amalgamation of U.S. and British global interests.

The Tory *Globe and Mail* took the lead, proclaiming in a series of editorials the connections between America's ward – Korea – and European imperial holdings. '[T]he United States, by its leadership in Korea,' they explained, 'is only catching up with Britain and France in the defence of Asiatic bridgeheads against the Red threat.' To the *Globe*, the basic difference between U.S. military operations in Korea and British and French operations against spurious 'nationalist' insurgencies in their colonies was that the European powers were 'putting down insurrection on home ground and [thus] do not require UN approval' (nor were they likely to received it!). 'In light of Asian events,' they continued with evident triumphalism, 'it should be clear that so-called Western "imperialism" and action in the name of the UN can have the same good intentions and use the same methods.' When the *Buffalo Evening News* charged that other UN members were not contributing enough to Korea and included Britain on its list of 'slackers,' the *Globe* was incensed, pointing to the thankless sacrifice by thousands of British troops in Malaya, 'a more important peninsula than Korea from the economic and military points of view.' An embittered *Calgary Herald* recalled the 'great deal of abuse from American critics' that the British had endured over efforts to 'pacify' Third World subjects inflamed by self-seeking communist agitators. 'The Americans ... were very slow to appreciate' what the British and French were dealing with in Asia, agreed *Saturday Night*'s Willson Woodside. *Winnipeg Tribune* editors concurred, cheering that the United States had at last joined 'Britain, France, and [Nationalist] China ... in trying to hold some line in Southeast Asia against the onrush of Communism.'[60] Those fearing that policies of containment could serve simply as the latest embodiment of Western domination would not have been soothed by these words.

Even the *Toronto Star*, which in debates over Indian independence had advised Britain to rescind both its colonial holdings and its associated 'delusions of national grandeur,' now reversed its view of that nation's global mandate. Though its resources were currently taxed by various flashpoints of 'communist-inspired' revolt, Britain had nonetheless determined to provide troops to Korea, for history's most extensive colonizer was, to the *Star*, 'ever in the forefront of struggles to preserve human liberty.' *Halifax Chronicle-Herald* editors agreed that Britain's struggle to maintain its imperial holdings against various insurgencies was not merely an attempt to shore up 'national grandeur.' Rather, Britain's overseas territories were 'essential to the protection of the sea lanes and the huge oil deposits upon which an increasing proportion of the world is dependent.' And because sustaining colonial administrations meant these lands remained in the 'Western sphere,' the paper recommended the common term 'Outposts of Empire' be replaced with the cringingly inappropriate 'Outposts of Democracy.'[61]

U.S. narratives treaded this ground with greater caution. They certainly did not deny the presence of communists in various indigenous insurgencies against foreign rule, or challenge the reductionist view that all 'slogans of freedom and independence' amounted to little more than Stalinist propaganda designed to forge 'heavier chains of slavery than even Asia had ever known.' Previous Western colonialism, in other words, was the kinder of two varieties of foreign domination, and might be useful as a short-term adjunct to the strategy of containment. The *Saturday Evening Post* went so far as to suggest that U.S. decolonization efforts had proven rash, as they had 'left a power vacuum in Asia' which the Russians were now exploiting.[62] Even so, the perpetuation of colonial empires was not recommended as a permanent solution to global governance, and few apologies were offered for earlier American condemnation of European colonialism. This overall bearing owes its impetus to both the anti-imperial sentiment at the core of U.S. ideology, as well as the belief that American involvement in the Third World was of an altogether different – that is, exceptional – character when juxtaposed to European colonialism.

Despite these views, U.S. officials did not deny that involvement in Korean affairs might carry the taint of previous Western intervention in Asia. While this was a UN mission comprising twenty-one member countries, in truth most of the non-Korean combatants in the UN coalition were from nations dominated by whites. This racial uniformity was in part a reflection of the U.S. military's hesitation to invite troops whose language, diet, and religion would prove difficult to integrate into existing U.S. operations. Still, Secretary of State Acheson and the State Department understood that participation by a strong contingent of Asian nations would have important symbolic value, and hoped for a more enthusiastic response from states in the region. India, for instance, an emerging spokesperson for Third World interests, offered just one field ambulance unit. Numerous mainstream American and Canadian publications lamented, and in many cases railed against, the alleged indifference of the non-white world to the plight of American-led efforts to defend South Korea: *Newsweek*'s Ernest Lindley regretted that his hope 'the free nations of Asia, large and small, would be quick to respond' was quickly dashed; the *Saturday Evening Post* condemned the 'deafening' apathy to the communist threat among Asians, attributing this unresponsiveness to the 'revolutionary rot which has made most of Asia so unreliable as a cold war asset'; *Time* blamed 'the Red propaganda line of "white man's aggression" in Asia'; Willson Woodside located the success of this transparent propaganda campaign in the region's backward populace and 'immature politicians,' the result being 'countless millions of deluded Asians [willing] to fight for Communist aims, while the Western nations must do their own fighting.'[63]

The few self-styled progressive voices that remained in both the United States and Canada, meanwhile, cited the history of Western imperialism as the logical basis of the disobliging Third World response to the UN mission. Both the *Canadian Forum* and the *Christian Century* made this a consistent theme in editorials published in the first months of the war, and held that only a truly multilateral solution to the Korean crisis – one that paid heed to the concerns of local inhabitants and other states in the region – would produce a lasting peace. Communism was indeed a concern in Asia, noted the *Forum*, but the West must also acknowledge 'a deep-rooted distrust of Western powers [and] a desire for independence' in the region. 'Make this truly a U.N. venture,' insisted the *Christian Century* in the first weeks of the war. 'It has hardly been so far. The impression so far has been that decisions have been made in Washington and communicated to Lake Success.' If this unilateralist approach to Asia continues, the journal feared, the United States would simply inherit the very 'stigma Britain is trying to eradicate' in the region. And like Britain, the United States would one day be shocked at the 'ingratitude' displayed by subject peoples who did not see the altruism in Western-imposed 'order and uplift.' Canada's *International Journal* published a summary of the roots of the Korean conflict by C. Clyde Mitchell, a specialist on Asia and Chair of the Department of Agricultural Economics at the University of Nebraska, who found U.S. assistance programs – funnelled to 'a reactionary property-owning class of feudal aristocracy' – redolent of neo-colonialism. Paul Robeson, though at this point maligned even by most in the black press, warned that the American action in Korea was a prelude to similar incursions into Africa. Even the pro-war *Saturday Night* conceded that state-sanctioned racism harmed the UN coalition's prospects, citing Canada's anti-Asian immigration policies as one reason South Koreans might choose to cooperate with invading communist forces.[64]

The most unexpected adherents to the idea that a legacy of Western domination in Asia was the UN coalition's 'Achilles heel' were publications that simultaneously extolled British imperialism as a force of global stability. The *Halifax Chronicle-Herald* maintained that 'the greatest need in the Far East, beyond firmness, is a solidarity of policy between the Democracies, founded on the nationalistic ambitions of the Eastern peoples most concerned.' The *Globe and Mail* was of similar mind, stating simply that the war could not be won without an affiliated commitment to democracy and the rule of law; both papers found the regime of Syngman Rhee decidedly lacking in these attributes. These emphatically Tory dailies were willing to undertake a judicious appraisal of recent Western machinations in Korea largely because those activities did not involve Britain, and in fact could be used to accentuate the alleged superiority of British governance. The *Herald* cited the Dutch in Indonesia and the United States in China and South Korea as evidence of how *not* to go about gaining local favour, while claiming that the 'liberation of India' had bolstered British prestige throughout the Far East. The *Globe* claimed that the United States habitually supports 'inefficient, corrupt and reactionary' leaders in Asia, while Britain grooms 'high-minded patriot[s]' with 'lofty ethical principles' like Nehru for leadership before they transfer power to their colonial subjects.[65]

Canada's Empire Loyalists played a rather transparent and defective card in maligning one type of foreign control while eulogizing another. Throughout the era, subject-peoples across the Third World actively challenged obstacles to 'home rule' regardless of which foreign entity limited their autonomy; to claim that resistance to U.S. control confirmed ineffective and unwelcome governance while (numerous) insurrections against Britain served merely as proof of Stalinist manipulation was patently simplistic, and fit too neatly into older patterns of anglophilia and its attendant anti-Americanism. Yet it is also true that Canadians from across the political, ethnic, and regional spectrum were more likely to scrutinize – and criticize – the type of regime the UN had pledged to prop up in South Korea. U.S. narratives rarely broached the subject of Rhee's flagrant corruption, brutality toward his own people, and contempt for transparency, democracy, and the rule of law – though here again, the *Christian Century* stands as something of a voice in the wilderness. The *New York Times* presented a simple and rather inflated polarity between the 'free and democratic government' of the South with the North's 'puppet regime' shored up by foreign armaments and advisors. *Time* and *Newsweek* made no mention of Rhee's objectionable conduct, choosing instead to depict the autocrat in language consonant with American ideals and identity. Rhee was 'the good doctor,' a freedom fighter and democrat possessing an Ivy-league education, an accomplished politician who was also an ordained Methodist minister.[66]

Canada's press corps appeared less charmed by the reverend. The *Canadian Forum* called both Chiang and Rhee 'stinkers'; *Saturday Night* labelled South Korea a 'dictatorship.' Blair Fraser of *Maclean's* warned that a truly democratic Korea-wide election might bring the communists to power, so loathed was the alternative – and, unlike the communists, so loath was it to take up the necessary issue of land reform. Syndicated columnist Elmore Philpott held that the United States could not win a psychological war or a shooting war if it continues to back 'crooks, corrupt ruling classes, or reactionaries. That fact – and not the Communist appeal – was the prime cause of the debacle in China.' While conservative voices like the *Globe and Mail* could use Rhee to underscore their preference for British global leadership, right-wing analysts from the Canadian West, who lacked the 'eastern establishment's' levels of affection for Britannia and coolness toward the United States, also denounced the regime. Three weeks into the fighting, and amid their strenuous efforts to compel the Canadian government to commit ground forces to Korea, *Calgary Herald* editors informed readers of recent mass executions by Rhee that, for the paper, confirmed the essentially anti-democratic character of the regime.[67]

These assessments of Rhee are based in part on the fact that Canada's UN delegation had protested as unrepresentative the elections that brought Rhee to power. Thus, the nation had little sense of direct responsibility for Rhee; he was not, in diplomatic parlance, 'their man.' But the willingness to emphasize complexities in the Korean situation, and to hold the West accountable to its own stated ideals, goes beyond the matter of Rhee: with notable exceptions, Canadian analysts, opinion polls, diplomats, and politicians displayed a greater accord with more idealistic and democratic currents of liberal internationalism in their representations of the Asian crisis than their American counterparts; the latter exhibited greater measures of 'realism,' conservatism, 'toughness,' and straightforward assessments of good and evil. This divergence points to a fourth means of encouraging Canadians to actively support the war effort: in addition to overplaying its multilateral character, stressing the folly of Canadian autonomy in a hostile, bipolar world, and depicting U.S. intervention as a redemption of British imperialism, war proponents believed that participation in Korea would provide Canadians with the means and licence to monitor and moderate American policy-making in the affair. Such a desire displays echoes of the heightened international role Canadians had enjoyed during the Second World War; too, it denotes a perception that American and Canadian international policies, interests, and values were not precisely analogous.

Once again, these general nation-based orientations point to the simple fact that more democratic and idealistic variants of liberal internationalism, as opposed to sheer power politics, better served the interests of less powerful nation-states. In addition, they indicate that the differing visions of global governance identified at the beginning of this study regarding the Bomb were not completely flattened by the often crude anti-communism of the Cold War. Importantly, these national distinctions also call attention to a circumstance apparent throughout the Canadian state's attempts to position itself in the early years of the Cold War, though perhaps most evident over the crucial question of war. Put simply, the presence of two major and distinct linguistic and cultural groups, each expressing what were often markedly different ideas on vital domestic and international issues, *and each possessing considerable electoral power*, proscribed a governing culture of unambiguous, unitary state action. To reprise John Ralston Saul, the nation's coexistent English and French blocs frustrated efforts to enforce 'a reality which could produce a centralized mythology.'[68] As such, policy questions frequently possessed more than one possible response, and successful management of matters of state depended upon at least the veneer of debate, negotiation, and compromise. This embedded heterodoxy, coupled with perennial fears of playing 'the tail to an American kite,' required that Canadian elites proceed with caution on matters of foreign policy, that they stake out positions that gave some impression of independence from the United States and consonance with this domestic multiplicity.

War in Korea brought aspects of these national characteristics to the fore: in the United States, the aforementioned amalgam of the Soviet detonation of the Bomb, McCarthyism, and the 'loss' of China had pushed political discourse further to the right, toward political realism, action, and certitude. Alternative visions, by definition, could be found almost exclusively to the left of these orientations, and toward an emphasis on the complexity and intractability of mid-century international affairs. Moreover, Canadian 'opinion-makers,' while certainly not immune to the spell of anti-communism, had learned from past experience that war in particular threatened to divide, even destroy, the nation along linguistic lines. When contemplating the deployment of armed forces abroad, Canadian officials were predisposed to proceed with a sensitivity to francophones' greater affinities for pacifism, isolationism, and anti-imperialism.

Elements of these discrepant national responses to the 1950 international setting are present in the aforementioned attitudes to unilateralism versus multilateralism, in polls asking whether to expel the Russians from the UN, and in evaluations of Rhee. A series of related questions that emerged at the beginning of the Korean crisis lent further clarity to the contours of these differing perspectives. For one, did open war with the communist bloc imply that military assistance should now supersede other forms of economic aid? In general, Canadian analysts placed greater emphasis on the notion that the global struggle could not be won by force alone. Even the hawkish *Saturday Night* warned of the 'danger of becoming pre-occupied by the techniques of force and extinction' and thereby neglecting the role of mediation and education in addressing the global rift. To the *New York Times,* by contrast, Korea proved that 'nothing counted' – not diplomacy, regional defence pacts, or economic assistance – 'except force in being.' Observing these contrasting national outlooks with disappointment, the *Calgary Herald*'s Richard Needham proposed a new and constructive way for Canada's bleeding hearts to find succour. 'While [the United States] held the fort,' he argued, 'we have been drooling over the underprivileged. The underprivileged, right now, are the American troops in Korea.' Ultimately Needham's view would carry the day, as after the fighting in Korea began, U.S. foreign aid moved from the economic to the military realm in dramatic fashion.[69]

A parallel debate centred on the question of whether to encourage attempts by Indian prime minister Nehru to negotiate a settlement between the Koreas, and to include other neutral and regional states in the process. Most Canadian publications held at least a measure of approval for the peace initiative of a fellow middle power and Commonwealth partner, agreeing with the *Ottawa Citizen*'s assessment that Nehru would bring to the crisis 'a powerful element of Asiatic opinion and nationalism that stands above suspicion in the eyes of millions of Asiatics.' Again, the *Calgary Herald* noted Canadians' apparent partiality for dialogue with alarm, wondering 'whether we have not been deluded into thinking that international conferences and patient negotiation are an alternative to well-girded defences.' Aside from the black press, which held Nehru in high regard, U.S. analysts tended to agree with their ambassador to the UN, Warren Austin, who considered Nehru at best meddlesome, at worst a tool of Stalin. For these reasons, Austin and the mainstream press opposed both negotiations with a malevolent communist state and any perceived rewards for aggression. *Maclean's* blamed the climate engendered by 'Senator McCarthy' for the stateside dismissal of Nehru's initiative as 'appeasement' and communist-inspired, and expressed gratitude that 'in Canada we have been relatively free of unbridled witch-hunting of this kind.'[70]

Similar issues surrounded a lingering question that gained prominence with the crisis in Korea: should the People's Republic of China be seated at the UN, or should the West back the Chinese Nationalists under Chiang? Greater per centages of Canadian politicians, journalists, and average citizens supported recognition of Mao's regime, and generally opposed attempts to link the defence of South Korea to that of Nationalist China. This refusal openly flummoxed leading U.S. correspondents in Asia, but underlined an appreciation for Chiang's corruption, Mao's nationalism, and the limits of Western power. On the eve of the Korean conflict, polls indicated a majority of 'informed' Canadians believed Canada should recognize the PRC, while 62 per cent of 'informed' Americans opposed recognition. Once the war was under way, many Canadian analysts, like their leaders, strenuously opposed the broadening of the UN mandate to include support for Nationalist forces in Formosa. The larger lesson, according to the *Canadian Forum*, was that the nation supported the fight against North Koreans, 'not because they are communists, *but because they are guilty of an act of aggression*' (italics in original).[71] Canada should not, in other words, hand a blank check to the Pentagon to help bankroll a global anti-communist campaign.

Differences would emerge, too, over the question of a suitable UN commander for the mission. Was Douglas MacArthur, a proponent of American 'neo-isolationist' internationalism, the 'Asia-first' school of thought, and the rollback of communism in the Far East, a judicious choice? While a select few in the United States expressed wariness regarding the general – the *Christian Century* found his imperiousness a threat to the Constitution and a detriment to America's relations with Asia – no observer attacked MacArthur earlier or harder than the *Canadian Forum*'s Frank Underhill, who referred to him as 'that phony demigod,' a man 'who may not be capable of thought.' At the outset, however, Canadians generally expressed approvals ranging from guarded to unequivocal. 'There can be no arguing over the choice of General MacArthur,' wrote *Regina Leader-Post* editors, calling him 'one of the most able soldiers in the world.' Support for the general would appear to imply approval of his confrontational stance toward Asia, and thus seems paradoxical alongside simultaneous Canadian endorsement of the PRC and of Nehru's peace initiative. Few openly acknowledged the contradiction beyond Willson Woodside, who subheaded a discussion of broad war methods 'Nehru or MacArthur?' – and endorsed the latter.[72]

Mass circulation publications in the United States, meanwhile, seemed locked in an Olympian battle to demonstrate greatest obsequiousness toward MacArthur. *Newsweek*'s Harry Kern caught up with the general in Tokyo, heralded the commander's latest 'rendez-vous with destiny,' and depicted MacArthur scoffing at the objections of his personal pilot and manfully ordering a June 29 reconnaissance trip to Korea, despite foul weather and the possibility of enemy attack: 'We go!'

was the brusque command to his hesitant charge. The *New York Times* dedicated an entire, and entirely fawning, editorial to his appointment – so reverent, in fact, that readers may have wondered why the general did not spare his pilot's nerves on June 29 and simply walk across the Sea of Japan to Korea.[73] *Time* bested its journalistic rivals, however, with the following homage, offered up with no subsequent analysis or qualification whatsoever:

> Inside the Dai Ichi Building [MacArthur's Tokyo headquarters], once the heart of a Japanese insurance empire, bleary-eyed staff officers looked up from stacks of paper, whispered proudly, 'God, the man is great.' General Almond, his chief of staff, said straight out, 'He's the greatest man alive.' And reverent Air Force General George E. Stratemeyer put it as strongly as it could be put (even in the Dai Ichi Building): 'He's the greatest man in history.'[74]

William Stueck, not the first to declare MacArthur 'vain and egotistical,' finds that 'those serving under him were for the most part sycophants and mediocrities who encouraged his least attractive qualities.' Stueck's model of cause and effect is substantiated rather pointedly by the foregoing exchange. Just as plainly, journalists who reported on MacArthur in tones that would make monotheists wince also bear a portion of the blame for puffing the general to proportions that would oblige unceremonious deflation. After Truman fired MacArthur for insubordination in April of 1951, public opinion surveys found that 56 per cent of Americans disapproved of the general's dismissal, while only 25 per cent of Canadians held the same view, statistics that echo the divergent tone of respective national media representations.[75]

Before his sacking, MacArthur's 'tough' stance and his 'grasp' of Asians' appreciation of ruthless force had led him to recommend extensive use of the ultimate weapon against his adversaries. The question of whether to drop the Bomb emerged almost immediately after U.S. intervention in Korea, and remained one of the most controversial issues throughout the conflict. In a testament to this sensitivity, news publications often placed calls for the use atomic weaponry in the mouths of others, especially unnamed average citizens. *Time*'s survey of the U.S. public mood in early August alleged a widespread desire to 'drop the atom bomb on Moscow. "Let's end it before it starts" was a phrase frequently heard.' The same magazine's summary of early Canadian opinion on the war included a quote from New Brunswick's

St. John Times Globe endorsing the use of the Bomb; *Time* presented no contrary views from north of the border, implying that the outlook was more or less representative.[76]

In fact, such opinions were atypical. The *Halifax Chronicle-Herald* sanctioned the use of the Bomb only as a last resort; more characteristic were the opinions of the *Ottawa Citizen* and *Regina Leader-Post*, which opposed the Bomb on strategic, political, and moral grounds – arguing that atomic bombing would stiffen North Korean resistance, turn all of Asia against the West, and place its practitioners on the same plane as terrorists and fascists. *Le Devoir* editors responded to the outbreak of war with an impassioned appeal to remove the atomic bomb from any discussions of combat strategy 'before,' as they noted in their title, 'it is too late.' *Time* later acknowledged that Canadian opinion ran strongly against the use of the Bomb, with objections loudest among Quebecers – though an anonymous Toronto 'oil truck driver' still urged UN forces to '"drop the damn bomb."'[77]

U.S. observers articulated a wider range of opinion on the issue. The *Saturday Evening Post* produced an especially forceful condemnation of the Bomb and an expression of regret for its past use. Noting that 'the wisdom of the decision to introduce atomic warfare to the world has since become increasingly debatable,' the publication argued that America's image would be damaged immeasurably by another bombing in Asia. Those favouring use of the Bomb included many of the Hearst and McCormick newspapers, as well as veterans' organizations, a number of elected representatives in Washington, and select members of the Truman administration and defence establishment. Truman himself did not rule out the use of the Bomb in a November 1950 press conference, a comment that provoked widespread anxiety among diplomats, politicians, and the general public throughout the globe, and one that led British prime minister Clement Attlee on an emergency visit to the White House. Howard Smith, London correspondent to the *Nation*, called the reaction in Western Europe 'a rebellion ... against the kind of leadership America was giving to the West on the Korean issue.' In Canada, too, there arose a general outcry over the president's remarks, as well as an increased resistance to the U.S. management of the war. Repeating a similar call by Britain, External Affairs Minister Pearson demanded that U.S. allies, including Canada, be permitted to participate in any discussions regarding the use of the Bomb. *Time*'s Ottawa correspondent observed that 'many newspapers across the nation splashed news that Prime Minister Attlee was flying to Washington almost as though the editors were turning to the old country for cautious guidance that the US had failed to provide.'[78]

Even before Truman's remark, the Canadian public, as did the nation's media and politicians, generally opposed the Allied use of atomic weapons in Korea. Only one-third of respondents to an October poll agreed that the Bomb would be justified 'under any circumstances,' including retaliation against an enemy atomic attack; 47 per cent opposed any use of the weapon whatsoever, while 20 per cent were undecided. Those who opposed the Bomb's use were far more likely to cite moral objections ('inhumane,' 'against civilization,' 'no one ever justified,' 'should be outlawed') than political or strategic considerations. Surprisingly, these findings bore a great deal of resemblance to results of a contemporaneous survey of the U.S. public.[79] In short, while those endorsing the use of the Bomb were concentrated in the United States, their calls did not conform to the views of most average Americans. On the surface, however, support for the Bomb by selected and highly visible individuals and groups gave the appearance that Americans as a whole took a harder line on the issue.

Responses to these crucial questions provide a brief précis of national attitudes in the opening months of the conflict. At the beginning of the war, *Newsweek* implied that American values and interests were synonymous with those of all non-communist nations, maintaining that President Truman 'spoke from the heart of his country, and indeed, of the free world. He spoke not only as Commander-in-Chief of American armed forces but as World Chief of Police.'[80] Divergence on key aspects of Korean War aims and strategies complicates this conflation of American interests and aims with those of the 'free world' as a whole. Rather, even among dominant voices within the two most 'like-minded' members of the UN coalition, 'liberal internationalism' took on different hues. Moreover, these national dissimilarities became more discernible as leaders sought to prosecute an overseas conflict to the satisfaction of domestic audiences, traditional allies, the UN, and lastly (and sadly, least of all) the Korean people. By February 1951, the *Canadian Forum* prepared a plainly exasperated editorial titled 'U.S. Foreign Policy,' which lamented what the journal considered a widening gulf between the war-related discourses of the United States and those of its allies. Debate in the U.S. Senate regarding Korea, held the journal,

> has touched the dormant isolationism of the American public which, like
> a sore not quite healed, can still be inflamed by irresponsible irritators ...

Attacks on the 'spy-infested' State Department ... have done incalculable harm to a Far Eastern policy which a year ago showed signs of developing on sane and sensible lines ... [F]or [Republican senator Robert] Taft, one of the most powerful and influential figures in the United States to announce to an anxious world at the most critical juncture of postwar history, a policy opposed on all fundamental issues to that worked out not only by the American government but by its allies, reveals a blindness to the realities of the modern world that is frightening. With his emphasis on America first, his contempt of the United Nations, his cynicism of the intentions of America's allies, his dislike of the Atlantic alliance, Mr. Taft would shatter the precious fabric of collective security that has been painfully woven during the past two years, and leave the Western world a shattered and drifting wreck.[81]

It is also important to note that from the outset of the Korean conflict, Canadian politicians and diplomats took positions regarding the crisis that were at odds with U.S. approaches and consonant with many of the views articulated by Canadians noted above. Canadian officials opposed proposals by former U.S. president Herbert Hoover to expel the Soviets from the UN or to turn the organization into a *de facto* anti-communist coalition, condemned the abuse of civil liberties under Rhee, and endorsed UN recognition of the PRC. Pearson and the diplomatic corps at External Affairs objected to the trend away from economic and toward military assistance to the Third World, urged adherence to the principle that the primary responsibility 'for solving a political problem should be left with the people who are immediately affected by it,' and sought to dissuade the United States from widening the war or resorting to the use of atomic weapons. As Denis Stairs observes, since advancing these aims required Canadian officials to constrain or censure the United States, 'friction in their official relations with their American counterparts was the result.'[82]

In December 1950, Pearson proposed his own peace plan, one closely resembling Nehru's. The plan advocated an immediate ceasefire, recognition of the PRC, and increased humanitarian aid to the post-colonial world. The independent Canadian initiative exasperated American leaders and journalists alike; *Time* called it 'even more conciliatory than Britain's,' a plan that 'looked strangely like peace at just about the price that Red China was likely to ask.'[83] It also reflected many of the attitudes expressed by Canadians.

The existence of this broad correlation between the Canadian government and the public on key matters relating to Korea places limits on the presumption that the era's Canadian foreign policy was a thoroughly 'mandarin' affair. Exponents of this 'mandarin thesis' contend that the elemental contours of Canadian foreign policy were crafted behind closed doors and only at the highest levels of government, and that the public was both indifferent and irrelevant to the process. Whitaker and Marcuse's insistence that the government determined a course of action and then marketed it to the public, rather than pursued policies that reflected the will of its constituents, is another way of making the same point.[84] At first glance, the above synchronicity between 'official' and public attitudes would appear to confirm this: here is a populace that simply reproduces the views of its rulers.

This assumption, however, ignores the singular obsession – and this is not too strong a term – that the ruling Liberal government displayed toward public opinion. Under the thirty-year leadership of Mackenzie King, the party had learned the art of caution on 'delicate' issues rather than resolute leadership, delays rather than action, all in the name of social harmony. King's famous 1942 declaration regarding the possibility of a wartime draft, 'Conscription if necessary, but not necessarily conscription,' is a distillation of this hesitant, fuzzy, waffling approach to important matters of state; Canadian historian and novelist Will Ferguson declares King 'had a weather vane where most people had a heart.'[85]

Louis St Laurent, King's carefully groomed successor, inherited aspects of this same chary approach to 'leadership.' As *Saturday Night* editors charged, the initial refusal to send troops to Korea proved that 'the prewar habits of the Mackenzie King regime still ruled ... that delay itself was being regarded as a virtue.' Contemporary political commentator James Laxer puts this another way, writing that Canada is a rare instance of an industrialized country 'where a centrist party has been dominant for decades, borrowing ideas from the left and right. Rarely innovative, always adaptive, the federal Liberals,' explains the former New Democratic Party operative, are 'detested by' many political opponents 'for their lack of principle.'[86] The unswerving attention to the public mood on significant issues might be considered the upside of the Liberals' chronic dithering. While many foreign policy decisions were indeed made behind closed doors, average Canadians' attitudes were instrumental in shaping those decisions nonetheless.

Indeed, King's initial opposition to Canadian involvement in UNT-

COK had much to do with triply paralyzing apprehensions of alarming Quebec, inviting war, and appearing an American pawn. These same concerns animated the St Laurent Liberals' careful management of the discourses surrounding NATO and the government's insistence on the inclusion of the treaty's article 2. All of this is to say that the Liberals tended not to act unless required and unless they believed they had public consent. The possibility of decisive action, meanwhile, increased when the government's own aims more closely matched those of the general populace. On the above issues concerning Korea, the dominant Canadian public mood was perceptible, displayed a general correlation to the thinking of the Canadian foreign policy establishment, *and* exhibited at least some distinction from views of the U.S. administration. Aware of this set of circumstances, the Liberals could at key junctures separate their Korea policy from that of the United States with confidence. In fact, to do otherwise would leave the government open to charges of capitulation to Washington.

While these intermittent expressions of non-alignment clearly served the interests of the Liberals at home, their impact on the wider conduct of the war was more ambiguous. Several authors maintain that when Canadian officials made independent gestures regarding the Korean situation, they lost influence over their U.S. counterparts. While it is true that U.S. officials consistently bemoaned the conciliatory, diplomatic approaches of Canadian officials over such issues as Korea and China, it would be a mistake to assume that these oppositional stances simply had no effect. Stueck finds, in his exhaustive and highly regarded examination of the international dimensions of the war, that U.S. allies exerted an undeniable impact over the general direction of the conflict. Foreign coalition members sought consistently and often successfully to reign in the excesses of unilateralist U.S. power in Korea, to keep the conflict from escalating, and to dissuade the American government from using the Bomb. He writes: 'In the West, at crucial times, U.S. allies, especially Great Britain and Canada, provided counterweights to tendencies in Washington to start along a road of escalation in Korea that could have ended in World War III.'[87] If the Canadian public did in fact embolden its leaders in these areas, the former deserves some credit for shaping the ultimate course of the war (just as public discourse in other Allied nations most certainly did). And if the early stages of the conflict carried the aura of a unilateralist undertaking, active participation, as opposed to mere token support, by a growing number of UN members served to blunt that aura.

Meaningful participation in the fighting in Korea was not the course initially selected by the Liberals. Rather, they had hoped their swift offer of three destroyers, a move initially lauded by the public, would suffice. Fears of damaging party fortunes in Quebec is a significant component of this stand – again demonstrating the influence of public opinion on the nation's foreign policy. Any lingering doubts about the ability of Canadian public discourse to stimulate government action on significant international matters during this era should be dispelled by the debates over whether to send ground troops to Korea. In short, the Liberals were compelled to reverse their position in large part by public irritation over the 'softness' of their response. This mounting anger among Canadians – combined with the protestations of U.S. officials, the American public, and UN Secretary General Trygve Lie over the perceived inadequacy of the Canadian contribution – resulted in a September 1950 commitment of ground forces. Canadians endorsing the move based their calls, variously, on their nation's responsibility to the UN, to the United States, to Britain and other Commonwealth nations who had already joined the ground war, and to a freedom directly imperilled by events in Korea. As was the case in the United States, the near-hysteria over the threat posed by global communism evident in these debates was one which the government itself had carefully built upon and employed for its own ends in the past, but one that now hamstrung their policy-making options.

By and large, English-Canadian journalists castigated the Liberals' initial refusal to provide ground forces; as *Le Devoir* noted with both incredulity and precision after the first week of battle, the greatest enthusiasm for the conflict emerged, not from government, but from 'the *Star* and the *Globe and Mail*.' While the anglophone press maintained that the nation's citizens shared their outrage over Canada's limited contribution, the sole survey to address the issue directly, conducted in the first weeks of the war and released on August 1, is somewhat less equivocal. The poll did suggest Canadian approval of Truman's initial action in Korea was nearly as strong as that of Americans (75 per cent and 81 per cent, respectively); after this, matters get murkier. In a follow-up question, 23 per cent of Canadians expressed the view that their nation should not 'send equipment to this war.' The remaining 77 per cent approving or undecided about equipment were then asked whether troops should also be sent. Less than half of these, or 34 per cent of all Canadians questioned, answered affirmatively. Sixteen per cent disapproved, 15 per cent provided qualified responses, and 12 per cent expressed no opinion.[88] If we are to share the pollster's assumption that those who declined to send equipment would also oppose the provision of troops, it would appear that as of July, roughly 4 in 10 Canadians objected to contributing troops, one-third endorsed the proposal, and nearly as many exhibited uncertainty over the issue.

The Canadian Institute of Public Opinion conducted no subsequent surveys on the issue, though for a number of reasons, it is probable that public support for troop deployment grew over the ensuing weeks. First, expectations of a quick victory by U.S.-led forces soon evaporated, a fact that would have brought unease to Canadians who had endorsed the UN action and not the provision of Canadian soldiers. Then, in mid-July, UN Secretary General Lie made a direct appeal for nations to send consequential, not merely token, assistance to Korea. In response, a number of foreign states committed to send forces, including other Commonwealth nations (most pointedly, Britain) and NATO allies. More and more, the Canadian response took on a comparatively minimalist air, something that many prominent Americans did not hesitate to point out. Likewise, irritation over the official response grew palpably in the Canadian media throughout July and August, a process that both reflected and fed the growing agitation.

Finally, and in a sure indication that the initial public recalcitrance suggested by the August 1 poll did not hold, the St Laurent government announced that it would provide ground forces in Korea. The about-face on the issue taken by the ever-opportunistic and exceptionally cautious Liberal government had roots in all of the above factors, though it is questionable whether the change would have come if the ruling party did not feel its electoral prospects would be harmed by 'staying the course' on its initial Korea policy. Ironically, at roughly the same time Canadian ground forces finally arrived in Korea in February of 1951, polls from Britain and the United States displayed a conspicuous souring of attitudes toward the now-stalemated conflict, with half of Britons and two-thirds of Americans calling for an immediate withdrawal of their nations' forces.[89] Had the Liberals maintained their original position on the issue, they may have experienced considerably less public hostility by the spring of 1951, and perhaps a sense of vindication over the matter.

In the first weeks of the war, however, such a response invited stinging criticism. *Saturday Night* editors first believed that Canadian troops would be unnecessary. But after Lie's appeal they accused the government of cowardice, of 'trying to find the easy way out,' and called for the resignation of Defence Minister Brooke Claxton. The *Globe and Mail*'s Dominion Day editorial expressed shame over the government's preference for 'standing on the sidelines making encouraging noises,' and linked such inaction to the nation's international reputation: 'It is not by performances like this that a country acquires the reputation and influence Canada aspires to.' Papers noted for their more progressive orientations, such as the *Ottawa Citizen* and *Toronto Star*, at first condemned the near-panic over the 'inadequacy' of Canada's commitment, citing the need for troops at home and possibly in Europe. But after a series of U.S. military setbacks in the first weeks of the war, the *Citizen* concluded that the West had 'miscalculated the world danger' represented by Korea, and that 'Canada's obligation to the United Nations' now mandated that the nation offer fighting forces to the peninsula.[90]

Publications from western Canada cut the government little to no slack on the issue; the 'embarrassment' over Canada's alleged cowardice and military weakness dominated the editorial pages throughout July and August. To the above arguments for sending troops, these analysts added a local rationale: anxiety that the fighting would cross the ocean to engulf the Canadian West. A July 8 cartoon in the *Vancouver Sun* depicts shiftless 'Sheriff' Brooke Claxton in an Old West town lazily flicking a cigarette, while a distressed proprietor of an establishment called 'West Coast Cities' demands protection; just across the street, another store-front designated 'Korea' belches smoke. Letter writer A.R. Reusch made a similar appeal for protection on the same page, believing 'Vancouver, Victoria, [and] Prince Rupert … are in real danger should the Korean trouble spread.' Unlike the politicians in Ottawa, 'we would be in the midst of it' if the conflict escalates, agreed another Vancouverite, who advocated the dissemination of civil defence information in preparation for possible bombing of area cities.[91]

As was the case during the last major conflict in the Pacific, some in the region also called for heightened attention to possible enemy collaborators among the local populace. This time, however, the fact that the 'enemy within' was distinguished by creed rather than physical appearance complicated vigilance. For that reason, the *Vancouver Sun* provided an ideological profile: anyone expressing 'fear,' 'doubt,' or 'pacifis[m]' could well be a 'slimy propagandist.' Attempts at sabotage would doubtless follow. 'Workers in the dockyards, communication centres, water and electrical distribution points,' the paper advised, 'all owe it to their fellow citizens to be on guard against disloyal elements secretly planning destruction in their midst.'[92] The idea that a conflict on the Korean peninsula might leapfrog the Pacific to North American shores provides a measure of the anxieties brought about by the gross exaggeration of

Soviet objectives and capabilities. The remedy for these fears involved sending ground troops to Asia to 'contain' the fighting to that region and at the same time building up civil defence, issues that were linked consistently in Canadian opinion pieces, particularly those from the West.

Canadians surmised with some justification, then, that their leaders' past and current expressions of alarm regarding the threat of global communism did not mesh with their actions (or inactions) in Korea. Adding to this sense of dissonance was Parliament's decision to recess for the summer at the end of June rather than extend the session in order to respond to the emergency – a decision ridiculed in the press. By contrast, as *Newsweek* reported, the United States exuded an 'electrifie[d]' atmosphere, a discrepancy noted with embarrassment by the *Winnipeg Tribune*. 'Washington seems to have [a] sense of urgency,' it noted; 'Ottawa does not.' The Liberals' true feelings regarding the threat to national security presented by the Korean conflict is perhaps best reflected in the July vacations taken by key cabinet members, as well as the prime minister himself, whilst retreating U.S. forces faced the prospect of being driven off the Korean peninsula altogether.[93]

St Laurent's government, as keenly anti-communist as any Western government outside Washington, was now depicted as naïve with respect to the communist threat – in terminology that bore insinuations of 'softness' so endemic south of the border. The *Toronto Telegram* wondered 'whether the Government is sufficiently awake to the dangers in the world situation today.' A *Globe and Mail* cartoonist juxtaposed cabinet ministers, dressed in summer garb and engaged in leisure activities, with a panicky male citizen wearing the vest and tie of the white-collar workplace. The latter wrings his hands as a radio reports 'GI's pushed further back in Korea ...' Noted *Saturday Night*: '... the Government – as if deliberately – has presented the world situation as though it were only a secondary concern of ours.' The magazine believed that this attitude had produced regrettable outcomes. Overlooking coincident polls which demonstrated that Canadians feared global war more than all other worries combined, that they believed their nation the second most likely theatre (after Europe) for the next global war, and that urbanites were strategizing responses to atomic bombings, the editors maintained that 'we do not think that the people of Canada generally recognize the terrible nature of the time in which we now find ourselves ...' As if to reverse this nonchalance, the editorial was followed by a story bearing the 'reassuring' title 'We CAN Prepare for Atom-Bombs.'[94]

Some in the pro-war press found an especially potent counterattack to government demurrals over Korea: the recent words of prominent Liberals themselves regarding the collective international responsibility toward communism. 'We have talked long and loud of our intention to resist aggression,' reminded the *Vancouver Sun*; now 'aggression stares us in the face.' The *Globe and Mail* reprinted portions of a St Laurent speech outlining the need for NATO, as well as the words of External Affairs Minister Pearson 'just six weeks ago' in Parliament that held that global communism could only be thwarted by an immediate, powerful, and collective response to any act of aggression. With Canadian ministers now 'stay[ing] on their verandas,' the *Globe* was led to wonder whether 'the fine speeches of Mr. St. Laurent and Mr. Pearson were nothing but wind ... It is a mercy, and a mercy we hardly deserve,' they concluded, 'that other countries are being better led.'[95] Harsh language indeed for a paper prone to revel in tired, anglophilic anti-Americanisms.

Influential observers from certain 'other countries' currently enjoying the type of leadership preferred by the *Globe* also expressed frustration over the Canadian response. American officials berated their Canadian counterparts in private, though they glossed over tensions in public statements. Blair Fraser of *Maclean's* pointed out that the blame for the bilateral strain was not Canada's alone: 'Ottawa may have been pretty inept in handling Canada-US relations over the Korean crisis ... but Washington wasn't very bright either.' Fraser went on to explain that American envoys had deliberately misled Ottawa about an impending announcement of troop contributions from Pakistan in an attempt to compel a similar move by Canada. But if U.S. officials exerted their coercions cautiously and behind closed doors, those outside of government circles held little back. In August, *Newsweek* called the Korean affair the Liberal cabinet's 'devil,' and noted the 'embarrassing news' that Britain, Australia, and New Zealand had announced troop commitments. 'What manner of allies are these?' asked an irate John Knight, publisher of the *Chicago Daily News.* Similar questions emerged from the *New York Times'* Arthur Krock, as well as the editors of the *Buffalo Evening News* and the *Chicago Tribune.*[96]

Arizona Star editors called Canada's refusal to supply troops 'a shocking spectacle,' declaring that one of the upsides to the otherwise gloomy July news about Korea was that the incident revealed America's true friends. Canada's weakness and indifference, the *Star* continued, was ultimately the fault of 'Britain and Washington,' who 'have treated her like a spoiled and pampered child'; only pressure from these guardians would inspire

Canada to offer 'the kind of help where blood is shed.' Accusations of this nature were particularly injurious to national identity, as Canadians frequently referenced their immediate entry into the two previous global conflicts as the measure of the nation's valour and sound judgment in the international arena. The handy counter-example, of course, was the United States, which had now turned the tables on this state of affairs. The *Calgary Herald* argued that Canada's past record of sacrifice did not give it a pass on Korea: 'The fact that the US was misguided enough to stand by while the West twice took a beating at the hands of the Germans,' they wrote (apparently unable to resist leading with the old jab), 'does not excuse Canada's failure to give her utmost in the Korean fight by one jot or tittle.'[97]

That Canadians from many quarters responded to U.S. criticisms in a similar manner serves as an abrupt reversal from earlier debates over the Bomb, the Gouzenko Affair, and decolonization, when American condemnation invited widespread counterattacks. Now, with their national self-image at stake, English- Canadian publications reprinted full texts of angry U.S. editorials, not as verification of American meddling, myopia, or self-righteousness, but as simple statements of fact that would spur their readers to demand fuller participation in Korea. Columnist Richard Needham cited one particularly caustic piece from the *Chicago Tribune* on the inclination among Canadians to pay lip service to collective security while allowing the United States to bear the burden: 'It was mean,' he granted, 'it was bitter, but fundamentally it was true.' To Needham, Canada's failure to act not only tarnished its reputation; it would also 'do irreparable harm to our relations with the United States.' 'Is it important for Canada to be well regarded by the American public?' he asked. 'We think that it is. We do not think it would be agreeable to have the situation arise, now or later, where Americans could look down on Canadians. And make no mistake, that situation is arising.' *Maclean's* expressed the same point of view in a piece titled 'Uncle Same Thinks We Let Him Down.' Should the United States be driven off the peninsula, warned the *Winnipeg Tribune*, the American people would reserve a special scorn for Canadians. To a public alarmed that the battle in Korea might be a harbinger of global nuclear confrontation, this was no time to antagonize their closest ally and only real defence against a potentially imminent Soviet invasion. And not for the last time, the notion that Canadians had let the United States down on the previous occasion Americans had appealed for assistance served as a powerful inducement to join a U.S.-led venture abroad. The ruling Liberals' refusals 'follow exactly the pattern of Canada's attitude to the Berlin Airlift,' the *Globe and Mail* lamented.[98] Evidently, rebuffing their American neighbour twice in succession is perceived as a dangerous game in Canada.

Quebecers, on the other hand, displayed a greater readiness to defy the pro-war offensive launched by English-speaking North Americans. In the first weeks of the conflict, just 21 per cent offered unqualified approval for sending Canadian ground troops to Korea; in Ontario, by contrast, 40 per cent supported the measure.[99] Though many influential Quebec politicians and media organizations offered various levels of support for Western military intervention and the provision of Canadian ground forces, the province was also home to the nation's most vocal and sustained opponents of the war.

Time magazine appeared wholly beguiled by the resistance in Quebec. Particularly galling were dispatches of the Asia correspondent for Montreal's *Le Devoir*, a daily *Time* contextualized as 'an ultra-nationalist newspaper closely associated with the Roman Catholic church.' Calling the correspondent a 'travelogue' writer masquerading as a political pundit, *Time* reprinted his 'strange opinions,' which, to the U.S. weekly, smacked of both 'appeasement' and '*Pravda*': namely, 'the West is defending a lost cause' in Korea, Formosa, and Indo-China; both the Soviets *and* the Western powers are responsible for global tensions; and by replicating official U.S. military reports uncritically, American war correspondents are distorting 'the opinions of millions.' *Time* ascribed the source of such ultimately prescient observations to the writer's 'French Canadian isolationist-pacifist sentiments.'[100]

English Canada was largely in agreement with this censure of francophones' opposition to the war and, like *Time*, ascribed the basis of this sentiment to simple isolationism. *Saturday Night* invoked the term for the much-maligned U.S. opponents to the old League of Nations, voicing regret that several Quebec 'irreconcilable' editorial boards opposed participation in the war. The *Globe and Mail* blamed the Liberals' hesitation on Korea to the undue influence the minority francophone population held over the party and, by extension, the rest of Canada. A *Maclean's* cartoonist depicted politicians fleeing in terror from a tiny firecracker representing Quebec isolationism and directly into an enormous bomb labelled 'Atom War.'[101]

However, few vestiges of true isolationist thinking can be perceived in the arguments against war that emerged from Quebec. The province's opposition MPs condemned the Liberals' Korea policy in a special Parliamentary session in early September, accusing the government of endorsing an imperial agenda, one that would kill innocent civilians in the name of liberty. The four MPs – two Progressive Conservative and two Independent – argued instead for supporting Nehru's mediation efforts, increasing non-military aid to the Third World, and reasserting Canadian autonomy in foreign affairs. The St Jean Baptiste Society, an organization created in 1834 to preserve French language and culture in Canada, called on national leaders to arbitrate an end to the conflict 'on morally acceptable bases.' Holding that their fellow citizens 'consider war a crime,' Quebec City's *Le Soleil* urged that Canada throw its efforts behind true self-determination in Asia rather than attempts to expand Western hegemony, arguing that their nation's very sovereignty was at stake. Montreal's *Le Devoir* concurred, stating that the West sought to impose on South Korea an unwanted and unrepresentative puppet regime, and that Canadians' desire to please the United States had now reached embarrassing proportions: 'We are like little dogs who are eager to show their master that they adore him, that one gesture from him is enough to throw themselves in the water,' wrote its editors.[102]

Quebec City's *L'Action Catholique*, a conservative and notoriously anti-communist daily subsidized by the archbishop's office, nonetheless endorsed North Korea's social reforms, land redistribution, and nationalization of industry, and condemned the corruption and human rights abuses of the Western-backed Rhee. Unless the West adopts a 'truly Christian policy' in Asia, held the journal, the entire region would gravitate toward communism.[103] All of these arguments took for granted a strong international role for the nation, though one that stressed diplomacy, support for human rights and humanitarian assistance, and a more autonomous Canada in a democratic, liberal international order. In this way, they anticipated the 'soft power' and peacekeeping orientations that would characterize Canadian foreign policy in the ensuing decades. Again, because a strong showing in Quebec was a prerequisite to any federal election victory, these views would need to be accommodated.

Le Devoir editors conveyed profound frustrations over the repeated conflation of oppositio to war and isolationism. 'Who defends *isolationism* among the French Canadians?' they demanded (emphasis in original). Instead, *Le Devoir* equated francophone sentiment with that of Nehru and the Indian people, who, though strongly internationalist, viewed armed conflict as both immoral and counterproductive. 'Both peoples have suffered from power politics and imperialism,' they explained, 'and both have had to rely on non-violent methods in their struggles for emancipation, methods which have in each case entered into the national tradition.' True isolationists, meanwhile, were those who had abrogated 'the idea of one world' by retreating into regional military alliances. 'From the world point of view,' concluded *Le Devoir*, 'the supreme act of isolationism consists in going to war against the other half of the human race.'[104]

The perspectives of war opponents, francophone and otherwise, gained increasing credibility as the war dragged on, death tolls multiplied, and the West pursued a negotiated settlement not unlike those proposed by Nehru and Pearson in the war's earliest days. In those first days, however, questioning the rectitude of a large-scale Western military response to a far-off civil conflict led to accusations of 'isolationism,' 'appeasement,' and 'softness' toward communism. The latter smear proved especially potent in tempering opposition to the war in Quebec, where church and state had long worked in tandem to cultivate an atmosphere particularly inimical to 'Reds.' As is evident above, this does not imply that francophones heartily sanctioned the war. Indeed, historian Robert Bothwell's claim that Korea produced 'no threat to national disunity' seems an oversimplification in light of polling data and the terse exchange between mainstream English Canadians and war opponents from Quebec; the nation *was* clearly disunited in the summer and autumn of 1950, and largely along familiar linguistic and regional lines. On the other hand, greater percentages of Quebec's average citizens and elites supported meaningful Canadian participation in Korea, and in the wider global anti-communist struggle, than had been the case in the nation's previous wars. This approval was both reflected and reinforced by the fact that francophones made up nearly one-third of Canadian forces in 1950, a figure that approached French Canadians' proportion of the total population.[105]

The unprecedented levels of francophone support provided the St Laurent administration with the capital and the nerve to pursue what was truly the only course of action available to them by September 1950. To a great degree, this bind was of the government's own making: the Liberals had faithfully played upon the communist threat in order to malign political opponents on their left, undercut those on their right, maintain dominance in Quebec, and gain consent for a regional defence agreement. Further, as a committed advocate of multilateralism conducted under the aegis of the UN, Canada could not afford to vote in favour of UN 'police action' in Korea and then withhold consequential military assistance while U.S. forces continued to lose ground – in short, to simultaneously condemn and facilitate America's unilateralist tendencies. For these reasons, Americans and Canadians alike were correct to call the

Liberals' initial response both tepid and disingenuous. Another aspect of this bind was beyond the Canadian government's control: the United States had settled on the appropriate Western response to the conflict before consulting with its allies, and then demanded UN endorsement of the policy. Canadian UN delegates could have opposed the UN resolutions on principle, and thereby isolated themselves from their European NATO allies (who were eager to support a venture that confirmed U.S. resolve), the wider non-communist world, and the United States. This clearly untenable course of action reinforced the impression that the most vital aspects of Canada's foreign policy were being preordained in Washington.

The friction between Canadian and American officials apparent at the outset of the Korean War owes much to the disparities in power and agency embedded in the bilateral relationship, and to the differing visions of liberal internationalism that marked the dominant self-perceptions of 'national character.' Fissures would be exacerbated by U.S. action and Canadian inaction in the conflict's early stages, though in this phase the most serious rupture ran, not along national lines, but between Canada's ruling Liberals and virtually all other discernible voices in the United States and English Canada. The unexpected duration and costliness of the war, features aggravated – to critics within and beyond the United States – by American blunders and mismanagement, would temper this congruity between public perceptions of Canadian and U.S. interests. As Defence Minister Pearson told a Toronto audience in April 1951, 'The days of relatively easy and automatic political relations with our neighbour are, I think, over.'[106]

Pearson was right. While American leaders would request military assistance from their northern neighbours in the ensuing decades, Canadian troops would not again engage in major military operations until the UN-authorized Gulf War of 1991. The consensus evident between citizens on both sides of the international divide at the beginning of the Korean War, by contrast, is without parallel in the history of Cold War Canadian-American relations. Though its assembly had hardly been 'easy and automatic,' the architects of this unanimity drew upon a unique alignment of global events, domestic circumstances, and their own interests to present a world view that appeared unassailable. Of equal importance is the fact that while a policy of militant anti-communism better served the aims and values of the United States, the construction of this consensus was a truly bilateral venture.

Conclusion

In February 1948, at the very moment the Soviets were coordinating a *coup d'état* in Czechoslovakia that would, for many, mark a point of no return in post-war East-West relations, *Saturday Night* columnist Mary Lowrey Ross puzzled over an unfamiliar epithet hurled toward her by an angry reader: that certain of her recently expressed views were 'un-Canadian.' What did it mean, responded Ross, to be an un-Canadian, and by extension an 'authentic' Canadian, in a nation that lacked even a national flag and anthem? Reflecting on the handling of alleged cases of Soviet espionage in both the United States and Canada, she observed:

> Un-Canadianism is still an unrecognized phenomenon in our country. When it was felt necessary to investigate Communist tactics in the United States, no one had any difficulty about labeling Communist activities. They were un-American. But it didn't occur to anyone to describe as un-Canadian the activities of our espionage participants. Nor did anyone condemn as un-Canadian the procedure of rounding up a group of espionage suspects and holding them without trial. We said it was un-British.

In casting about for markers that would help delineate a national identity, Ross considered the aptness of Canada's national animal. 'The beaver,' she wrote, 'is industrious home-loving, and constructive ... It is also timid, conservative and vegetarian ...' More ominously for those concerned over issues of the nation's autonomy and/or its very survival, she noted dryly: 'It is chiefly valuable when skinned.' Ross concluded that the dilemma in fixing a national identity concerned the commonly held assumption 'that there are two frames of reference, one English and one American,' and that Canadians are expected to simultaneously reflect *and* – if they hope to retain their collective skins – resist both referents. While some Canadians 'feel it is only possible to be Canadian by being British,' others consider it 'un-Canadian to feel British or even Canadian to feel un-British.' At the same time, 'it is possible also to seem un-Canadian and conceivably un-British by not appearing to be sufficiently un-American, though not of course,' wrote Ross, at a time of accelerated HUAC investigations in the United States, 'in the sense that "un-American" is used by Americans themselves.' Even with Ross's complete erasure of Canadians of First Nations, francophone, or non-Anglo or American heritage, understanding or establishing a cohesive national identity appeared a complicated and ambiguous undertaking.

The same irate reader who prompted these musings also proposed a remedy for Ross's perceived failure to conform to attitudes and values expected of Canada's citizens: that she 'go and live in the United States.'[1] While the concept of un-Canadianism *per se* might have been novel, and the demarcation of a genuine collective identity paradoxical and contested (to the point of being unattainable), the depository for those living north of the U.S. border who could not or would not accommodate themselves to social 'norms' was not. Ross's perceived disloyalty to a largely ineffable national character had rendered her little more than a symbolic American, a definitive and time-honoured slight among those who considered their national experiment somehow nobler and more enlightened than that of their southern neighbour.

The columnist-reader altercation cited above raises a number of issues germane to this project. For one, Canadians, it seemed, possessed a clearer notion of 'Other' than they did of 'Self'; identity was most easily defined in the negative. It is also noteworthy that un-Canadianism was not, for this reader at least, equated with pro-communism. That is, the phrase could be understood in terms that were roughly opposite to connotations of un-Americanism among mid-century Americans. Thus, while 'un-Americans' such as Emma Goldman were herded onto the 'Soviet Ark' for a transatlantic voyage to Russia, un-Canadians were encouraged to simply cross their southern border in order to fraternize with others of their ilk. Yet as the preceding study has shown, it was during this moment that the already shadowy map of national identities and allegiances became considerably more convoluted.

I began this project with two assumptions: (1) that the Canadian public had been manoeuvred toward the pro-U.S. anti-communist consensus to a significant degree by American voices, most notably those associated with, or presented through, mass media organizations; (2) that mapping this general process – that is, proving the first assumption – would be a relatively straightforward matter. I do not retract the first hypothesis entirely, though I found the practices of cultural borrowing, adaptation, coercion, and resistance much more complex and contingent than anticipated; in consequence, I found the latter supposition to be groundless, at least in my own hands.

It is true that the U.S. popular and public culture possessed the means to reach a higher percentage of Canadians than it did in any other foreign context. I suggested in the introduction that Canada was likely spared U.S. government-sponsored cultural initiatives in large part because policy-makers assumed their neighbouring citizens shared basic views regarding the desirability of liberal internationalism and the anathema of domestic and international communism. It is also possible that the State Department did not sponsor cultural programs in Canada because they understood that the cultural incursion had already occurred. Canada's theatres screened Hollywood films (to the exclusion of nearly all others); its radio and print media included high percentages of American material; its citizens tuned in to American broadcasting directly and read many more U.S. magazines than they did Canadian. And clearly, these two processes are linked: U.S. media dominance in Canada contributed to similar viewpoints between Canadians and Americans; shared outlooks made U.S. cultural products more amenable to Canadian consumers.

As a result of this market saturation, Canadians were presented with a predominance of views that would support the establishment of a pro-U.S. Cold War consensus in Canada. To restate but a few: that atomic weaponry, having been used prudently against Japan, should be possessed by the United States alone, and that the nation's leaders and scientists could be trusted to usher in a benign atomic future; that American values and institutions exhibited a universal suitability and appeal; that post-war American expansionism was of an entirely different character than Soviet expansionism; that domestic and international communism posed an unparalleled threat to liberal democracy. Variations on some of these assumptions, and particularly the last one, were shared and promulgated by Canada's ruling Liberal government in service of their own electoral fortunes and by many of the nation's more conservative media outlets. What American post-war discourse added to the mix was the notion that a preponderant, nuclear-armed United States would be the best, or only, answer to this threat for Canadians and Americans alike – as opposed to a non-aligned Canada, a United Nations strengthened by its sole possession (or its eradication) of nuclear weapons, renewed efforts in East-West dialogue, and so on. The solution endorsed by U.S. Cold Warriors was not necessarily the one preferred by the Liberal government, External Affairs bureaucrats, or other Canadian elites, but these groups had clearly prepared the public for this reorientation through their consistent reiterations of the communist threat.

As noted at several points throughout this narrative, views expressed by Americans on any given issue were always far more diverse than those represented in the nation's 'leading,' or largest circulating, publications – in those, namely, which were available in Canada. Further, this narrowing of perspectives in the mainstream press only accelerated as the 'communist conspiracy' became an article of faith. This does not mean that all views that reached Canada endorsed an anti-communist crusade under U.S. leadership, and I have pointed to several instances where Canadians drew upon ideas that emerged from the American context in order to challenge the general drift toward bipolar entrenchment. As an aggregate, however, U.S. messages regarding post-war international affairs were more bellicose and unambiguous than those produced in Canada.

Of course, these tendencies toward exclusion and unanimity are not unique to the U.S. communications industry or to the Cold War, although these tendencies were especially powerful under this geographical and temporal combination. Canadians, however, frequently seized upon the narrow range of views as proof of the violence, intolerance, shallowness, materialism, arrogance, unilateralism (and on and on) that 'defined' the American 'character.' Americans did not resist similarly reductionist representations of Canadians on the rare occasions they considered them at all, depicting their northern neighbours as amusingly naïve and provincial in their reactions to Soviet espionage, and as little more than effete colonial subjects with resources to plunder in debates over the ownership of Canadian uranium. Again, Canadian attempts to map out and inhabit difference, to celebrate openness and a tolerance for a diversity of views, may have rendered elements of Canadian society more democratic and less deferential to privilege, at least in their rhetoric. In this sense, Canadian society may be characterized as becoming increasingly 'American' through these processes – if the term is used to connote the more radical democracy promoted by U.S. ideals, if not always practices, and by the greater racial and ethnic diversity observable in mid-century America.

By the end of the period under study, however, much of the vitriol had vanished from Canadian depictions of the United States – or rather, had been transferred to communists and Russians. In Canadian discourses surrounding NATO and Korea, Americans had largely been transformed from 'Other' to an extension of self, an essential prerequisite for signing on to an anti-communist campaign under U.S. leadership.

The specific means of arriving at this position is central to this study, as it goes directly to the issue of American influences in Canada. Stephen Whitfield has written that the United States was alone among its post-war social democratic allies in permitting attacks on civil liberties and 'cultural distortions' in the name of anti-communism.[2] Like many other historians of American society and culture, Whitfield overlooks Canada, the site of what was arguably the second most disproportionate response to the communist threat in the West. It is no mere coincidence that the nation whose Cold War climate most closely resembled that of the United States was and remains the globe's most avid consumer of American popular and public culture. Many Canadians came to emphasize the positive aspects of the nuclear age, replicated without question the exaggerated claims of U.S. reporter Drew Pearson regarding Soviet espionage, and obeyed orders from their American-controlled unions to purge suspected communists from their ranks. Canadians trusted the interpretations offered by the Associated Press, Douglas MacArthur, and John Foster Dulles about Asia – where few Canadian politicians or reporters had ventured – aped President Truman's characterization of North Koreans as 'bandits and thugs,' and expressed alarm when U.S. editors condemned Canada's initial refusal to send ground troops to Korea. Clearly, Canadians were influenced to varying degrees by the frequently monolithic anti-communist messages emanating from the south.

Yet it is also clear from the foregoing that the mere presence of American viewpoints in Canada did not amount to a simple and uncritical adoption of those views. At many points in this survey, Canadians of a variety of identities and political leanings – progressives, imperialists, anglophiles, francophones, rural populists, trade unionists – appear to actively seek out U.S. mainstream opinion on an issue precisely to establish an oppositional position on the same matter (or at least to emphasize, and delight in, their disconnection from perceived American viewpoints). As historians S.F. Wise and Robert Craig Brown have demonstrated, nineteenth-century Canadians were often inordinately curious and knowledgeable about goings on in the United States for this same reason; this survey shows this tradition to be alive and well in the aftermath of the Second World War.[3]

In other words, a variety of Canadians had long been conditioned, perhaps more so than citizens of any other nationality, to 'stand on guard' against creeping Americanism. This was not, then, analogous to the situation in post-war Western Europe, where residents were rather suddenly confronted with unprecedented degrees of American mass culture, consumer products, and State Department coercions. Canadians were, or thought themselves to be, savvy observers and consumers of all things American. This state of affairs does not lend itself to a straightforward depiction of the nation's citizens as victims of cultural imperialism.

All the more striking, then, that some of the more dependable sources of anti-Americanism at the beginning of this survey quietly or enthusiastically endorsed U.S. global leadership by 1950. As I suggest at the conclusion of chapter 4, it seems unlikely that individuals and organizations noted for their independence and careful and critical scrutiny of U.S. policy would have characterized themselves as cowed by American pressures, as victims of foreign ideological domination. Real fear of communist expansionism appears to be the salient feature of this reorientation, and while U.S. popular and public culture certainly played a role in exacerbating those fears, many Canadians at least believed themselves to have agency in this process, to have made this choice based on their own assessment of the costs and benefits. Thus, even among those who might lament the submission to a U.S.-led ideological crusade, this compliance lacks the tragic overtones that characterize the frequently violent absorption of Eastern European or Latin America nations into Cold War blocs. Canada became a satellite, in part, through an act of volition. And some, like columnist Willson Woodside, clearly understood what this meant for the nation's sovereignty, but feared the only plausible alternative – world slavery – far more. The sense of crisis did not lend itself to a nuanced appraisal of a broad variety of possible options and outcomes.

If Canada's post-war international orientation represents an act of volition, it is also important to underscore the broad, democratic impulsion toward this new bearing. Past appraisals of this policy shift have been heavily influenced by the interpretations of Canada's 'new nationalists,' a loose collection of public intellectuals from across the political spectrum – including such figures as Walter Gordon, George Grant, Donald Creighton, Farley Mowat, and Margaret Atwood – whose condemnations of U.S. influence over Canada gained prominence in the 1960s and '70s. Rallying around Grant's 1965 publication *Lament for a Nation*, the new nationalists framed Canada's turning from Britain and toward the United States in decidedly autocratic and conspiratorial tones: Liberal governments under King, St Laurent, and Pearson, so the argument went, along with influential collaborators from big business and the Canadian bureaucracy who advocated both continentalism and U.S.-style liberalism, manoeuvred an unsuspecting public toward acceptance of an alliance with the United States. Strategic, economic, and cultural domination followed, though by the time the Canadian people realized the depth of their servitude, little could be done to reverse the process.[4]

Close examination of public debates surrounding the steps taken toward Cold War continental integration casts doubt on straightforward acceptance of the 'Liberal conspiracy' thesis. In fact, mid-century Canadian citizens, stirred from their inward-looking and isolationist tendencies by a global war of unfathomable proportions, constituted active agents in the interpretation and making of their nation's post-war foreign affairs. Episodes of perceived crisis which appeared to threaten both national security and the wider liberal world order – including the prospect of nuclear annihilation, Soviet espionage, fears of communist expansion in Europe and the Third World, and war in Korea – led traumatized citizens to insist that their often hesitant Liberal Party leaders take a leading role in international affairs; for many Canadians, the starting point for that role was a firm alliance with the globe's most powerful exponent of liberalism. Nowhere is this process more evident than in the St Laurent government's acquiescence to calls for Canadian ground forces in Korea; the Canadian public, rather than the ever cautious Liberals, was ultimately responsible for the nation's most tangible commitment to America's Cold War policy of containment.[5]

Finally, it is common for scholars to speak of transnational identities and efforts to bring about a climate of trans- or post-nationalism. These analyses generally focus on aggrieved communities, who because of structural exclusions embedded in state ideals and practices, seek affiliations with like-minded individuals and groups both within and beyond the boundaries of the nation-state.[6] These phenomena are certainly apparent in both the United States and Canada during the period under study – among African Americans, who forged fertile alliances with colonized peoples and promoted notions of pan-Africanism, and among opponents of imperialism and supporters of a robust UN and greater world federalism. However, attempts to make cross-border linkages among dissenting and marginalized groups in Canada and the United States are frequently indiscernible in the earliest years of the Cold War. This may be a partial consequence of the narrow range of media exchange addressed above; knowledge of the existence and activities of nonconforming, 'inassimilable' actors was often not readily available.

In fact, the strongest force in favour of transnationalism – of fostering a sense of community not bounded by the nation-state – was advanced in service of state objectives: that is, the campaigns to convince citizens to support a North Atlantic alliance and a war against communism in a distant and largely unknown Asian nation.[7] In retrospect, many Canadians felt that they had made a miscalculation, and that Canadian nationalism and sovereignty had been scuttled under false pretenses. And if the U.S. establishment built an anti-communist consensus on a pre-existing foundation of American nationalism, Canadian elites embarked on a somewhat thornier path. The latter attempted to construct their own Cold War consensus on a combination of Canadian nationalism – which they employed to discredit the internationalist spirit of communism, to manage recent, non-Nordic and potentially leftist immigrants, to discredit dissenting francophones, to uphold imperialism as a check against Soviet expansion, and so on – and, with NATO and Korea, subservience to the United States and its increasingly nationalistic anti-communist foreign policy. For a brief period at mid-century, fear and coercion served to occlude the paradoxical foundations of Canadian consensus. Over time, however, the contradiction inherent to this project became clear, and citizens of various identities and political affiliations would come to wield Canadian nationalism as a tool *against* simple quiescence to Cold War conventions.

Notes

Introduction

1 Truman press release cited in 'Challenge Accepted,' *Time*, 3 July 1950, p. 8 (all references to *Time* are from the magazine's split-run Canadian edition); 'Uncle Sam Takes Role as World Cop,' *Newsweek*, 3 July 1950, p. 17. For a discussion of Truman's political ideology, see Offner, *Another Such Victory*.

2 For a summary of the opinions of the era's Canadian intellectuals toward mid-century continentalism, including the vehement opposition of such figures as Harold Innis, George Grant, and Donald Creighton to this process, see Massolin, *Canadian Intellectuals*, and Edwardson, '"Kicking Uncle Sam out of the Peaceable Kingdom."' A sampling of works which present various takes on the relationship between the Cold War and continental integration includes Minifie, *Peacemaker or Powder-Monkey*; Grant, *Lament for a Nation*; Hertzman et al., *Alliances and Illusions*; Warnock, *Partner to Behemoth*; Cuff and Granatstein, *Canadian-American Relations in Wartime*; Creighton, *The Forked Road*; Holmes, *The Shaping of Peace*; Littleton, *Target Nation*; Clark-Jones, *A Staple State*; Smith, *Diplomacy of Fear*; Whitaker and Marcuse, *Cold War Canada*; Bothwell, *The Big Chill*; Mahant and Mount, *Invisible and Inaudible in Washington*; Keating, *Canada and World Order*.

3 Ericson et al., *Negotiating Control*, 397, 174 (quote); Willis, *The Media Effect*, xii; Curran, 'Rethinking the Media as a Public Sphere,' 29. See also Cook, *Governing with the News*, and Miller, *Media Pressure on Foreign Policy*.

4 Rutherford, *The Making of the Canadian Media*, 81, 84, 75 (quote). Mary Vipond notes that "the idea of communication ... has always been central to both the material and the mythological definition of Canada" (Vipond, *Listening In*, 23).

5 Chomsky, *Manufacturing Consent*; Gitlin, *The World Is Watching*; Hall, 'Cul-

ture, the Media and the '"Ideological Effect"'; Hall, 'The Rediscovery of "Ideology." ' The absence of broadcasting records is perhaps less detrimental in analysing the American context, where large, private corporations dominated both publishing and broadcasting, resulting in more homogenized news coverage; in Canada, however, the state-owned Canadian Broadcasting Corporation (CBC) dominated the airwaves and was frequently targeted by conservative commentators for its perceived left-wing bias. The ability to scrutinize CBC broadcasts, therefore, would allow for an analysis of the full range of views available to Canadians. For a comparison between U.S. commercial broadcasting and the CBC, see Vipond, *The Mass Media in Canada*, 37–42.

6 For a summary of this body of scholarship, including an exhaustive (until 2000) bibliography, see Griffith, 'The Cultural Turn in Cold War Studies.' More recent examples in the field include Rotter, *Comrades at Odds*; Ryan, *US Foreign Policy in World History*; Kuznick and Gilbert, *Rethinking Cold War Culture*; McAlister, *Epic Encounters*; Klein, *Cold War Orientalism*; Morgan, *Reds*; Richmond, *Cultural Exchange and the Cold War*; Endy, *Cold War Holidays*; Logevall, 'A Critique of Containment'; Field, *American Cold War Culture*.

7 Eric Foner, 'Introduction,' in Prevots, *Dance for Export*, 1.

8 For a rare comparative study of differing Canadian and American attitudes toward the Cold War conflict, see Valerie Korinek, '"It's a Tough Time to Be in Love": The Darker Side of *Chatelaine* during the Cold War,' in Cavell, *Love, Hate, and Fear in Canada's Cold War*, 159–82. Korinek provides a more comprehensive analysis of *Chatelaine* and its Cold War–era readers in *Roughing It in the Suburbs*.

9 Whitaker and Marcuse, *Cold War Canada*, 282, 7; Smith, *Diplomacy of Fear*, 4.

10 Acheson cited in Smith, *Diplomacy of Fear*, 164; Mahant and Mount, *Invisible and Inaudible in Washington*, 33; Gaddis cited in Logevall, 'A Critique of Containment,' 494–5.

11 Bothwell, *The Big Chill*, 73; Smith, *Diplomacy of Fear*, 4, 7.

12 Mahant and Mount, 'The U.S. Cultural Impact upon Canada,' 451–3; Vipond, *The Mass Media in Canada*, 26.

13 Edwardson, *Canadian Content*, 9; McKinnon, 'Can-Con vs. Neo-Con,' 136.

14 For a thorough discussion of the evolving theoretical framework guiding scholars of Cold War cultural exchange, see Gienow-Hecht, 'Shame on US?'

15 Wagnleitner, *Coca-Colonization*. Ravault's term is taken from page three of this same volume.

16 New, *Borderlands*, 50.

1. The Bomb: 'Pax Anglo-Saxonia' or 'Too Much Power'?

1 Ross Harkness, 'Atom May Give Canada California's Winter,' *Toronto Star*, 8 August 1945.

2 Some of the more prominent works that deal specifically with the Americans' responses to the Bomb include Boyer, *By the Bomb's Early Light* and *Fallout*; Oakes, *The Imaginary War*; Henrickson, *Dr. Strangelove's America*; Fried, *The Russians Are Coming*.

3 Some examples of works which incorporate elements of this view include Minifie, *Peacemaker or Powder-Monkey;* Grant, *Lament for a Nation;* Creighton, *The Forked Road.*

4 C.R. Blackburn, 'Atomic Bomb Rocks Japan,' *Globe and Mail*, 7 August 1945.

5 A.C. Cummings, 'Terrifying Power Menaces Globe,' *Ottawa Citizen*, 7 August 1945; 'Jap City "Seared to Death" by One Bomb,' *Ottawa Citizen*, 8 August 1945; 'Atom Bomb Could Destroy Civilization,' *Globe and Mail*, 7 August 1945; 'Sees Atomic Bomb as Best Means to Maintain Peace,' *Ottawa Citizen*, 7 August 1945; Szilard cited in Boyer, *By the Bomb's Early Light*, 61; *Canadian Tribune* cited in Wittner, *One World or None*, 172.

6 Austin Cross, 'Ottawa Scientists Helped Develop Uranium for Use as Atomic Power,' *Ottawa Citizen*, 14 August 1945.

7 Bothwell, *Eldorado*, 157.

8 Fousek, *To Lead the Free World*, 17; 'The Atomic Age: That Flash Showed Where Man's Real Problems Are: Not under the Bed but in the Cellar,' *Life*, 20 August 1945, p. 32; Kaltenborn cited in Boyer, *By the Bomb's Early Light*, 5; Blackburn, 'Atomic Bomb Rocks Japan'; 'Our Responsibilities,' *Halifax Chronicle-Herald*, 9 August 1945; Lawrence J. Burpee to editor, 'Our Scientists Absent?' *Saturday Night*, 11 August 1945, p. 2.

9 'Canada's Uranium Resources,' *Vancouver Sun*, 8 August 1945.

10 Wittner, *One World or None*, 56; A U.S. Gallup poll conducted in August 1945 found that 85 per cent approved of the bombing, 10 per cent disapproved, and 5 per cent were undecided; a Canadian survey from October of that same year found percentages of 77, 12, and 11, respectively. The polls are less reliable measures of national difference than they might seem, since they were conducted months apart and asked substantively different questions: The U.S poll specifically referenced the targeting of civilians, asking, 'Do you approve or disapprove of using the new atomic bomb on Japanese cities?' The Canadian version omitted reference to the Bomb's specific target. Instead, it provided a not-so-subtle connection between the Bomb and Japanese surrender, and framed the bombing as an

Allied, rather than U.S., action, asking, 'Now that it's all over, do you think the Allies should or should not have used the atomic bomb against Japan?' (U.S. Gallup Poll, 27 August 1945; Canadian Institute of Public Opinion [hereafter, 'CIPO'] news release, 3 October 1945).

11 'Pre-eminence of the Anglo-Saxon,' *Canadian Forum*, September 1945, p. 127.

12 'Genie out of the Bottle,' *Saturday Night*, 11 August 1945, p. 1; the characterizations of the magazine's politics and audience are taken from Rutherford, *The Making of the Canadian Media*, 46, 81.

13 'Should We Have Used It?' *Saturday Night*, 8 September 1945, p. 1.

14 'Atomic Bombing – the Moral Issue,' *Vancouver Sun*, 10 August 1945; 'Our Pledge to Youth,' *Canadian Home Journal*, September 1945, p. 88; Dyson Carter, 'Pill Bottle May Hold 50 Years' House Heat,' *Toronto Star*, 7 August 1945.

15 'The Atomic Age,' p. 32; Cecil Swanson, Letter to the editor, *Canadian Churchman*, 6 September 1945, p. 7; 'A Noose to Hang the Human Race,' *Calgary Herald*, 7 August 1945; 'Pre-eminence of the Anglo-Saxon,' 127.

16 Janet Besse and Harold D. Lasswell, 'Our Columnists and the A-Bomb,' *World Politics* 3 (October 1950): 78.

17 Willson Woodside, 'U.S. Strength, Peace-Time Draft, Will Closely Concern Canada,' *Saturday Night*, 8 September 1945, p. 15; Paul Sauriol, 'La Bombe atomique: Nouvelle arme des Alliés contre le Japon,' *Le Devoir*, 7 August 1945; Paul Sauriol, 'La Bombe atomique a détruit 60 pour cent de Hiroshima,' *Le Devoir*, 8 August 1945, author's translation ('Mais les Mongols ne se battaient pas au nom de la civilisation démocratique'). (At the request of the publisher, I have provided English translations of all quotations taken directly from French-language publications.) Canadian Fellowship of Reconciliation cited in Wittner, *One World or None*, 98.

18 Harold C. Francis, 'A Pessimistic View,' *Saturday Night*, 22 September 1945, p. 2.

19 Dower, *War without Mercy*, 4; Hollinger, *Postethnic America*, 55.

20 Dower, *War without Mercy*, 9.

21 'We Are Not Proud of It,' *Omaha Morning World Herald*, 8 August 1945; 'Hot Enough for Satan Himself,' *Vancouver Sun*, 9 August 1945.

22 'Avenging Genii,' *Globe and Mail*, 9 August 1945.

23 Elizabeth Saville to editor, 'No Ordinary Enemy Met the "Atomic,"' *Globe and Mail*, 29 August 1945; Fred Gregg to editor, 'Quickest Way Best for Fighting Japs,' *Globe and Mail*, 11 August 1945; King cited in Smith, *Diplomacy of Fear*, 93.

24 Dower, *War without Mercy*, 48–53; Bercuson, *Blood on the Hills*, 29.

25 Dower, *War without Mercy*, 61–6.
26 Gerald Bonwick to editor, 'Atomic Bombing of Japanese Area Said "Not War at All,"' *Globe and Mail*, 9 August 1945; Margaret Baldwin to editor, 'Sorry Anglo-Saxons Produced Atomic Bomb,' 15 August 1945; J. Preston to editor, 'Things Japs Have Done Called for Retribution,' *Globe and Mail*, 17 August 1945.
27 Cited in Boyer, *By the Bomb's Early Light*, 184.
28 'Negro Scientists Help Produce 1st Atom Bomb,' *Chicago Defender*, 18 August 1945; Fousek, *To Lead the Free World*, 29–33.
29 Boyer, *By the Bomb's Early Light*, 183.
30 Winks, *The Blacks in Canada*, 394; Whitaker and Marcuse, *Cold War Canada*, 7-10.
31 Boyer, *By the Bomb's Early Light*, 126.
32 Howard W. Blakeslee, 'Public Jitters Concerning Perils of Atomic Bomb Held Unjustified,' *Ottawa Citizen*, 9 August 1945.
33 Boyer, *By the Bomb's Early Light*, 124; Cottrell and Eberhart cited on page 23 of the same volume.
34 Wittner, *One World or None*, 81; A.C. Cummings, 'Implications of Bomb Still Amaze Britons,' *Ottawa Citizen*, 8 August 1945; Mahant and Mount, 'The U.S. Cultural Impact upon Canada,' 451.
35 Wittner, *One World or None*, 98; CIPO Press Release, 26 January 1946; Kuffert, *A Great Duty*, 109.
36 'The New Age,' *Ottawa Citizen*, 16 August 1945; Stuart Armour, 'Atomic Energy Brings Problems for Canada,' *Saturday Night*, 1 September 1945, p. 7; 'Can We Control Atomic Power?' *Financial Post*, 18 August 1945; Coldwell cited in J.A. Hume, 'Sees Atomic Bomb as Powerful Weapon for Peace,' *Ottawa Citizen*, 8 August 1945.
37 Packenham, *Liberal America*; Hartz cited in Peceny, *Democracy at the Point of Bayonets*, 27.
38 Logevall, 'A Critique of Containment,' 490 (quote), 487.
39 Dolan, *Allegories of America*, 62, 65; Hartz, cited in Peceny, *Democracy at the Point of Bayonets*, 27.
40 Singh, 'Culture/Wars,' 510 (quote), 471–522.
41 'The Atomic Age,' 32; Fousek, *To Lead the Free World*, 2; Boyer, *By the Bomb's Early Light*, 40.
42 Richard J. Needham, 'One Man's Opinion,' *Calgary Herald*, 9 August 1945.
43 J.F. Boland to editor, 'Secrecy Is Urged for Atomic Bomb,' *Globe and Mail*, 10 August 1945.
44 Stuart Armour, 'Atomic Energy Brings Problems for Canada,' *Saturday Night*, 1 September 1945, pp. 6, 7.

45 As political scientist Tom Keating's study of Canadian post-war foreign policy demonstrates, 'multilateralism has frequently been viewed as the most effective strategy for pursuing national policy objectives' (*Canada and World Order*, 5).

46 McKinnon, 'Can-Con vs. Neo Con,' 131, 139; New, *Borderlands*, 12.

47 Finkel, *Our Lives*, 12; Whitaker and Hewitt, *Canada and the Cold War*, 19, 84; Whitaker and Marcuse, *Cold War Canada*, 10.

48 This imagined disparity between state repression in Canada and the United States is a central theme in both Whitaker and Marcuse, *Cold War Canada*, and Whitaker and Hewitt, *Canada and the Cold War*.

49 Saul, *Reflections of a Siamese Twin*, 8, 13; Coleman, *White Civility*, 5. For other appraisals of the origins and functions of Canadian multiculturalism, see Mackey, *The House of Difference*; Bannerji, *The Dark Side of the Nation*; Walcott, *Black Like Who?*; Day, *Multiculturalism and the History of Canadian Diversity*.

50 For a more sanguine view on Canadian multiculturalism than those cited in the previous reference, see Kymlicka, *Finding Our Way*.

51 Cited in Boyer, *By the Bomb's Early Light*, 36.

52 'Fear of Atom Bomb's Future Use Grows and Spreads in Britain,' *Ottawa Citizen*, 10 August 1945.

53 'For Good or for Evil,' *Maclean's*, 15 September 1945, p. 1; *Saturday Night*, 8 September 1945, p. 2; Willson Woodside, 'Emperor's Position the Key to Surrender and Future,' *Saturday Night*, 18 August 1945, p. 13.

54 W.R. Inge, 'No Winning Side Left in Any Future War,' *Saturday Night*, 29 September 1945, p. 11; Percy Price, 'We Must Now Develop World Patriotism,' *Saturday Night*, 20 October 1945, pp. 6–7.

55 'Sharing the Secret,' *Saturday Night*, 15 September 1945, p. 1; 'And Now Atomic Bombs,' *Toronto Star*, 7 August 1945; Elmore Philpott, 'Real Atomic Peril,' *Ottawa Citizen*, 28 August 1945.

56 'Too Much Power,' *Saturday Night*, 25 August 1945, p. 1; *Le Droit* cited in 'Views from French Canada,' *Winnipeg Tribune*, 15 August 1945; 'What Do Women Think? We Must Determine If Bomb Will Be Used for Good or Evil,' *Winnipeg Tribune*, 8 August 1945.

57 Whitaker and Marcuse, *Cold War Canada*, 11; 'Allied Clash in Germany,' *Saturday Night*, 22 September 1945, p. 3; Willson Woodside, 'Deadlock on Italy Emphasizes Dangers of Influence Spheres,' *Saturday Night*, 22 September 1945, p. 12.

58 Whitaker and Marcuse, *Cold War Canada*, 11.

59 'The Split Atom,' *New York Daily News*, 8 August 1945; 'Canada's Empire,' *Montreal Gazette*, reprinted in the *Winnipeg Tribune*, 14 August 1945.

60 Jones-Imhotep, 'Communicating the Nation,' 35.
61 Ibid.; Whitaker and Marcuse, *Cold War Canada*, 43.
62 'It's Our Uranium,' *Saturday Night*, 8 August 1945, p. 1; '"Thou Shalt Not Covet,"' *Financial Post*, 18 August 1945.
63 'It's Our Uranium,' 3; 'Wisdom Has Governed So Far,' *Globe and Mail*, 10 August 1945.
64 Wittner, *One World or None*, 101.
65 Mary Lowrey Ross, 'Miss A. Meets the Atomic World and Puts It in Its Place,' *Saturday Night*, 1 September 1945, p. 10.
66 To cite a further example: prior to the Second World War, as Paul Rutherford observes, 'the front page of the *Montreal Gazette* displayed a fascination with American vice and crime, much more so than for signs of Canadian or British depravity' (Rutherford, *The Making of the Canadian Media*, 58).

2. Espionage: 'Soviet Method Revealed!'

1 'Charge and Counter-charge,' *Ottawa Citizen*, 25 February 1946.
2 Whitaker and Hewitt, *Canada and the Cold War*, 17.
3 Mary Lowrey Ross, 'As Spy Story "The Iron Curtain" Is Exciting Entertainment,' *Saturday Night*, 17 May 1948, p. 26; 'The New Pictures,' *Time*, 17 May 1948, p. 102; 'Winnipeg Service Clubs to Boycott "Iron Curtain,"' *Canadian Moving Picture Digest*, 28 February 1948, p. 5; Jack Droy, 'Vancouver News,' *Canadian Moving Picture Digest*, 5 June 1948, p. 9.
4 'The New Pictures,' 102; Ross, 'As Spy Story,' 26; D. Mosdell, 'Film Review,' *Canadian Forum*, July 1948, p. 89; 'Dynamite!' *Canadian Moving Picture Digest*, 10 April, 1948, p. 1; Bosley Crowther, '"The Iron Curtain"' – New Roxy Film Poses a Question: Is It Being Raised or Lowered?' *New York Times*, 16 May 1948.
5 'The New Pictures,' 102; Ross, 'As Spy Story,' 26; Crowther, '"The Iron Curtain"'; Mosdell, 'Film Review,' 89.
6 Ibid.; Crowther, '"The Iron Curtain."'
7 Knight, *How the Cold War Began*, 102–6; Bothwell, *The Big Chill*, 19; Drew Pearson, '"Inside" Government Men Co-operating with Soviet Named by Russian Agent,' *Toronto Telegram*, 16 February 1946.
8 Weisbord, *The Strangest Dream*, 146–56; Whitaker and Marcuse, *Cold War Canada*, 56–80.
9 Weisbord, *The Strangest Dream*, 172–3; Whitaker and Marcuse, *Cold War Canada*, 71.
10 Ibid., 70–4 (quote); Kristmanson, *Plateaus of Freedom*, 139.
11 Smith, *Diplomacy of Fear*, 133–4; Kristmanson, *Plateaus of Freedom*, 154.

12 Weisbord, The *Strangest Dream,* 4.
13 Whitaker and Marcuse, *Cold War Canada,* 71; Weisbord, *The Strangest Dream,* 152.
14 Whitaker and Marcuse, *Cold War Canada,* 74; Weisbord, *The Strangest Dream,* 4; Knight, *How the Cold War Began,* 12–13.
15 Whitaker and Marcuse, *Cold War Canada,* 72; Clément, 'Spies, Lies, and a Commission,' 53-79. Historian Frank Clarke makes a similar case for the affair's role in spurring demands for increased protection for civil liberties, though he points out that the era's civil rights organizations remained bitterly divided over the issue of communist participation in the movement (Frank K. Clarke, 'Debilitating Divisions: The Civil Liberties Movement in Early Cold War Canada 1946-48,' in Kinsman et al., *Whose National Security?* 171). Because of the extensive work already done in this area, and because it does not lend itself well to a cross-cultural comparison, I have chosen not to re-examine the Gouzenko Affair's impact on civil liberties. U.S. commentators virtually ignored this aspect of the incident, focusing instead – and understandably – on its implications for international relations and national security. In general, centrist and left-leaning publications and organizations protested government handling of the case, while those on the right and some publications from Quebec defended it. That said, concerns over government secrecy and the suspension of *habeas corpus* were tabled by many on the right as well.
16 Knight, *How the Cold War Began,* 34–44.
17 Ibid., 104–5; Pearson, '"Inside" Government Men.'
18 Weisbord, *The Strangest Dream,* 155; Elmore Philpott, 'Ottawa Spy Case,' *Vancouver Sun,* 22 February 1946.
19 Pearson, ' "Inside" Government Men.'
20 Lackenbauer and Farish, 'The Cold War on Canadian Soil,' 920; 'Exercise Musk Ox,' *Life,* 11 March 1946, p. 40.
21 Dorothy Thompson, 'What Kind of One World?' *Globe and Mail,* 22 February 1946; Willson Woodside, 'Sees Spy Case as Outstanding Treason Affair,' *Toronto Telegram,* 21 February 1946.
22 Weisbord, *The Strangest Dream,* 4; 'Atomic Secret Leaks to Soviet,' *Globe and Mail,* 16 February 1946; J.H. Fisher, 'Plot to Sell to Russians Secret of Atomic Bomb,' *Toronto Telegram,* 16 February 1946; 'Soviet Note Reveals Situation Fraught with Terrible Possibilities,' *Toronto Telegram,* 22 February 1946; 'Loose Talk of "Invasion,"' *Ottawa Citizen,* 12 March 1946; Whitaker and Marcuse, *Cold War Canada,* 91; NRC president cited in Knight, *How the Cold War Began,* 148.
23 P.J. Philip, 'Documents Included in Roundup,' *Globe and Mail,* 18 Febru-

ary 1946. 'London Papers Claim Spy Ring World-Wide,' *Globe and Mail*, 18 February 1946.

24 'Spies across Canada: Soviet Method Revealed,' *Toronto Telegram*, 16 February 1946; 'The Cost of Friendship,' *Globe and Mail*, 18 February 1946.

25 J.H. Fisher, 'Plot to Sell Russians Secrets of Atomic Bomb,' *Toronto Telegram*, 16 February 1946; 'RCMP Barracks Used as "Cells" for Prisoners,' *Toronto Telegram*, 16 February 1946; 'Russia Building "Fifth Column" Spy Ring in Canada,' *Vancouver Sun*, 16 February 1946; 'Spying in Canada,' *Saturday Night*, 23 February 1946; Irving Plaunt, 'The "Spy Ring" in Perspective,' *Ottawa Citizen*, 28 February 1946.

26 'Charge Russia Sought Metal Stock Here,' *Globe and Mail*, 19 February 1946; 'Ottawa RCMP Detain Girl in Code Office,' *Vancouver Sun*, 19 February 1946; 'Big Russian Spy Ring Bared in Theft of Atom Secrets,' *Calgary Herald*, 16 February 1946.

27 'Red Propagandist Busy in Mine Areas for Years,' *Toronto Telegram*, 18 February 1946; 'Russian Spy Activities Exposed in Canada,' *Calgary Herald*, 18 February 1946; 'Communists Fomenting Trouble in India,' *Toronto Telegram*, 23 February 1946.

28 'Duplessis Offers Spy-Hunt Help,' *Globe and Mail*, 20 February 1946; Whitaker and Hewitt, *Canada and the Cold War*, 85.

29 'Communism Threatens Democracy in Canada, Drew Warns Audience,' *Globe and Mail*, 22 February 1946.

30 Whitaker and Hewitt, *Canada and the Cold War*, 36–7.

31 Niebuhr cited in Fousek, *To Lead the Free World*, 121; 'The Cost of Friendship.' The commission phrased it this way: the accused 'had a loyalty which took priority over the loyalty owed by them to their country' (cited in 'Higher Loyalties,' *Ottawa Citizen*, 26 March 1946). The *Ottawa Citizen* editorial which reprinted the phrase rejected this line of reasoning, arguing that scientists with 'higher loyalties' (to humanity rather than the nation-state) should be applauded for rejecting demands that they produce atomic weapons.

32 'Is Canada a Nation?' *Canadian Forum*, June 1946, p. 53.

33 Foster cited in Day, *Multiculturalism and the History of Canadian Diversity*, 151, 153.

34 Ibid., 173. On Canadian attitudes toward non-traditional immigrants, see CIPO press release, 30 October 1946, which finds Canadians eager to ban a series of immigrants on the basis of nationality, ethnicity, religion, and race. This poll is discussed in greater detail in chapter 4.

35 Kristmanson, *Plateaus of Freedom*, 48; Gregory S. Kealey, 'Spymasters, Spies, and Their Subjects: The RCMP and Canadian State Repression, 1914–1939,' in Kinsman et al., *Whose National Security?* 19.

36 Franca Iacovetta, 'Making Model Citizens: Gender, Corrupted Democracy, and Immigrant and Refugee Reception Work in Cold War Canada,' in Kinsman et al., *Whose National Security?* 154 (quote), 155; Kristmanson, *Plateaus of Freedom*, xiv. Thorough analysis of the Massey Commission can be found in Litt, *The Muses, the Masses, and the Massey Commission*, and in Edwardson, *Canadian Content*. Subsequent commissions addressed radio and television broadcasting, magazine publishing, and bilingualism and biculturalism; see Mackey, *The House of Difference*, 54.

37 Mackey, *The House of Difference*, 13.

38 S.F. Wise, 'Colonial Attitudes from the Era of the War of 1812 to the Rebellions of 1837,' in Wise and Brown, *Canada Views the United States*, 23. Of course, Americans were not the only, nor always the primary, counterpoint to Canadians' self-conception. The 'national character' has been framed in opposition to a series of identities – including Indigenous Peoples, the French, and a variety of immigrant ethnicities – depending on shifting national requirements and contexts. As Mackey notes, however, the United States constitutes the 'external and threatening "other" which has consistently been central in the defining of Canadian identity' (Mackey, *The House of Difference*, 57). For the author, the 'othering' of a more powerful entity casts Canada as a feminized victim of the United States, and serves to elide the victimizations *within* Canadian society.

39 Edwardson, *Canadian Content*, 51–77.

40 'Duplessis Offers Spy-Hunt Help'; King cited in Knight, *How the Cold War Began*, 113 (see also page 172 of the same volume); 'The Espionage Case,' *Halifax Chronicle-Herald*, 18 February 1946.

41 Edgar Kelley, 'Capital Shocked by Revelations,' *Halifax Chronicle-Herald*, 18 February 1946; Omer Heroux, 'L'Enquête sur l'espionnage,' *Le Devoir*, 18 February 1946, author's translation ('un parti nationaliste étranger'); editorial cartoon, *Calgary Herald*, 20 February 1946; Philip cited in Knight, *How the Cold War Began*, 154–5.

42 Walden cited in Whitaker and Marcuse, *Cold War Canada*, 264. The reorientation in fictional accounts identified by Walden provides an accurate reflection of the changing mandate of the real RCMP, as G. Kealey notes: 'Initially imperialist, and closely identified with the interests of the British Empire, the Service later switched metropolitan allegiance from London to Washington' (Kealey, 'Spymasters, Spies, and Their Subjects,' 19).

43 Drew Pearson's initial story is the most significant of these reports that foreground the continental nature of the espionage operations. See also W.H. Lawrence, 'Atomic Bomb Know-How Remains a U.S. Secret, State Secretary Says,' *New York Times*, 20 February 1946; 'FBI "In Thick of" Probe to Get U.S. Atom Secrets,' *Toronto Telegram*, 19 February 1946.

44 Joseph E. Davies, 'Says Soviet Right in Seeking Bomb,' *Globe and Mail*, 19 February 1946; 'Canadian Reds Rally to Russia's Defense,' *Calgary Herald*, 20 February 1946; Paul Sauriol, 'Le Complot d'espionnage et la course au secret atomique,' *Le Devoir*, 19 February 1946, author's translation ('C'est pour la Russie une question de légitime défense que de rechercher les secrets de la bombe atomique et qu'elle a absolument le droit moral de la faire'). For examples of editorials and articles that adopted Davies' line of reasoning, see 'Bare the Facts Fully and Quickly,' *Regina Leader-Post*, 19 February 1946; 'Wait for the Facts,' *Ottawa Citizen*, 19 February 1946; 'Spies in Ottawa,' *Canadian Forum*, March 1946, p. 275.

45 George Fielding Eliot, 'U.S. Military Analyst Reviews the Spy Issue,' *Toronto Star*, 22 February 1946. p. 6; 'Protocol and Espionage,' *Globe and Mail*, 23 February 1946; *New York Times* cited in Knight, *How the Cold War Began*, 140.

46 See, for example, 'Canada,' *Time*, 4 March 1946, which provides an amused summary of the more sensational rumours appearing in the Canadian press. (Example: 'The Windsor *Daily Star* heard about a "large black sedan" crossing from Canada to the U.S., hinted that it was probably loaded with escaping Russians.')

47 Fousek, *To Lead the Free World*, 118–23; 'American Foreign Policy,' *New York Times*, 1 March 1946.

48 Fousek, *To Lead the Free World*, 120; Gwinn cited in '"Certain" Foreign Powers Said Using Endless Funds to Get U.S. Atomic Secrets,' *Toronto Telegram*, 19 February 1946.

49 CIPO press releases, 23 June 1945, 18 March 1946, 18 September 1946. Note that a portion of the 44 per cent who did not perceive a change in the Russians could well have been admirers of the Soviets all along. Among those who believed that 'one country wishes to dominate the world,' on the other hand, Canadians were most likely to cite Russia as the power seeking world domination. Canadians were much less inclined to finger fellow Commonwealth member Britain as the aspiring hegemon than were Americans (who rarely cited their own nation), and much less apt than France and Australia to identify the United States – the source of much Canadian news about world affairs – for the same title. To a large degree, Russia dominated Canadian responses by default. Several other public opinion surveys are relevant here: Polls conducted in late 1945 revealed that 70 per cent of Americans favoured a retention of the nuclear monopoly; the figure in Canada was 58 per cent (CIPO press release, 5 December 1945). A CIPO poll taken in the midst of the spy trials revealed 32 per cent of Canadians still expressed sentiments favourable or neutral toward Russia's international objectives, while 52 per cent voiced unfavourable views (CIPO press release, 13 April 1946). A survey conducted after the royal commission's final report

on the Gouzenko Affair indicated that 38 per cent of Canadians felt more friendly or about the same toward Russia as they had a year ago, while 51 per cent felt less friendly. U.S. figures for the same question were 30 per cent and 62 per cent, respectively (CIPO press release, 5 October 1946).

50 M. Pryor to editor, 'In Defence of Russia,' *Calgary Herald*, 22 February 1946; Harry Youngman to editor, 'Russia Does Not Want War,' *Calgary Herald*, 23 February 1946; S.T. Jones to editor, 'Accusations against the USSR,' *Ottawa Citizen*, 21 February 1946; Betty Simpson to editor, 'An Anti-Soviet Witch-Hunt,' *Ottawa Citizen*, 21 February 1946.

51 Simpson, 'An Anti-Soviet Witch-Hunt'; D.R. Smith to editor, 'Browned Off,' *Vancouver Sun*, 26 February 1946; 'Seamen Score "Undemocratic" Spy Probe,' *Vancouver Sun*, 28 February 1946.

52 Michael Fellman, 'Sleeping with the Elephant: Reflections of an American-Canadian on Americanization and Anti-Americanism in Canada,' in Findlay and Coates, *Parallel Destinies*, 282; Day, *Multiculturalism*, 5; Knight, *How the Cold War Began*, 155.

53 *Financial Post* cited in Whitaker and Marcuse, *Cold War Canada*, 287; 'The Spy Scare,' *Vancouver Sun*, 18 February 1946; 'Primarily a Canadian Concern,' *Winnipeg Tribune*, 26 February 1946. 'Bare the Facts Fully and Quickly,' *Regina Leader-Post*, 19 February 1946; *Hamilton Spectator* cited in 'Russia Has Devoted Supporters in Canada,' *Calgary Herald*, 25 February 1946.

54 'Time for a Report,' *Globe and Mail*, 20 February 1946; 'The Cost of Friend-ship.'

55 J.H. Fisher, 'Staff of 100 in Capital Runs Information Machine That Works but One Way,' *Toronto Telegram*, 18 February 1946; 'False Prophets Responsible for Creating Fifth Column in Canada,' *Toronto Telegram*, 21 February 1946.

56 'Suspended Animation,' *Globe and Mail*, 21 February 1946.

57 H.R. Armstrong, 'International Feeling Major Spy Case Worry,' *Toronto Star*, 20 February 1946.

58 'Those 12,000,000 Names,' *Toronto Star*, 20 February 1946.

59 'Mr. King and the Soviet Union,' *Toronto Star*, 22 February 1946; 'Canadian Government Took the Only Possible Course,' *Toronto Star*, 5 March 1946.

60 Cited in Clarke, 'Debilitating Divisions,' 173.

61 'Wide Speculation in U.S. Press over Spy Revelations in Ottawa,' *Ottawa Citizen*, 19 February 1946; Simpson, 'An Anti-Soviet Witch-Hunt'; 'U.S. Shocked: Bitterness of Russia Is Noted,' *Globe and Mail*, 21 February 1946.

62 'Trial by Newspaper?' *Ottawa Citizen*, 20 February 1946; 'Charge and Coun-ter-charge,' *Ottawa Citizen*, 25 February 1946.

63 'Charge and Counter-charge'; Untitled editorial, *Ottawa Citizen*, 28 February 1946. The *Citizen* faced similar attacks from Canadian dailies as well, particularly the *Ottawa Journal* and the French-language press.
64 Cited in Logevall, 'A Critique of Containment,' 478–9.
65 Whitaker and Marcuse, *Cold War Canada*, xi.

3. The Cold War and the Third World: 'Time to Lay Bogey of British Imperialism'

1 James Madison, 'Thinking about Wendell Willkie,' in Madison, *Wendell Willkie*, xvii. Willkie cited in F.F. Hunter, 'India Is Not a Nation, and Cannot Become One,' *Saturday Night*, 21 November 1942, p. 16.
2 Madison, 'Thinking about Wendell Willkie,' xvii; Hunter, 'India Is Not a Nation,' 16.
3 Whitaker and Marcuse, *Cold War Canada*, 388.
4 Hillmer and Granatstein, *Empire to Umpire*, 255–6; *Globe and Mail* and *Ottawa Journal* cited on 255.
5 Mackey, *The House of Difference*, 30–1. Of course, U.S. immigration policies were also highly restrictive, establishing quotas and outright bans for those considered undesirable. Still, the nation contained much higher percentages of non-whites and East- and South-Europeans than did Canada, a state of affairs that Canadian elites blamed for the higher levels of social unrest they ascribed to the United States.
6 Ibid.; King cited in Harney, '"So Great a Heritage as Ours,"' 54.
7 Mackey, *The House of Difference*, 31. See also Berger, 'The True North Strong and Free,' 3–26, and Berger, *The Sense of Power*, 129–49.
8 Berger, *The Sense of Power*, 5; Coleman, *White Civility*, 138; Massolin, *Canadian Intellectuals*, 241, 5. The 'quid pro quo' was one of the pragmatic arguments made by Canadian imperialists in support of their nation's participation in the Boer War, the First World War, and in more general financial and armaments support for Britain. See Miller, 'Loyalty, Patriotism and Resistance.'
9 Massolin, *Canadian Intellectuals*, 8.
10 Finlay and Sprague, *The Structure of Canadian History*, 341, 414; see also Trofimenkoff, *The Dream of Nation*.
11 Miller, 'Loyalty, Patriotism and Resistance'; Brown, 'Goldwin Smith and Anti-imperialism'; Stiles, '"The Dragon of Imperialism"'; Regina Manifesto cited in Naylor, 'Pacifism or Anti-imperialism?' 217.
12 Naylor, 'Pacifism or Anti-imperialism?' 214, 236–7.
13 Innis cited in Massolin, *Canadian Intellectuals*, 199. In the words of Arthur

Burns, an official from the Ford administration, 'Canada has a special relationship with the Third World which can be useful to us. It has no colonial history, and has played a leading role in peacekeeping operations. As a bilingual country, it has ties with both the Commonwealth and the francophone Third World. It is the world's sixth largest aid donor' (cited in Mahant and Mount, *Invisible and Inaudible in Washington*, 77).

14 Cited in Keating, *Canada and World Order*, 11.

15 Day, *Multiculturalism and the History of Canadian Diversity*, 3–5, 157–76; Mackay, *The House of Difference*, 50.

16 For a discussion of the relationship between Wilson's and Roosevelt's attitudes to colonialism and the broader tradition of American anti-imperialism, see Heiss, 'The Evolution of the Imperial Idea and US National Identity,' and Orders, '"Adjusting to a New Period in History."' For works that describe the anti-imperial activities of American racial minorities, see Von Eschen, *Race against Empire*; Plummer, *Rising Wind*; Borstelmann, *Apartheid's Reluctant Uncle*; Krenn, *Black Diplomacy*; and Dudziak, *Cold War Civil Rights*.

17 Michael Ignatieff, 'The Burden,' *New York Times Magazine*, 5 January 2003, p. 24; Ninkovich, *The United States and Imperialism*, 249.

18 Williams, *The Tragedy of American Diplomacy*; Kaplan, '"Left Alone with America": The Absence of Empire in the Study of American Culture,' in Kaplan and Pease, *Cultures of United States Imperialism*, 3–21.

19 Rotter, *Comrades at Odds*, 161; OSS memorandum cited in Heiss, 'The Evolution of the Imperial Idea,' 535.

20 Young, *Postcolonialism*, 180.

21 Ibid. Penny Von Eschen acknowledges that the intensive anti-communism of the 1950s, along with the acceleration of domestic civil rights struggles which diverted attention from international matters, did lead to an amelioration of anti-imperialist rhetoric among African Americans. However, even in mainline organizations such as the NAACP, the issue remained on the table throughout the period (Von Eschen, *Race against Empire*, 112–21).

22 H. Ford Wilkins, 'Philippine Republic Is Born as U.S. Rule Ends in Glory,' *New York Times*, 4 July 1946; 'The Philippine Republic,' *New York Times*, 4 July 1946.

23 'New Republic Is Born in Philippines,' *Life*, 22 July 1946, p. 19; McNutt cited in Fousek, *To Lead the Free World*, 80–1.

24 Ninkovich, *The United States and Imperialism*, 80.

25 Fousek, *To Lead the Free World*, 80.

26 Cited in ibid., 82–3.

27 *Canadian Periodical Index, 1938–1947* (Toronto: University of Toronto Press, 1948).

28 In the words of Philip Massolin, Canadian elites 'explained that Canada was an advanced political entity – far superior to the republic – because of its British connection. The British nexus implied a set of moral virtues that placed the Anglo-Canadian world above other civilizations' (*Canadian Intellectuals*, 6).

29 Young, *Postcolonialism*, 180.

30 H.S.L. Polak, 'India's Contribution to the Empire's War,' *Saturday Night*, 30 August 1941, p. 6; Sadhu Singh Dhami, 'India and the War: Gandhi, Nehru, and Cripps,' *Saturday Night*, 16 May 1942, p. 7; Willson Woodside, 'India as Another Eire,' *Saturday Night*, 14 March 1942, p. 16; J. Lewis Milligan, 'India at the Cross-Roads,' *Saturday Night*,' 7 March 1942, p. 9.

31 R.C. Tute, 'Democratic Self-Government Impossible in India,' *Saturday Night*, 17 October 1942, p. 6; Hunter, 'India Is Not a Nation,' 16.

32 CIPO press release, 1 April 1946.

33 Margaret R. Kirkland, 'Time to Lay Bogey of British Imperialism,' *Saturday Night*, 23 March 1946, p. 11.

34 David England, 'British Rule Has Meant More Food for India,' *Saturday Night*, 23 March 1946, p. 10; James McCook, 'Free India, Turbulent, Unafraid,' *Regina Leader-Post*, 15 August 1947; 'May Yet Yearn for Pax Britannica,' *Halifax Chronicle-Herald*, 15 August 1947.

35 'Independence Plus,' *Globe and Mail*, 15 August 1947; McCook, 'Free India.'

36 'Independence Plus'; Alexander Inglis, 'Mr. Nehru's India,' *Queen's Quarterly* 53.4 (1946): 417; 'Hail India and Pakistan,' *Regina Leader-Post*, 16 August 1947.

37 J. Hennessy, 'India's First Problem Is National Tongue,' *Saturday Night*, 6 September 1947, p. 7; McCook, 'Free India.' Michael Hunt makes the same point in his discussion of the post-war turn in U.S. foreign policy from the language of race to that of 'development,' which ranked societies according to their relative relationship to 'modernity.' 'Not surprisingly,' he writes, 'the resulting rankings were strikingly similar to the ones assigned two centuries earlier by race-conscious ancestors' (*Ideology and US Foreign Policy*, 162).

38 'Independence Plus.'

39 'Your Babies Now,' *Winnipeg Tribune*, 16 August 1947. Rotter, *Comrades at Odds*, 85; Francis cited in Coleman, *White Civility*, 171. My use of gender-exclusive language is intentional, as the 'white civility' described by Coleman was organized around the ideals of 'whiteness, masculinity, and Britishness' (10).

40 'May Yet Yearn.'

41 Kirkland, 'Time to Lay Bogey,' 11; 'Communists Fomenting Trouble in India,' *Toronto Telegram*, 23 February 1946; 'Consider the Source,' *Globe and Mail*, 1 August 1947.

42 J.A. Stevenson, 'Topics of the Day,' *Dalhousie Review* 26 (April 1946): 102; 'India's Great Day,' *Toronto Star*, 15 August 1947; second quote cited in 'Consider the Source.'
43 Elmore Philpott, 'Gandhi the Great,' *Vancouver Sun*, 18 August 1947.
44 N. Dharmarajan to editor, 'India Also Has Her Pride,' *Globe and Mail*, 8 August 1947.
45 Pierre Vigeant, 'La Naissance de deux états indépendants dans l'Inde,' *Le Devoir*, 14 August 1947, author's translation ('Les 14 et 15 août 1947 marquent une grande date dans l'histoire du monde'; 'la domination des premiers sur les seconds').
46 Berger, *The Writing of Canadian History*, 61–2; Underhill cited in ibid., 64. The controversial nature of Underhill's views, as well as the continued dominance of anglophilia among English-Canadian elites between the wars, can be illustrated by two incidents which resulted in attempts to fire Underhill from the University of Toronto's history department. The first occurred when he taught that Britain bore some responsibility, along with Germany, for causing the First World War; the second, when Underhill wrote an article in the *Canadian Forum* condemning the anti-Americanism of Canadian politicians. On both occasions, the premier of Ontario himself, G. Howard Ferguson, threatened Underhill with dismissal. See Massolin, *Canadian Intellectuals*, 81–2.
47 Brown, 'Goldwin Smith,' 105; Michael Fellman, 'Sleeping with the Elephant: Reflections of an American-Canadian on Americanization and Anti-Americanism in Canada,' in Findlay and Coates, *Parallel Destinies*, 278.
48 Bruce Woodsworth, 'Equatorial Conflict – a Study in Black and White,' *Canadian Forum*, May 1944, pp. 42–3.
49 'India in Transition,' *Canadian Forum*, October 1946, p. 147; 'The New India,' *Canadian Forum*, October 1947, p. 148; 'The Two Dominions,' *Canadian Forum*, November 1947, p. 172.
50 Heiss, 'The Evolution of the Imperial Idea,' 534; *Life* cited on the same page; Hunter, 'India Is Not a Nation,' 16.
51 'Foreign News,' *Time*, 18 August 1947, p. 34.
52 Dorothy Thompson, 'Gandhi in the Day of Triumph,' *Globe and Mail*, 20 August 1947; Robert Trumbull, 'Civil Strife Threatens India's Future,' *Globe and Mail*, 18 August 1947; 'Foreign News'; 'India Is Free,' *New York Times*, 15 August 1947.
53 'Consider the Source'; 'Independence Plus.'
54 Tute, 'Democratic Self-Government Impossible,' 6; Hunter, 'India Is Not a Nation,' 16.
55 Polak, 'India's Contribution to the Empire's War,' 6; Woodside, 'India as Another Eire,' 16.

56 Kirkland, 'Time to Lay Bogey,' 11; Cuff and Granatstein cited in Whitaker and Marcuse, *Cold War Canada*, 140; Massolin, *Canadian Intellectuals*, 11; George Ferguson, 'Are the Yanks Invading Canada?' *Maclean's*, 1 September 1947, p. 6.
57 'The American Way,' *Canadian Forum*, May 1944, p. 27; 'Indonesian Tea Party,' *Canadian Forum*, September 1947, p. 125.
58 'The Two Dominions,' *Canadian Forum*, November 1947, p. 172; Fousek, *To Lead the Free World*, 81, 82.

4. NATO: 'Our Only Present Means of Salvation'

1 'Spring Thaw: Prediction Colder,' *Canadian Forum*, February 1949, p. 242.
2 'The Atlantic Pact,' *Canadian Forum*, April, 1949, p. 3.
3 Finlay and Sprague, *The Structure of Canadian History*, 432.
4 George Kennan, 'The Sources of Soviet Conduct,' *Foreign Affairs* 25 (July 1947): 566–82; Logevall, 'A Critique of Containment,' 473.
5 Whitaker and Marcuse, *Cold War Canada*, 127–30, 270.
6 Ibid., 314–16; Kennan, 'The Sources of Soviet Conduct,' 576.
7 Ibid. On NATO and the United States, see especially Ambrose and Brinkley, *Rise to Globalism*; Cook, *Forging the Alliance*; Kaplan, *NATO and the United States*; Leffler, *A Preponderance of Power*; McCormick, *America's Half-Century;* and Pach, *Arming the Free World*. For the diplomatic reasoning behind Canada's participation in NATO, see Haglund, *The North Atlantic Triangle Revisited*; Keating, *Canada and World Order*; Macmillan and Sorenson, *Canada and NATO*; Reid, *Time of Fear and Hope*; and Smith, *Diplomacy of Fear.*
8 Mackenzie, *Documents on Canadian External Relations*, 414–16.
9 'The Stockade,' *Time*, 28 March 1949, p. 17.
10 Willson Woodside, 'Red Seizure of Czechoslovakia Makes Western Union Urgent,' *Saturday Night*, 6 March 1948, p. 12; Willson Woodside, 'The War Is On Now, Next "Battle" in Italy, Not a Rain of A-Bombs,' *Saturday Night*, 13 March 1948, p. 14; Willson Woodside, 'Democracies Must Go Still Further, Form Transatlantic Union,' *Saturday Night*, 27 March 1948, p. 12; Willson Woodside, 'Does Canada Hope to Hitchhike on North Atlantic Pact?' *Saturday Night*, 23 October 1948, p. 14.
11 Woodside, 'Red Seizure,' 12; Woodside, 'Does Canada Hope to Hitchhike?' 14.
12 Von Eschen, *Race against Empire*, 112; Plummer, *Rising Wind*, 167–216.
13 CIPO press releases, 18 March 1946, 6 August 1947, 11 August 1948.
14 CIPO press releases, 6 April 1946, 24 July 1946, 27 November 1946, 6 January 1947, 12 April 1947, 20 September 1947, 16 February 1949.

15 CIPO press release, 17 July 1948.

16 McCormick, *America's Half-Century*, 87.

17 Plummer, *Rising Wind*, 125–65.

18 NAACP Branches resolution cited in Plummer, *Rising Wind*, 189; ibid, 184; Fousek, *To Lead the Free World*, 145.

19 'The Next Great Choice,' *Christian Century*, 24 November 1948, p. 1266; 'Shall the Generals Run Our Foreign Policy?' *Christian Century*, 23 February 1949, p. 230; 'Europe's Forgotten Man,' *Christian Century*, 8 December 1948, p. 1327.

20 McCormick, *America's Half Century*, 87.

21 *Le Canada* and first quote from *Le Devoir* cited in the *Winnipeg Tribune*, 7 April 1949; 'Le Pact à l'envers,' *Le Devoir*, 5 August 1949, author's translation ('les manœuvres du capitalisme sanguinaire'; 'Qu'en dites-vous?').

22 'The Peace Council Men,' *Saturday Night*, 29 March 1949, p. 1; 'Peace Split in the CCF,' *Saturday Night*, 17 May 1949, p. 1.

23 Berger, *The Writing of Canadian History*, 178, 238.

24 Winnipeg Study Group, 'Canada and the North Atlantic Treaty,' *International Journal* 4(3): 244–9.

25 Cited in Finlay and Sprague, *The Structure of Canadian History*, 432.

26 Keating, *Canada and World Order*, 82; Acheson cited in ibid.

27 'Antidote to Fear,' *Time*, 24 January 1949, p. 17.

28 Cook, *Forging the Alliance*, viii; 'After 173 Years, a Step into Europe,' *Newsweek*, 28 March 1949, p. 17; 'The Shape of Things,' *Nation*, 19 March 1949, p. 323.

29 Whitaker and Marcuse, *Cold War Canada*, 266; St Laurent cited in 'Hands across the Sea,' *Time*, 8 November 1948, p. 43.

30 Woodside, 'Does Canada Hope to Hitchhike?' 14; 'Isolationism in Its Grave,' *Maclean's*, 1 May 1949, p. 2.

31 'The Peace Council Men,' 1; 'CCF-ers out of Step,' *Vancouver Sun*, 6 April 1949; 'In Unity Is Strength,' *Regina Leader-Post*, 4 April 1949; 'Ce que M. Churchill a dit du Pacte,' *Le Devoir*, 5 April 1949, author's translation ('dans une certain mesure l'influence de la propagande officielle').

32 'The Stockade,' 17; 'Despite Hysteria, Pacts Are Signed to Protect Peace,' *Saturday Evening Post*, 26 March 1949, p. 10; 'Leadership They Don't Deserve,' *New Republic*, 28 February 1949, p. 6.

33 'A Historic Week,' *New York Times*, 4 April 1949, p. 22. For a summary of the contributions of Willkie, Kinsey, and Steichen to mid-century universalist discourse, see Hollinger, *Postethnic America*.

34 Willson Woodside, 'From Pact to Atlantic Union,' *Saturday Night*, 29 March 1949, p. 12.

35 For studies on the changing dimensions of 'Whiteness' that look specifically at this moment in the United States, see Jacobson, *Whiteness of a Different Color*; Rogin, *Blackface, White Noise*; and Lipsitz, 'The Meaning of Memory.' Canada's relationship to whiteness is best outlined in Coleman, *White Civility*.

36 CIPO press release, 30 October 1946. As historian Michael Hunt has demonstrated, this fusion of racial hierarchy and international affairs was also a fixture of American policy-making (*Ideology and US Foreign Policy*).

37 Attlee cited in Mackenzie, *Documents on Canadian External Relations*, 401. Pearson cited in ibid., 429. For examples of religious terminology appearing in diplomatic correspondence related to the proposed alliance, see ibid., 403, 405, 429, and 438.

38 Woodside, 'Does Canada Hope to Hitchhike?' 14; Whitaker and Marcuse, *Cold War Canada*, 265–6; CIPO press release, 18 August 1948.

39 Acheson cited in 'Historic Document Is Signed,' *Halifax Chronicle-Herald*, 5 April 1949; 'Destiny at the Door,' *New York Times*, 3 April 1949; 'The Peace Council Men,' 1.

40 Willson Woodside, 'Highlights and Personalities: A Great Week in Washington,' *Saturday Night*, 19 April 1949, p. 12. David Haglund's recent work, for instance, notes that the alliance constituted 'balancing within the family' (Haglund, *The North Atlantic Triangle Revisited*, 25).

41 Wendt cited in Haglund, *The North Atlantic Triangle Revisited*, 40; 'Destiny at the Door.'

42 Cited in Haglund, *The North Atlantic Triangle Revisited*, 42.

43 Cited in Fousek, *To Lead the Free World*, 145.

44 'CCF-ers out of Step'; 'Destiny at the Door.'

45 Finlay and Sprague, *The Structure of Canadian History*, 595; Whitfield, *The Culture of the Cold War*, 4.

46 'Under False Auspices,' *Hamilton Spectator*, 1 April 1949; Winnipeg Study Group, 'Canada and the North Atlantic Treaty,' 244; 'In Unity Is Strength.'

47 'Freedom of Belief,' letter from 'Not a Communist' to the editor, *Vancouver Sun*, 4 April 1949.

48 'The Case for the Treaty,' *Saturday Night*, 19 April 1949, p. 1.

49 'The Peace Advocates,' *Saturday Night*, 3 May 1949, p. 5.

50 Ibid.

51 Woodside, 'The War Is On Now,' 14; 'Yes, We Must Be Strong!' *Saturday Night*, 17 May 1949, p. 5.

52 'A Wider Roof,' *Time*, 28 March 1949, p. 24.

53 'Taking Sides,' *Time*, 28 February 1949, p. 19.

252 Notes to pages 157–64

54 'Lessons Learned,' *Time*, 28 March 1949, p. 18. 'After 173 Years, a Step into Europe,' 17; Woodside, 'Highlights and Personalities,' 12. As John McNay's study of Acheson shows, *Time*'s equation of the secretary and state with the Bard is apt. Acheson, the son of British parents who moved from Canada to Connecticut, was a committed anglophile whose policy-making was influenced by romantic idealism regarding the British Empire and its benevolent promotion of Western civilization (McNay, *Acheson and Empire*).

55 'Mr. Churchill at Boston,' *Globe and Mail*, 2 April 1949. See also 'From Fulton to Boston,' *Halifax Chronicle-Herald*, 7 April 1949.

56 Willson Woodside, 'Churchill Credits Pact to Soviets,' *Saturday Night*, 12 April 1949, p. 12; Haglund, *The North Atlantic Triangle Revisited*, 41; 'Mr. Churchill at Boston.'

57 Woodside, 'Does Canada Hope to Hitchhike?' 14.

58 Willson Woodside, 'Few Words Make a Lot of Trouble over the North Atlantic Pact,' *Saturday Night*, 1 March 1949, p. 14.

59 Willson Woodside, 'Sharing Out the Pact's Burdens,' *Saturday Night*, 5 April 1949, p. 12; Whitaker and Marcuse, *Cold War Canada*, 131–2, 388.

60 'Destiny at the Door.'

61 James Reston, 'We Assume World Role but Cost Bothers Us,' *New York Times*, 3 April 1949; 'Leadership They Don't Deserve,' 6–7. The first cartoon is depicted in the article 'Europe's Fear, America's Frontier,' *Newsweek*, 28 February 1949, p. 26; the second is reprinted in 'Lessons Learned,' *Time*, 28 March 1949, p. 18.

62 'The Good Right Arm,' *New York Times*, 3 April 1949; 'Destiny at the Door'; 'All Fine,' *Time*, 21 March 1949, p. 27; Ambrose and Brinkley, *Rise to Globalism*, 104.

63 'CCF-ers out of Step'; Peter Inglis, 'Will Atlantic Pact Prevent War or Hasten It? Asks Europe,' *Saturday Night*, 26 April 1949, p. 6; 'The Atlantic Treaty,' *Halifax Chronicle-Herald*, 7 April 1949.

64 Woodside, 'Sharing Out the Pact's Burdens,' 12; Woodside, 'Highlights and Personalities,' 12; 'Walter Lippmann, the Pact and Mr. Churchill,' *Globe and Mail*, 7 April 1949.

65 'Atlantic Pact: The Cold Reality,' *Calgary Herald*, 4 April 1949; Winnipeg Study Group, 'Canada and the North Atlantic Treaty,' 244.

66 'No Mere Fox-Hole from Fear' *Winnipeg Tribune*, 5 April 1949; 'The Atlantic Treaty.'

67 'The Case for the Treaty,' 1; 'Isolationism in Its Grave,' 2; 'Ce que M. Churchill a dit du Pacte,' author's translation ('Si l'on en croit ce qui se dit a Lake Success, il semble que, malgré le préambule du pacte, cette alliance relègue l'O.N.U. au second plan ...').

68 'Despite Hysteria.'

69 'As Churchill Sees It,' *Ottawa Citizen*, 2 April 1949; 'UN's Vital Role,' *Ottawa Citizen*, 5 April 1949; 'The Atlantic Treaty Vote,' *Ottawa Citizen*, 7 April 1949; 'Former Victims of Aggression Sign the Pact,' *Toronto Star*, 5 April 1949.

70 'On the Right Hand,' *Time*, 21 March 1949; CIPO press releases, 28 March, 1949, 30 April 1949.

71 'The Stockade,' 17; 'Atlantic Pact: The Cold Reality'; Woodside, 'From Pact to Atlantic Union,' 12.

72 CIPO press release, 30 April 1949.

73 Cited in Massolin, *Canadian Intellectuals*, 242.

5. Korea: 'From an Imperial Frying Pan into an American Fire'

1 Blair Fraser, 'New Role for Canadians?,' *Maclean's*, 15 December 1950, pp. 4, 41; Fraser, 'Was the Tibet Invasion Our Fault?' *Maclean's*, 1 January 1951, p. 39; Fraser, 'Win or Lose, Russians May Get Korea,' *Maclean's*, 1 January 1951, p. 9.

2 Fraser, 'Was the Tibet Invasion Our Fault?' 39.

3 Haglund, *The North Atlantic Triangle Revisited*, 83–5.

4 Keating, *Canada and World Order*, 33; King cited in ibid.; Hillmer and Granatstein, *Empire to Umpire*, 208; Stueck, *The Korean War*, 26–7.

5 Fousek, *To Lead the Free World*, 163; Keylor, *A World of Nations*, 189; Keylor and Bannister, *The Twentieth-Century World*, 273–7; Thompson and Randall, *Canada and the United States*, 195.

6 'Crisis in Korea,' *Halifax Chronicle-Herald*, 27 June 1950; 'A Matter between Sponsors,' *Halifax Chronicle-Herald*, 28 June 1950; 'An Inexhaustible Supply,' *Halifax Chronicle-Herald*, 6 July 1950.

7 CIPO press release, 5 July 1950; Foot, *The Wrong War*, 56, 59.

8 'The Choice Is Russia's,' *New York Times*, 29 June 1950; 'US Throws Forces into Korean War,' *Newsweek*, 3 July 1950, p. 11; 'US Flexes for a Bitter Struggle,' *Newsweek*, 17 July 1950, p. 14; 'The Enemy,' *Time*, 17 July 1950, p. 21; 'Aggression Threatens Peace of the World,' *Christian Century*, 5 July 1950, p. 811; Keylor, *A World of Nations*, 190. The first authoritative English-language account to cast doubt on the idea that Stalin ordered the invasion was Cumings's *Origins of the Korean War*. More recent studies, beginning with Goncharov et al., *Uncertain Partners*, assign Stalin and Mao a greater role in the planning and execution of the war than Cumings. However, the civil character of the conflict's origins, long denied in Western scholarship, can no longer be dismissed. For an excellent summary of Korean War historiography, see Stueck, *Rethinking the Korean War*.

9 'Behind the Attack on Korea,' *Ottawa Citizen*, 4 July 1950; 'Military Censorship,' *Canadian Forum*, February 1951, p. 243; Whitfield, *The Culture of the Cold War*, 156–60.

10 Cited in 'Challenge Accepted,' *Time*, 3 July 1950, p. 8.

11 'War in Korea,' *Globe and Mail*, 27 June 1950; 'Moscow Turns On the Heat in Asia, Our Weakest Spot,' *Saturday Evening Post*, 15 July 1950, p. 10; Ernest Lindley, 'Korea: Austria of the Next War?' *Newsweek*, 3 July 1950, p. 16; Sebastian Haffner, 'The Future of Korea,' *Saturday Night*, 17 October 1950, p. 15.

12 'Summer Travel Plans,' *Calgary Herald*, 29 June 1950; 'The Pattern of Aggression,' *Regina Leader-Post*, 28 June 1950; Foot, *The Wrong War*, 59.

13 'Senators Declare Neutrality No Longer Possible,' *Toronto Telegram*, 11 July 1950, 'Powder Keg Ignited by Red Match,' *Newsweek*, 3 July 1950, p. 22.

14 Lindley, 'Korea: Austria of the Next War?' 16; CIPO press releases, 30 June 1950, 26 August 1950, 6 January 1951, 17 February 1951, 3 March 1951.

15 Graham cited in 'The Kidding Stopped,' *Time*, 24 July 1950, p. 11; CIPO press release, 4 November 1950; 'Truman's Stand Electrifies Nation,' *Newsweek*, 10 July 1950, p. 24; 'The Time in Korea,' *Time*, 10 July 1950, p. 9.

16 CIPO press release, 1 August 1950; Pierce, 'Liberals and the Cold War,' abstract; Gary L. Huey, 'Public Opinion and the Korean War,' in Brune, *The Korean War*, 409–71; Foot, *The Wrong War*, 62–3. For the CCF endorsement, see comments of party member Stanley Knowles, Canada House of Commons Debates, 29 July 1950, p. 4386.

17 Acheson cited in Thompson and Randall, *Canada and the United States*, 193; Carl Spaatz, 'Why We Face a Tough Fight in Korea,' *Newsweek*, 10 July 1950, p. 23; Ernest Lindley, 'The Great Results of Korea,' *Newsweek*, 7 August 1950, p. 25; text of NSC-68 cited in Thompson and Randall, *Canada and the United States*, 186.

18 'Anticipating the President,' *Vancouver Sun*, 19 July 1950; Michael Barkway, 'How Does Our Defence Look Now?' *Saturday Night*, 1 August 1950, p. 9; *Winnipeg Free Press* cited in 'Viewpoints of Canada,' *Calgary Herald*, 25 July 1950; 'What Price Adequate Defence?' *Saturday Night*, 19 September 1950, p. 3. 'Response to Aggression,' *Ottawa Citizen*, 20 July 1950; 'We Must Be Strong,' *Halifax Chronicle-Herald*, 29 June 1950. For expressions of disappointment with Canadian military readiness, see 'What Answer from Canada,' *Globe and Mail*, 15 July 1950, and 'How Badly Were We Misled?' *Globe and Mail*, 17 July 1950.

19 King cited in Bercuson, *Blood on the Hills*, 15; 'Cut Down Building,' *Saturday Night*, 19 September 1950, p. 2. For a summary of the perceived differences in national values, see Lipset, *Continental Divide*; 'What Happened to All the Money?' *Calgary Herald*, 18 July 1950.

20 Richard Needham, 'One Man's Opinion,' *Calgary Herald*, 27 July 1950; 'Informed Canadian Opinion Aid to National Strength,' *Toronto Telegram*, 12 July 1950; Willson Woodside, 'No Time to Lose,' *Saturday Night*, 25 July 1950, p. 15.

21 Bercuson, *Blood on the Hills*, 17-18; Haglund, *The North Atlantic Triangle Revisited*, 83; Keating, *Canada and World Order*, 85.

22 Backhouse, "Legal Discrimination against the Chinese in Canada," 24; CIPO press release, 30 October 1946; Robert Bothwell, 'Eyes West: Canada and the Cold War in Asia,' in Donaghy, *Canada and the Early Cold War*, 81; Statistics Canada, 2001 Census; Bercuson, *Blood on the Fields*, 29.

23 'Not Too Late?' *Time*, 3 July 1950, p. 15; 'The Time in Korea,' 9; 'Ear to the Ground,' *Saturday Night*, 11 July 1950, p. 2; Andre Laurendeau, 'Quelle cause défendons-nous en Corée?' *Le Devoir*, 4 July 1950, author's translation ('Probablement pas dix sur cent'); 'The Fathers … and Sons,' *Globe and Mail*, 1 July 1950.

24 Woodside, 'No Time to Lose,' 15; 'Those Korean Names,' *Time*, 17 July 1950, p. 20; 'Uncle Same Takes Role as World Cop,' *Newsweek*, 10 July 1950, pp. 17–19; Leong, *The China Mystique*.

25 'In the Cause of Peace,' *Time*, 10 July 1950, p. 6; Willson Woodside, 'Will the Koreans Fight?' *Saturday Night*, 18 July 1950, p. 16; Richard Needham, 'One Man's Opinion,' *Calgary Herald*, 29 June 1950; O.M. Green, 'The People of Korea,' *Globe and Mail*, 15 July 1950; Nehru cited in 'Moves behind the Korean Front,' *Christian Century*, 16 August 1950, p. 963. The first and most influential work on Western representations of the East is Said, *Orientalism*. See also Tchen, *New York before Chinatown*; Klein, *Cold War Orientalism*; Yoshihara, *Embracing the East*.

26 Blair Fraser, 'Win or Lose,' 9; 'A Reborn UN Bares Its Teeth,' *Maclean's* 15 August 1950, p. 54; Frank Underhill, 'Korea,' *Canadian Forum*, August 1950, p. 102.

27 'In Korea as Liberators,' *Toronto Star*, 28 July 1950.

28 'On Whom We Rely,' *Globe and Mail*, 21 July 1950. The classic study on the topic of race and East-West conflict remains Dower, *War without Mercy*.

29 Mark Bradley, 'Slouching toward Bethlehem: Culture, Diplomacy, and the Origins of the Cold War in Vietnam,' in Appy, *Cold War Constructions*, 11–34.

30 MacArthur cited in 'How Not to Handle Orientals,' *Christian Century*, 13 September 1950, p. 1067; Wallace Goforth, 'We Didn't Plan for This Kind of War,' *Saturday Night*, 15 August 1950, p. 9.

31 'Down the Peninsula,' *Time*, 17 July 1950, p. 17; Sebastian Haffner, 'The Next Trouble Spot,' *Saturday Night*, 15 August 1950, p. 14. Haffner's use of

the term 'gooks' is confusing, rendered as it is in quotation marks. Perhaps his punctuation simply indicates that the term is slang; perhaps he is pointing to the common use of the term by the aforementioned U.S. troops, who must now reconsider their underestimation of supposed racial inferiors. Either way the employment of the word in such a context is arresting, particularly as the author offers no clear explanation for his use of an epithet that would alarm many readers (in fact, the piece ends with this sentence). Haffner's description of North Korean 'cunning' and 'savagery' in the lead-up to 'gook' offers some clue as to his own impressions of the region's inhabitants.

32 'US Flexes for a Bitter Struggle,' 13; 'The Road Ahead,' *Halifax Chronicle-Herald*, 28 July 1950; Goforth, 'We Didn't Plan for This Kind of War,' 9.

33 'What They Must Understand,' *Halifax Chronicle-Herald*, 8 August 1950.

34 'The West Gropes for Unity,' *Globe and Mail*, 4 July 1950; 'It's Never Premature,'' *Vancouver Sun*, 27 July 1950; Kennan cited in Donaghy, *Documents on Canadian External Relations*, 25.

35 'We're Fighting for Our Own Survival,' *Calgary Herald*, 17 July 1950; R.H. Babbage to editor, 'Wants Full-Dress Debate on Korea,' *Globe and Mail*, 21 July 1950; Bothwell, 'Eyes West,' 67.

36 Fraser, 'Was the Tibet Invasion Our Fault?' 39; Fraser, 'Win or Lose,' 8–9, 38; CIPO press releases, 2 December and 1 August 1950; U.S. survey cited in CIPO press release, 5 March 1951. The poll reported that 56 per cent of Americans questioned in a September 1950 poll felt that 'stopping Russia in Asia' was either more important than, or equally important to, 'stopping Russia in Europe'; only 31 per cent expressed 'Europe-first' sentiments. By January, only 37 per cent held the former view, while 49 per cent believed the latter.

37 CIPO press releases, 6 May and 23 August 1950.

38 CIPO press release, 20 December 1950.

39 'Out of Darkness, Hope!' *Christian Century*, 12 July 1950, pp. 837–9; Lippmann cited in 'The UN Proves Its Worth with the Blue Chips Down,' *Maclean's*, 1 August 1950, p. 1.

40 'Ibid.; 'The UN and World Security,' *Canadian Forum*, November 1950, p. 171; 'Death of the Veto,' *Globe and Mail*, 30 June 1950; 'Korea: Is It the Start of a New Deal?' *Calgary Herald*, 11 July 1950.

41 Peceny, *Democracy at the Point of Bayonets*, 27; Dolan, *Allegories of America*; Foot, *The Wrong War*, 43; Stueck, *The Korean War*, 66.

42 Logevall, 'A Critique of Containment'; Fousek, *To Lead the Free World*, 173.

43 Foot, *The Wrong War*, 43.

44 Offner, *Another Such Victory*.

45 Whitaker and Marcuse, *Cold War Canada*, 388.

46 Truman cited in 'Challenge Accepted.'

47 Huey, 'Public Opinion and the Korean War'; Stueck, *The Korean War*, 54; Foot, *The Wrong War*, 63; Ernest Lindley, 'Rebirth of the UN, Thanks to Truman,' *Newsweek*, 10 July 1950, p. 22. 'United Nations: "We Are Determined,"' *Time*, 3 July 1950, p. 15; 'The Spotlight Shifts from France to Washington,' *New York Times*, 28 June 1950; 'Support from the Free World,' *New York Times*, 29 June 1950; 'War in Asia,' *Time*, 10 July 1950, pp. 8–17.

48 'Backstage at Ottawa,' *Maclean's*, 15 August 1950, p. 54; Pearson cited in 'Canada and the Korean Crisis,' *External Affairs*, August 1950, p. 291.

49 Keating, *Canada and World Order*, 34; Hillmer and Granatstein, *From Empire to Umpire*, 213.

50 Donaghy, *Documents on Canadian External Relations*, 22–3.

51 'U.N., Not U.S. Show,' *Saturday Night*, 11 July 1950, p. 3; 'All the Way on Korea,' *Ottawa Citizen*, 29 June 1950; 'War in Korea,' *Globe and Mail*, 27 June 1950; 'US Defends Korea,' *Globe and Mail*, 28 June 1950; 'Death of the Veto.'

52 'Canada and the Korean Crisis,' 292–3; 'The West Gropes for Unity'; 'This Is Our Fight, Too,' *Vancouver Sun*, 15 July 1950; 'A U.N. Flag, a U.N. Commander,' *Regina Leader-Post*, 10 July 1950.

53 Donaghy, *Documents on Canadian External Relations*, 36, 39–40.

54 'Fighting under United Nations' Light Blue Flag,' *Toronto Star*, 11 July 1950; Coldwell cited in 'International Police Force,' *Vancouver Sun*, 20 July 1950; 'Responsibilities in Korea,' *Globe and Mail*, 13 July 1950; 'Cautious Guidance?' *Time*, 11 December 1950, p. 36.

55 'Arms for the Men,' *Time*, 21 August 1950, p. 35; 'The Sooner They're in High Gear the Better,' *Saturday Night*, 3 October 1950, p. 5; 'Standardization?' *Saturday Night*, 29 August 1950, p. 2.

56 Department of External Affairs, 'Canada and the United States,' reprinted in the 'The Yanks and Us,' *Ottawa Citizen*, 8 July 1950.

57 'Later than We Think,' *Halifax Chronicle-Herald*, 5 July 1950; 'We Must Hang Together,' *Halifax Chronicle-Herald*, 15 July 1950. 'When Colors Go By,' *Halifax Chronicle-Herald*, 1 August 1950; Elmore Philpott, 'Canada Leads West,' *Vancouver Sun*, 14 July 1950.

58 Philpott, 'Canada Leads West'; Pearson cited in 'Later than We Think.'

59 'A New Recruiting Drive Opens,' *Globe and Mail*, 13 July 1950; 'Finally, a Leader and a Rallying Point,' *Toronto Star*, 29 June 1950; 'Strong Figures Emerge,' *Saturday Night*, 18 July 1950, p. 5; 'The Dawn Comes Up like Thunder,' *Regina Leader-Post*, 5 July 1950; '"US" – That Also Spells "Us,"' *Regina Leader-Post*, 31 July 1950.

60 'All the Same Operation,' *Globe and Mail*, 7 July 1950. 'Are There Slackers in the UN?' *Globe and Mail*, 18 July 1950; 'Grave Questions for Canada,' *Calgary Herald*, 20 July 1950; Willson Woodside, 'Does the U.N. Mean It?' *Saturday Night*, 1 August 1950, p. 14; 'In Union There Is Strength,' *Winnipeg Tribune*, 12 July 1950. This is not to deny the presence of communist factions among the many groups seeking independence from European powers. According to many of these accounts, however, nationalist sentiment was little more than a communist ruse utilized to deliver a European colony into the Stalinist orbit.

61 'Britain Gives Ground Forces,' *Toronto Star*, 27 July 1950; 'Playing an Impressive Part,' *Halifax Chronicle-Herald*, 14 July 1950.

62 'Strategy,' *Time*, 10 July 1950, p. 14; 'Moscow Turns On the Heat in Asia.'

63 Lindley, 'Will the United Nations Fight as One?' *Newsweek*, 24 July 1950, p. 2; 'Moscow Turns On the Heat in Asia'; 'Answers to Aggression,' *Time*, 24 July 1950, p. 27; Willson Woodside, 'Stalin's Next Move,' *Saturday Night*, 8 August 1950, p. 14; Stueck, *The Korean War*, 58–9, 72. As Stueck notes, 'Other than Nationalist China [whose offer was flatly rejected as being too sensitive and as having obvious ulterior motives] the only Asian states to volunteer troops were Turkey, which did not consider itself Asian at all, and the Philippines and Thailand, neither of which had substantial influence in the region and both of whose troops were poorly trained and equipped for action in Korea' (72).

64 'Korea, Canada and the Far East,' *Canadian Forum*, September 1950, p. 124; 'Out of Darkness, Hope!' 838; C. Clyde Mitchell, 'Political and Economic Significance of the Korean War,' *International Journal* 5.4 (Autumn 1950): 301; Dudziak, *Cold War Civil Rights*, 62; 'Plague o' Both Houses,' *Saturday Night*, 8 August 1950, p. 5.

65 'Need for Solidarity,' *Halifax Chronicle-Herald*, 3 July 1950; 'The Main Battle,' *Halifax Chronicle-Herald*, 19 July 1950; 'Lessons of Korea,' *Globe and Mail*, 3 July 1950.

66 'Situations of Strength,' *Christian Century*, 26 July 1950, p. 886; 'War in Korea,' *New York Times*, 26 July 1950; 'The Allies,' *Time*, 17 July 1950, p. 20; 'Powder Keg Ignited by Red Match,' 22.

67 Underhill, 'Korea,' 102; 'Anxiety over Korea,' *Saturday Night*, 9 May 1950, p. 16; Fraser, 'Win or Lose,' 9; Elmore Philpott, 'Korean Boys Write,' *Vancouver Sun*, 6 July 1950; 'We're Fighting for Our Own Survival.'

68 Saul, *Reflections of a Siamese Twin*, 8.

69 Wilfrid Eggleston, 'After Korean War, What Then?' *Saturday Night*, 15 August 1950, p. 3; McCormick, 'The Spotlight Shifts'; Richard Needham, 'One Man's Opinion,' *Calgary Herald*, 25 July 1950; Stueck, *The Korean War*, 5.

70 'Nehru's Peace Politics,' *Ottawa Citizen*, 15 July 1950; Haffner, 'The Next Trouble Spot,' 14; 'Grave Questions for Canada'; Rotter, *Comrades at Odds*, 172; Foot, *The Wrong War*, 69; 'The Nehru Case Shows Up One of Our Bad Habits,' *Maclean's*, 15 September 1950, p. 3.

71 CIPO press release, 14 June 1950; 'Korea, Canada and the Far East,' *Canadian Forum*, September 1950, p. 124. John Osborne, *Time-Life* senior correspondent in the Far East, called the refusal to offer full and immediate military support to Chiang a 'crime against the vital interests of our country.' The patent necessity of such support, he believed, 'stems entirely from what any child can observe in Taipei today' ('War in Asia,' *Time*, 17 July 1950, p. 22). For opposing views, see 'No Canadian Help for Formosa,' *Ottawa Citizen*, 14 July 1950; Elmore Philpott, 'Where Uncle Sam Erred,' *Vancouver Sun*, 29 July 1950.

72 'MacArthur Tries to Make Policy,' *Christian Century*, 13 September 1950, 1067–8; Underhill, 'Korea,' 97; Frank Underhill, 'The Cole War,' *Canadian Forum*, April 1951, p. 1; 'A U.N. Flag'; Willson Woodside, 'War without Policy,' *Saturday Night*, 19 September 1950, p. 14.

73 Harry Kern, 'MacArthur in Action,' *Newsweek*, 10 July 1950, p. 20; 'MacArthur in Command,' *New York Times*, 29 June 1950.

74 'Strategy,' 15.

75 Stueck, *The Korean War*, 66; CIPO press release, 13 June 1951.

76 'August Mood,' *Time*, 14 August 1950, p. 7; 'Respect through Strength,' *Time*, 17 July 1950, p. 36.

77 'What Realism Dictates,' *Halifax Chronicle-Herald*, 15 July 1950; 'The Atomic Bomb and Korea,' *Ottawa Citizen*, 27 July 1950; 'No Place for the Atom Bomb,' *Regina Leader-Post*, 15 July 1950; Paul Sauriol, 'Avant qu'il soit trop tard,' *Le Devoir*, 29 June 1950; 'Cautious Guidance?' 36. For a survey of the Truman and Eisenhower administrations' deliberations regarding the Bomb, see Edward C. Keefer, 'Truman and Eisenhower: Strategic Options for Atomic War and Diplomacy in Korea,' in Brune, *The Korean War*, 285–308.

78 'America Mustn't Open the Way to Atomic Conflict,' *Saturday Evening Post*, 5 August 1950, p. 10; Foot, *The Wrong War*, 115; Stueck, *The Korean War*, 131–2 (Smith cited 132), 181; 'Cautious Guidance?' 36.

79 CIPO press release, 11 October 1950.

80 'Uncle Sam Takes Role as World Cop,' 17.

81 'U.S. Foreign Policy,' *Canadian Forum*, February 1951, pp. 241–2.

82 Keating, *Canada and World Order*, 32 (quote)–38, 127; Whitaker and Marcuse, *Cold War Canada*, 394; Mahant and Mount, *Invisible and Inaudible in Washington*, 35; Stairs, *The Diplomacy of Constraint*, 53.

83 'Accommodations Wanted,' *Time*, 18 December 1950, p. 37.
84 Whitaker and Marcuse, *Cold War Canada*, 14–15; 286; Smith, *Diplomacy of Fear*, 4.
85 Ferguson, *Bastards and Boneheads*, 168.
86 'Political Background,' *Saturday Night*, 15 August 1950, p. 2; James Laxer, 'Fake Left, Go Right: An Insider's Take on Jack Layton's Game of Chance,' *The Walrus*, May 2006, p. 48.
87 Stueck, *The Korean War*, 4. For accounts which emphasize the limits of Canadian influence over U.S. policy, see Mahant and Mount, *Invisible and Inaudible in Washington*, 34–9; Whitaker and Marcuse, *Cold War Canada*, 388–9; Prince, 'The Limits of Constraint.' Keating allows that Canada exerted a relatively minor, though perceptible, influence over U.S. policy in Korea (*Canada and World Order*, 34–5, 38).
88 'Quelle cause défendons-nous en Corée?'; CIPO press release, 1 August 1950.
89 CIPO press release, 19 February 1951.
90 'What Will it Take?' *Saturday Night*, 11 July 1950, p. 2; 'The Challenge Is Now Clear,' *Saturday Night*, 25 July 1950, pp. 5–6; 'Change Needed at Defence,' *Saturday Night*, 1 August 1950, p. 5. 'Canada on the Sidelines,' *Globe and Mail*, 1 July 1950; 'Canada to Do Her Share,' *Toronto Star*, 21 July 1950; 'Shrill Voices and Loose Thoughts,' *Ottawa Citizen*, 19 July 1950; 'The Inevitable Step,' *Ottawa Citizen*, 28 July 1950.
91 'The Helpful Sheriff,' *Vancouver Sun*, 8 July 1950; A.R. Reusch to editor, 'West Coast Defenses,' *Vancouver Sun*, 8 July 1950; 'A.G.' to editor, 'Civilian Defense,' *Vancouver Sun*, 11 July 1950.
92 'We're All in the Home Guard,' *Vancouver Sun*, 31 July 1950.
93 'Truman's Stand Electrifies Nation'; 'More That Must Be Told,' *Winnipeg Tribune*, 24 July 1950.
94 'Informed Canadian Opinion'; 'This Is Our Fight, Too'; 'Politician's Holiday,' *Globe and Mail*, 14 July 1950; 'Masterly Inactivity?' *Saturday Night*, 8 August 1950, p. 6; 'In a Dangerous Time,' *Saturday Night*, 26 September 1950, p. 7; Larry Smith, 'We CAN Prepare for Atom-Bombs,' *Saturday Night*, 26 September 1950, p. 8.
95 'Time We Awoke,' *Vancouver Sun*, 25 July 1950; 'What Sort of People?' *Globe and Mail*, 22 July 1950.
96 Blair Fraser, 'Wartime Taxes? Not Yet,' *Maclean's*, 15 September 1950, p. 66; 'Laying the Foundation,' *Newsweek*, 7 August 1950, p. 34; John S. Knight, 'What Sort of Allies?' reprinted in the *Calgary Herald*, 28 July 1950; Blair Fraser, 'Uncle Same Thinks We Let Him Down,' *Maclean's*, 1 September 1950, p. 4.

97 'O Canada,' *Arizona Star*, reprinted in the *Calgary Herald*, 27 July 1950;
   Canada's Hesitation and Canada's Shame,' *Calgary Herald*, 28 July 1950.

98 Needham, 'One Man's Opinion,' 25 July 1950; 'Grave Questions for Canada,' *Calgary Herald*, 20 July 1950; Fraser, 'Uncle Same Thinks We Let Him
   Down,' 4; 'It Is Parliament's Job,' *Winnipeg Tribune*, 27 July 1950; 'Canada
   on the Sidelines.'

99 CIPO press release, 1 August 1950.

100 'Parallel Lines,' *Time*, 18 September 1950, p. 46.

101 'Press Reactions Noted,' *Saturday Night*, 18 July 1950, p. 2; untitled edito-
    rial, *Globe and Mail*, 8 July 1950; *Maclean's*, 15 October 1950, p. 4.

102 Gordon O. Rothney, 'Quebec and Korea,' *Canadian Forum*, June 1951, p.
    56; St Jean Baptiste Society cited in 'The Voice of Quebec,' *Saturday Night*,
    12 September 1950, p. 7; 'Il en est temps encore,' *Le Soleil*, 28 June 1950,
    author's translation ('Les Canadiens ... considèrent la guerre comme un
    crime'); 'Quelle cause défendons-nous en Corée?' author's translation.
    ('Nous sommes comme ces petits chiens qui brûlent de montrer à leur
    maître qu'ils l'adorent, qu'il suffira d'un geste et qu'ils se jetteront à
    l'eau').

103 André Patry, 'L'Affaire coréenne et le mercantilisme américain,' *Action
    Catholique*, reprinted in *Le Devoir*, 3 July 1950, author's translation ('une
    politique vraiment chrétienne').

104 Cited in 'Quebec and Korea,' *Canadian Forum*, June 1951, pp. 55–7.

105 Bothwell, *The Big Chill*, 38.

106 Cited in ibid.

Conclusion

1 Mary Lowrey Ross, 'Canadians and Un-Canadians,' *Saturday Night*, 28
  February 1948, p. 10.

2 Whitfield, *The Culture of the Cold War*, 4, 24.

3 Wise and Brown, *Canada Views the United States*.

4 Grant, *Lament for a Nation*; for a concise examination of Canadian intellectual life from this era, and of the 'new nationalist' critique of the
  perceived Americanization of Canada, see Edwardson, '"Kicking Uncle
  Sam out of the Peaceable Kingdom."'

5 My thanks to the anonymous reader at University of Toronto Press whose
  comments precipitated this discussion on the 'New Nationalist' thesis
  regarding continentalism.

6 For an excellent historical analysis of the intersection of racial exclusion,

liberalism, and the nation-state, see two studies by David Goldberg: *Racist Culture* and *The Racial State*.

7 As chapter 5 makes clear, official 'state objectives' regarding Canada's appropriate contributions to the Korean War changed markedly in the first months of the conflict. From the beginning, however, Canadian leaders sought to marshal public support for some sort of contribution to the war effort, despite their private reservations about the rectitude of the U.S.-led mission.

Bibliography

Ambrose, Stephen, and Douglas Brinkley. *Rise to Globalism: American Foreign Policy since 1938*. 8th ed. New York: Penguin Books, 1997.

Appy, Christian G., ed. *Cold War Constructions: The Political Culture of United States Imperialism, 1945–1966*. Amherst: University of Massachusetts Press, 2000.

Aronson, Lawrence R. *American National Security and Economic Relations with Canada, 1945–1954*. Westport, CT: Praeger Publishers, 1997.

Backhouse, Constance. 'Legal Discrimination against the Chinese in Canada: The Historical Framework.' In David Dyzenhaus and Mayo Moran, eds. *Calling Power to Account: Law, Reparations, and the Chinese Canadian Head Tax Case*. Toronto: University of Toronto Press, 2005. 24–59.

Bannerji, Himani. *The Dark Side of the Nation: Essays on Multiculturalism, Nationalism, and Gender*. Toronto: Canadian Scholar's Press, 2000.

Bercuson, David. *Blood on the Hills: The Canadian Army in the Korean War*. Toronto: University of Toronto Press, 1999.

Berger, Carl. *The Sense of Power: Studies in the Ideas of Canadian Imperialism, 1867–1914*. Toronto: University of Toronto Press, 1970.

– 'The True North Strong and Free.' In Peter Russell, ed. *Nationalism in Canada*. Toronto: McGraw-Hill, 1966. 3–26.

– *The Writing of Canadian History: Aspects of English-Canadian Historical Writing since 1900*. 2nd ed. Toronto: University of Toronto Press, 1986.

Borstelmann, Thomas. *Apartheid's Reluctant Uncle: The United States and Southern Africa in the Early Cold War*. New York: Oxford University Press, 1993.

Bothwell, Robert. *The Big Chill: Canada and the Cold War*. Toronto: Irwin Publishers, 1998.

– *Canada and the United States: The Politics of Partnership*. New York: Twayne, 1992.

– *Eldorado: Canada's National Uranium Company*. Toronto: University of Toronto Press, 1984.

Boyer, Paul. *By the Bomb's Early Light: American Thought and Culture at the Dawn of the Atomic Age.* Chapel Hill: University of North Carolina Press, 1985.

– *Fallout: A Historian Reflects on America's Half-century Encounter with Nuclear Weapons.* Columbus: Ohio State University Press, 1998.

Brown, Robert Craig. 'Goldwin Smith and Anti-imperialism.' *Canadian Historical Review* 43 (1962): 93–105.

Brune, Lester H., ed. *The Korean War: Handbook of Literature and Research.* Westport, CT: Greenwood Press, 1996.

Cavell, Richard., ed. *Love, Hate, and Fear in Canada's Cold War.* Toronto: University of Toronto Press, 2004.

Chomsky, Noam. *Manufacturing Consent: The Political Economy of the Mass Media.* New York: Pantheon, 1988.

Clark-Jones, Melissa. *A Staple State: Canadian Industrial Resources in the Cold War.* Toronto: University of Toronto Press, 1987.

Clément, Dominique. 'Spies, Lies, and a Commission: A Case Study in the Mobilization of the Canadian Civil Liberties Movement.' *Left History* 7.2 (2000): 53–79.

Coleman, Daniel. *White Civility: The Literary Project of English Canada.* Toronto: University of Toronto Press, 2006.

Cook, Don. *Forging the Alliance: NATO, 1945–1950.* New York: Arbor House / William Morrow, 1989.

Cook, Timothy. *Governing with the News: The News Media as a Political Institution.* Chicago: University of Chicago Press, 1998.

Creighton, Donald. *The Forked Road.* Toronto: McClelland and Stewart, 1976.

Cuff, R.D., and J.L. Granatstein. *Canadian-American Relations in Wartime: From the Great War to the Cold War.* Toronto: Hakkert, 1975.

Cumings, Bruce. *Origins of the Korean War: Liberation and the Emergence of Separate Regimes.* Princeton: Princeton University Press, 1981.

Curran, James. 'Rethinking the Media as a Public Sphere.' In Peter Dahlgren and Colin Sparks, eds. *Communication and Citizenship: Journalism and the Public Sphere.* London: Routledge, 1991. 27–57.

Day, Richard. *Multiculturalism and the History of Canadian Diversity.* Toronto: University of Toronto Press, 2000.

Dolan, Frederick. *Allegories of America: Narratives, Metaphysics, Politics.* Ithaca, NY: Cornell University Press, 1994.

Donaghy, Greg, ed. *Canada and the Early Cold War, 1943–1957.* Ottawa: Department of Foreign Affairs and International Trade, 1998.

– *Documents on Canadian External Relations, Volume 16: 1950.* Ottawa, 1995.

Dower, John. *War without Mercy: Race and Power in the Pacific War.* New York: Pantheon Books, 1986.

Dudziak, Mary. *Cold War Civil Rights: Race and the Image of American Democracy.*
Princeton: Princeton University Press, 2000.

Edwardson, Ryan. *Canadian Content: Culture and the Quest for Nationhood.* Toronto: University of Toronto Press, 2008.

– '"Kicking Uncle Sam out of the Peaceable Kingdom": English-Canadian "New
Nationalism" and Americanization.' *Journal of Canadian Studies* 37.4 (Winter
2003): 131–50.

Eldridge, C.C., ed. *Kith and Kin: Canada, Britain and the United States from the
Revolution to the Cold War.* Cardiff: University of Wales Press, 1997.

Endy, Christopher. *Cold War Holidays: American Tourism in France.* Chapel Hill:
University of North Carolina Press, 2004.

Ericson, Richard, Patricia Baranek, and Janet Chan. *Negotiating Control: A Study
of News Sources.* Toronto: University of Toronto Press, 1989.

Ferguson, Will. *Bastards and Boneheads: Canada's Glorious Leaders Past and Present.*
Vancouver: Douglas and McIntyre, 1999.

Field, Douglas, ed. *American Cold War Culture.* Edinburgh: Edinburgh University
Press, 2005.

Findlay, John M., and Ken S. Coates, eds. *Parallel Destinies: Canadian-American
Relations West of the Rockies.* Montreal: McGill-Queen's University Press, 2002.

Finkel, Alvin. *Our Lives: Canada after 1945.* Toronto: James Lorimer & Company,
1997.

Finlay, J.F., and D.N. Sprague. *The Structure of Canadian History.* 6th ed. Scarbor-
ough, ON: Prentice Hall Canada Inc., 2000.

Flaherty, David H., and Frank E. Manning, eds. *The Beaver Bites Back? American
Popular Culture in Canada.* Montreal: McGill-Queen's University Press, 1993.

Foot, Rosemary. *The Wrong War: American Policy and the Dimensions of the Korean
Conflict, 1950–1953.* Ithaca, NY: Cornell University Press, 1985.

Fousek, John. *To Lead the Free World: American Nationalism and the Cultural Roots of
the Cold War.* Chapel Hill: University of North Carolina Press, 2000.

Fried, Richard. *The Russians Are Coming, the Russians Are Coming: Pageantry and
Patriotism in Cold War America.* New York: Oxford University Press, 1998.

Gienow-Hecht, Jessica. 'Shame on US? Academics, Cultural Transfer, and the
Cold War – a Critical Review.' *Diplomatic History* 24.3 (Summer 2000): 465–94.

Gitlin, Todd. *The World Is Watching: The Mass Media and the Making and Unmak-
ing of the New Left.* Berkeley: University of California Press, 1980.

Goldberg, David. *The Racial State.* Malden, MA: Blackwell Publishers, 2001.

– *Racist Culture: Philosophy and the Politics of Meaning.* Malden, MA: Blackwell
Publishers, 1993.

Goncharov, Sergei N., John W. Lewis, Xue Litai, and Litai Xue. *Uncertain Partners: Stalin, Mao and the Korean War.* Stanford: Stanford University Press, 1993.

Granatstein, J.L., and Norman Hillmer. *For Better or for Worse: Canada and the United States to the 1990s.* Toronto: Copp Clark Pitman, 1990.

Grant, George. *Lament for a Nation: The Defeat of Canadian Nationalism.* 40th anniversary ed. Montreal: McGill-Queen's University Press, 2005.

Griffith, Robert. 'The Cultural Turn in Cold War Studies.' *Reviews in American History* 29 (2001): 150–7.

Haglund, David. *The North Atlantic Triangle Revisited: Canadian Grand Strategy at Century's End.* Toronto: Irwin Publishing, 2000.

Hall, Stuart. 'Culture, the Media and the "Ideological Effect."' In James Curran, Michael Gurevitch, and Janet Woollacott, eds. *Mass Communication and Society.* Beverly Hills, CA: Sage, 1977. 315–48.

– 'The Rediscovery of "Ideology": Return of the Repressed in Media Studies.' In Michael Gurevitch, Tony Bennett, James Curran, and Janet Woollacott, eds. *Culture, Society, and the Media.* New York: Methuen, 1982. 56–90.

Harney, Robert F. '"So Great a Heritage as Ours": Immigration and the Survival of the Canadian Polity.' In Stephen R. Grabaurd, ed. *In Search of Canada.* Edison, NJ: Transaction Publishers, 1991. 51–98.

Hartz, Louis. *The Liberal Tradition in America: An Interpretation of American Political Thought since the Revolution.* New York: Harcourt Brace Jovanovich, 1955.

Heiss, Mary Ann. 'The Evolution of the Imperial Idea and US National Identity.' *Diplomatic History* 26.4 (2002): 511–41.

Henrickson, Margot. *Dr. Strangelove's America: Society and Culture in the Atomic Age.* Berkeley: University of California Press, 1997.

Hertzman, Lewis, John W. Warnock, and Thomas A Hockin. *Alliances and Illusions: Canada and the NATO-NORAD Question.* Edmonton: M.G. Hurtig Ltd, 1969.

Hillmer, Norman, and J.L. Granatstein. *Empire to Umpire.* Toronto: Irwin Publishing, 1994.

Hollinger, David. *Postethnic America: Beyond Multiculturalism.* New York: Basic Books, 1995.

Holmes, John. *The Shaping of Peace: Canada and the Search for World Order, 1943–1957.* 2 vols. Toronto: University of Toronto Press, 1979.

Hunt, Michael. *Ideology and US Foreign Policy.* New Haven: Yale University Press, 1987.

Jacobson, Matthew Frye. *Whiteness of a Different Color: European Immigrants and the Alchemy of Race.* Cambridge: Harvard University Press, 1998.

Jones-Imhotep, Edward. 'Communicating the Nation: Northern Radio, National Identity and the Ionospheric Laboratory in Canada.' Ph.D. diss., Harvard University, 2001.

Kackman, Michael. *Citizen Spy: Television, Espionage, and Cold War Culture*. Minneapolis: University of Minnesota Press, 2005.

Kaplan, Amy, and Donald Pease, eds. *Cultures of United States Imperialism*. Durham, NC: Duke University Press, 1993.

Kaplan, Lawrence. *NATO and the United States: The Enduring Alliance*. Boston: Twayne Publishers, 1988.

Keating, Tom. *Canada and World Order: The Multilateralist Tradition in Canadian Foreign Policy*. 2nd ed. Toronto: Oxford University Press, 2002.

Keylor, William. *A World of Nations: The International Order since 1945*. New York: Oxford University Press, 2003.

Keylor, William, and Jerry Bannister. *The Twentieth-Century World: An International History, Canadian Edition*. Don Mills, ON: Oxford University Press, 2005.

Kinsman, Gary, Dieter K. Buse, and Mercedes Steedman, eds. *Whose National Security? Canadian State Surveillance and the Creation of Enemies*. Toronto: Between the Lines, 2000.

Klein, Christina. *Cold War Orientalism: Asia in the Middlebrow Imagination, 1945–1961*. Berkeley: University of California Press, 2003.

Knight, Amy. *How the Cold War Began: The Gouzenko Affair and the Hunt for Soviet Spies*. Toronto: McClelland and Stewart, 2005.

Korinek, Valerie. *Roughing It in the Suburbs: Reading Chatelaine Magazine in the Fifties and Sixties*. Toronto: University of Toronto Press, 2000.

Krenn, Michael. *Black Diplomacy: African Americans and the State Department, 1945–1969*. New York: ME Sharpe, 1999.

Kristmanson, Mark. *Plateaus of Freedom: Nationality, Culture, and State Security in Canada, 1940–1960*. Don Mills, ON: Oxford University Press, 2003.

Kuffert, L.B. *A Great Duty: Canadian Responses to Modern Life and Mass Culture, 1939-1967*. Montreal: McGill-Queen's University Press, 2003.

Kuznick, Peter J., and James Gilbert, eds. *Rethinking Cold War Culture*. Washington, DC: Smithsonian Institution Press, 2001.

Kymlicka, William. *Finding Our Way: Rethinking Ethnocultural Relations in Canada*. Toronto: Oxford University Press, 1998.

Lackenbauer, P. Whitney, and Matthew Farish. 'The Cold War on Canadian Soil: Militarizing a Northern Environment.' *Environmental History* 12.4 (October 2007): 920–50.

Leffler, Melvyn P. *A Preponderance of Power: National Security, the Truman Administration, and the Cold War*. Stanford: Stanford University Press, 1992.

Leong, Karen J. *The China Mystique: Pearl S. Buck, Anna May Wong, Mayling Soong, and the Transformation of American Orientalism*. Berkeley: University of California Press, 2005.

Lipset, Seymour Martin. *Continental Divide: The Values and Institutions of the United States and Canada*. New York: Routledge, 1990.

Lipsitz, George. 'The Meaning of Memory: Family, Class, and Ethnicity in Early Television Programs.' In Lynn Spigel and Denise Mann, eds. *Television and the Female Consumer*. Minneapolis: University of Minnesota Press, 1992. 97–121.

Litt, Paul. *The Muses, the Masses, and the Massey Commission*. Toronto: University of Toronto Press, 1992.

Littleton, James. *Target Nation: Canada and the Western Intelligence Network*. Toronto: Lester & Orpen Dennys / CBC Enterprises, 1986.

Logevall, Fredrik. 'A Critique of Containment.' *Diplomatic History* 28.4 (September 2004): 473–99.

Luhan, Gordon. *The Making of a Spy*. Toronto: Robert Davies Publishing, 1995.

Mackenzie, Hector, ed. *Documents on Canadian External Relations, Volume 14: 1948*. Ottawa, 1994. 291.

Mackey, Eva. *The House of Difference: Cultural Politics and National Identity in Canada*. 2nd ed. Toronto: University of Toronto Press, 2002.

Macmillan, Margaret, and David Sorenson, eds. *Canada and NATO: Uneasy Past, Uncertain Future*. Waterloo, ON: University of Waterloo Press, 1990.

Madison, James H., ed. *Wendell Willkie: Hoosier Internationalist*. Bloomington: Indiana University Press, 1992.

Mahant, Edelgard E., and Graeme S. Mount. *Invisible and Inaudible in Washington: American Policies toward Canada*. Vancouver: University of British Columbia Press, 1999.

– 'The U.S. Cultural Impact upon Canada.' *American Review of Canadian Studies* 31.3 (September 2001): 449–65.

Massolin, Philip. *Canadian Intellectuals, the Tory Tradition, and the Challenge of Modernity, 1939–1970*. Toronto: University of Toronto Press, 2001.

McAlister, Melani. *Epic Encounters: Culture, Media, and US Interests in the Middle East, 1945–2000*. Berkeley: University of California Press, 2001.

McCormick, Thomas. *America's Half-Century: United States Foreign Policy in the Cold War and After*. 2nd ed. Baltimore: Johns Hopkins University Press, 1995.

McKinnon, Ann. 'Can-Con vs. Neo Con: Television Studies in Canada.' *Textual Studies in Canada* 13/14 (Summer 2001): 131–52.

McNay, John. *Acheson and Empire: The British Accent in American Foreign Policy*. Columbia: University of Missouri Press, 2001.

Miller, Carman. 'Loyalty, Patriotism and Resistance: Canada's Response to the Anglo-Boer War, 1899–1902.' *South African History Journal* 41 (2000): 312–23.

Miller, Derek. *Media Pressure on Foreign Policy: The Evolving Theoretical Framework*. New York: Palgrave Macmillan, 2007.

Minifie, James M. *Peacemaker or Powder-Monkey: Canada's Role in a Revolutionary World*. Toronto: McClelland and Stewart, 1960.

Morgan, Ted. *Reds: McCarthyism in Twentieth-Century America*. New York: Random House, 2003.

Naylor, James. 'Pacifism or Anti-imperialism? The CCF Response to the Outbreak of World War II.' *Journal of the Canadian Historical Association* 8 (1997): 213–37.

New, W.H. *Borderlands: How We Talk about Canada*. Vancouver: UBC Press, 1998.

Ninkovich, Frank A. *The Diplomacy of Ideas: U.S. Foreign Policy and Cultural Relations, 1938–1950*. Cambridge: Cambridge University Press, 1981.

– *The United States and Imperialism*. London: Blackwell Publishing, 2001.

Oakes, Guy. *The Imaginary War: Civil Defense and American Cold War Culture*. New York: Oxford University Press, 1994.

Offner, Arnold. *Another Such Victory: President Truman and the Cold War, 1945-1953*. Stanford: Stanford University Press, 2002.

Omi, Michael, and Howard Winant. *Racial Formation in the United States*. 2nd ed. New York: Routledge, 1994.

Orders, Paul. '"Adjusting to a New Period in History": Franklin Roosevelt and European Colonialism.' In David Ryan and Victor Pungong, eds. *The United States and Decolonization: Power and Freedom*. New York: Palgrave Macmillan, 2000. 63–84.

Pach, Chester. *Arming the Free World: The Origins of the United States Military Assistance Program, 1945–1950*. Chapel Hill: University of North Carolina Press, 1991.

Packenham, Robert. *Liberal America and the Third World*. Princeton: Princeton University Press, 1973.

Peceny, Mark. *Democracy at the Point of Bayonets*. University Park: Pennsylvania State University Press, 1999.

Pierce, Robert Clayton. 'Liberals and the Cold War: Union for Democratic Action and Americans for Democratic Action, 1940–1949.' Ph.D. diss., University of Wisconsin, 1979.

Plummer, Brenda Gayle. *Rising Wind: Black Americans and US Foreign Affairs, 1935–1960*. Chapel Hill: University of North Carolina Press, 1996.

Prevots, Naima. *Dance for Export: Cultural Diplomacy and the Cold War*. Hanover: Wesleyan University Press, 1998.

Prince, Robert S. 'The Limits of Constraint: Canadian-American Relations and the Korean War, 1950–51.' *Journal of Canadian Studies* 27.4 (1992–3): 129–52.

Reid, Escott. *Time of Fear and Hope: The Making of the North Atlantic Treaty, 1947–1949*. Toronto: McClelland and Stewart, 1977.

Richmond, Yale. *Cultural Exchange and the Cold War: Raising the Iron Curtain.*
University Park: Pennsylvania State University Press, 2003.

Rogin, Michael. *Blackface, White Noise: Jewish Immigrants in the Hollywood Melting Pot.* Berkeley: University of California Press, 1998.

Rotter, Andrew J. *Comrades at Odds: The United States and India, 1947–1964.* Ithaca, NY: Cornell University Press, 2000.

Russell, Peter, ed. *Nationalism in Canada.* Toronto: McGraw-Hill, 1966.

Rutherford, Paul. *The Making of the Canadian Media.* Toronto: McGraw-Hill Ryerson, 1978.

Ryan, David. *US Foreign Policy in World History.* New York: Routledge, 2000.

Said, Edward. *Culture and Imperialism.* New York: Vintage Books, 1993.

– *Orientalism.* New York: Vintage Books, 1989.

Saul, John Ralston. *Reflections of a Siamese Twin: Canada at the End of the Twentieth Century.* Toronto: Penguin Books, 1998.

Scher, Len. *The Un-Canadians: True Stories of the Blacklist Era.* Toronto: Tower City Publications, 1992.

Singh, Nikhil Pal. 'Culture/Wars: Recoding Empire in an Age of Democracy.' *American Quarterly* 50.3 (September 1998): 471–522.

Smith, Denis. *Diplomacy of Fear: Canada and the Cold War, 1941-1948.* Toronto: University of Toronto Press, 1988.

Stairs, Denis. *The Diplomacy of Constraint: Canada, the Korean War, and the United States.* Toronto: University of Toronto Press, 1974.

Stiles, Deborah. '"The Dragon of Imperialism": Martin Butler, *Butler's Journal,* the *Canadian Democrat,* and Anti-Imperialism, 1899–1902.' *Canadian Historical Review* 85.3 (2004): 481–505.

Stuart, Reginald C. 'Continentalism Revisited: Recent Narratives on the History of Canadian-American Relations.' *Diplomatic History* 18.3 (Summer 1994): 405–14.

Stueck, William. *The Korean War: An International History.* Princeton: Princeton University Press, 1995.

– *Rethinking the Korean War: A New Diplomatic and Strategic History.* Princeton: Princeton University Press, 2002.

Tchen, John Kuo. *New York before Chinatown: Orientalism and the Shaping of American Culture, 1776–1882.* Baltimore: Johns Hopkins University Press, 1999.

Thompson, John Herd, and Stephen J. Randall. *Canada and the United States: Ambivalent Allies.* 3rd ed. Athens: University of Georgia Press, 2002.

Trofimenkoff, Susan Mann. *The Dream of Nation: A Social and Intellectual History of Quebec.* Toronto: Macmillan, 1982.

Vipond, Mary. 'Canadian Nationalism and the Plight of Canadian Magazines in the 1920s.' *Canadian Historical Review* 58 (March 1977): 43–63.

– *Listening In: The First Decade of Canadian Broadcasting, 1922–1932.* Montreal: McGill-Queen's University Press, 1992.
– *The Mass Media in Canada.* 3rd ed. Toronto: James Lormier & Company, 2000.
Von Eschen, Penny. *Race against Empire: Black Americans and Anticolonialism, 1937–1957.* Ithaca, NY: Cornell University Press, 1997.
Wagnleitner, Reinhold. *Coca-Colonization and the Cold War: The Cultural Mission of the United States in Austria after the Second World War.* Trans. Diana M. Wolf. Chapel Hill: University of North Carolina Press, 1994.
Wagnleitner, Reinhold, and Elaine Tyler May, eds. *'Here, There and Everywhere': The Foreign Politics of American Popular Culture.* Hanover: University Press of New England, 2000.
Walcott, Rinaldo. *Black like Who? Writing Black Canada.* Toronto: Insomniac Press, 1997.
Warnock, John W. *Partner to Behemoth: The Military Policy of a Satellite Canada.* Toronto: New Press, 1970.
Weisbord, Merrily. *The Strangest Dream: Canadian Communists, the Spy Trials, and the Cold War.* 2nd ed. Montreal: Véhicule Press, 1994.
Whitaker, Reginald, and Steve Hewitt. *Canada and the Cold War.* Toronto: Lorimer Press, 2002.
Whitaker, Reginald, and Gary Marcuse. *Cold War Canada: The Making of a National Insecurity State, 1945–1957.* Toronto: University of Toronto Press, 1994.
Whitfield, Stephen J. *The Culture of the Cold War.* Baltimore: Johns Hopkins University Press, 1991.
Williams, William Appleman. *The Tragedy of American Diplomacy.* New York: Dell Publishing, 1959.
Willis, Jim. *The Media Effect: How the News Influences Politics and Government.* Westport, CT: Praeger, 2007.
Winks, Robin. *The Blacks in Canada: A History.* 2nd ed. Montreal: McGill-Queen's University Press, 1997.
Wise, S.F., and Robert Craig Brown, eds. *Canada Views the United States: Nineteenth-Century Political Attitudes.* Toronto: Macmillan, 1967.
Wittner, Lawrence. *One World or None: A History of the World Nuclear Disarmament Movement through 1953.* Palo Alto: Stanford University Press, 1995.
Yoshihara, Mari. *Embracing the East: White Women and American Orientalism.* Oxford: Oxford University Press, 2003.
Young, Robert. *Postcolonialism: An Historical Introduction.* Oxford: Blackwell Publishers, 2001.

Index

Acheson, Dean: and Korea, 178, 193, 195, 202; and NATO, 11, 143, 150, 157, 161, 252n54
Action Catholique, L', 222
Africa, 103, 117, 120, 152, 203
African Americans: and anti-communism, 141, 246n21; and anti-imperialism, 104, 107, 123, 139, 246n21; and atomic bomb, 32–4; and internationalism, 40, 78, 139, 231; and NATO, 136, 139, 152; and Soviet Union, 33
African Canadians, 34, 43
Ambrose, Stephen, 161
American Federation of Labor, 131
American Revolution, 96, 101, 115
Americans for Democratic Action, 178
Anglican Church, Canada, 28, 141, 146
anglophiles, Canadian: anti-Americanism of, 12, 73, 92–4, 98, 107, 120–6, 157, 204, 219, 229, 248n46; and anti-communism, 16, 114, 120–6, 200–4; and atomic bomb, 41, 50; and decolonization, 16, 93–4, 96–8, 109–26; and franco-

phones, 41, 70; and Gouzenko Affair, 70; and Korea, 200–4; and NATO, 157–8, 164. *See also* Anglo-Saxon identity
Anglo-Saxon identity, 25, 30, 32–3, 41–2, 148–9
anti-Americanism, 10, 226, 229–30, 242n39; and anglophiles, 12, 73, 92–4, 98, 107, 120–6, 157, 204, 219, 229–30, 248n46; and atomic bomb, 22, 41, 50–3; and decolonization, 92–4, 98, 101, 107, 120–6; European, 140; and Gouzenko Affair, 58, 71, 73; and Korean War, 179, 204, 206, 219; and NATO, 157
anti-colonialism. *See* anti-imperialism
anti-communism: and African Americans, 141, 246n21; and anglophiles, 16, 114, 120–6, 200–4; and atomic bomb, 47–8, 57, 70; and Canada–United States relations, 4, 8–9, 164, 178, 205–6, 224, 226, 228–9; and Canadian citizenship, 73; and Canadian identity, 53, 70–5; and decolonization, 16, 93–4, 100, 103–4, 108, 111, 114, 121–6; and francophones, 69, 140,

146, 223; and Gouzenko Affair,
16, 54–7, 63, 68–70, 74, 76–7,
80–1, 83–6; and Korean War, 17,
169–70, 208, 212, 223–4; of Liberal
Party, 170, 218; and NATO, 127,
130–2, 134, 138–9, 140–2, 146,
152–5, 164–7; of RCMP, 72; and
U.S. imperialism, 93, 142; and U.S.
nationalism, 232. *See also* containment policy; Truman Doctrine
anti-imperialism: Canadian, 16, 28,
98–101, 114–18, 122–3, 126, 206,
222–3; U.S., 16, 92–4, 101, 104–7,
116–26, 139, 202, 246n16, 246 n21
Anti-Imperialist League, 101
Armour, Stuart, 37, 41–2, 148
arms race: and atomic bomb, 20,
45, 47, 64, 76, 87; and Korea, 180;
and NATO, 128, 140, 180. *See also*
military budgets
Asia: Canadian policy toward, 172,
181–2, 208, 229; and imperialism,
92, 103, 111, 117, 119, 123, 200–4;
and Korean War, 174–5, 177,
180–224, 258n63; and NATO, 127,
135, 147, 152; U.S policy toward,
181, 192–3, 208. *See also specific
countries*
'Asia-first' idea, 192, 208
Asian peoples: in Canada, 82, 182;
Canadian attitudes toward, 17, 43,
96, 181–90, 203; and Korean War,
17, 173,181–90, 209; and Orientalism, 185–7; U.S. attitudes toward,
181. *See also* race; *and specific
nationalities*
Atlantic Charter, 83, 94, 104, 107–8,
118, 125
atomic bomb: and African Americans, 32–4; and anglophiles, 41,

50; and anti-Americanism, 22, 41,
50–3; and anti-communism, 47–8,
57, 70; attitudes toward atomic age,
19–20, 34–8, 227; Britain and, 36,
45, 66; Canada's role in developing, 21, 23–5, 65–6; and Canada-
U.S. relations, 7, 15, 20–2, 36–7,
41, 47–50, 212, 227, 231; and Canadian nationalism, 26, 41, 50–1, 53;
and Cold War consensus, 53; and
espionage, 192; and francophones,
28, 76; and Gouzenko Affair, 58,
63–7, 125; impact on international
relations, 38–51; international
control of, 45–7, 53, 61, 63, 76,
78–9, 86, 90, 129, 227, 243n50;
and Korean War, 171, 177, 209–12,
214, 218, 220; morality of, 25–34,
186, 210–11; and NATO, 133, 141,
148, 164; and opinion polls, 211,
236n10; and race, 29–34, 45–6,
181; and Soviet Union, 21, 40, 45,
47, 65–6, 76, 128, 192, 206; and
UN, 38, 42, 45, 47, 50, 76, 129; and
U.S. nationalism, 40–1, 46; and
U.S. unilateralism, 24–5, 40–1, 45,
47, 49–50, 125, 133, 227
Atomic Energy Commission, 35
Attlee, Clement, 150, 210
Atwood, Margaret, 230
Austin, Warren, 207
Australia, 79, 152, 172, 188, 219,
243n50
autonomy, Canadian. *See* sovereignty,
Canadian
Axis powers, 26, 29, 92, 109–10, 121,
176. *See also* Nazi Germany

Baruch, Bernard, 123
Bataan Death March, 31

Beard, Charles, 116
Belgian Congo, 25, 95
Benes, Eduard, 88
Bennett, R.B., 82
Bercuson, David, 180
Berger, Carl, 97, 116, 142
Berlin, 127; and airlift, 169, 221; blockade of, 130, 144
Bikini Atoll, 181
bilateralism, Canada-U.S., 4, 11, 17, 122, 133, 198, 224
Bill of Rights: Canadian, 62; U.S., 101
Boer War, 98–9, 245n8
Bothwell, Robert, 11–12, 189, 223
Boxer Rebellion, 181
Boyer, Raymond, 59
Bradley, Mark, 185
Bretton Woods Agreement, 122
Brinkley, Douglas, 161
Britain: and atomic bomb, 36, 45, 47, 66; and Canadian identity, 12–13, 41, 44, 52, 71, 82–3, 88–9, 95–8, 108, 116, 151, 226; Canadian relationship to, 4–5, 10–12, 17, 42, 47–8, 50, 54, 79, 96–100, 108, 122, 132–3, 140, 198, 205, 219, 230, 243n50, 245n8; and cultural influence in Canada, 14, 36–7, 45, 59–60; and Gouzenko Affair, 59–60, 62, 66, 77; and imperialism, 42, 69, 92, 109–26, 200–1, 203–5; and Korean War, 17, 188, 197, 200–1, 203–5, 210, 212, 214, 215–16, 219; and NATO, 132–3, 136, 146, 157–9. See also British Commonwealth; British Empire
British Columbia, 82, 141, 182
British Commonwealth: and Canada, 5, 42, 50, 96–7, 100, 109–10, 133, 215–16, 243n50, 246n13; and

India, 120–1, 207; and Korean War, 215–16; and NATO, 150
British Empire: and Canada, 5, 17, 46, 83, 98, 100, 108–9, 113, 116–17, 242n43; and Gouzenko Affair, 80; and India and Pakistan, 109–26; and United States, 92, 98, 103, 118, 252n54
Brown, Robert Craig, 229
Brussels Pact, 127
Burma, 95
Byrnes, James, 78

Calgary Herald: and atomic bomb, 28, 41; and Gouzenko Affair, 68–9, 74, 76, 80; and Korean War, 175, 179, 183, 188, 191, 201, 205, 207, 220; and NATO, 162, 165
Camsell, Charles, 24
Canada, Le, 141
'Canada and the North Atlantic Treaty,' 141–3
Canadian Broadcasting Corporation (CBC), 22, 82, 92, 234n5
Canadian Churchman, 28
Canadian Citizenship Act (1946), 72
Canadian Forum, 6; and anti-imperialism, 94, 116–20, 122–3; and atomic bomb, 26, 28; and Gouzenko Affair, 56, 71; and Korean War, 165, 174, 184, 191, 203–4, 208, 211; and NATO, 127–8
Canadian Home Journal, 27
Canadian Moving Picture Digest, 56
Canadian Seamen's Union, 81, 131
Canadian Tribune, 24, 178
Carr, Sam, 59, 131
Catholic Church, 28, 48, 70, 140, 221
Chiang Kai-shek, 204, 207–8, 259n71
Chicago Defender, 33

China: Canadian policy toward, 129, 182, 207–8, 214; and decolonization, 103; 'fall' of, 7, 130, 187, 192; and Korean War, 172, 198, 201, 212, 258n63; and Second World War, 27; and United Nations, 190, 207; U.S. policy toward, 129, 166, 194, 204–8

'China lobby,' 192–3

Chinese Exclusion Act, 181–2

Chinese peoples, 149, 173, 181–2

Chomsky, Noam, 7, 41

Christian Century, 140, 143, 174, 191, 203–4, 208

Churchill, Winston, 78, 108, 158, 176

CIA, 173

citizenship, Canadian, 72–5

civil liberties: Canada, 44, 61–2, 83, 86, 131, 154–5, 229; United States, 229

Clark, S.D., 10

Clarke, Frank, 240n15

Claxton, Brooke, 216–17

Clément, Dominique, 62

Cold War: Baruch and Orwell on term, 123; and Canada-U.S. relations, overview, 4–5, 9–15, 226–32; general description, 4–9; origins, 22; and public opinion, 10–15; scholarship on, 9–12. *See also* anti-communism; consensus; Truman Doctrine

Coldwell, M.J., 37, 119, 197

Coleman, Daniel, 44, 97

collective security, 50, 57, 128, 142–4, 163, 192, 212, 220. *See also* North Atlantic Treaty Organization (NATO); United Nations

colonialism. *See* imperialism

Colony to Nation, 100

Communist Party, 80, 135, 150, 154–5; Canadian, 43, 140, 153; U.S., 153, 156. *See also* Labour-Progressive Party

Congress of International Organizations (CIO), 64, 85

Connally Tom, 157

conscription, Canada, 5, 98, 177, 213

consensus, Cold War: and atomic bomb, 53; and Canada-U.S. relations, 4–5, 9–11, 13–14, 17, 226–7, 232; and decolonization, 94, 108, 114, 124–5; and Gouzenko Affair, 75; and Korean War, 173, 224; and NATO, 133–4, 136, 167. *See also* anti-communism

constitution, U.S., 101, 208

containment policy, 4; as imperialist, 16, 106, 127, 201; Kennan on, 130–2; and Korean War, 7, 169–70, 177, 189, 201–2, 231; and NATO, 16, 130–2; Niebuhr on, 70. *See also* Truman Doctrine

continentalism, 5, 75–6, 100, 125, 199, 231, 233n2

Cook, Don, 144

Co-operative Commonwealth Federation (CCF) Party: and anti-imperialism, 94, 99, 119; and atomic bomb, 37; and Korean War, 178, 197; and Marshall Plan, 130; and NATO, 141, 154, 161, 165; and United States, 122

Council of the Empire Press Union, 121

Creighton, Donald, 230, 233n2

Criminal Code (Canada), 59

Crisis, 33–4

Cuff, R.D., 122

cultural mosaic, Canadian, 43, 71–2, 101, 149, 159

culture: Cold War and, 8–9, 13–14;
    elitism of Canadian culture,
    12–13, 72–3; government-spon-
    sored culture in Canada, 22; and
    international hierarchy, 71, 93,
    111–12, 115–16; and international
    relations, 10–12; theories of, 6–8,
    13–14; U.S. culture in Canada,
    12–15, 227–30
Czechoslovakia, 7, 88, 130, 132, 135,
    176, 225

Dalhousie Review, 114, 116
Davies, Joseph, 76, 78
Day, Richard, 71–2
decolonization: in Africa, 103; and
    African Americans, 104, 107, 123;
    and anglophiles, 16, 93–4, 96–8,
    109–26; and anti-Americanism,
    92–4, 98, 101, 107, 120–6; and anti-
    communism, 16, 93–4, 100, 103–4,
    108, 111, 114, 121–6; in Asia, 103,
    202; and Canada, 96–101, 107–26;
    and Canada-U.S. relations, 92–4,
    107–8, 116–17, 120–6, 220; and
    China, 103; and Cold War consen-
    sus, 94, 108, 114, 124–5; Cold War
    impact on, 7, 102–5, 109, 111, 114,
    121–6; and Gouzenko Affair, 114,
    124–5; and India, 92–4, 109–26;
    and Korean War, 171, 202; and
    Pakistan, 109–26; and Philippines,
    94–5, 105–9, 111–12, 181; and
    Second World War, 92–3, 94–5, 97,
    109–11, 121, 123; and Soviet Un-
    ion, 16, 103–6, 111, 114, 120–6; and
    United States, 101–7, 116–26. See
    also anti-imperialism; imperialism
Democratic Party, 63–4, 138, 140,
    178, 192

Denmark, 156, 161
Department of Citizenship and Im-
    migration (Canada), 72
destiny, U.S. sense of, 3, 40–1, 102,
    160, 192
Devoir, Le: and atomic bomb, 28;
    and decolonization, 116; and
    Gouzenko Affair, 74, 76; and
    Korean War, 183, 210, 215, 221–3;
    and NATO, 141, 146, 163
disarmament. See peace movement
Dolan, Frederick, 39
Donnell, Forest, 156
Doolittle flyers, 31
Dower, John, 29–30, 33
Dresden, firebombing of, 27
Drew, George, 69–70
Droit, Le, 47
Du Bois, W.E.B., 40, 139
Dulles, John Foster, 78, 174, 183, 229
Duplessis, Maurice, 69, 74, 140

Eastern Europe, 106, 130, 149–50,
    230. See also specific countries
Ebony, 33–4
Edwardson, Ryan, 12–13
Eisenhower, Dwight, 178
Ellison, Ralph, 40
England, David, 111
espionage, 60, 192–3, 212, 225. See
    also Gouzenko Affair
Europe: and anti-Americanism, 140;
    Cold War division of, 128; rebuild-
    ing of, 128, 140; U.S. attitudes to-
    ward, 132. See also Eastern Europe;
    Western Europe
exceptionalism, U.S., 3, 105–6, 192,
    202

Family of Man, The, 148, 188

fascism: and African Americans, 40; and atomic bomb, 210; and Canadian policy, 43, 72; and decolonization, 121; and Gouzenko Affair, 80, 85, 87; and War Measures Act, 34. *See also* Hitler, Adolf; Nazi Germany

FBI, 63–4, 87

Fellowship of Reconciliation, 29

Ferguson, Will, 213

First Nations. *See* indigenous peoples

First World War, 98–9, 245n8, 248n46

Fisk University, 139

Fitzgerald, Maureen, 32

Foner, Eric, 8

Foot, Rosemary, 193

Foster, Kate, 71

Four Freedoms, 94, 104, 108, 117–18, 125

Fousek, John, 24, 40, 78, 123

France: and Cold War, 79, 243n50; and imperialism, 42, 46, 92, 96, 103, 115, 194, 200–1; and Korean War, 195, 200–1; and NATO, 156

francophones, Canadian: and anglophiles, 41, 70; and anti-communism, 48, 69–70, 79, 140; and anti-imperialism, 5, 28, 98–9, 110, 116, 221–3; and atomic bomb, 28, 76; and Canadian identity, 41, 44, 72, 96, 153–4, 206, 226, 242n39; and Gouzenko Affair, 69–70, 74–6; and isolationism, 140, 221–3; and Korean War, 178, 206, 210, 214, 221–4; and nationalism, 5, 98–9, 101, 232; and NATO, 140–1, 150–1, 153, 164; and pacifism, 5, 28, 206, 221–3; and United States, 12, 18, 229. *See also* Quebec

Fraser, Blair, 168–9, 184, 189, 204, 219

free-world leadership, U.S., 3, 8, 103–4, 129, 159, 195, 211

Frye, Northrop, 7

Gaddis, John Lewis, 11

Gandhi, Mahatma, 112, 115

gender: and anti-communism, 9, 199; and atomic bomb, 47, 50; and Canada-U.S. relations, 242n39; and Canadian identity, 247n39; and imperialism, 97; and Soviet Union, 89; and U.S.-European relations, 160; and Western ideals, 56

German Canadians, 99

Germany, 136, 138, 149, 220, 248n46

Gitlin, Todd, 7

Globe and Mail: and atomic bomb, 23, 25, 29–30, 32, 41, 50; and decolonization, 95, 111–15, 119–20; and Gouzenko Affair, 66–7, 70, 77, 83–5; and Korean War, 175, 179, 183, 185, 188, 191, 196–8, 200, 203, 205, 215–16, 218–19, 221; and NATO, 158

Goforth, Wallace, 186–7

Goldman, Emma, 226

Gordon, Walter, 230

Gouzenko, Igor, 21, 54–60, 62–3, 68–9

Gouzenko, Svetlana, 56

Gouzenko Affair: and anglophiles, 70; and anti-Americanism, 58, 71, 73; and anti-communism, 16, 54–7, 63, 68–70, 74, 76–7, 80–1, 83–6; and atomic bomb, 54, 63–7, 85; and attitudes toward Soviets, 67, 78–91, 243n50; and Britain, 59–60, 62, 66, 77; and Canada-U.S. relations, 54–7, 58–9, 62–3, 75–7, 87–9; and Canadian identity, 70–5; and

Canadian nationalism, 15, 57–8, 70–5, 88–9; and Cold War consensus, 75; and decolonization, 114, 124–5; and francophones, 69–70, 74–6; and immigration, 71–5; *The Iron Curtain*, 55–7; and Kellock-Taschereau Commission, 59, 61–2, 67–8, 70, 73, 77; and Korean War, 220; and labour movement, 61, 64, 68–9, 72, 78, 82, 85; and NATO, 131; summary of, 7, 15, 58–62; and U.S. nationalism, 78. *See also Iron Curtain, The*
Graham, Billy, 177
Granatstein, J.L., 95, 122
Grant, George, 230, 233n2
Groves, Leslie, 63, 76
Gwinn, Ralph, 78

Haffner, Sebastian, 175, 187
Haglund, David, 158, 251n40
Halifax Chronicle-Herald: and atomic bomb, 25; and decolonization, 111, 114; and Gouzenko Affair, 74; and Korean War 173, 179, 187, 198, 201, 203, 210; and NATO, 162–3
Hall, Stuart, 7
Hamilton Spectator, 83, 153
Harkness, Ross, 19
Hartz, Louis, 39–40
Hearst newspaper chain, 87, 192, 210
Heiss, Mary Ann, 118
Hewitt, Steve, 55, 69
Hiroshima. *See* atomic bomb
Hiss, Alger, 131
Hitler, Adolf: and atomic bomb, 50; and Gouzenko Affair, 67, 80; and imperialism, 110, 122; and Korean War, 176, 179; and NATO, 135, 146, 159; and 'One World,' 65;

Stalin as, 67, 122, 176, 185. *See also* fascism; Nazi Germany
Holland. *See* Netherlands
Hollywood, 14, 31, 55–6, 131, 227
Holmes, John, 100
Holocaust, 29, 72, 112
Hong Kong, 31, 48, 182
Hoover, Herbert, 212
House Un-American Activities Committee (HUAC), U.S., 55, 113, 156, 226
How the Cold War Began, 62
Howe, C.D., 24, 66
Hunt, Michael, 247n37
Hunter, F. Fraser, 92–3, 121

Iacovetta, Franca, 72
Ickes, Harold, 106–7, 181
Ignatieff, Michael, 102
immigration: Canadian, 5, 48, 71–2, 82, 96–7, 101, 149, 182, 203; U.S., 71, 96, 181
imperialism: British, 42, 69, 92, 109–26, 200–1, 203–4; Canadian experience of, 42, 52, 95–6; Canadian support for, 16, 46, 93, 96–8, 108–26, 200–5; as check against communist expansion, 94, 103, 111, 114, 121–6, 200–5; and Cold War consensus, 94, 108, 114, 124–5; French, 42, 46, 92, 96, 103, 115, 194, 200–1; U.S., 40, 42, 94, 101–4, 122, 132, 142, 145, 158, 161–2, 203; U.S. in Canada, 42, 48–51, 93, 100, 122. *See also* British Empire; containment policy
India: and Bengal Famine, 118; as 'childlike,' 113; cultural and religious diversity of, 109–10, 112, 114–16, 118; and independence,

92–4, 109–26; and Korean War, 184, 202, 204, 207, 222–3; poverty of, 119; and Second World War, 92–3, 109–10

indigenous peoples, Canadian, 42–3, 82, 95, 99, 122; U.S., 95, 122

Indochina, 95, 120. *See also* Vietnam War

Indonesia, 95, 123, 204

Innis, Harold, 7, 100, 233n2

International Journal, 141–3, 203

internationalism, 5, 11, 38, 41–2, 152; Canadian, 47, 93, 99–100, 129, 140–1, 144, 148–9, 190–1, 195, 205, 211, 224, 227; communist, 70–5; U.S., 40–1, 51, 94, 102, 123, 131, 138, 140, 190–2, 205, 208, 211, 224, 227. *See also* liberalism

Iran, 176

Iraq War (2003), 3

Irish Canadians, 99

Iron Curtain, The, 55–7

isolationism: Canadian, 28, 38, 132, 140, 150, 206, 221–3, 231; U.S., 38, 94, 123, 128, 132–3, 138–9, 143, 156–7, 159–60, 176, 192, 208, 211

Italy, 135, 148, 156

Japanese peoples: Canadian attitudes toward, 30–2, 43, 84–5, 149, 182; internment of, 30, 154–5, 181–2; U.S. attitudes toward, 30–2, 181, 184

Jews, 46, 74, 85, 149

Jinnah, Muhammad Ali, 113

Johnson, Charles S., 139

Jones-Imhotep, Edward, 49

Kaplan, Amy, 102

Kealey, Gregory, 72, 242n43

Keating, Tom, 143, 171, 238n45, 260n87

Kelley, Edgar, 74

Kellock-Taschereau Commission, 59, 61–2, 67–8, 70, 73, 77

Kennan, George, 129–32, 188

Kim Il Sung, 172, 174, 176

King, William Lyon Mackenzie: and atomic bomb, 31, 33; and continentalism, 230–1; and Gouzenko Affair, 59, 74, 85–6; and immigration, 96–7; and India, 119; and Korea, 171–2, 182, 214; leadership style of, 213–14; and military budgets, 179; and NATO, 150; and War Measures Act, 10, 59; and Western Canada, 82

King, Jr, Martin Luther, 40

Kinsey reports, 148

Kirkland, Margaret, 111, 114, 121–2

Knight, Amy, 61–2

Korea. *See* Korean War

Korean War, 17; as 'American' war, 3–4,190–8, 224; and anglophiles, 200–4; and anti-Americanism, 179, 204, 206, 219; and anti-communism,17, 169–70, 208, 212, 223–4; and atomic bomb, 171, 177, 209–12, 214, 218, 220; background and summary, 17, 171–2; and Britain, 17, 188, 197, 200–1, 203–5, 210, 212, 214, 215–16, 219; and Canada-U.S relations, 8, 11, 169–72, 174, 198–200, 212–14, 219–24; Canadian debate over ground troops, 215–24, 231; and Canadian nationalism, 17, 170–1, 195, 199; Canadian-U.S. disagreements over, 204–11; and China, 172, 198, 201, 212, 258n63; and Cold War consensus, 173, 224; and containment, 7, 169–70, 177, 189, 201–2; and continental integration, 198–200; and decolonization, 171, 202; and francophones, 178, 206, 210, 214, 221–4; and Gouzenko Affair, 220; and imperialism, 200–4; and India, 184, 202, 204, 207, 222–3; and Liberal Party, 170–2, 212–20, 223–4; and 'mandarin thesis,' 213–14; and military budgets, 178–81; and NATO, 129, 169–70, 175–6, 180, 188, 212, 214, 216, 219, 224; public support for, 177–8, 189, 215–21, 231; and race, 171, 181–90; Soviet role in, 173–7, 185–7, 189; and UN, 168–72, 179–80, 183–208, 210–17, 223–4; and UNTCOK, 171–2; and U.S. nationalism, 3–4, 171

Korinek, Valerie, 234n8
Kristmanson, Mark, 60–1, 72
Kuffert, L.B., 36

labour movement: and anti-communism, 9, 229; and anti-imperialism, 99; and atomic bomb, 52; and Gouzenko Affair, 61, 64, 68–9, 72, 78, 82, 85; and Korean War, 198; and NATO, 130–1, 136. *See also* Canadian Seamen's Union; Congress of International Organizations
Labour-Progressive Party, 59, 85, 89, 153. *See also* Communist Party
Ladies' Home Journal, 12
Lament for a Nation, 230
Latin America, 230
League of Nations, 197, 221
Liberal Party: and anti-communism, 170, 218; and Gouzenko Affair, 59,

62, 69; and Korean War, 3–4, 11, 170–2, 196–7, 213–24; and NATO, 145; and War Measures Act, 10, 59
liberalism: and Canada, 11, 42, 46, 52, 57, 62–3, 81, 93, 98–9, 107, 128, 231; and immigration, 72; and imperialism, 103, 115, 122, 200; and Korean War, 186; and the media, 6; and NATO, 128; and United States, 9, 11, 14, 38–40, 46, 53, 57, 101–4, 106, 117, 120, 126, 160, 231. *See also* internationalism
Lie, Trygve, 170, 194, 215–16
Life, 6, 14; and atomic bomb, 25, 28, 40; and imperialism, 105, 118, 121; and NATO, 156; Niebuhr in, 70; and Operation Musk-Ox, 65
Lindley, Ernest, 175–6, 178, 194, 202
Lippmann, Walter, 90, 162, 191
Logevall, Fredrik, 39, 130, 192
Lower, A.R.M., 100
Loyalists, 73. *See also* anglophiles
Luce, Henry, 40, 192

MacArthur, Douglas, 186, 195, 199, 208–9, 229
Mackey, Eva, 73, 96–7, 242n39
Maclean's, 6, 46, 122, 146, 163, 167–8, 184, 191, 195, 204, 207, 219–21
'mandarin thesis' of Canadian policymaking, 10–11, 213, 230–1
Manhattan Project, 21, 24, 32
Mao Zedong, 192, 207–8, 253n8
Marcuse, Gary, 47–8, 60–2, 93–4, 213
Maritime provinces, 19
Marshall Plan, 129–30, 133, 138, 140, 141, 150
mass media: characteristics of Canadian, 33–4, 45, 81, 107–8, 134, 144; characteristics of U.S., 33–4, 51–2,

87, 134, 144; influence on policy
and public opinion, 6–7, 11–12,
14–15
Massey, Vincent, 12
Massey Commission, 72–3, 242n37
Massolin, Philip, 97, 247n28
McCalls, 12
McCarthy, Joseph, 43, 62, 69, 78, 194,
207
McCarthyism, 10, 62, 70, 104, 154,
189, 193, 206
McCormick, Thomas, 138, 140
McCormick newspaper chain, 87,
192, 210
McKinnon, Ann, 13, 42
McLuhan, Marshall, 7
McWilliams, Carey, 40, 44
'melting pot,' U.S., 43, 71
Meredith, James, 43
Métis peoples, 82
Middle East, 48, 123, 129, 135, 175
military budgets, 128, 178–81. *See also*
arms race
Montreal Gazette, 49
Morton, W.L., 142
movies. *See* Hollywood
Mowat, Farley, 230
multiculturalism: Canada, 42–4, 52,
71–2, 101; United States, 40, 52. *See
also* cultural mosaic
multilateralism: and Canada, 5,
15–17, 42, 44–5, 53, 57, 90, 100,
132–3, 149, 195, 197–8, 203, 223,
238n45; and United States, 15–16,
51–2, 57, 78, 123, 134, 191, 203
Munich Agreement, 134–5, 176
Murray Hill Area Project, 49
Mussolini, Benito, 80

Nagasaki. *See* atomic bomb

Nation, 145–6, 160, 166, 210
National Association for the Ad-
vancement of Colored Peoples
(NAACP), 136, 139, 141, 152
National Film Board (NFB), 22, 82
national identity, Canadian, 15, 16;
as American, 37, 75, 116, 129, 151,
226; as anti-American, 22, 51–2,
53, 58, 71, 73, 101, 179, 206, 226,
242n39; as anti-communist, 53, 58,
70–5, 151; and Britain, 12–13, 41,
44, 52, 71, 82–3, 88–9, 95–8, 108,
116, 151, 226; and Cold War, 4–5,
9–10; and francophones, 41, 44,
72, 96, 153–4, 206, 226, 242n39;
and Gouzenko Affair, 70–5; and
Korean War, 206, 224; and military
history, 22, 159, 220; and multiculturalism, 42–4, 52, 71–2, 101, 149,
159; and race, 96–7, 148–9, 152;
and religion, 18, 148–51; and science, 35–6; state management of,
22, 44, 72–3; and the Third World,
95; and tolerance, 17, 43–4, 57,
71–2, 82, 84, 96; and the welfare
state, 179–80. *See also* anglophiles;
francophones; nationalism,
Canadian
national identity, U.S: and anti-
imperialism, 16, 92–4, 101, 104–7,
116–26, 139, 202, 246n16, 246n21;
Canadian perceptions of, 10, 22,
58, 179; and Cold War, 4, 9–10,
15, 16; and destiny, 3, 40–1, 102,
160, 192; and exceptionalism, 3,
105–6, 192, 202; and individualism,
179; and Korean War, 204, 206,
224; and 'melting pot,' 43, 71; and
prosperity, 24; and race, 148; and
religion, 148–51; and republican-

ism, 46, 93–4, 96, 101, 104, 117,
126; and science, 24, 35–6; and
utopianism, 35, 42
National Research Council (Canada), 66
national security state, Canadian, 58,
72, 131
nationalism, 38, 45–6, 57, 70, 132,
148, 186, 200–3, 208
nationalism, Canadian: and atomic
bomb, 26, 41, 50–1, 53; and Cold
War, 4, 15, 17, 22, 230–2; and
culture, 72; and francophones,
5, 98–9, 101, 232; and Gouzenko
Affair, 15, 57–8, 70–5, 88–9; as
imperialist, 97–8; as leftist, 98; and
liberalism, 98; and Korean War, 17,
170–1, 195, 199; and NATO, 129,
157, 164; and Second World War,
70–1; state promotion of, 22, 70–5;
and U.S. influence, 13, 88–9, 93,
122, 195, 199, 230–2
nationalism, U.S.: and atomic bomb,
40–1, 46; and Cold War, 3–4, 15,
232; and decolonization, 106, 123;
and Gouzenko Affair, 78; and
Korean War, 171, 192–3; and
NATO, 134; and Second World
War, 70–1
NATO. See North Atlantic Treaty
Organization
Naylor, James, 99
Nazi Germany: and atomic bomb,
27–9, 32, 43; and decolonization,
104, 110–11, 117; and Gouzenko
Affair, 56, 60, 67, 80; and Korean
War, 176; and NATO, 149. See also
fascism; Germany; Hitler, Adolf
Needham, Richard, 41, 180, 183, 207,
220

Nehru, Jawaharlal, 112–13, 118, 184,
204, 207–8, 212, 222–3
Netherlands, 46, 103, 123, 204
New, W.H., 14
New Deal, 9, 80, 123
'new history,' 116
New Republic, 146, 160
New Statesman, 45
New York Daily News, 49, 160
New York Times, 14; and decoloniza-
tion, 105, 119; and Gouzenko
Affair, 56, 66, 74, 77–8; and Korean
War, 173, 194, 204, 207, 209, 219;
and NATO, 148, 151–2, 160–1, 163
New Zealand, 152, 188, 219
Newsweek, 3; and Korean War, 173,
175–8, 183, 187, 194, 202, 204, 208,
211, 218–19; and NATO, 156–7,
160
Niebuhr, Reinhold, 70
Ninkovich, Frank A., 102, 106
North American Air Defence (NO-
RAD), 129
North Atlantic Treaty Organization
(NATO): and African Americans,
136, 139, 152; and anglophiles,
157–8, 164; and anti-Americanism,
157; and anti-communism, 127,
130–2, 134, 138–9, 140–2, 146,
152–5, 164–7; and appeasement,
134–5, 159; Article 2 of, 11, 143,
162, 164; and atomic bomb, 133,
141, 148, 164; and Britain, 132–3,
136, 146, 157–9; and Canada-U.S.
relations, 127, 129, 132–4, 142,
148–51, 157–67; Canada's role in
creating, 132, 159; and Canadian
nationalism, 129, 157, 164; and
Canadian sovereignty, 129, 147,
161–2, 167; and CCF, 141, 154,

161, 165; and Cold War consensus,
133–4, 136, 167; and colonized
world, 139, 152–3; and containment, 16, 130–2; and francophones, 140–1, 150–1, 153, 164; and
Gouzenko Affair, 131; impact on
Canada, 5, 16, 129, 167; impact on
Cold War, 128; impact on United
States, 128–9; and Korean War,
129, 169–70, 175–6, 180, 188, 212,
214, 216, 219, 224; and military
budgets, 180–1; and opinion polls,
165–6; opposition to, 138–43,
167; perceived need for, 129–35;
press support for, 143–7, 154–67;
and race, 139, 148–9, 152–3; and
relationship to UN, 128–9, 132,
134, 136–8, 140, 142–3, 158, 162–6;
and religion, 127–8, 149–51, 153;
U.S. dominance of, 132, 160–2;
and U.S. isolationism, 128, 132–3,
138–9, 143, 156–7, 159–60; and
U.S. nationalism, 134; and Western
values, 133–4, 147–53
North Korea, 3, 172–6, 185–8, 193,
195, 198, 208, 210, 222, 229
northern Canada, 49, 64–5, 68
Northern Citizen, 68
Norway, 156
NSC-68, 178
nuclear weapons. *See* atomic bomb

Office of Strategic Services, 103
Official Secrets Act (OSA) (Canada),
59, 61
Offner, Arnold, 193, 233n1
Ogdensburg Agreement, 122
One World, 38, 92, 148
'One World,' concept of, 5, 16;
and atomic bomb, 38, 41, 47, 51;

and decolonization, 112; and
Gouzenko Affair, 65; and Korean
War, 188; and NATO, 128
Ontario, 43, 69, 98, 221
Operation Musk-Ox, 64–5
Orientalism, 185–7
Orwell, George, 123
Osservatore Romano, 28
Ottawa Citizen: and atomic bomb,
35–6, 45; and Gouzenko Affair, 54,
68, 80, 87–9; and Korean War, 174,
179, 196, 207, 210, 217; and NATO
164–5
Our Canadian Mosaic, 71

Packenham, Robert, 39
Padlock Law, 69
Pakistan: and independence, 109–26;
and Korean War, 219
Palestine, 127, 166
Parkin, George, 97
Parrington, Vernon, 116
peace movement, 18, 20, 29, 50–1,
55, 139–41, 146
peacekeeping, 95, 100, 222, 245n13
Pearl Harbor, 30–1, 63, 176, 182
Pearson, Drew, 63–4, 67–8, 78, 85, 88,
229, 242n44
Pearson, Lester B., 145, 150, 195–9,
210, 212, 219, 223–4, 230, 258n63
Peceny, Mark, 192
Philip, P.J., 66, 74
Philippines, 94–5, 105–9, 111–12,
181, 194
Philpott, Elmore, 45, 63–4, 115, 120,
199, 204
Pittsburgh Courier, 33, 107
Plummer, Brenda Gayle, 139
Polak, H.S.L., 121
Popular Front, 61, 67, 99

Portugal, 148
Progressive Conservative Party,
    69–70, 82, 110, 222
Purple Heart, The, 31

Quebec, 28, 43, 69–70, 74, 98–9, 140,
    146, 214–15. *See also* francophones
Queen's Quarterly, 116

race: and Anglo-Saxon identity, 25,
    30, 32–3, 41–2, 148–9; and atomic
    bomb, 29–34, 45–6, 181; and Cana-
    dian immigration policy, 71–2; and
    Canadian society, 43, 71, 74–5, 95,
    148–51; and capitalism, 103, 115;
    and Gouzenko Affair, 71–5, 85;
    and imperialism, 93, 111–12, 117;
    and international relations, 38,
    45, 95, 106; and Korean War, 171,
    181–90; and NATO, 148–53; and
    Orientalism,185–7; and Slavic peo-
    ples, 56–7, 149; and Soviet Union,
    89; and United States, 40, 95; and
    whiteness, 44, 149
radio broadcasting, 6–7, 14, 92
Ravault, René-Jean, 14
RCMP: and espionage against Sovi-
    ets, 60; and Gouzenko Affair, 59,
    64, 67, 80–1; ideology of, 72, 75;
    and immigration, 72
Reader's Digest, 12
Red-baiting. *See* anti-communism
Regina Leader-Post, 112, 146, 153, 161,
    176, 197, 200, 208, 210
religion: and anti-communism, 48,
    222–3; and atomic bomb, 27–30,
    32, 41, 46, 52; and Gouzenko Af-
    fair, 69–70, 87; and India, 109–10,
    112, 114–16, 118, 121; and Ko-
    rean War, 174, 177, 202, 222; and

NATO, 127–8, 139–40, 148–51,
    153; and Western identity, 7–8, 18,
    27, 32, 148–51
Republican Party, 38; and anti-
    communism, 9, 70, 78; and Ko-
    rean War, 174, 192, 194, 212; and
    NATO, 132, 138, 156
republicanism, 46, 93–4, 96, 101, 104,
    117, 126
Rhee, Syngman, 172, 203–6, 212, 222
Robeson, Paul, 203
Robinson, James Harvey, 116
Roosevelt, Franklin Delano, 11, 30,
    101, 108, 178, 181, 246n16
Rose, Fred, 59
Ross, Mary Lowrey, 50, 225–6
Rotter, Andrew J., 103, 113
Royal Commission on National De-
    velopment in the Arts, Letters and
    Sciences. *See* Massey Commission
Russia. *See* Soviet Union
Rutherford, Ernest, 23
Rutherford, Paul, 7, 236n12, 239n66

St Jean Baptiste Society, 222
St Laurent, Louis, 145, 150, 159, 213
Saturday Evening Post, 6, 12, 146, 164,
    175, 202, 210
Saturday Night, 6; and atomic bomb,
    26–8, 37, 41, 46–50; and decoloni-
    zation, 92, 109–11, 114, 121; and
    Gouzenko Affair, 55–6, 67, 225;
    and Korean War, 175, 179, 182–3,
    187, 196, 198, 201, 203–4, 207, 213,
    216, 218, 221; and NATO, 135,
    146, 148, 151, 154–6, 159, 161, 163
Saul, John Ralston, 44, 206
Sauriol, Paul, 76
Second World War: and Canada-U.S.
    relations, 20, 49; and Canadian

domestic policy, 10, 34, 43; and Canadian international policy, 54, 205; and decolonization, 92–3, 94–5, 97, 109–11, 121, 123; as 'Good War,' 27; and imperialism, 98–9, 103–4; and interpretation of Cold War, 146, 175–6; and Korea, 171, 175–6; and race, 29–34, 148; and Soviet alliance, 24–5, 43, 47–8, 60, 67, 79–80, 121; as 'total war,' 27; U.S. responsibility for, 159; as 'U.S. victory,' 24

self-determination: and Canada, 16, 42, 44, 96–7, 108, 110, 113, 121, 222; and United States, 16, 40, 93, 101, 104–7, 118, 123

self-government. *See* self-determination

Singapore, 48

Singh, Nikhil Pal, 40

Smith, Denis, 10–12, 60

Smith, Goldwin, 117

Soleil, Le, 222

'Sources of Soviet Conduct, The,' 129–32

South Korea, 168, 171, 181, 185–7, 190, 194, 196–7, 202–4, 208, 222

sovereignty, Canadian: and atomic bomb, 22, 37, 41, 49–50; and Britain, 50, 96, 99–100, 133; and Gouzenko Affair, 75, 79, 88–9; and Korean War, 197, 199, 205, 222; and NATO, 129, 147, 162; and U.S. containment strategy, 4–5, 93, 100, 124, 133, 230, 232

Soviet friendship societies, 55, 67, 82, 89

Soviet Union: African-American views of, 33; and anti-imperialism, 103; and atomic bomb, 21, 40, 45, 47,

65–6, 76, 128, 192, 206; Canadian relations with, 55, 60–3, 67, 79, 82, 85–6; Canadian views of, 48–9, 60, 64–5, 79–91, 108, 128, 136, 149, 151–2, 173, 189, 221; and Czechoslovakian coup, 7, 88, 130, 132, 135, 176, 225; and decolonization, 16, 103–6, 111–12, 114, 120–6; global ambitions of, 4–5, 16, 65, 70, 75, 106, 130, 132, 135, 173–7, 189, 218, 220, 227; and Gouzenko Affair, 7, 15, 21, 54–91; and Korean War, 171–7, 186–9; and Marshall Plan, 129; and NATO, 128, 145–6, 151, 162, 164; Second World War alliance, 24–5, 43, 47–8, 60, 67, 79–80, 121; and Truman Doctrine, 129; and UN, 127, 165, 172, 212; U.S. relations with, 63, 67; U.S views of, 65, 67, 76, 78–9, 87, 128–30, 136, 151–2, 189. *See also* anti-communism; Gouzenko Affair

Spain, 166

Spanish-American War, 101, 105

Stairs, Denis, 212

Stalin, Joseph: and atomic bomb, 33; Canadian views of, 48, 79, 88–90; and Gouzenko Affair, 78; as Hitler, 67, 122, 176, 185; and Korean War, 173–5, 207, 253n8; and NATO, 153, 155

Stars and Stripes, 168–9

State Department, U.S.: and cultural exchange, 14, 227; and decolonization, 123; and Gouzenko Affair, 63–4, 78, 87; and Korean War, 170, 172, 174, 178, 193–4, 197, 202, 212; and NATO, 131, 144, 161, 166

Steichen, Edward, 148

Stueck, William, 209, 214, 258n63
Szilard, Leo, 24, 45

Taft, Robert, 212
television, 43, 55
Thompson, Dorothy, 65, 119
Time, 6, 12, 14; and decolonization,
    119; and Gouzenko Affair, 55–6;
    and Korean War, 174, 177, 182–3,
    186, 192, 194–5, 198, 202, 204,
    209–10, 212, 221; and NATO,
    134–5, 144–6, 156–7, 161, 165–6
Tokyo, 27–8, 208–9
Toronto Star: and atomic bomb, 19,
    27, 47; and decolonization, 114,
    120; and Gouzenko Affair, 83–
    6, 89–90; and Korean War, 184,
    188, 197, 201, 217; and NATO,
    165
Toronto Telegram, 48, 66–9, 79, 83–4,
    114, 176, 180, 218
total war, 27
Trades and Labour Congress, 131
Tragedy of American Diplomacy, The,
    102
trans-nationalism, 70, 232
Truman, Harry: and atomic bomb,
    27, 30, 40; and Canada, 11, 79;
    and domestic politics, 11; and
    Gouzenko Affair, 63; and Korean
    War, 3; and nationalism, 46, 78;
    and NATO, 127
Truman Doctrine, 22, 106, 109,
    129–30, 138, 140, 152, 171, 183. *See
    also* containment policy
Tute, Richard C., 110, 121
Twentieth Century Fox, 55

Underhill, Frank, 116, 184, 208,
    248n46

unilateralism, U.S., 3, 24, 40–1, 78,
    81, 100
United Nations, 23; and atomic
    bomb, 5, 23, 38, 42, 45, 47, 50, 76,
    129; Canadian attitudes toward, 79,
    93, 99, 137–8, 150, 190–1, 195–201,
    212, 223–4; Charter/principles
    of, 104, 106, 108, 112, 142–3, 196;
    East-West disputes over, 48, 64,
    127; and Korean War, 168–72, 179–
    80, 183–208, 210–16, 223–4; and
    NATO, 128–9, 132, 134, 136–8,
    140–3, 158, 162–6; peacekeeping,
    95, 100; perceived need for, 5, 38,
    92, 99; Security Council, 142, 172;
    and Soviet Union, 127, 165, 172,
    212; U.S. attitudes toward, 79,
    92–3, 137–8, 168, 190–1, 193–5,
    212, 223–4
United Nations Temporary Commis-
    sion on Korea (UNTCOK), 171–2
universalism, 38–40, 44–5, 70
USSR. *See* Soviet Union
utopianism, U.S., 35, 42

Vancouver Sun: and atomic bomb, 25,
    27, 30; and Gouzenko Affair, 67,
    80, 82; and Korean War, 178, 188,
    197, 217, 219; and NATO, 146,
    152, 154, 161
Vandenberg, Arthur, 13, 78, 146
Vietnam War, 170, 174, 185
Vipond, Mary, 12, 233n4
Von Eschen, Penny, 246n21

Wagnleitner, Reinhold, 14
Walden, Keith, 75
Wallace, Henry, 40, 44, 64, 140
War Measures Act, 10, 34, 59
Warnock, John, 42, 233n1

Warsaw Pact, 128
Weisbord, Merrily, 61–2
Western Canada, 82–3, 217–18
Western civilization, 17, 33, 40, 92,
    128, 148–51, 188, 195, 252n54
Western Europe, 39, 103, 127–8, 130,
    131, 152, 161, 195, 210, 230. *See
    also specific countries*
Whitaker, Reginald, 47–8, 55, 60–2,
    69, 93–4, 213
White, Walter, 152
whiteness, 44, 149
Whitfield, Stephen J., 153, 174, 229
Williams, William Appleman, 102
Willkie, Wendell, 38, 92–3, 118–19,
    121, 123, 148
Wilson, Woodrow, 101, 246n16
Winks, Robin, 34
Winnipeg General Strike, 82
Winnipeg Study Group, 141–3, 153,
    162–3, 167

Winnipeg Tribune, 47, 82, 113, 163,
    201, 218, 220
Wittner, Lawrence, 25, 50
Women's Christian Temperance
    Union, 47
Woodside, Willson: and atomic
    bomb, 28, 46; and decolonization,
    121; and Gouzenko Affair, 65;
    and Korean War, 180, 183, 201–2,
    208; and NATO, 135, 145–6, 148,
    150–1, 155, 157–8, 162, 166, 230
world federalists. *See* world
    government
world government, 5, 38, 42, 50, 55,
    76–8, 86, 90. *See also One World;*
    'One World,' concept of
Wrong, Hume, 11, 197

Young, Robert, 103–4, 108